Traversals of Affect

Also available from Bloomsbury

Libidinal Economy, Jean-Francois Lyotard
Lyotard and Theology, Lieven Boeve
Lyotard and the 'figural' in Performance, Art and Writing, Kiff Bamford
Philosophy, Sophistry, Antiphilosophy, Matthew R. McLennan

Traversals of Affect

On Jean-François Lyotard

Edited by
Julie Gaillard, Claire Nouvet, and Mark Stoholski

Bloomsbury Academic
An imprint of Bloomsbury Publishing Plc

B L O O M S B U R Y

LONDON · OXFORD · NEW YORK · NEW DELHI · SYDNEY

Bloomsbury Academic

An imprint of Bloomsbury Publishing Plc

50 Bedford Square	1385 Broadway
London	New York
WC1B 3DP	NY 10018
UK	USA

www.bloomsbury.com

BLOOMSBURY and the Diana logo are trademarks of Bloomsbury Publishing Plc

First published 2016

British Library Cataloguing-in-Publication Data
A catalogue record for this book is available from the British Library.

ISBN: HB: 9781474257886
ePDF: 9781474257893
ePub: 9781474257909

Library of Congress Cataloging-in-Publication Data
A catalog record for this book is available from the Library of Congress.

Typeset by RefineCatch Limited, Bungay, Suffolk
Printed and bound in Great Britain

Contents

List of Contributors

Kiff Bamford is senior lecturer in contemporary art & graphic design, School of Art, Architecture and Design, Leeds Beckett University, UK. Recent publications include *Lyotard and the 'figural' in Performance, Art and Writing* (Continuum, 2012); chapter "A Late Performance: Intimate Distance" in *Rereading Jean-François Lyotard* (eds Bickis & Shields, Ashgate, 2013); article "Acconci's Pied-à-terre: Taking the archive for a walk," *Performance Research 17:2* (April 2012) and "Desire, Absence and Art in Deleuze and Lyotard," *Parrhesia: A Journal of Critical Philosophy* (2013).

Geoffrey Bennington is Asa G. Candler Professor of Modern French Thought at Emory University. He has published extensively on the work of Jean-François Lyotard, Jacques Derrida, and deconstruction. Amongst his many published works are *Lyotard: Writing the Event* (Columbia, 1988), *Late Lyotard* (CreateSpace, 2005), *Legislations: The Politics of Deconstruction* (Verso, 1994), *Frontières kantiennes* (Editions Galilée, 2000), and *Jacques Derrida* (in collaboration with Jacques Derrida) (Chicago, 1993). His next volume, *Scatter 1: The Politics of Politics in Foucault, Heidegger and Derrida* is forthcoming from Fordham University Press in 2016. He has translated numerous works by Lyotard and Derrida. A member of the French editorial team preparing Jacques Derrida's seminars for publication (Editions Galilée), and general editor (with Peggy Kamuf) of the English translation of those seminars, he is also a collaborator of the editorial board of the series *Jean-François Lyotard: Ecrits sur l'art contemporain et les artistes / Writings on Contemporary Art and Artists* (Leuven University Press, 2009–13).

Heidi Bickis recently graduated from the University of Alberta with a PhD in sociology. Her dissertation examines the conceptual significance of the line for social theory and, in particular, for analyzing the complexity of the lived body. She was co-organizer of "Rewriting Lyotard," an international conference at the University of Alberta in 2011, and is co-editor of (with Rob Shields) and contributor to *Rereading Jean-François Lyotard: Essays on His Later Works* (Ashgate, 2013). She has worked as a lecturer at the University of Alberta and the University of Saskatchewan.

Julie Gaillard is a doctoral candidate in the Department of French and Italian at Emory University, and an Andrew W. Mellon Graduate Teaching Fellow at Morehouse College. She is preparing a dissertation on proper names, referentiality and mediality in French literature and arts at the turn of the twenty-first century.

Kirsten Locke is lecturer in philosophy of education at the School of Critical Studies in Education in the Faculty of Education and Social Work, University of Auckland, New Zealand. Her research brings poststructuralist and feminist theories and methodologies to bear on a range of intersecting and overlapping interests in education that encompass architecture, gender, policy, and music.

Peter Milne is assistant professor of aesthetics at Seoul National University, where he teaches contemporary French aesthetics and philosophy. He is the author of numerous articles on Jean-François Lyotard, and is associate editor and one of the translators of the multi-volume, *Jean-François Lyotard: Writings on Contemporary Art and Artists*, Leuven University Press (2009–13). He is also co-editor of *Rewriting Lyotard: Figuration, Presentation, Resistance*, a special issue of *Cultural Politics* (2013). He is presently working on a book length study of Lyotard's reading of Kant's sublime.

Claire Nouvet is associate professor in the Department of French and Italian at Emory University. She is the co-editor of *Minima Memoria: In the Wake of Jean-Francois Lyotard* (Stanford, 2007), the author of *Enfances Narcisse* (Galilée, 2009), *Abélard et Héloïse: la passion de la maîtrise* (Presses Universitaires du Septentrion, 2009), and the editor of *Literature and the Ethical Question* (Yale French Studies, 1991).

Erin Obodiac received her PhD in comparative literature from the University of California, Irvine and has held teaching and research appointments at UC Irvine, the University of Leeds, SUNY Albany, and Cornell University. Her writings assemble residual questions from the deconstructive legacy with emergent discourses on technics and animality, robotics, and biomedia. She is currently a Mellon postdoctoral fellow at Cornell University, completing a book called *Robots at Risk: Transgenic Art and Corporate Personhood*.

Kas Saghafi is associate professor of philosophy at the University of Memphis. He is the author of *Apparitions—Of Derrida's Other* (Fordham University Press, 2010). He is currently co-editing, with Geoffrey Bennington, a two-volume collection of Derrida's writings entitled *Thinking What Comes* (Edinburgh University Press). He is the editor of the Spindel Supplement of the *Southern Journal of Philosophy*, "Derrida and the Theologico-political" (2012).

Jana V. Schmidt holds a PhD in comparative literature from the University at Buffalo. She currently is the Klemens von Klemperer Hannah Arendt Center Fellow at Bard College where she works on Hannah Arendt's aesthetics, image theory, postwar literatures, and notions of intersubjectivity.

Kent Still holds a PhD in philosophy from Emory University. He is the co-editor of *Minima Memoria: In the Wake of Jean-Francois Lyotard* (Stanford, 2007), *Addressing Levinas* (Northwestern, 2005), and *Rewriting Lyotard: Figuration, Presentation, Resistance*, a special issue of *Cultural Politics* (2013). He is co-translator of Lyotard's "What To Paint?" (Cultural Politics, 2013).

Mark Stoholski is a Mellon/ACLS dissertation completion fellow in the Department of Comparative Literature at Emory University and a candidate at the Emory University Psychoanalytic Institute. He is preparing a dissertation on affect via the ancient sophists and their reception in modern literature and psychoanalysis.

Anne Tomiche is professor of comparative literature at the university Paris-Sorbonne-Paris IV. She is the author of *La Naissance des avant-gardes occidentales* (Armand Colin, 2015), *"L'Intraduisible dont je suis fait," Artaud et les avant-gardes occidentales* (Editions du Manuscrit, 2012), and *Métamorphoses du lyrisme. Philomèle, le Rossignol et la modernité occidentale* (Classiques Garnier, 2010), and the editor of a number of other books. She has published many works on Lyotard, including book chapters in *Afterwords. Essays in Memory of Jean-François Lyotard* (Humanities Institute, 2000), *Philosophies of the Visible* (Continuum, 2002) and *Les Transformateurs Lyotard* (Sens & Tonka, 2008), and articles in journals including *Diacritics, L'Esprit créateur, Yale French Studies* and *Europe*.

Ashley Woodward is lecturer in philosophy, University of Dundee. He is author and editor of a number of books, including *Nihilism in Postmodernity: Lyotard, Baudrillard, Vattimo* (The Davies Group, 2009) and is an editor for *Parrhesia: A Journal of Critical Philosophy*. His book *Lyotard and the Inhuman Condition: Reflections on Nihilism, Information, and Art* is forthcoming with Edinburgh University Press in 2016.

Introduction

Claire Nouvet, Julie Gaillard, and Mark Stoholski

To think "affect," as that which escapes the bounds of formalization and the grasp of articulation, is one of the tasks that Jean-François Lyotard sets out for philosophy, while always acknowledging the radical challenge that affect poses to thinking itself. Across the span of his work and under various names, he pursued a reflection on affect through the multiple fields he engaged. Affect does not indeed belong to any particular field that might determine its modes of presentation. Instead, it traverses the fields that it destabilizes, as is manifest in and across Lyotard's texts. To render an account of these traversals and attempt to do them justice is the task of this volume.

Affect: an unarticulated phrase

To trace Lyotard's reflections on affect across his *oeuvre*, one needs the vantage provided by his later texts—after *The Differend* (1983)—where he addresses most explicitly the question of "affect." Informed by the shift that *The Differend* performs, this approach to affect significantly differs from the "libidinal approach" used in earlier works.

The Differend is commonly regarded as a turning point in Lyotard's philosophical reflection. As he moves from a libidinal approach to a pragmatics of phrases, Freud goes into abeyance, and the Kant of the third *Critique* (the division of the faculties) and the Wittgenstein of the *Philosophical Investigations* (the "language games") become central interlocutors. This interest in the pragmatics of language concerns itself with the dynamics that underlie the production of meaning. The notions of "phrase" and of "differend" elaborated in *The Differend* lay the ground that will later allow him to insist on the radical incommensurability of affect with discourse, representation, and articulation in general.

An articulated phrase manifests a universe organized according to four poles:[1] it presents a referent (what is the case), a meaning (what is signified about this referent), an addressor, and an addressee. It can have several referents, several meanings, several addressors, and several addressees. A genre of discourse provides the rules according to which phrases obeying different regimes (assertions, interrogations, orders, etc.) are *linked* with one another. The kind of linkage between phrases varies according to the aim that is set by the genre of discourse—be it knowing, teaching, being just, controlling, moving.[2] It is in the very moment of that linkage that Lyotard situates the differend, which he defines as a conflict between two parties whose means of articulation are radically heterogeneous, such that there is no common rule that can decide between the two. For lack of a common rule of judgment, the conflict cannot be settled, or even phrased, without wronging one of the parties. This wrong results from the imposition of the rules of one genre of discourse upon another to which they are foreign, thereby foreclosing the claims of one party.[3]

Lyotard gives as an example of a differend the hypothetical case of a Martinican who deems that he has been treated unjustly in having been given French citizenship.[4] The case cannot be pleaded since the available tribunal is the French court, which considers him a French citizen. This citizenship is presumed, and cannot be investigated by the terms of the court. To appear before an international court, he would need to not be a French citizen; there would be, then, no damage of which he could complain. In either case, the tribunal is constitutively unable to appraise the presumed damage. The damage is thus nullified: he cannot have been a victim. This nullification of the damage constitutes a wrong: "This is what a wrong [*tort*] would be: a damage [*dommage*] accompanied by the loss of the means to prove the damage."[5] In the face of the differend, new idioms must be created to articulate the wrong inflicted upon those victims who are condemned to silence, deprived of the means to attest the damage that they have suffered.

As Lyotard remarks, "[i]n the differend, something 'asks' to be put into phrases, and suffers from the wrong of not being able to be put into phrases right away."[6] This state is accompanied by a "feeling": "This state is signaled by what one ordinarily calls a feeling. 'One cannot find the words,' etc."[7] While he evoked the "feeling" of inarticulation attached to the differend, it is only in later texts that he focuses specifically on the question of affect, in part through a return to Freud. This return marks a significant departure from his previous use of Freudian theory in his "libidinal" period. After *The Differend* and its philosophy of phrases, Lyotard indeed no longer relies on what he calls Freud's "metaphysics of forces."[8] Consequently, affect is not considered, as Freud had, as a "quantum of energy," but as a phrase. This phrase, Lyotard insists, has the peculiarity of being "unarticulated": "The sentiment is a phrase. I call it affect-phrase. It distinguishes itself in that it is *unarticulated*."[9] The affect-phrase is unarticulated insofar as it ignores the fundamental categories of articulation: it has no addressor, no addressee, no referent, and no meaning.[10] To account for the inarticulation of the affect-phrase, Lyotard relies analogically on the Freudian notions of infantile sexuality and primary narcissism.

The Freudian elaboration of primary narcissism permits a thinking of affectivity anterior to the formation of the ego, in the indivision of subject and object. Affect springs before there is the possibility of an "I." It is in this sense that the affect-phrase has no addressor, that affect is "a feeling felt by no 'I' and no 'one.'"[11] Affect is there before there is an "I" to receive it. Nor is this condition restricted to infancy conceived as a mere developmental stage. Seized by affect, the adult falls back into an infancy that precedes the ego and consciousness, and which resists any conscious apperception.[12] As s/he is affected, s/he is overtaken in infancy, that is, muteness.

Correlatively, affect has no addressee, not even originally,[13] since the mother's body does not constitute an object for the infant. The Freudian notion of polymorphous perversity allows a thinking of affectivity that is not attached to any specific object, but circulates in an undifferentiated manner across numerous erogenous zones, whose excitation produces pleasure. The object is but the contingent occasion of pleasure or displeasure.[14] For that matter, and insofar as infantile affect precedes any division of the ego from the exterior world, what is affected is an undifferentiated "incorporeal chaos" that does not yet constitute a unified body distinct from a "world" and that knows neither object nor organ.[15] In this sense, the affect-phrase has no referent. Finally, affect has no meaning. It is a tautegorical signal—that is, at once, an affective state and the signal of that state.[16] It bears no meaning, being nothing more than that raw and minimal sentiment of pleasure and/or pain.[17]

Affect is thus non-articulated: it has no addressor, no addressee, no referent, and no definite meaning. To justify the apparently paradoxical usage of the term "affect-phrase" to describe something that ignores the four poles of articulation, Lyotard evokes the Aristotelian distinction between *phōnē* (voice) and *logos* (here, taken as articulated discourse).[18] The human, possessing the privilege of articulated discourse, nevertheless shares with animals the "confused voice," the *phōnē*, which has an affective valor insofar as it signals, but does not signify, pleasure and/or pain. Knowing neither past nor future, its presence is foreign to representation, referentiality, and the pragmatics of discursive communication where the political community that "deliberates and decides the useful and the just" inscribes itself. After Aristotle, Lyotard affirms that pleasure and pain are communicable without the mediation of the *logos*, through the *phōnē* alone which allows for "a transitivity of affects without expectation of a return."[19]

Between "the *phōnē*, the inarticulate phrase," and "the *logos*, the articulated phrase,"[20] there is no continuity, but rather a radical heterogeneity, a differend: "The *phōnē* and the *logos* can only meet each other, and not link to each other."[21] This differend between affect and articulated discourse serves as a limit case, indeed as "the differend itself" (*le différend même*), as the original title of "The Affect Phrase" indicates.[22] Articulation necessarily wrongs the affect-phrase, the *phōnē*, which Aristotle—who excludes those genres of discourse that do not belong to argumentation, let alone to articulation—banished from the *logos*.[23] Although wronged by articulation, the inarticulate affect nevertheless "occupies" articulated discourse in a clandestine fashion.[24]

The first section of this volume, titled "Affect: An Unarticulated Phrase," explores Lyotard's thinking of the inarticulacy of affect (and its differend with articulation) as it unfolds in those key texts that follow *The Differend*: "The Affect-Phrase: From a Supplement to the Differend" (1990) and "Emma" (1989). In "The Affect-Phrase," it is no longer the case that, in the differend between affect and articulation, something "asks" to be put into phrases. As Mark Stoholski notes in "Apathēmata," affect is indifferent to articulation, to the relations that it posits, and to determinate ends. It makes its presence felt in articulated discourse while remaining silent. The *logos*, which wrongs affect by denying it its silence, is nonetheless continually troubled by an impassive affective remainder. Unarticulated, affect is, for Lyotard, unconscious in a sense that Claire Nouvet explores in "For 'Emma,'" where she distinguishes affect from conscious feeling. This distinction is central to Lyotard's rereading of Freud's Emma case, where he examines the peculiar temporality of affect ("belatedness," *Nachträglichkeit*), its relation to subjectivity, the radical differend between infantile and adult sexuality, and, more generally, between affect and articulation.

Affect in the work of art and commentary

Throughout his philosophical reflection, Lyotard repeatedly engaged the question of the work of art and of its commentary.[25] Several of his texts were devoted to commentary on artists such as Duchamp, Buren, Adami, Arakawa, Appel, Ettinger, or Francis. No less important (although less extensive) was his engagement with literature (Kafka, Valéry, Quignard, or Malraux), as well as with music (Boulez, Cage) and cinema.

Lyotard's first major writings—*Discourse, Figure* (1971) and *Libidinal Economy* (1974)—are concerned with the work of art as an affective transmitter and transformer, a commitment that remains constant through the various forms it takes in his corpus. The work of painting, of music, of literature and other arts features large in *Duchamp's TRANS/formers* (1977), *The Inhuman* (1986), *What to Paint?* (1987), *Misère de la philosophie* (2000), and a number of other books commenting on particular artistic corpuses. For Lyotard, commentary is not merely a matter of categorizing works according to periods, but of following the affective gestures that they manifest. As he writes:

> It is a grave and common error to impose a classification by periods or schools on works of art. In reality, you're only classifying cultural products, which belong in effect to observable phenomena of historical reality, like political events, demographical mutations, and economic changes. But what there is that is art in works of art is independent of these contexts, even if art shows itself only within those contexts and on their occasion. . . . Gestures, which are neither contents nor forms but the absolutely emotive power of the work, make no progress in the course of history. There is no history of art as gesture, only as cultural product. The power to affect sensibility beyond what it can sense does not belong to chronological time. Only what is called the "function" of art, the gesture's trace recollected within human communities, is what is transformed, and what may be periodized.[26]

The practice of art commentary must attest to this affective dimension, as the texts in this section demonstrate. They focus indeed on some of the major movements in Lyotard's conception of the work of art and its commentary as affective work.

This section begins by considering Lyotard's pragmatic approach (in the late 1970s and early 1980s) which, as Ashley Woodward shows in "Pragmatics and Affect in Art and Commentary," understands the artwork as a pragmatic force of transformation, commentary as a pragmatic effect of the work, and theory as a "transformation group" allowing the passage from the work to its commentary. This pragmatic approach functions, Woodward argues, as a transitional period. Insofar as it focuses on the ways in which a work of art can affect its receiver, it prolongs the concern with affect in Lyotard's libidinal philosophy while preparing his return to affect in terms of phrases after *The Differend*. As Anne Tomiche demonstrates in "Anamnesis," after *The Differend* and "The Affect-Phrase," Lyotard indeed rethinks art both in terms of "phrases" and of a "working-through" or "anamnesis." Art is neither the product of a conscious subject, nor simply the work of forces, as was the case in *Discourse, Figure*, but an anamnesis that works through articulated phrases and forms to testify to the presence, within articulation and the visible, of something that both escapes and inhabits them. Art, as opposed to history, does not represent something that has happened, but makes present an event of color, of words, of sound, opening a passage toward the affect-phrase. This passage, Kas Saghafi argues in "Lyotard's Gesture," is opened by the work's gesture. Focusing on Lyotard's *Karel Appel: A Gesture of Colour* (1998) that, as he points out, contains Lyotard's most extensive reflections on painting after *What to Paint?*, Saghafi unfolds Lyotard's understanding of art as a complex "gesture" that challenges sensibility by pointing (gesturing) towards another time, space, and matter. This gesture calls for what Lyotard calls an "account of affect" which, Saghafi explains, is not a "report" on affect but an affected writing inhabited by the gesture. In "No Place for Complacency: The Resistance of Gesture," Kiff Bamford extends Lyotard's notion of gesture to rethink the archiving of performance art as the working-through of an affect each time remobilized. The affective trace of the gesture may recur again, although not attestable as the return of the "same," since such attestation would require the articulation of that which does not lend itself to articulation. The "commentary" of art transfers this affective trace in a gesture of its own, as Bamford does, when he responds to the video performance of the artist Yingmei Duan with a video piece of his own.

Affect as figure

Section III of this book returns to Lyotard's earlier reflections on aesthetics in *Discourse, Figure*, from the vantage point of his later texts on affect. *Discourse, Figure* is reread and, as it were, extended in light of this later elaboration of affect.

Acknowledged as the first of Lyotard's major works, *Discourse, Figure* undertakes a critique of structuralism and of phenomenology, proposing a thought of the figure and of the figural that exceeds the binary opposition between body and language. "Discourse," understood as a closed system of signification, deploys itself as a surface that ignores the depth of the sensible as well as the eye that apperceives. For Lyotard, art has an interruptive power that points to an other of discourse. As Kiff Bamford notes:

> The figural is the transgression of signification which shows that alternatives to established forms of discourse—not only language and critical philosophy but

also visual methods—are possible. It ... draws attention to the need to find a mode of presentation for that which has been repressed—an inevitably unending search which confronts the paradox that the unsignifiable aspect of the figure is changed through attempts to make it "present."[27]

Art and psychoanalysis (with its notion of "dream-work") are the privileged milieux for observing the figural that perturbs discourse, "an exteriority it cannot interiorize as signification."[28] Discourse, however, also carries some figural element within it since it not only signifies, but also expresses. "Language is not a homogenous environment: it is divisive, because it exteriorizes the sensory into a *vis-à-vis*, an object, and divided, because it interiorizes the figural in the articulated."[29] As the *logos* poses the sensible as an object for a subject, the sensible returns at its core, under the thrust of the figural that pushes through the pores of discourse. From *Discourse, Figure* onward, Lyotard focuses on this "outsider within" to undermine the discursive hegemony of the Ego, taken as a constituted and unitary instance, by opposing to it the Freudian Id. The figural, understood not only as the very opening of plastic space, but also as the action, within this plastic and sensible space, of a "force" that ignores the operations of binding, is in part tied to the primary processes which Lyotard will again evoke when he elaborates the notion of the affect-phrase.[30] The silence of the figure, which cannot be heard but as the white noise of discourse, is "a silence that precedes speech":[31] that of the non-differentiation of the ego and objects, of the aleatory wandering of the psychic energies according to unconscious, primary processes. And, just as with the inarticulation of affect, this silence is "impossible": "there is simply no way to go to the other side of discourse. Only from within language can one get to and enter the figure."[32] In the course of this complex work, Lyotard traces the contours of the operations of the figural within discourse according to an "energetic" perspective that he will develop within the "libidinal" writings, such as *Libidinal Economy* and the texts immediately preceding.

Primary processes of condensation and displacement can distort, fold, transform the images and forms given to quotidian perception. They transgress the contours and lines that make images recognizable. As Heidi Bickis shows in "Following Lyotard's Lines: Affect and Figure in Guillermo Kuitca's *Acoustic Mass VI* and *Mozart Da-Ponte VIII*," Lyotard distinguishes discursive lines, which trace boundaries, from the figural lines that confound them. The "figural" line transgresses the discursivity of the code to which a line is usually attached. Extending Lyotard's reflections on the figural line to the question of affect, she argues that the figural lines in Kuitca's works signal the trace of an unarticulate affect by disrupting orientation, suspending bodily discourse, and shifting things "out of line" towards an "elsewhere" that exceeds the line. In "Philip Guston's Piles," Jana V. Schmidt argues that Philip Guston's late "figurative" paintings provide an example of how the work of the figural within the language of forms produces an oblique, affective way of witnessing, which arises from the failure of representation, and comes to signal, within representation, that something remains in excess. In these paintings, the language of forms neither depicts nor signifies, but undergoes processes of displacement and condensation that disrupt symbolic interpretation and, in so doing, "figure" the relation to the Shoah as an affective "working-through."

Affect and the sublime in the age of new technologies

The texts in Section IV address the relation between the conception of affect that Lyotard elaborated through his engagement with Kant—specifically on the "sublime"—and the new technologies that challenge or complicate this sublime conception of affect. While Lyotard's best known writings on affect are concerned with psychoanalysis, his thinking of affect was not tied to Freud alone. Following a cue from Kant's Third *Critique* and *The Conflict of the Faculties*, Lyotard insists that a thinking of affect must engage in a "reflection" akin to Kant's reflective judgment. Lyotard takes as his point of departure the place that the Third *Critique* accords to the faculty of judgment. Unlike the other faculties, each of which has its proper domain, the power of judgment has none. Its role is rather to regulate genres of discourse by validating presentations under a rule according to which they would be the case. Judgment decides that a given presentation is the case that accords with the rule of a certain genre of discourse, and determines which genre of discourse is pertinent.[33] If, as Lyotard depicts them in *Enthusiasm: The Kantian Critique of History* (1986), genres of discourse are like the islands of an archipelago, the faculty of judgment is the admiral who sends expeditions between these islands. It determines their boundaries and regulates the commerce—whether interchange or warfare—between them.

For Lyotard, affect requires the type of thinking that Kant defined as "reflective judgment," which deals with the presentation of a case for which a rule is not yet available. Kant holds aesthetic judgment to be a model for reflective judgment in general, an emphasis that Lyotard redoubles.[34] Having no principle to guide it, aesthetic judgment attends to a singular presentation, to the sentiment that it entails. For Lyotard, it is this sentiment that animates thought. Affected by a sentiment that does not yet belong to articulated discourse, the task of thought is to go off in search of terms according to which this unpresentable sentiment might come to representation.[35]

The Kantian thematic of the sublime provides Lyotard with the limit case and model for this exposure of the faculties to what is radically heterogeneous. The sublime presentation, according to Kant, does not merely bring pleasure, but a mixed sentiment of pleasure and pain induced by the failure of the faculties to apprehend what presents itself. The faculties cannot assert their power against it; they find themselves overthrown, wanting. Understanding fails. As such, Lyotard often links the modality of the sublime to affect, as a presence that is incommensurate with representation. As he remarks in *Lessons on the Analytic of the Sublime* (1991): "What awakens the 'intellectual feeling' (*Geistesgefühl*), the sublime, is not nature, which is an artist in forms and in the work of forms, but rather magnitude, force, quantity, in its purest state, a 'presence' that exceeds what imaginative thought can grasp at once in a form—what it can *form*."[36] This "presence" that remains unpresentable returns under the heading of affect: radically heterogeneous to articulated discourse, affect is also an "unpresentable presentation" that catches thought unprepared, and awakens it by exceeding it. While this Kantian line of thinking provides a resource for engaging affect, Lyotard is nonetheless attentive to the changes in the modes of presentation wrought since Kant's day, particularly with the advent of new technologies. His writings—most notably *The Inhuman* and *Postmodern Fables* (1993)—often reflect on their stakes for art and for the task of thinking itself. The texts in this section turn to Lyotard's thinking of the sublime affect and its vicissitudes in the face of the technologies of postmodernity.

In "Gods, Angels and Puppets: Lyotard's Lessons on Listening," Kirsten Locke argues that Lyotard listened in music for the presence of a sonic matter that surpasses the mind's synthetic capacity: to be affected by it, the subject must, in sublime fashion, lose itself. Lost and emptied of intentionality, it can then respond to sound exclusively and, as it were, automatically, in a puppet-like passivity. While new technologies allow for exact recordings, Lyotard listened in music for the unrepeatable and inaudible genesis of sound and set for contemporary music (with its computerized and digitalized technologies) the task to extend it. In "Autoaffection and Lyotard's Cinematic Sublime," Erin Obodiac explores, for her part, the affinity between the technical and the sublime. In his reading of Kant's *Critique of Aesthetic Judgment*, Lyotard suggests indeed that there is "an affinity of aesthetic sublimes with an era of technique."[37] As she follows Lyotard's analogy of the operations of comprehension and synthesis to that of a camera, she shows that the notion of a technical sublime emerges that binds the human to the technical, the inhuman. What Lyotard calls "autoaffection"—the affect proper to aesthetic reflective judgment—belongs, she argues, to a transhuman technics that finds its machinic analogue in his notion of the "acinema."

Affect in postmodern politics

In his Anglophone reception, Lyotard has best been known for his engagements with politics, which remain a focal point from his early writings as part of the collective *Socialism or Barbarism* to the different perspectives offered in the wake of May '68, under the various headings of the "pagan," the politics of the sublime, and the "postmodern." As Lyotard famously put it, one of the characteristics of postmodernity is its incredulity towards meta-narratives: "In contemporary society and culture—postindustrial society, postmodern culture—the question of the legitimation of knowledge is formulated in different terms. The grand narrative has lost its credibility, regardless of what mode of unification it uses, regardless of whether it is a speculative narrative or a narrative of emancipation."[38]

In terms of politics, the postmodern turns from a "modern" politics based on grand narratives that construe history as the teleological movement leading a universal subject of History towards emancipation: "the great Tale of Emancipation which modern politics produced is no longer credible and we are now dealing with an enormous System, once called capitalism, which today has no 'challenger.' We are dealing with a system without any end apart from its own development, a system that grows in and of itself, stands on its own."[39] It knows only the logic of performativity: to achieve the best ratio of input and output, to increase its own efficiency, and to gain time. Digital technologies have enabled messages to be exchanged "in real time," thus increasing the performativity of the system and making the horizon of universal intelligibility draw nearer. In many of his later works, such as *Postmodern Fables* or *The Inhuman*, Lyotard devoted much of his attention to the analysis of the workings of the system, its pervasion of all fields of human activity, and its "inhumanity."[40]

Does this mean that the system can "treat," that is, "process" everything according to the law of optimal performativity? Is there no "intractable" left, the kind of intractable that Lyotard said he was pursuing under other names from the very beginning of his political engagement? Looking back on *Socialism or Barbarism*, he insisted that "the idea that guided *Socialism or Barbarism* was ultimately, even if it was expressed in other terms, the idea that there is something within the system that it cannot, in principle, *deal with* [traiter]."[41] This emphasis persists in his later works. Lyotard insists: however invasive the system and its pervasive development might be, "[t]his does not mean that the system has digested the intractable."[42] With the system's overwhelming emphasis on performativity, what indeed happens to affect? Affect, as that which lends nothing to representation and thus cannot be assimilated, resists the inhumanity of development, which the thinker of *The Postmodern Condition* identified as the rule of the system turned global.[43] The texts in this section turn to the specific thinking of the political relative to the postmodern, and the place that affect occupies in this postmodern politics.

In "A New Kind of Sublime: Lyotard's Affect-Phrase and the '*Begebenheit* of Our Time,'" Peter Milne explores the political possibilities of the sublime in light of Lyotard's later shift to affect. Taking as his point of departure the criticisms of Jacques Rancière and others that Lyotard's turn towards the sublime (and affect more generally) signifies a turn away from politics, he examines Lyotard's reading of the sublime in its most political context, that of Kantian enthusiasm. Lyotard's discussion of enthusiasm, where he suggests that the so-called "postmodern" constitutes an occurrence, an event—a "*Begebenheit* of our time"—allows us, as Milne argues, to see more fully the political implications of Lyotard's later turn towards affect. In "Lyotard on Affect and Media: Or the Postmodern-Version 2.0 Explained by Orwell's *1984*," Kent Still elaborates what he calls "the postmodern-version 2.0" (the reassessment of *The Postmodern Condition* in Lyotard's later works) by focusing on Lyotard's engagement with Orwell's *1984*, especially his citation of Winston's journal as a model of resistance. Since Winston's political resistance fails abjectly, such a claim seems to validate the criticism that postmodernism abandons hope of changing the world. Still argues, however, that Lyotard elaborates the contemporary relevance of *1984*, especially the overlapping of the public/political and of the private/psychological, the maintenance of power through the mobilization of affect, and the role of media in such mobilization.

Affect and the task of thinking

Although Lyotard's works have often been placed under the heading of "French Theory," his invocations of the term "theory" are, at best, ambivalent; affect unsettles any theory that would attempt to come to terms with it. In "Apathie dans la théorie" ("Apathy in Theory," 1977), an essay devoted to Freud's renunciation of conviction when confronted with affect, Lyotard announces that "the moment has come to interrupt the terror of theory."[44] What is at issue, here and in his works of this period, is neither resistance to a particular doctrine, nor a call to develop new theories, but a challenge to the privilege that theory has enjoyed since Plato and Aristotle. The founding gesture of the theoretical position entails making of ontology a master discourse, thereby disqualifying those who do not acknowledge its preeminence, such as those minor Greeks— Lyotard lists the sophists, cynics and Megarans—who treat argumentation as an art form, who delight in paradox and in making the weaker argument the stronger.[45] As Lyotard presents it, "[t]he friends of wisdom—Plato and Aristotle— seek to establish masterful accounts, to fix a non-referable reference, to determine a term that escapes relation and dominates all relations."[46] Thus axiomatically posited, this absolute term serves as the point from which judgment will be rendered upon all other genres of discourse. Whether he insists on "being," on "communication," or any other idea that could be instrumentalized for this sort of discursive police action, the philosopher who performs this gesture establishes his mastery by ignoring the heterogeneity of genres of discourse, and setting aside the troubling presence of affect, which remains apart from any discourse.

This depiction does not aim at rejecting philosophy, but instead calls upon it to resist the desire for possession of the truth. As Lyotard writes, philosophy must become to a certain extent apathetic: "[t]heoretical apathy is not a depressive state, it comports itself with the greatest intransigence with regard to those discourses that place themselves under the law of the true and the false."[47] This apathy regards with intransigent detachment the hegemonic purchase on truth asserted by any discourse that would presume mastery. The respective claims to truth of various discourses may have pertinence, but the very diversity of these claims makes them heterogeneous to one another. This attention to the heterogeneity of discourses, already present in Lyotard's "pagan" period, finds fuller expression in *The Differend*. The task of that book, which Lyotard sets for philosophy writ large, is to attest to differends, as those sites of irreconcilable differences between genres of discourse that arise in the absence of a universal standard. After *The Differend* and with the turn (or return) to affect, philosophy finds itself under yet another obligation: to acquit the debt of thought owed to affect as the intractable that exceeds the mind. This is the last inflection in what Dolorès Lyotard calls Lyotard's distinctive practice of "reflective writing." This mode of "reflective writing" puts itself under the obligation "to interrogate its place and its foundation, its mode of inscription"; philosophical investigation becomes an "incessant anamnesis of that which it believes to have, for a moment, elucidated."[48] It is this kind of philosophical anamnesis that Kent Still traces through Lyotard's critical reassessments of *The Postmodern Condition,* and that Anne Tomiche foregrounds. If Lyotard comes to designate the work of art as anamnesis, it is, as she shows, by performing a philosophical anamnesis (a critical "working through") of his own texts that opens to a thinking of affect in light of which the very task of thinking must yet again be reassessed. The texts of this section consider this reassessment.

In "The Task of Thinking (in) The Postmodern Space of 'The Zone,'" Julie Gaillard examines the role of thinking in the postmodern megalopolis. From its origin, philosophy has posited ideals that repress the absolute nothing of affect, a nothing that nonetheless motivates its investigation. To resist the "pathetic nihilism" of the system, which relays and worsens this occultation in its drive towards the increase of its own performativity, Lyotard calls upon an "active nihilism": philosophy is to attest to what remains outside of the system, to signal the silent passings of affect. One of the names that Lyotard grants this signaling is "grace," as Mark Stoholski claims in "*Coups de Grâce.*" Lyotard mobilizes the language of Jansenism to speak of affect as what remains outside of articulation and which cannot be reconciled to it. This grace is never a given, it belongs to no doctrine; philosophy attends to it by surrendering itself, becoming a matter of writing, albeit one that can never definitively escape the grasp of the law. In "Impious Thinking," Geoffrey Bennington elaborates upon Lyotard's turn to affect after *The Differend,* his engagement with sexual difference in "The Affect-Phrase" (and the texts surrounding it), as well as the radical sense in which he understands reflective judgment and its import for politics. He argues that philosophy is, for Lyotard, an interminable and tenuous work that attests its debt to a "mute exteriority," whose event relegates the subject, and thinking, in a secondary position—an exteriority that no subject will ever master. If it is to gesture towards what resists articulation and representation, philosophical thinking must necessarily be oblique, aporetic, and inventive, in a way that knows no definite end, nor even result.

Affect mobilizes a thought that belatedly attempts to "catch up" and render an account of its having been affected. Obeying no regime of articulation, it traverses fields, transgresses the categories that might attempt to determine it, even as thought continues to pursue it. Incommensurable with the *logos* in all of its modalities, it will always have resisted the attempt to seize and articulate it. It remains intractable, impassable; what is left is the labor of an interminable working through. And, in that sense, this impassability is itself a passage. This book seeks to locate itself within that passage, and to extend it.

Notes

1   Jean-François Lyotard, *The Differend: Phrases in Dispute,* trans. Georges Van Den
    Abbeele (Minneapolis: University of Minnesota Press, 1988), 14.
2   Ibid., xii.
3   On the stakes of "thinking" in *The Differend,* see Rodolphe Gasché, *The Honor of
    Thinking: Critique, Philosophy, History* (Stanford: Stanford University Press, 2007),
    275–96.
4   Lyotard, *The Differend,* 27.
5   Ibid., 5.
6   Ibid., 13.
7   Ibid.
8   Jean-François Lyotard, "Emma," in *Lyotard: Politics, Philosophy, and the Sublime,* ed.
    Hugh Silverman (New York: Routledge, 2002), 30.
9   Jean-François Lyotard, "The Affect-Phrase (From a Supplement to *The Differend*),"
    trans. Keith Crome, in *The Lyotard Reader and Guide,* eds Keith Crome and James
    Williams (New York: Columbia University Press, 2006), 104.
10 See Claire Nouvet, "The Inarticulate Affect. Lyotard and Psychoanalytic Testimony,"
    in *Minima Memoria,* eds Claire Nouvet, Kent Still, and Zrinka Stahuljak (Stanford:
    Stanford University Press, 2007), 108, especially her study of the ways in which the
    affect-phrase ignores the four poles of the articulated phrase. See also, on the notion
    of affect, Anne Tomiche, "Rephrasing the Freudian Unconscious: Lyotard's Affect-
    Phrase," *Diacritics* 24.1 (1994): 43–62.
11 Nouvet, "Inarticulate Affect", 109.
12 Ibid., 108.
13 Lyotard, "Affect-Phrase," 105–6, 109.
14 Nouvet, "Inarticulate Affect," 110.
15 Lyotard, "Affect-Phrase," 109–10.
16 This notion of affect as a tautegorical signal resembles the conception of affect that
    has become influential through Eve Kosofsky Sedgwick's rereading of the works of
    Sylvan Tomkins. In her essay "Shame and the Cybernetic Fold: Reading Sylvan
    Tomkins" (co-written with Adam Frank), she quotes Tomkins on the autoreferential
    character of affect: "Affect is self-validating with or without any further referent,"
    which, for Sedgwick and Frank, makes affect theory a "useful site of resistance to
    teleological presumptions." For them, as for Lyotard, affect remains outside of what
    the latter calls articulation. Divorced from the definite realms of cognitive
    organization, affect intervenes outside of any definite notion of linear causality; its
    movements betray a radical contingency. There remain key differences between
    Lyotard's philosophical approach and the phenomenological psychology of Tomkins,
    but in both affect shows itself transgressive in nature. See Eve Kosofsky Sedgwick,

Touching Feeling: Affect, Performance, Pedagogy (Durham, NC: Duke University, 2003), esp. 99–101.

17 Nouvet, "Inarticulate Affect," 111.

18 Lyotard, "Affect-Phrase," 107.

19 Ibid., 109–10.

20 Ibid., 108.

21 Ibid., 109.

22 As the original title of the essay indicates: "L'Inarticulé, ou le différend même" (The Unarticulated, or the Differend Itself).

23 Ibid., 108–9.

24 Lyotard's definition of affect, as an unarticulated phrase that interrupts the articulation of *logos*, may seem to intersect with the view of affect as a non-signifying and non-subjective intensity proposed by Brian Massumi in *Parables for the Virtual: Movement, Affect, Sensation* (Durham, NC and London: Duke University Press, 2002), a view which allows him to make a crucial distinction between "affect" and qualified "emotion." Massumi defines affect as an "event" that "momentarily suspend[s] the linear progress of the narrative present from past to future" and provokes the "collapse of structured distinction into intensity" (see 26–7). This "hole in time" creates an "expectant suspension," out of which the new emerges. Affect is a potentiality at the crossroads of the virtual and the actual, a "bifurcation point" (32) where everything is (still) possible: once the expectant suspension fades, one potentiality is selected, actualized. The move from virtual to actual is phrased in terms of a differential emergence, affect being the non-signifying intensity that is actualized, and also the autonomic remainder that falls out from such actualization. Lyotard, for his part, does not conceive of the relation between affect and *logos* as a differential emergence but, as we pointed out, as a differend which emphasizes the radical heterogeneity of affect to articulation.

25 As evidenced by the recent publication of his collected texts on art and aesthetics. See Jean-François Lyotard, *Ecrits sur l'art contemporain et les artistes/Writings on Contemporary Art and Artists*, eds Herman Parret et al. (Leuven: Leuven University Press, 2009–13).

26 Jean-François Lyotard, *Postmodern Fables*, trans. Georges Van Den Abbeele (Minneapolis: University of Minnesota Press, 1997), 217–18.

27 Kiff Bamford, *Lyotard and the "figural" in Performance, Art and Writing* (London and New York: Continuum, 2012), 21.

28 Lyotard, *Discourse, Figure*, trans. Anthony Hudek and Mary Lydon (Minneapolis: University of Minnesota Press, 2011), 7.

29 Ibid., 7–8.

30 In her essay "Phrasing the Disruptiveness of the Visible in Freudian Terms: Lyotard and the Visual," Anne Tomiche traces the continuities and ruptures between

Discourse, Figure and later works such as *Postmodern Fables*, and highlights how Lyotard evolves from a thinking of desire as energy to a thinking of the unconscious as phrase, keeping the question of the radically heterogeneous as the core concern of his thinking. See *Afterwords. Essays in memory of Jean-François Lyotard*, ed. Robert Harvey (New York: Occasional Papers of the Humanities Institute University at Stony Brook, 2000), 29–54.

31 Lyotard, *Discourse, Figure*, 7.

32 Ibid.

33 *Enthusiasm: The Kantian Critique of History*, trans. Georges Van Den Abbeele (Stanford: Stanford University Press, 2009), 12.

34 Jean-François Lyotard, *Lessons on the Analytic of the Sublime: Kant's Critique of Judgment*, 23–9, trans. Elizabeth Rottenberg (Stanford: Stanford University Press, 1994), 6.

35 Ibid., 81–3.

36 Ibid., 53.

37 Ibid., 70.

38 Jean-François Lyotard, *The Postmodern Condition: A Report on Knowledge*, trans. Geoffrey Bennington and Brian Massumi (Minneapolis: University of Minnesota Press, 1985), 37.

39 "Resistances: A Conversation of Sergio Benvenuto with Jean-François Lyotard," *JEP: European Journal of Psychoanalysis* 2 (1995–6), n. pag., accessed March 12, 2014, www.psychomedia.it/jep/number2/lyotard.htm.

40 Against a widely spread idea, according to which Lyotard would have turned away from politics as he turned toward a philosophy of phrases in *The Differend*, Geoffrey Bennington reminds us, in his article "Political Animals," that the task of politics in Lyotard is to bear witness to the differend, whose paradigmatic case would be affect—as "the differend itself" (*le différend même*). *Diacritics* 39.2 (2009): 23f. On Lyotard and politics, see in particular James Williams, *Lyotard and the Political* (London: Routledge, 2000); and Bill Readings, *Introducing Lyotard. Art and Politics* (London and New York: Routledge, 1991).

41 Jean-François Lyotard, *Political Writings*, trans. Bill Readings, Kevin Paul, and Kevin P. Geiman (Minneapolis: University of Minnesota Press, 1993), 166.

42 Ibid., 169.

43 The paradoxical relation of affect to temporality in Lyotard's writings, related to Freudian *Nachträglichkeit*, intersects with a central concern in affect theory, where Spinoza remains a central reference. According to the Spinozan reception, affect, between activity and passivity, the psychic and the somatic, refers both to the capacity to be acted upon and the ability to act. Confounding linear causality, it is construed as an indefinite potentiality, unrelated to definite means and ends; one does not know in advance the capabilities of the affected body or mind, as more than

one introductory text to affect theory forcefully asserts. A present horizon that indicates an "otherwise" of the *hic et nunc*, affect serves, for Muñoz in particular, as motivation for a radical politics that finds in the work of art means for a politics of the otherwise, a "queer" politics—José Esteban Muñoz, *Cruising Utopia: The Then and There of Queer Futurity* (New York: NYU Press, 2009). But, he admits, this politics of the otherwise cannot necessarily exclude the potential for evil (ibid., 166), a concern that is central to Lyotard's writings on politics and affect; affect may yet be put to use for uncertain political ends (see Gaillard and Still, in this volume). It is this problematic continuity between affect and politics that Lyotard questions by insisting on the critical role of reflective judgment in politics (see Milne in this volume) as well as on the distinction between affect (often tightly associated with what Lyotard calls "the Thing") and the "Law" (see Still in this volume). On the question of non-programmatic politics, see also Bennington in this volume.

44 Jean-François Lyotard, *Rudiments païens: Genre dissertatif* (Paris: UGE, 1977), 9.

45 Jean-François Lyotard, *Toward the Postmodern*, eds Robert Harvey and Mark S. Roberts (Atlantic Highlands, NJ: Humanities Press, 1993), 64.

46 Ibid., 63.

47 Lyotard, *Rudiments,* 30, our translation. For an examination of Lyotard's "apathy" within the realm of psychoanalytic practice, see Laurence Kahn, *Le Psychanalyste apathique et le patient postmoderne* (Paris: Editions de l'Olivier, 2014), 97–115.

48 Dolorès Lyotard, "L'écriture migrante de Jean-François Lyotard," *Contemporary French and Francophone Studies* 18.1 (2014): 18–30, here pp. 18–19, our translation.

Section I

Affect: An Unarticulated Phrase

1

Apathēmata

Mark Stoholski

"And why would it be necessary that a forgotten (repressed) sentiment necessarily have to come back? Is it necessary to admit the hypothesis, hazy even in the eyes of Freud, of a repetition compulsion? Of an eternal return of the same?"[1] The question stands as a provocation, one central to Lyotard's later work on affect. There is a hesitation here, a reflection of the disarming position that affect inflicts upon theoretical discourse, whether philosophical, psychoanalytic, or any other. A pause, perhaps unavoidable, afflicts any attempt to come to terms with affect, whether that found in Lyotard's essay "The Affect-Phrase," where the question is posed, or those that might seek to follow. What returns with affect, or the question of affect, brings a halt to the simple application of received discourses. The return that is posed here is not the recurrence of an object or a motif that could be tracked. Rather, faced with what lies beyond their bounds, the interruption worked by affect forces these knowledges to return upon themselves. Before the question of affect, philosophy, or any other genre of discourse, finds its own authority called into question and thereby is forced to once more interrogate its own constitution, to attempt to account for the disturbance that has been inflicted upon it, and thus to give an account of its own limits.

It is as such that "The Affect-Phrase" can be said to manifest a kind of return. The subtitle of the text—"From a supplement to *The Differend*"—announces it as marking what had been left unaddressed by the earlier work. It is in that work that Lyotard lays out his philosophy of the phrase, a deliberate attempt to break with his own earlier work as it had appeared in *Libidinal Economy* and the texts preceding. Dispensing with the motif of libidinal *dispositifs* (apparatuses) that had characterized his works in the 1970s and before, which he would later deride as yet attached to a "metaphysics of forces," *The Differend* takes as its motif a pragmatics of events of presentation, which he terms "phrases."[2] Despite the immediate association to which the term might well lead, the phrase is not necessarily a linguistic formation in a spoken or written language, though particular phrases might well be. To put it in its most simple form (though, as we will see, the notion is anything but simple): a phrase happens, it is the minimal instance of an event, what presents itself as the case without reference to any pre-given framework. The phrase is, within *The Differend* and also in those works that follow, the most elementary unit of analysis; that there is a phrase lies beyond doubt. Geoffrey Bennington summarizes the notion thus: "What is indubitable about a [phrase] is not its meaning, nor even its existence, its reality. Simply that there is a [phrase] is indubitable. That there is a phrase is presupposed in saying anything at all. In this conception, neither reality nor the subject stands prior to and in principle independent of a [phrase]."[3] The search for what remains beyond doubt, a gesture that Lyotard borrows from Descartes, nonetheless remains almost parodic; although it offers the basic unit of the analysis that runs through *The Differend*, the phrase is in no way a stable foundation upon which any certain knowledge might rest. It is rather to the contrary. The phrase presents, but what it will have presented—in other words, what it furnishes for representation—is left in abeyance, it is dependent upon further phrases that link onto it. As Lyotard writes, "[f]or there to be no phrase is impossible, for there to be *And a phrase* is necessary. It is necessary to make linkage. This is not an obligation, a *Sollen*, but a necessity, a *Müssen*. To link is necessary, but how to link is not."[4] A phrase, insofar as it is said to have been articulated, will have given a "phrase universe" constituted by four poles: those of its addressor, its addressee, its sense, and its referent. The linkage of phrases presupposes of the "prior" phrase that someone (addressor) will have said something (sense) to someone (addressee) about something (referent). These poles, as Lyotard remarks, are closer to transcendental conditions of articulation than they are to empirical facts; an everyday phrase, such as the command "get out," remains entirely comprehensible according to this framework, despite not explicitly marking three of the four poles.[5] Any of these four poles may serve as grounds for the linkage of phrases, either individually or together. Some examples, linking to the aforementioned command: "You can't tell me that!" (addressor), "who, me?" (addressee), "that is an imperative" (sense), "get out of where, exactly?" (referent). Or, of course, one might simply leave, implicitly affirming at least one, if not all four, of these poles. In each case, the former phrase is taken, through whichever poles, as a referent of that phrase which links onto it. The presentation is thereby represented, albeit via an important transformation; it is no longer a matter of the "it happens" of a current phrase-event, but the "what has happened" that the latter phrase determines through the response that it formulates. As one sees from the examples given, the multiple ways of linking onto a phrase show that there are multiple (and indeed, probably innumerable) ways in which this determination might take place, each yielding a different representation of the prior phrase.

This is to say that the presentation does not, in itself, determine the mode or the content of the latter phrase that represents it. That a phrase presents a universe at all is not necessarily given in the mode of its presentation; the four instances that constitute the universe are themselves only determined by the representations that are furnished by subsequent phrases that will have linked onto it. To further draw upon the same example; B stands to leave the room in response to the command, "get out," addressed by A; the linkage here affirms that A has addressed this phrase to B, its sense is clear, and its referent is the room that the two currently occupy. Seeing B head for the door, A then says, "I wasn't talking to you, I want C to leave." This third phrase undercuts the representation of the initial phrase that it discovers in the second phrase (leaving the room)—the representation of the first phrase given by the second is held to be incorrect, and another is rendered in its place. It is important to note that it is, as Lyotard declares, not the case that the second phrase would have misrepresented the universe of the initial presentation; there is no last phrase, no final word that would belong to a "reality" somehow given where presentation and representation would be set in accord, such that might serve as a universal final determinant for judgment.[6] Absent such a rule, there is only the interminable work of determination that is operated by the linkage of phrases, one that knows no ultimate finality; presentation and representation are radically heterogeneous modes. While the representation of a given phrase might claim, implicitly or explicitly, to reproduce a given presentation "faithfully," there is something of a ruse here; as Gérald Sfez remarks, "[e]ach time, the event arrives or not and time guarantees nothing. One is always in the apparent time of the first phrase and in the real time of the second."[7] The reconstruction is only ever fashioned belatedly, in the manner of the psychoanalytic *Nachträglichkeit* (belatedness), important to Lyotard's works following *The Differend*, yet already pertinent in that book, though not explicitly marked. While the instance of a phrase remains indubitable, its happening in no way renders beyond doubt the representation of what has happened. As Lyotard writes: "there are events: something happens which is not tautological with what has happened ... The case, *der Fall*, would be that something happens, *quod*, rather than what happens, *quid* ... The case is not that which is the case. The case is: *There is, It happens*. That is to say: *Is it happening?*"[8]

Despite the work of representation, the presentation remains in abeyance, in the lingering question that accompanies all determination. That there is this remainder is indicated by the fact that the poles which a given phrase presents remain open to dispute; it may yet be argued that there have been instances of misinterpretation and the question reopened as to who addressed a given phrase to whom, what it might have meant, or what its referent may have been.

Nevertheless, there remains the necessity that linkage be furnished; although presentation leaves its inevitable remainder, this does not by itself interrupt the linkage of phrases. The lack of a universal criterion does not imply that there are not local criteria belonging to genres of discourse, in their heterogeneity and their multiplicity. These genres serve to determine the linkage of phrases, each according to its own particular mode. These genres direct the linkage of phrases of different regimes (cognitive, interrogative, descriptive, etc.) towards a particular pragmatic end, according to which certain modes of linkage are deemed pertinent, and others not.[9] These genres, as Lyotard argues, provide means to link together phrases of different regimes, which are not translatable one into another, by subordinating them to a common purpose, be it to educate, to know, to persuade, and so on; the number of genres of discourse is perhaps, at least in principle, infinite.[10] However, precisely according to the heterogeneity of phrases, conflicts will arise; this is inevitable. It is here that the notion of the differend emerges:

> As distinguished from a litigation, a differend would be a case of conflict between (at least) two parties that cannot be equitably resolved for lack of a rule of judgment applicable to both arguments. One side's legitimacy does not imply the other's lack of legitimacy. However, applying a single rule of judgment to both in order to settle their differend as though it were merely a litigation would wrong (at least) one of them (and both of them if neither side admits this rule).[11]

A differend marks a certain discord in the process of the linkage, where the heterogeneity of phrases is not respected. It does not imply the cessation of this process; this would be impossible. Rather, it is that a phrase that links onto a prior phrase fails to do the former justice, in discounting the singular nature of its idiom. If there were a tribunal, or a third party to which the conflict could be referred, this would merely be a litigation; it would be a matter of considering the damage inflicted upon the phrase in the course of its violent translation. The differend is otherwise, in that such a rule of judgment does not avail itself; the damage is accompanied by the loss of means to articulate this injustice.[12] The idiom in which the damage could be asserted is disqualified *a priori* from the idiom in which it would necessarily be taken up, presenting a double bind. If the damage cannot be asserted because it entails the loss of the means to articulate this damage, then there is no damage. Lyotard terms this privation a wrong; there is a lack of a means where one should avail itself.[13] Lyotard further elucidates it:

> The differend is the unstable state and instant of language wherein something which must be able to be put into phrases cannot yet be. This state includes silence, which is a negative phrase, but it also calls upon phrases which are in principle possible. This state is signaled by what one ordinarily calls a feeling: "One cannot find the words," etc.[14]

Although the differend lends itself to no immediate articulation, as Lyotard indicates, it nonetheless signals itself at the level of sentiment, in a degree of pain, of frustration, or the vague sense that something has been left unsaid. This state refers to another mode of linkage, one that is in principle possible, even if it is not presently so, in which this unsaid might be brought to articulation. Despite the conflict between idioms, there remains the possibility that another means of linkage, one not yet available, might arrive to resolve this conflict, or at least to allow for its litigation. In short, the lack of a means of linkage does not imply that linkage is impossible; as Lyotard indicates in the quotation above, it is not yet available. The pain that indicates a case of differend signs a deprivation with regard to a linkage that, in principle, ought to be possible. This does not imply any practical guarantee of a result that could be made universal and the concomitant progressive unfolding of the capacities of linkage. Hegel remains one of the principal opponents of *The Differend*; borrowing from Adorno's *Negative Dialectics*, Lyotard asserts that this transcendental possibility of saying what remains yet unsaid might simply be to report upon the singularity of the case.[15] Nonetheless, it is important to note here that the differend, as it is theorized in the eponymous work, depends upon this projection of a possible means of linkage that would do justice to those entangled in a state of differend. Lyotard remarks that a break in phrasing that disavows the possibility of linkage to another idiom is not a differend.[16]

"The Affect-Phrase," then, marks a return to the notion of the differend, as a supplement to the earlier work; moreover, the title under which it was originally delivered, "*L'Inarticulé ou le différend même*" ("The Inarticulate, or the Differend Itself"), can only strike one as contradictory, if not bizarre. What is at stake in the later piece is not only an expansion of the notion of the differend, the differend itself, but also another kind of differend, precisely at the point where it refuses any sort of accord with itself, at the level of that sentiment that Lyotard had, in the earlier work, taken as the sign of a case of differend. The title, which Lyotard confesses to having modeled after that of Duchamp's *La mariée mise à nu par ses célibataires, même* (The Bride Stripped Bare by Her Bachelors, Even), in its own way lays bare the problem of the linkage between presentation and representation through the difficulty it presents for any translation.[17] The *même*, the "itself" of the title is equivocal, lending itself just as well to a reading of its sense as an "even so," where what was the same is already no longer the same. The title forces upon the translator a decision that necessarily leaves something unsaid; one decides upon the sense of the title (in various contexts, one might render *même* "itself," "the same," "exact," "even," "very," leaving aside a host of idiomatic constructions) and leaves other possible readings in abeyance. The mode here is, of course, the mode of affected language that Freud had discovered in the *Witz* (joke), the doubling, duplicity or intimation of sense through which the workings of the unconscious are indicated, while remaining themselves inarticulate. It is a matter of what presents itself within the domain of articulation while remaining heterogeneous to it, what presents itself apart from representation, and, in this sense, Lyotard reopens the problem of presentation and its linkage through the Freudian problematic of affect.

Affect, as Lyotard declares, is a phrase. However, this class of phrase, the "affect-phrase" of the essay's title, presents itself in a way that is little amenable to the analyses put forth in the earlier work. In contrast to those phrases that will have articulated a universe according to those four poles, addressor, addressee, sense, and referent, the affect-phrase appears as deficient; in presenting, it will have not furnished a universe. This is to say that it has no addressor, no addressee, no referent, and, from the standpoint of articulated discourse, it has no sense. Lyotard describes it thus:

> A phrase can be more or less articulated, its polarizations more or less marked. But the affect-phrase does not admit of these gradations. Inarticulate would signify: this phrase does not present a phrase-universe; it signals something of sense [*elle signale du sens*]; this sense is of one kind, pleasure and/or pain; this sense is not related to any referent ... this sense does not emanate from any sender (I) and does not address itself to any recipient (you). The signal that is the affect-phrase is tautegorical: *aisthēsis, Empfindung*. It is at once an affective state (pleasure or pain) and the sign of this state, that which Kant wrote of as aesthetic sentiment. Equally Freud separates affects from representations of a thing or of a word. They are testimonies, but testimonies that represent nothing to anyone.[18]

In contradistinction to an articulated phrase, the affect-phrase says nothing about any referent. It does not pass from any sender to any receiver. It is, like any phrase, an event, but one signaled only by the sentiment of pleasure and/or pain. But it would be overhasty to say that it is something felt. Precisely insofar as it has no addressee, the affect-phrase is not felt by anyone or anything, be it a subject, an organism, a consciousness. There is an excitation and concomitant pleasure and/or pain; that is all that one might say; to assume that it has a context, even a minimal one, is already to presuppose a ground that could be furnished only by the linkage of articulated phrases that here remains foreign. That is to say that the affect occurs, it excites "before" there is yet anyone or anything who could claim it as something undergone or experienced, who could claim to have felt it.[19] Thus divorced from articulated discourse, the affect-phrase implies nothing; it belongs to no regime of causality, nor to the schema of temporal unfolding that would undergird these regimes. As Lyotard indicates, "the time of sentiment is *now* [maintenant]."[20] This now is not one that belongs to the mapping of chronological time, which is the product of articulated phrases; it is the now of presentation, which remains otherwise than the now that is indicated by those phrases that attempt to represent it. This now is what is lacking in the movement of articulated phrases, which can only map temporality according to their linkage, designating a before and an after. Even as a "now" can be articulated, and is necessary to the establishment of chronology, this articulated "now" is not coterminous with the now of the affect phrase, insofar as what is articulated only appears "after," belatedly, according to the *nachträglich* (belated) determination of representation.

Divorced from the linkage of phrases and their temporality, affect could be construed to be indifferent. As Lyotard remarks, "[a]ffectivity is independent from its possible articulation. It does not await it ... it has no need of it to complete itself ... It is perhaps indifferent to articulation."[21] It neither presumes nor seeks an interlocutor, it neither responds nor does it await a response. It simply happens, apparently without regard to what precedes and what follows. Yet the phrase that declares the affect-phrase to be indifferent takes this affect-phrase as referent, after all, and thus should give pause. But just the same, that it should be brought into relation to articulated discourse is inevitable. Nevertheless, the model that Lyotard proposes in "The Affect-Phrase" differs in a significant fashion from that set forth in the earlier text, precisely insofar as what is here at stake is no longer a conflict between modes of articulated discourse. He writes:

> Many noteworthy characteristics follow from the fact that the affect-phrase is unarticulated. Here are three: 1. The affect-phrase appears not to let itself be linked

on to according to the rules of any genre of discourse; on the contrary, it appears only to be able to suspend or interrupt the linkages, whatever they are; 2. The affect phrase injures the rules of the genres of discourse; it creates a damage; 3. This damage in its turn gives rise to a wrong, because the damage suffered by discourse can be settled within the rules, but argumentation is in all cases inappropriate to the affect-phrase, if it is true that it does not give rise to a genre and cannot be argued. Consequently the damage that the affect-phrase makes the genres of discourse suffer transforms itself into a wrong suffered by the affect-phrase. The articulated phrase and the affect phrase can "meet" only in missing one another. From their differend, there results a wrong. If articulation and inarticulation are irreducible to one another, this wrong could be said to be radical.[22]

As inarticulate, the affect-phrase does not furnish other phrases with means by which it might be linked; its occurrence merely serves to interrupt or to suspend the process of linking phrases that might otherwise occur. These interruptions might be the imposition of silence, or the work of deformation that affect inflicts on articulated discourse, whether in the form of the *Witz*, of parapraxis, or other instances in which discourse shows itself to be affected, animated by something other than what one wanted to say. But where Freud, or at least a certain Freudianism, would there inaugurate a work of translation whereby it could be asserted that the affect is but a deformed instance of articulation, Lyotard does not turn in this direction. As he notes, affect inflicts a damage upon the rules of the genres of discourse; it does not inflict a wrong. This is to say that, following the definition set out in *The Differend*, this is not yet a case of differend. The damage inflicted upon articulated discourse does not in any way impede its ability to argue the case, since any argumentation can and will be carried out at the level of articulated discourse. The damage inflicted on articulated discourse is only a damage because there is no deprivation; indeed, the disturbance worked by affect will, in its own way, incite argumentation, even if only in the manner of a "what was that?" It is only in the third movement outlined in the passage above that the differend is introduced. The discourse or discourses, whatever they may be, that attempt to give an account of the occurrence of the affect-phrase necessarily wrong it. This is not, in any way, because the affect-phrase is silenced by articulated discourse; indeed, the affect-phrase is already silent. It gives nothing to be heard, it does not demand a response. The differend emerges precisely at the point where articulation presupposes that the affect-phrase, despite appearances, does indeed intend something, signifies something. The case becomes a differend insofar as the affect is made to "speak," treated as if it furnished material for articulation. Whereas the relation between affect and articulated discourse is only "initially" a damage inflicted upon discourse, it becomes a wrong when discourse attempts to treat affect in this way—in effect, articulated discourse deprives the affect-phrase of its very silence.

Thus construed, the status of the differend between the inarticulate and articulated phrases appears in a somewhat different light than Lyotard had developed in *The Differend*. Where, in the earlier work, perhaps owing to the legal framework that permeates many of its examples, one could say that something sought to be phrased, signaled by the frustration that something had been left unsaid; with affect, it is otherwise. Affect does not "want" to be heard. It remains indifferent to articulation. The wrong that is inflicted by articulated discourse dishonors this very indifference. It cannot let the remainder rest; a double bind emerges precisely at that point where articulated discourse goes after the affect-phrase, according to the necessity that linkage be furnished, in spite of the lack of means provided by the affect-phrase. To do justice to the affect-phrase, to respect its own impossible idiom, it would perhaps be necessary not to link onto it; this, precisely, is something that is not allowed to articulated discourse. There is, and indeed must be, an attempted "transcription" of affect into articulated discourse. As Lyotard writes:

> It appears that this transcription is inevitable, if only because within the order of discourse the affect phrase is inopportune, unseemly, and even disquieting. Your joy, your suffering, will be shown, despite everything, to have been legitimate all along; they would only have been upsetting because their "logic" was misunderstood. It could almost be said that the affect-phrase demands to be articulated in this way and even argued—as if the scandal that it procures from discourse was unsupportable. Discourse does not seem to be able to support for long an unarticulated and unargued remnant remaining outside its grasp.[23]

One could almost say that the affect-phrase demands to be articulated, but this demand is not imposed by the inarticulate phrase. It is attributed to that phrase by the articulated discourse that can neither admit nor tolerate this remainder that speaks nothing. The "nothing" that the affect speaks is, as Lyotard indicates, manifest within the order of discourse, as that disquieting presence that intrudes upon articulated discourse and disrupts it thereby attesting that which remains outside the grasp of any articulation. Though there is a differend between affect and articulated discourse whereby affect is wronged, affect is in no way troubled by this differend. It is rather the opposite. It is the *logos* that suffers the presence of affect, and which finds the presence of this remainder to be insufferable. As Jacob Rogozinski notes, articulated discourse is made to suffer a situation in which all of its possible means are found wanting. It is confronted with the possibility of the impossible, the presence of "that which could not happen, in any case, and which however happened."[24] That the affect-phrase should befall, in the manner of a presentation, does not in any way serve to dispel the sense in which it remains impossible according to the regimes of representation. In happening, it does not enter the register of events that may be identified, described, and known. Rather, its occurrence is the occurrence of the impossible *qua* impossible.

The suffering of the *logos* nonetheless does manifest itself through these disturbances within the movements of discourse, not as an articulation of sense, but in those breakages where the voice is let to show through. This voice, Lyotard argues, is to be read in the manner of the Aristotelian *phōnē*, as distinguished from articulated discourse, the *logos*. The human, as the well-known definition goes, is the animal endowed with *logos*, but like other animals, it also possesses *phōnē*. This voice, as Aristotle indicates, "is itself the sign of pain and of pleasure," means by which the tautegorical signal of affect is presented.[25] Thus construed, the voice serves as an immediate signal of affective states—*pathēmata*—that owe nothing to signification. Its mode of presentation is aesthetic, indicating via tone, tempo, and rhythm. Moreover, these phonic presentations, according to Aristotle, are *teleia*—perfect, entirely accomplished—insofar as they befall absolutely, without reference to what might come before or after; Lyotard accordingly notes that they await nothing.[26] It might be said then, that the *pathēmata* are themselves apathetic, indifferent to articulation, its chronology, and its sense; they stand unmoved by any possible term of temporal or positional relation. Moreover, they want nothing, suffer nothing, enjoy nothing, and, in a sense, are nothing. Faced with this nothing, the *logos* tries to make something of this nothing; in the attempt, it undergoes a disturbance that remains anterior to any logic.

Lyotard calls the mode of the affect-phrase, its impossible presentation, *infantia*, infancy. It lies anterior to representation, remaining outside of its means. Following its etymology, the infant is *in-fans*, unspeaking—the term serves to mark a state that the Aristotelian definition evokes, but nonetheless elides. The human might well be the animal that is endowed with *logos*, but it is not thus gifted from the moment of its birth. Lyotard gestures towards a dimension anterior to the human, an inhumanity that remains, or will have remained, constitutive of the human: the infant is born to affectability, not to the *logos*. This infancy is not to be construed as a historical childhood—such would be already to displace infancy in making it the referent of articulated phrases belonging to the narrative genre. Lyotard instead relates the term to the Freudian notions of primary narcissism and the polymorphous perversity of infantile sexuality; it indicates a state that stubbornly remains anterior to and outside the domain of the *logos*, adult genital sexuality, and the modes of linkage and relation that are there implied. Nonetheless, Lyotard sounds a note of dissatisfaction with this portrayal. The question demands also another approach; the Freudian depictions of infancy "remain anthropological. It is a question of elaborating the transcendental status of *infantia*."[27] Infancy designates what remains unlinked to articulation and the concomitant domains of the human and of possibility. This is to say that the notion of *infantia* cannot be derived from an empirical approach, whether in the conventional sense, or the extended one in which analytic observation might be included. *Infantia* does not yield itself to observation. It must be derived about the constitutive aporia that is found in the *logos*' differend with affect; however one might formulate the role played by affect, it remains within the umbra of its unyielding impossibility, giving nothing to representation. The affect-phrase neither knows nor cares for any interlocution, nor any *telos*. It does not communicate anything, but all the same it makes itself heard. The infant, for lack of the *logos*, does not speak the affect-phrase, but via the *phōnē*, such phrases are nonetheless signaled in the tone of a cry of pain and/or pleasure. As Lyotard indicates, this cry does not communicate anything; that would require that the affect-phrase be addressed. It signals, to no one, and from no one, the nothing of affect.

Removed as they are from representation, the *pathēmata* cannot be construed as bodily states, in which pain and/or pleasure is the effect of some cause inflicted upon a body conceived in terms of physiology or biology. As Lyotard writes:

> There is a body only as the referent of one or several cognitive phrases, attested to by the procedures for the establishment of reality. There are many sorts of body, according to the nature of the knowledge sought. Bodies thus suppose the *logos* for their existence. Only the logical animal *has* a body. The *phōnē* does not have a body since it is not referential. The pleasures and pains experienced in the adventure of the *infans* are only attributed to the excitation of such and such an erogenous zone by the articulate discourse of adults, which takes the organism as its referent. It is necessary to elaborate the status of the world or of the incorporeal chaos associated with affect, the status of the Thing (*la Chose*) ... Freud might have persisted in wanting to name this infantile affectivity sexuality, yet it is certain that it ignores completely the polarization linked to sexual difference.[28]

Deprived of the *logos*, the infant does not have a body; the assertion of such possession depends upon the body being the referent of an articulated phrase.

The presentation of the infantile affect-phrase is rather associated with an "incorporeal chaos," unmapped and unmappable, without position (which is to say not even the body of physics), the absolute site of affectability. This chaos does not belong to a world. It is rather the nothing of affect. Borrowing the term, though perhaps not the exact sense, from Lacan, Lyotard refers to this affective "nothing," the negated universe that it presents, as *la Chose*. Nevertheless, the pleasures and pains that the *infans* undergoes will be explained according to the phrases of adults, which attempt to link onto them, positioning the infant's cries according to a regime of causality that would allow it to be heard as if it were articulated. Despite the inarticulation of the affect phrase—it is unaddressed, and without sense or referent—the *logos* of the adult takes it as if it were a report on a bodily state that the infant addresses to another. The adult rationalizes the infantile cry, taking it as if it were an articulated phrase (albeit one that is articulated quite badly, in a rudimentary fashion) along the lines of, "I, the infant, ask you, the adult, for relief of my discomfort." In a quotidian fashion, this inevitable work of translation serves to preserve the child's life; nonetheless it mistakes the nature of the affective cry, thus inscribing the differend between *phōnē* and *logos*. The *logos* sets itself to work, "correcting" the affect-phrase. A phrase-universe is imputed to the affect-phrase, no matter the wrong.

One might well say, transforming the epicurean dictum, "If my infancy is, I am not; if I am, my infancy is not." Even so, the "I" of articulation will be inserted into narratives of origin, and will thus link itself to an infancy that is "mine." The infantile pleasures and pains that belong to no "I" are claimed, belatedly, by an "I"; they thereby constitute it through instating an account of its origin. The one who declares "I was indeed that child," errs in the assertion, but only up to a point. I was not that infant, but, in narration, I will have been the infant who rejoiced and who suffered; identity is asserted via the pronoun. Where I should not, could not have been, beyond the limit where the "I" is able to identify itself, recognition is nonetheless forced. In this equation, the "I" makes itself accountable for the excitements of infantile sexuality. The "I" discovers itself responsible for the infantile, for all the sordid pleasures and humiliations of its sexuality. These excitements, as Lyotard indicates, are "obscene"—they do not lend themselves to the stagings proffered by the *logos*, the attempts at representation that would make them apparent, understood, or even understandable. The movements of the *logos* cannot contain them.

Accordingly, the presence of affect inspires a constitutive disquiet, a state from which one does not depart. As Lyotard writes:

The infantile *phōnē* is innocent not because it has no fault, but because the question of what is just and what unjust is unknown to it, given that this question demands the *logos*. This question only poses itself with phrases that can present referents, senders and recipients—that is, all instances necessary to the thought of distribution, equality, and the communicability of proper names upon the instances of destination, which permit debate and argumentation. Infancy, like the first Adam, does not know that it is naked. And as much as the *logos* recovers the *phōnē* (redresses it, or dresses it over), it only suppresses it, or, the same, domesticates it, this ashamed innocence will always be able to surge forth in the course of articulated phrases in an impromptu fashion. But in that case one will be ashamed of it for being naked. The immodesty of affect will be culpable. Innocence and culpability arrive together, under the name of anxiety.[29]

The infant, Lyotard notes, is innocent. Unable to know relation, it necessarily ignores the question of what is just and what is unjust. It is not innocent in the eyes of the law; it is innocent of the law, precisely insofar as this knowledge depends upon articulate *logos*. Remaining outside of and anterior to the law, it would be impossible for the infant to submit to the dictates of articulated discourse. Only belatedly, when it learns to articulate, does the human acquire the knowledge of good and evil; as Lyotard indicates, with this knowledge, there arrives a concomitant shame. With articulation, one discovers one's own supposed sins of the past, of having been unaware, of having openly flaunted the sordid pleasures and pains of infantile sexuality, and, accordingly, of already having transgressed. Shame arrives in arrears, shame at having been incapable of shame when it was called for; therefore one is guilty of shameless transgression. Lyotard indicates that, like that first Adam, the infant is insapient, not knowing its own nakedness. Seduced by the serpent, and called to account by the divine, this Adam is introduced to articulation as already culpable, for having been an infant who paraded about nakedly. This nakedness is perhaps not one of a body, but the crime of having put infantile sexuality openly on display, of having flaunted before the *logos* its intolerable other. For this, the "I" will be held culpable, no matter its absence from the occasion of the purported crime; this is cause enough for anxiety. Accordingly, the *logos* vests (*vêt*) the infantile with an intention to which the *phōnē*, in its apathetic indifference, is entirely foreign. But, as Lyotard notes, it also revests the infantile. The verb *revêtir* may designate the clothing of what is naked, but also the granting of a function. With the supposed intention that is granted to the infantile, a legitimation of sorts is granted; genres of discourse will interpret the infantile cry as if it related to one *telos* or another. Affect is taken as if it could be made to serve, its indifference ignored. Thus its obscene nudity is covered over, one pretends that it had always been clothed. In attempting to cover over the infantile affect-phrase, the *logos* claims responsibility for it, and thus becomes culpable for its obscene crimes. The "I" is made guilty, by association to that which knows no sociation.

Thus the infantile affect persists in spite of its articulation by the *logos*, its attempt to domesticate it. It will not have been treated by articulated discourse, it will not been done away with; as Anne Tomiche remarks, "affect is excluded inside; it inhabits articulated discourse while being its radical other. The Thing and the affect-phrase name an otherness that can never be assimilated, an irreducible otherness that inhabits articulated discourse while being its radical other."[30] The affective thing persists as that impossible remainder, because of which one will have always remained an infant, party to affect. The human bears with its affective remnant, even as it would try to master it, or to forget its unruliness by articulating it; this unspeaking, animal, or inhuman remainder persists as integral, even constitutive of the human. The voice, as voice, never ceases to comport something of a cry; it is never a pure medium, it remains sonic matter that stands to give way to something other than the movements of articulation. This matter, signaled in the aesthetic, which is to say affective, movements of the voice remains singular, removed from the exchanges of signification; as Claire Nouvet argues, "the *phōnē* is neither the absolute other nor the absolute outside of articulated language. It can inhabit articulated language, but as a squatter, a clandestine guest, an 'outside within,' the presence of which articulated language does not even suspect."[31] This suspicion is deferred so long as the affected voice does not reassert itself through interruption, in the breaking of linguistic sense, announcing itself as an obstacle to the articulation of good sense. Though one might never anticipate its impossible befalling, affect stands always to assert itself in the progressions of articulated sense, thereby leaving one who presumes to speak once again exposed.

No matter what attempts might be made to dress over the affect-phrase, the presumptions of the *logos* are never realized. Articulation is made to suffer the failure of its means in the face of the anxiety provoked by the unrepresentable affect, and the humiliation of the discovery that its means have again proved fruitless. The *logos* suffers from the frustrations worked by the impossible presence of the affect-phrase, which remains outside any regime of possibility. Articulation here finds itself shaken, and made to differ from itself on account of its encounter with this other, an other that remains for it a source of the shame and imagined mockery that continually torment it. In this "meeting" of affect and the *logos*, culpability emerges, and articulated discourse becomes accountable for the disturbance. No matter the attempt, it can only reinscribe the wrong that it inflicts upon affect, at every turn. It is here, that one—or call it an "I," if you wish—emerges as inextricably responsible for the activity of that which does not belong to it, and which demands no response.

Notes

1   Jean-François Lyotard, "The Affect-Phrase," in *The Lyotard Reader and Guide,* eds Keith Crome and James Williams (New York: Columbia University Press, 2006), 106.

2   Jean-François Lyotard, "Emma," in *Lyotard: Politics, Philosophy and the Sublime,* ed. Hugh J. Silverman (New York: Routledge, 2003), 25.

3   Geoffrey Bennington, *Lyotard: Writing the Event* (New York: Columbia University Press, 1988), 124–5. Simply for the sake of consistency, I have replaced his rendering of the French *phrase* as "sentence" with its English cognate; the term has been translated both ways in the various editions of Lyotard's works in English.

4   Jean-François Lyotard, *The Differend: Phrases in Dispute,* trans. Georges Van Den Abbeele (Minneapolis: University of Minnesota, 1988), 66.

5   Lyotard, "The Affect-Phrase," 104–5.

6   Lyotard, *Differend,* 17.

7   Gérald Sfez, *Jean-François Lyotard, la faculté d'une phrase* (Paris: Galilée, 2000), 91, my translation.

8   Ibid., 79.

9   Lyotard, *Differend,* 29.

10 Ibid.

11 Ibid., 84.

12 Ibid., xi.

13 Ibid.

14 Ibid., 13.

15 Ibid., 86–8.

16 Ibid., 106.

17 Niels Brügger, "Examen oral: Entretien avec Jean-François Lyotard," in *Lyotard, Les Déplacements philosophiques,* eds Niels Brügger, Finn Fransen, and Dominique Pirotte (Brussels: DeBoeck-Wesmael, 1993), 141–2, my translation. On the *même* of this title, see also Geoffrey Bennington's "The Same, Even, Itself," in his *Late Lyotard* (Lexington: Createspace, 2005), 43–64.

18 Lyotard, "The Affect-Phrase," 106, translation modified.

19 For a greater exposition of the consequences of inarticulation, see Claire Nouvet, "The Inarticulate Affect: Lyotard and Psychoanalytic Testimony," in *Minima Memoria: In the Wake of Jean-François Lyotard,* eds Claire Nouvet, Zrinka Stahuljak, and Kent Still (Stanford: Stanford University Press, 2007), 107–13.

20 Lyotard, "The Affect-Phrase," 106, translation modified.

21 Ibid., 109.

22 Ibid., 105.

23 Ibid., 106, translation modified.

24 Jacob Rogozinski, "Lyotard, Le Différend, La Présence," in *Témoigner du Différend : quand phraser ne se peut* (Paris: Editions Osiris, 1989), 68, my translation.

25 Aristotle, *Politics* 1253 a15; the quotation is given in "The Affect-Phrase," 107.

26 Lyotard, "The Affect-Phrase," 105.

27 Ibid., 109.

28 Ibid.

29 Lyotard, "The Affect-Phrase," 110, translation modified.

30 Anne Tomiche, "Rephrasing the Freudian Unconscious: Lyotard's Affect-Phrase," *Diacritics* 24.1 (Spring 1994), 59.

31 Nouvet, "The Inarticulate Affect," 114.

2

For "Emma"

Claire Nouvet

Why write "Emma" as a kind of philosophical companion piece to "The Affect-Phrase"? Why turn, yet again, to this psychoanalytic case already evoked in *Heidegger and "the jews"*? If Lyotard returns to Emma in *Misère de la philosophie*, it is, he insists, to pursue an idea that is not "psychoanalytic" but "philosophical." Through the Emma case and under her name, as it were,[1] he writes indeed one of his most complex philosophical reflections on affect as an inarticulate phrase and its differend with articulation, a differend to which this case gives a distinctly sexual twist. I propose to follow this philosophical reflection before turning to aspects of the case that it leaves aside, but which a certain thought of the differend gives us the means to approach.

Emma comes to analysis because she is unable to go into stores alone. She traces this phobia to an incident that happened when she was twelve years old: "She went into a shop to buy something, saw the two shop assistants ... laughing together, and ran away in some kind of *affect of fright*."[2] But, as Freud points out, this conscious memory explains "neither the compulsion nor the determination of the symptom."[3] Analysis reaches another memory: "On two occasions when she was a child of eight, she had gone into a small shop to buy some sweets, and the shopkeeper had grabbed at her genitals through her clothes. In spite of the first experience she had gone there a second time; after the second time she stopped away."[4] After reconstructing the network of unconscious associations that linked the two scenes (Emma is again alone in a store, and the shop assistants' laughter at her clothes reminds her of the shopkeeper's grin as he grabbed her genitals though her dress), Freud concludes: "Here we have the case of a memory arousing an affect which it did not arouse as an experience, because in the meantime the change [brought about] in puberty had made possible a different understanding of what was remembered."[5]

With the Emma case, Freud elaborates the temporality of *Nachträglichkeit* (afterwardsness) or "*après-coup*," as Lyotard calls it, an expression that underlines both the "*coup*," the "blow," and the "strike" of the affect as well as the temporal gap between the two. When is Emma struck—that is, affected—by the blow that the shopkeeper delivers? For Freud, not at the time of the event, but much later, at puberty. And, then, it is not the event that strikes, but its reactivated memory. The memory, not the event, produces the affect (fright) that triggers repression. Why did the event not provoke any affect? Because Emma, at the time of the event, had not yet reached puberty, the stage of psychological development that would allow her to understand the sexual nature of the shopkeeper's gesture. Nor had she reached the stage of physiological maturation that would allow her to respond to his gesture. It is only afterwards, at puberty, that she will be equipped to both understand and respond to the sexual significance of the scene. Then, and only then, will she be affected by it.

Lyotard opposes Freud's interpretation, which turns the alteration due to puberty into a "birth to passibility."[6] At eight years old, Emma had been affected, as evidenced by her return to the store where she had been assaulted. But, then, how can one account for her lack of emotional response? This requires an elaboration of the notion of affect that Lyotard began in *Heidegger and "the jews"* where he reminds us that, for Freud, excitations can shock the psychic apparatus to such a degree that the psyche cannot register them. These excitations are excessive in the precise sense that they exceed all available representation. They nevertheless have an "effect": "Even so, there is an 'effect.' Freud calls it 'unconscious affect.'"[7] However, as the quotation marks around this "effect" signal, Lyotard maintains reservations regarding the "metaphysics of forces" that underlies Freud's early metapsychology. To avoid this metaphysics by rethinking affect as an unarticulated phrase is the task pursued in "Emma" as well as "Voix" ("Voice"), a reading of Freud's Rat Man case, where Lyotard reflects "upon the unconscious affect, that is, intensity in non-metaphysical terms, in terms, strictly, of sentences."[8] While distancing himself from Freud's "metaphysics," Lyotard nevertheless elaborates on Freud's unconscious affect to correct, in "Emma," Freud's reading. Far from signaling an impassibility (as it did for Freud), the absence of representation signals, for Lyotard, the affect that seized Emma.

This lack of representation dooms affect to forgetting. As Lyotard points out, the scene with the shopkeeper "has been forgotten, put to sleep."[9] Does this mean that it has been repressed? Not quite. Emma forgets it not through secondary repression (which bears upon representations), but through primal repression, which, as he puts it somewhat enigmatically, "consists in not repressing."[10] While secondary repression "forgets" that which is remembered in a representation, primal repression "forgets" that for which there is no representation. Emma "forgets" the scene because she cannot attach any representation to the affect that it generated. And it is not that images of the event would be "too blurred or too pale, they are not at all."[11] In place of an image: a blank. Two types of forgetting need therefore to be distinguished: a "representational, reversible forgetting" (the forgetting of secondary repression) and "a forgetting that thwarts all representation," which is at stake in primal repression.[12] As it "thwarts all representation," affect is both forgotten and unforgettable. It is forgotten since it lacks the representation that would allow it to be inscribed as a "memory." And it is unforgettable precisely because it is not inscribed as a memory, a mnemic representation, that one can then proceed to "forget." These two types of forgetting (or repression) lead to the distinction between two kinds of unconscious. Besides the unconscious constituted through secondary repression and composed of thing-representations (representations of things), Lyotard insists that Freud had to hypothesize another unconscious, constituted through primal repression, "where there are no representations, not even disguised, indirect, reworked, reshaped ones."[13] Affect belongs to this second kind: it is unconscious because it was never attached to a representation.

What is at stake in the Emma case is an unconscious that is not constituted of representations, but of these "traces" devoid of representation that affects are. As Lyotard notes, Freud's interpretation of the case presupposes the existence of mnesic traces to which Emma attaches, at puberty, sexual representations which trigger the generation of affect. But what are these traces? Lyotard sets up an alternative: either they are representations of the event made in a prepubescent language, or they are the affects themselves. And he decides for the second option: "It seems to me that one must opt for this second interpretation: these traces are what must be read or represented; they are not preceding representations. . . . And in this case, these traces being affects, puberty in no way creates them; it creates only another 'reading' of an affect already there."[14] The adolescent does not reinterpret (with the representations provided by the language of sexuality) mnesic traces that would be already representations, such as those that a prepubescent language would afford. Instead, s/he attaches "sexual" representations to affect-traces devoid of representation in order to make sense of them. This interpretation is, in principle, interminable: one will keep interpreting, that is, representing in various languages and over the course of a lifetime, a trace-affect that is indeterminate because it is devoid of representation.[15]

Forgotten for lack of representation, the unconscious affect is inarticulate in Lyotard's precise sense of "inarticulacy." It ignores the four poles that articulate a phrase and allow for its linkage with another phrase: addressor, addressee, meaning, and referent. Since it is unrepresentable, it is indeterminate and cannot therefore convey any qualifiable meaning. Lyotard indeed links the question of meaning to the question of quality when, recalling the Freudian distinction between "affect as quantity" and "affect as quality," he translates "quality of affect" as "sentimental meaning": "in terms of its quality (its sentimental meaning) and its addressedness (addressor/addressee), the affect can repeatedly assume any number of meanings."[16] Meaning requires a qualification of affect. When Lyotard states that a qualified affect has a "sentimental meaning," this qualified affect is, then, a "feeling." Once qualified, affect becomes a feeling which belongs to articulation: "quality and address are still, or already, what in affect pertains, however much removed, to the representative, to articulation, and to time."[17] This qualified affect, this "feeling," is not the affect that he is trying to approach through the Emma case. Feelings, insofar as they are qualified (i.e., have a "sentimental" meaning), are distinct from affects that are indeterminate, unqualifiable, devoid of "sentimental meaning," since they are not tied to a representation. In other words, the very indeterminacy of affect (which is the mark of its excessive intensity) distinguishes it from a determinate and qualified feeling. And if Lyotard does not stress this distinction between affect and feeling, it is, I believe, because, in other texts, he thinks affect through the notion of "feeling" used by the philosophical corpus he engages. However, the "feelings" that interest him are not those endowed with "sentimental meaning," but rather those close to the Freudian unconscious affect, feelings that preempt representation and therefore qualification, such as Kant's sublime. Lyotard reminds us that, for Kant, a feeling is sublime insofar as it is "energetic," an energetic notion of the sublime that he ties to the Freudian affect as the indeterminate quantity that "overloads" (*surcharge*) the psychic apparatus.[18] In other words, the "feeling" of the sublime is akin to what Freud called an unconscious affect and what Lyotard rephrases in "Emma" as the inarticulate affect.

Devoid of "sentimental meaning" because of its lack of representation, "[t]he affect is not lived."[19] It is not lived as a first-person experience, since it is so "off the charts" that the subject cannot consciously register it in a representation that would allow her to feel it according to the spectrum of available feelings at her disposal. Lyotard compares it to ultrasound or infrared light: "It is like a whistle that is inaudible to humans but not to dogs, or like infrared or ultraviolet light."[20] It is that which the subject cannot perceive, feel or hear. It follows that it cannot be addressed from an "I" to a "you," since there is no "I" to "live" it. In Emma's case, her lack of feeling and emotional response is the indication that the ego is overwhelmed and, as it were, dismissed by an affect so intense that it exceeds what it knows how to feel. Apathy signals the overwhelming excess that is the inarticulate affect.

Finally, affect does not have a referent. Referentiality implies that phrases speak "about" an object. Since the constitution of an object presupposes representation, affect cannot have an "object." Devoid of representation (either word-representation or thing-representation), it cannot be attached to any "thing," any object that could function as the object, the referent of a discourse. The unconscious affect is therefore "no-thing": "The phrase of affect 'says' that there is something, as *Da*, here and now, inasmuch as this something is *nothing*, not meaning, not referent, not address."[21] Affect is this "something," "here and now," which, for lack of representation, escapes chronological time, cannot be topographically situated in the psyche, does not convey any meaning, and is not consciously "lived" or felt by the subject, whose powers of representation and synthesis it defeats and whose consciousness it overwhelms. It cannot be addressed by an "I" to a "you," as the referent of a communication that could presume to say its "meaning." Its unrepresentability condemns affect both to inarticulacy and "unconsciousness," which are not the mark of a specific category of affects to be distinguished from other conscious and articulate affects. Through the Emma case, Lyotard points to the forgetting and inarticulacy that distinguishes "*affects*" that exceed representation from "*feelings*" that can still be bound to a representation.

One may wonder at this point about their status. If the inarticulate affect is unconscious due to a process akin to primal repression, *how* is it unconscious? How to conceive of the "existence" in the psyche of an affect devoid of representation? Strictly speaking, it is not "in" the psyche, as Lyotard points out in his commentary on Freud: "It is an excitation that is not 'introduced': it affects, but does not enter; it has not been introduced ... and remains unpresented."[22] Since it does not present/introduce itself to the psyche bound to a representation, affect does not enter/introduce itself into the psychic apparatus. "Deposited outside representation,"[23] it is not localizable "within" a psychic apparatus composed of representations. It is "outside" (it "ek-sists" as Lyotard puts it),[24] because it is "in excess" of the representations that the psyche processes. As such, it is that which the psyche cannot treat, fashion, transform, or put to work. Devoid of representation, it floats like a "cloud," an indeterminate and shapeless excitation that cannot be organized in thoughts, words, or images of things: "I imagine the effect of the shock, the unconscious affect, to be like a cloud of energy particles ... that are not organized into sets that can be thought in terms of words or images."[25] This affective "cloud" (the metaphorical representation that Lyotard favors for an affect that precludes representation) does not stand simply "outside" the psyche as an "outside" that could neatly be separated from an "inside." It "floats" through it and in-fuses it without having any place within it. It diffuses itself throughout the psyche as the excitation "in excess" that it cannot bind to its representative formations. It does not "take place" in it, since it lacks the representation necessary to be inscribed either in a topography or a chronology. Devoid of representation, it is not a "present" that could ever become a "past." Time passes; its intensity neither passes nor wears away. It remains, immune to the tempering that chronological time inflicts even on the most intense of qualified feelings. Unregistered in space and time, the unconscious affect stagnates outside representation in a stasis that preserves in-tact (i.e., untouched by any qualification) its inarticulate and indeterminate intensity: "An 'excitation' occurs, and it remains in place. This stasis is the affect-phrase."[26]

As it stagnates, the unconscious and inarticulate affect insists. An event that cannot be tied to any representable scene, it "ek-sists inside, in-sisting, as what exceeds every imaginative, conceptual, rational synthesis."[27] As Mark Stoholski argues, we should not conclude that this insistence "demands" anything. Lyotard makes this crucial point in "Emma." Since "[a] demand is an expectation of linking,"[28] the affect-phrase, insofar as it does not provide any of the poles (addressor, addressee, meaning, referent) necessary for another phrase to link onto it, cannot demand anything. And yet, as Stoholski also notes: "*logos* ... suffers the presence of affect, and ... finds the presence of this remainder to be insufferable."[29] Like the drive that extracts labor from the psychic apparatus without asking for it, affect "insists," because it exceeds the mind's powers of representation and synthesis. It is in this sense that Lyotard sometimes calls it an "affliction" and a "misery": its excess "afflicts" the mind by defeating its powers and showing its insufficiency, its "misery." (This misery is also the "misery" of philosophical thought when it takes affect as the object of its reflection, as indicated in the title of the book where "Emma" is included: *Misère de la philosophie.*) Although it knows nothing of the affect that clandestinely occupies it, the mind, Lyotard suggests, nevertheless suffers from this "no-thing" that infuses it through and through without ever being localizable "within" any of its representations. For a psyche that requires binding in order to work, for a mind that requires linkages in order to think, the unqualified affective "cloud" can only be "bad" because it is the indeterminate excess that remains inarticulate "within" the linkages of articulation. As Lyotard puts it in "Emma," the affect-phrase is a "stasis" which "remains in place" (*stationne*) without moving, a stoppage of sorts that interrupts movement by not participating in it. As stasis, the inarticulate affect-phrase "stops" articulation by stagnating within it. Unlinked and unmovable, it stands still in the very midst of articulation and of the movements that its linkages afford. This stasis rephrases the Freudian notion of affect as a quantity that "overloads" (*surcharge*) the psyche: "By 'overload' (a mechanistic metaphor), one indicates the 'presence' of a non-significative phrase (pleasure or pain?), neither destined (from whom to whom?) nor referenced (about what?), which occurs unexpectedly in the course of the phrases."[30] Under the insistence of this inarticulate excess, the mind sets itself to work in order to work it "out," to get rid of it. And to do so, it will seize any occasion to bind the unconscious inarticulate affect to a representation.

In Emma's case, the scene with the two shop assistants provides such an occasion. While he does not tackle the details of this scene, Lyotard suggests a way of reading it when he mentions that puberty is the time when one can interpret in the "language of sexuality" affective traces devoid of representation. What this remark suggests (but leaves undeveloped) is that Emma, at twelve years old, tries unconsciously to bind the affective trace left by the shopkeeper's gesture to the scene with the shop assistants. This binding produces an "anxiety" that Lyotard interprets as the recurrence of the unconscious affect. Anxiety, he suggests, marks the failure to bind the unconscious affect to the representation that the scene with the shop assistants provided. Instead, the unconscious affect seizes this occasion to re-present itself, that is, to present itself again, because it cannot represent itself in any representation: "If it re-presents (itself), it is precisely because it represents nothing. It only keeps occurring, now and now."[31] A presence without representation, it presents itself over and over again, without ever representing itself, each time as if it were the first time, a temporal complication that the French expression "*une nouvelle fois*" ("once again") captures, as Lyotard notes: each time of the reiteration is as "new" as a "first" time.[32]

As it keeps presenting itself without ever representing itself, the inarticulate affect traverses chronological time. It also traverses Emma with anxiety attacks that reduce her to a mere blank: she "forgets herself" during the phobic episodes that "interrupt" the "continuity of her adult time,"[33] that is, the chronological time of an "adult" state which "minimally determines itself by a preponderance of the articulated phrase."[34] Can we, then, still call her "Emma" when, in the grip of affect, she loses herself? Identity indeed is a matter of articulation insofar as "the articulated phrase" "gathers an entity (now an addressor, now an addressee) under the same name. . . . Emma is the same in all the instances of address and of reference presented by the adult phrases that concern her, simply because she always and everywhere names herself or is named 'Emma.'"[35] Different meanings can be articulated about "Emma" as long as her name is attached to the three poles that she can alternatively occupy, addressor ("I"), addressee ("You"), and referent. But when she is seized by affect, "Emma" is no longer the identifiable "someone" that could address and be addressed, the nameable "subject" that one can posit as the referent of a discourse which could claim to articulate meanings about "her." In short, she is no longer "Emma," no longer a "person" to whom a proper name can be attached that (by its alternative occupation of the poles of addressor, addressee and referent) guarantees her self-identity and self-continuity through the chronology of an adult life that could be called her own. When affect strikes, the very notion of person:

> can be a lie with respect to the "presence" that is the affect-phrase. What is *pseudos* here is the articulation, which I reduce, for convenience, to the triple instantiation of the pronominal person, when it applies itself to "presence." The "excitation" is nothing but the affect, and if it is disturbing, that is because it dissipates (to what degree it does not matter) the triple disposition which is the guarantee of identity.[36]

How, then, are we to read the title of Lyotard's text: "Emma"? Is it simply a proper name? I do not think so. Under this name is written a text that denounces the lies and the deceptions that are the proper name and the very notion of person as far as affect is concerned. "Emma," in other words, is a pseudonym of sorts, a false proper name for the dissipation of identity and of proper names that affect inflicts. To write about "Emma," as the title indicates, is to write about an inarticulate affect that turns all proper names into pseudo-names that hide its obliteration of the proper name.

Affect "dissipates" the very notion of "person" as well as the distinction between persons, a dissipation that Lyotard reads in another "Emma," the "Emma" of Flaubert's *Madame Bovary*. While, in Freud's report, "Emma" functions as a referent, an "objectified third person," such is not the case in Flaubert's use of "free indirect style" which "condenses" "referent and addressor."[37] To illustrate the difference, Lyotard gives two sentences: "She returns to the store" and "No, she would not return to the store." In this last sentence, which exemplifies free indirect style, "she" is a "false [*fausse*] third person,"[38] "false" because Emma seems to be speaking/addressing through the "she" that the narrative voice posits as its referent. By condensing referent and addressor, free indirect style disrupts articulation and, in so doing, signals an inarticulate affect. For Lyotard, it is the task of literature "to try to write an inarticulate affect that cannot be written," to give a sense of its inarticulacy by inflicting stylistic "infringements" upon linguistic articulation that can be as "modest" as Flaubert's free indirect style.[39] However modest, this disturbance of articulation is nevertheless "analogous to the occurrence of an affect, oblivious to the distinctions of person."[40] Through the condensation of the positions of addressor and referent, literature attests to the occurrence of an affect that obliterates the very notion of a "person" and, therefore, the distinction between "persons."

If literature is dedicated to the task of signaling affect through its singular disarticulations, is Freud's report as disaffected as Lyotard implies when he insists that it posits "Emma" as an "objectified third person"? After all, Lyotard himself notes a strange error in Freud's report. As he argues that it is the memory of the event that generates an affect, Freud writes: "The memory awakens ... what it was evidently unable [to do] then, a sexual release." Lyotard comments: *"Was sie damals gewiss nicht konnte"* (what it/she—*sie*—at the time clearly could not do). The German *sie* grammatically echoes *die Erinnerung*. But the echo is semantically inconsistent, since *then* the memory was not a memory. Rather she—*sie*—Emma was then not capable of this 'sexual discharge.'"[41] Freud makes this error twice, as Lyotard remarks when he quotes again Freud: "Here is a case where a memory awakens [*erweckt*] an affect that it would not have awakened when it was actually experienced [*als Erlebnis*, same semantico-grammatical paradox as the preceding]."[42] Lyotard signals the repeated mistake, but does not explain. I will try. Freud loses control of his syntax and ends up confusing the event ("before") and its memory ("after"), thereby disarticulating the logic of the argument that he is trying to articulate, ironically enough, about the very generation of an affect. This disarticulation signals, I believe, the "presence" of an inarticulate affect that traverses, resists and confuses the chronology as well as the logical articulation of Freud's report.

And what of philosophy? Does it simply write a disaffected discourse "about" Emma? Or is it also writing, in a way, about what affects philosophy? This is indeed what Lyotard suggests, in a complicated manner, when he turns "Emma" into the pseudo-name for the "nothing" that is the inarticulate affect, insofar as it negates the poles of articulation (addressor, addressee, referent, meaning). In so doing, he transforms Emma, the eight year old little girl assaulted in a store, into a version of the "nothing" that, as he points out, philosophy is tempted to resist precisely because this nothing "resists understanding and reason."[43] But this nothing is also that which under different names or maybe pseudo-names (absolute skepticism, nihilism, *taedium vitae spiritus*, *desperatio cogitandi*, Kant's *Unding*) excites philosophy, at least the kind of philosophy that interests Lyotard.

Philosophical thinking is indeed excited by what he calls a "contradictory affect, pain and pleasure, pleasure caused by pain" which is "without doubt the first stirring of philosophy—its *excitatio*—the recurrent occasion for the act of philosophizing."[44] In other words, philosophical thinking is excited by the "pain" that some "thing," or rather a "no-thing," exceeds thought and its linkages, and by the "pleasure" derived from this very excess, which excites thought to think what challenges its power and surpasses what it knows how to think. To write about "Emma" is, then, to write about the nothing that excites philosophy into thinking, the kind of "nothing" that excites Lyotard to "do" philosophy, not as a performance of knowledge, but as a pursuit. And what excites this thinking is not just the nothing of affect, but its differend with articulation.

It is indeed this philosophical idea that Lyotard is excited to pursue through "Emma," even at the cost of allegorizing her in the process, first by turning her into the figure for the inarticulacy of affect, and, then, for what he calls "infantile affectability." In Lyotard's account, Emma is indeed no longer an eight-year-old child. She represents an infantile affectability that, insofar as it ignores the articulation of sexual difference, is incommensurate with the adult articulation of affectability in terms of sexual difference that the shopkeeper represents. Here is Lyotard's translation of the shopkeeper's gesture as he grabs Emma's genitals: "His gesture 'says': listen to the difference of the sexes, i.e. to genitality. He places the child all at once in the position of a 'you' in an exchange she doesn't understand, as well as in the position of a woman in a sexual division which she also doesn't comprehend."[45] And he adds that, in so doing, his gesture forces infantile affectivity "to identify itself with one of the sexes, to refer to the other as an entity, namely as an object, that it cannot embody, and to finally address itself to that object as its intended partner."[46] Lyotard, in other words, turns the shopkeeper into the representative of an adult sexuality that is articulated in terms of sexed persons whose sexual object or intended partner is the one "they cannot embody," that is, the other sex.[47] His grabbing of Emma's genitals is read metaphorically as the violent imposition that this adult and "normative" articulation of sexuality inflicts on an infantile affectivity that ignores it. We are witnessing a philosophical allegorization of the case that changes the cast of characters. Emma stands for an infantile affectivity that is not articulated in terms of sexual difference, and the shopkeeper for an adult sexuality that "grabs" infantile affectivity, that is, forces upon it the articulation of sexual difference. Their encounter stages the differend between inarticulate infantile affectivity and articulated adult sexuality. As for this infantile affectivity, "[a]nthropologically speaking, it is bound up with childhood. Transcendentally (in the Kantian sense), it is nothing other than the faculty of pleasure and pain, 'pure' because it is derived from no other faculty.... In the 'phrasistics' where I venture, it signals a passibility more 'archaic' than all articulation and irreducible to it."[48]

As he turns "Emma" into the pseudo-name both for a possibility irreducible to articulation and for an infantile affectability that ignores "sexual division," Lyotard knows that he performs an erasure to which he himself calls attention when he remarks that "[o]ne will say that she was not ignorant of these matters [sexual division] when she was eight years old. I admit this, although it is not essential to the idea, philosophical and not psychoanalytic, that I pursue [*"l'idée philosophique, et non psychanalytique, que je poursuis"*].[49] It indeed does not matter for the idea that he pursues through "Emma." But, in so doing, Lyotard (like many other readers before him) leaves aside another aspect of the case, to which I will now turn.

In Lyotard's account, the shopkeeper represents, metaphorically as it were, the imposition that adult sexual articulation inflicts on an affectivity that ignores it. While useful for the philosophical point that he wishes to make, this metaphorical reading depathologizes the abusive literality of the phrase. There is indeed a more troubling aspect of the shopkeeper that is ignored when he becomes the representative of adult articulation in general, as it violently imposes itself on an infantile affectivity that ignores articulation. To put it simply, not every grown-up imposes the articulation of adult sexuality on infantile affectivity by grabbing the genitals of an eight-year-old girl. In other words, what is hidden in plain sight in the Emma case is, I believe, another differend than the "general" differend between inarticulate affectivity and adult articulation. What is lurking in this case is the singular differend of sexual abuse, a differend that the philosophical allegorization of the case leaves aside, but which Lyotard also gives us the means to think, or at least to begin to think, as precisely being a differend, the kind of differend that Annie Leclerc tries to articulate in *Paedophilia ou l'amour des enfants (Paedophilia or the Love of Children).*[50] In this book, which was only published after her death, she attempts to explain the silence of sexually abused children, a silence that she shared, although she was the victim of what she calls "minor" pedophilic aggressions. She does not narrate—not in detail—what happened at the hands of a familiar figure who, much like the shopkeeper of the Emma case, grabbed her repeatedly. Instead of a narration, a figure is proposed: the figure of the closed parental bedroom door, which protects by forbidding access to adult sexuality, thereby allowing the child to conduct her own sexual investigation, in a place of her own, separate from theirs, where she is "neither guilty of her desire nor guilty of her secret."[51] The parental interdiction figured by the closed door also protects by underlining an impossibility: the child *should* not enter the bedroom of the adult because she *cannot* enter it. It protects by marking the radical incommensurability between adult sexuality and infantile affectability. Pedophilia, says Leclerc, opens the door between these two incompatible spaces. The child is made to stand where she literally cannot stand. And to stand where one cannot stand cuts one's legs, which weaken, and one's tongue, which petrifies.

The pedophile transgresses the limit. The child tries to reinstate it by pretending that what is happening is not happening: "One is forced to act as if all this did not exist. What needs to be saved is the intangible authority of the Law. . . . One closes one's eyes. One submits."[52] But this "as if," which tries to obey the law by ignoring its transgression, comes at the cost of a confusion. Everything gets "muddled." Words are "blurred," for they have lost the distinctions that allow them to make sense. They have become a disgusting magma where obedience to the parental Law has been inverted into submission to the transgression of the Law, where one no longer knows "what a grown-up is, what a child is, what she is,"[53] where one also no longer knows what she, as a child, might have wanted in the first place. This confusion, I will suggest, is the "affect" of this specific kind of differend.

And it is with an attention to this "affect" that I would like to return to Emma and to the translation that Lyotard proposes of the shopkeeper's gesture:

> what breaks into Emma's affective phrase . . . is that the shopkeeper *addressed himself* to her as "you [*toi*], a woman." His gesture "says": listen to the difference of the sexes, i.e. to genitality. He places the child all at once in the position of a "you" in an exchange she doesn't understand, as well as in the position of a woman in a sexual division which she also doesn't comprehend.[54]

A few remarks. First, the gesture of the shopkeeper is not simply a demand to listen to the difference of the sexes. At eight years old, Emma, as Lyotard himself points out, has probably already listened to it, in her own way. It is not a listening that is demanded, but a placing that is imposed, as he also suggests. I would therefore propose the following translation of this phrasing: "I am addressing you as a woman precisely because you are not a woman, but a child." The shopkeeper does not seek the "genitalized woman" that the child cannot be. He seeks the child, and a child to abuse by placing her in the position that she cannot occupy: that of a genitalized woman. Although difficult to articulate, this difference seems to me essential. The shopkeeper is not merely a party in the creation of the differend, a party that would be on the side of an "adult" and "genitally" articulated sexuality according to the division of the sexes. What he seeks is the very imposition of the differend upon the child, that is, of the incommensurability between infantile affectivity and adult sexuality. He targets infancy, not to teach it the difference of the sexes, but to impose upon it a performance of sexed division that it precisely cannot perform.

My second remark will elaborate on a dimension that Lyotard is the only one, to my knowledge, to bring to the foreground: the dimension of address, and more specifically the distinction between what he calls, in English, "addressedness" and "affectedness." In his philosophical rewriting of the case, Emma stands for an infantile affectivity that is "affectable," but not "addressable."[55] She cannot be addressed, because infantile affectivity as such does not belong to an "I," a fully constituted subject who could permute into the "you" of an address. But the shopkeeper does address her, an address that, according to Lyotard, breaks into Emma's affective phrase. He addresses the child as "You, woman." To give a sense of the difference that is at stake, Lyotard relies on a comparison. It is as if the shopkeeper addressed Emma in a foreign language that she does not know, cannot translate, and to which she cannot respond. And he concludes: "The speaker addresses us, but we are only affected by this 'address' and not properly addressed. In this way, Emma would be affected by the phrase that is the gesture of the shopkeeper despite being unable to be 'addressed' by him."[56]

Emma is not properly addressed. This is indeed the case as long as we conceive of the address as relying on the permutation of roles that Lyotard singles out, in "Voix," as the distinct feature that temporalizes the articulated phrase:

What is *I*? That in the name of which the phrase articulates itself now ... What is *you*? That to which the phrase now addresses itself but also that which later ... will come to occupy the place of "I" ... *I* and *you* are therefore potentially exchangeable on the poles of destination.... To this faculty of permutation immediately corresponds a temporalization.[57]

But it is here that one may have to think of abuse as a "negative address," an address that abuses precisely by negating the permutation of roles from "you" to "I." By taking as his addressee a child whom he addresses as that which she cannot be, "woman," the shopkeeper places his addressee in the place where she precisely cannot be an addressee, that is, a "you" who could ever permute into an "I." The French word "*tu*," which means both "you" and "silenced," captures the muting inherent in that "you" position. "*On est tu*" writes Leclerc:[58] "one is silenced, muted" by being stuck in the position of a "you" that cannot permute into an "I," that cannot speak, address the shopkeeper, or anyone else for that matter. And it is indeed "one" who is muted, not "I," since "I" has been made to stand where "I" precisely cannot stand to be. The very infliction of the differend ensures that it cannot be spoken. Abuse protects itself from disclosure in its very perpetration. Nor will time pass for the one who is stuck in this specific "you" position.

How, then, can one speak, as Annie Leclerc apparently does? This speaking "I" is not the result of a simple permutation:

> This little girl, it was me, of this I am sure, but I have been suddenly removed from her head, and now I can only look at her from the outside with the words of now, words that were not at her disposal since her tongue had been cut off—which means that I can only give an approximate account of her suffering. What I am about to say, it is sure that she could not say it.[59]

There is no permutation from the muted "you" to the speaking "I." An "I" now speaks what "you" could not speak and, in so doing, cuts herself from the little girl, then. As for this speaking "I," it is not a "me":

> If I did not write to you, if I did not try to transform into words the oppressive density of the emotion, it seems to me that I would not really be alive.[60]

> Without the words that I form for you . . . I would be nothing. . . . It is I who write to you because I need you in order to be me.[61]

The semblance of an "I," a pseudo-subject of sorts, is trying to write, to articulate, and to address "now" the muting that took place "then" to a "you," an addressee, that it is trying to create in that very gesture, an addressee who might be able to hear it as such. Then, and only then, will "I," maybe, have spoken.

At eight years old, Emma does not speak. Not even with that kind of "I." Instead she returns to the store, a return that is, for Lyotard, the strongest evidence that she has been affected. Then she stops, because she reproaches herself for having gone back "as if" she had wanted to provoke the assault, reports Freud: "She now reproached herself for having gone there the second time, *as though* she had wanted in that way to provoke the assault. In fact a state of 'oppressive bad conscience' is to be traced back to this experience."[62] She returns "as if" she had wanted to seduce or be seduced, says Lyotard, who both underlines and leaves aside this "as if": "This lived experience (*dieses Erlebnis*) seems to me to indicate the temptation or the *quasi*-temptation (the '*as if*') of seducing and being seduced."[63] According to Lyotard, the "seduction" would not only be on the part of the grown-up, but also on the part of the child who, having been seduced, repeats compulsively the scene of seduction. In this line of thinking, one could even say that, from the very first time she steps into the store, she was already "seducing," an interpretation that Jean Laplanche in fact proposed early on when he wonders if she did not go to the store "moved by some obscure sexual presentiment."[64] After all, and after Freud, we no longer need to posit an innocent little girl immune from fantasies of seducing or being seduced. But, I will insist, this infantile "seduction" is incommensurate to the "seduction" that the shopkeeper inflicts. Lyotard points out the difference and, again, in passing, as it were: if Emma "seduces," it is "under the guise [*sous couvert*] of candy, I suppose, but this is of little importance."[65] This "cover" actually matters, for it marks the difference between two incommensurate "seductions." One takes place under the guise of asking for sweets, a demand that might very well cover other demands, the object of which remains, thanks to this cover, indeterminate, unarticulated for both child and adult. In response, whatever is given will also be given under the cover of the infantile oral craving for "sweets." The shopkeeper strips the infantile cover. In response to the demand, he does not give sweets, but instead takes away their indeterminacy, and substitutes for it his own perversely fixed and determinate object: the genitalia of a little girl. He does not give. He takes. Put another way, if infancy can play at seduction in the mode of "as if" that Lyotard himself singled out as its distinct privilege, the shopkeeper, for his part, does not play and, even more, crushes any future possibility of playing.

Why, then, go back to subject herself, yet again, to this differend? Is it because, having been seduced, she is tempted in turn to seduce? Is this the affect of the differend that took place? To repeat it? To want it to happen, yet again?

To claim that she returned to seduce the shopkeeper ignores the temporal torsion in the phrasing of her self-reproaches. It is *after* the differend has happened again that retroactively, *après-coup*, she reinterprets her decision to go back to the store as her "seduction." Yes, after it happened yet again, it looks "as if" this is what she wanted to begin with. And not just the second time, but the first time as well. But the one who lends her voice to this statement detaches herself from it in the very gesture of voicing it. "As if" withdraws the explanation that it proposes in the very gesture of proposing it, leaving the return unexplained.

Laplanche, who kept returning to the Emma case, proposed, in one of his later interpretations, a different explanation of her return. She returns because what was signified *to* her remains in her "as a sequence that is absolutely not comprehended."[66] What is incomprehensible, I would suggest, is precisely the differend that was inflicted. And it is the affect of this differend that attacks and excites her to go back, only to be struck again by its incomprehensibility. Then she stops—and begins to reproach herself "as if" she had wanted to seduce and be seduced, that is, "as if" what she received, a determinate grabbing, was commensurate with whatever she asked for in the first place, a whatever that remains indeterminate. I will propose to hear this "as if" as the very mark of the aftershock of the differend and of its affect. As it pretends to mend the incommensurability, "as if" underlines this incommensurability all the more, and denounces any commensurability as being but a pretense, the kind of pretense that abused children maintain, without believing in it, when they go on "as if" they were guilty and "as if" nothing had happened. And this "as if" is no longer any child's play.

Notes

1 In *Misère de la philosophie*, the title is simply "Emma." The English translation of the title is: "Emma: Between Philosophy and Psychoanalysis," in *Lyotard. Philosophy, Politics, and the Sublime*, ed. Hugh J. Silverman (New York and London: Routledge, 2002).

2 Sigmund Freud, *Project for a Scientific Psychology*, in *The Standard Edition of the Complete Psychological Works of Sigmund Freud*, trans. James Strachey et al. (London: The Hogarth Press, 1957), volume I, 353.

3 Ibid.

4 Ibid., 354.

5 Ibid., 356.

6 Jean-François Lyotard, "Emma," 35, translation modified. The translation renders "*une véritable naissance à la passibilité*" in *Misère de la philosophie* (Paris: Galilée, 2000), 78, as "true source of susceptibility." Although maybe a bit odd in English, I prefer "passibility."

7 Jean-François Lyotard, *Heidegger and "the jews"* trans. Andreas Michel and Mark Roberts (Minneapolis: University of Minnesota Press, 1990), 12.

8 "Freud, Energy and Chance. A Conversation with Jean-François Lyotard," in *Tekhnema* 5, "Energy and Chance" (fall 1999): 92.

9 Lyotard, "Emma," 35, translation modified.

10 Ibid., 34.

11 Ibid., 32, translation modified.

12 Lyotard, *Heidegger*, 5.

13 Ibid., 11.

14 Lyotard, "Emma," 36, translation modified.

15 Avital Ronell addresses the question of adolescence in "*Was war Aufklärung?*/What Was Enlightenment? The Turn of the Screwed," in *Loser Sons: Politics and Authority* (Champaign: The University of Illinois Press, 2012), 175–80.

16 Lyotard, "Emma," 32, translation modified.

17 Ibid., 32, translation modified.

18 "What is important in the affect is how much it loads, overloads the thought-body, the psychic apparatus [*l'appareil psychique*]. (Kant said that, whatever its qualitative variety may be [*quelle que soit sa variété qualitative*], and there are many, feeling is sublime only insofar as it is "energetic." ["*le sentiment n'est sublime qu'autant qu'il est énergétique*"]. Ibid., 33, translation modified. French text, *Misère*, 75.

19 Lyotard, "Emma," 33.

20 Lyotard, *Heidegger*, 15.

21 Lyotard, "Emma," 33, translation modified.

22 Lyotard, *Heidegger*, 12.

23 Ibid., 16.

24 Ibid., 19.

25 Ibid., 15.

26 Lyotard, "Emma," 34, translation modified.

27 Lyotard, *Heidegger*, 19.

28 Lyotard, "Emma," 39.

29 Mark Stoholski, "*Apathēmata*," in this volume, p. 29.

30 Lyotard, "Emma," 33, translation modified.

31 Ibid., 33, translation modified. "It only keeps occurring, now and now." "*Il ne fait que survenir, maintenant, et maintenant*" (*Misère*, 74). This sentence is omitted from the English translation.

32 Ibid., 30.

33 Ibid., 41, translation modified.

34 Ibid., 40, translation modified.

35 Ibid., 41.

36 Ibid., 40, translation modified.

37 Ibid., 41, translation modified.

38 Ibid., translation modified.

39 Ibid., translation modified.

40 Ibid., translation modified. For a reading of Lyotard's own use of "free indirect style" according to "a logic of countersignature," see Geoffrey Bennington, "Childish Things," in *Minima Memoria: In the Wake of Jean-François Lyotard*, eds Claire Nouvet, Zrinka Stahuljak, and Kent Still (Stanford: Stanford University Press, 2007).

41 Lyotard, "Emma," 34–5.

42 Ibid., 35.

43 Ibid., 24.

44 Lyotard, "Emma," 24, translation modified.

45 Lyotard, "Emma," 42.

46 Ibid., 43–4.

47 Ibid.

48 Ibid., 44.

49 Ibid., 42, translation modified. French text, *Misère*, 91.

50 Annie Leclerc, *Paedophilia ou l'amour des enfants* (Arles: Actes Sud, 2010). Hereafter *Paedophilia*. All translations mine.

51 Leclerc, *Paedophilia*, 39.

52 Ibid., 45.

53 Ibid., 39

54 Lyotard, "Emma," 42.

55 Ibid., 42.

56 Ibid., 42–3. For a reading of this address in a different perspective, see Avital Ronell, "*Was war Aufklärung?*/What Was Enlightenment? The Turn of the Screwed."

57 Lyotard, "Voix," in *Lectures d'enfance* (Paris: Galilée, 1991), 135, translation mine.

58 Leclerc, *Paedophilia*, 39.

59 Ibid., 37.

60 Ibid., 27.

61 Ibid., 25.

62 Freud, *Project*, 354. Emphasis mine.

63 Lyotard, "Emma," 35. Emphasis mine.

64 Jean Laplanche, *Life and Death in Psychoanalysis*, trans. Jeffrey Mehlman (Baltimore: Johns Hopkins University Press, 1976), 39.

65 Lyotard, "Emma," 35. "*Sous le couvert*" literally means in French "under the cover."

66 Jean Laplanche, *The Unconscious and the Id* (London: Karnac Books, 1999), 103.

Section II

Affect in the Work of Art and in Commentary

3

Pragmatics and Affect in Art
and Commentary

Ashley Woodward

My topic here is perhaps the most unlikely in a book dedicated to affect in Jean-François Lyotard's work: it is his approach to art and commentary in the period in which he seems least of all concerned with affect. While increasing attention has recently been given to Lyotard's aesthetics,[1] his "pragmatic" approach to artworks and art commentary, developed in the late 1970s and early 1980s, has been all but neglected. Lyotard scholarship so far has taken up primarily one side of his thought, the sensitivity to feeling, the openness to the "unthought," the insistence on the limits of rationality, and the recourse to the artistic and literary. Yet Lyotard would be a much less interesting thinker and writer than he is if there were not also another side to his thought, an attraction to formalization and a penchant for writing which is sparse, punctual, and precise. Lyotard's writings on the pragmatics of art and commentary fall on this side of his thought. They are of great interest not only for the inventive approach to the philosophy of art they suggest, but in the context of his entire *oeuvre*. Lyotard's pragmatics develops the role played by affect in his earlier libidinal philosophy, insofar as he continues to be concerned with how a work of art can affect its receiver. This power of the artwork to affect is now understood as a pragmatic force, and initially as a transformative energetics. Moreover, this period acts as groundwork for Lyotard's later work on the affect-phrase, a return to affect in a different register. Overall, I argue, we can understand Lyotard's pragmatic period as a transitional one in which he seeks to divest his aesthetics of metaphysical commitments, and which prepares the way for a later return to a consideration of affect in terms of phrases, rather than of libidinal energies.

Lyotard's pragmatic turn

It is well known that Lyotard's work seems to undergo a dramatic shift in both style and content in the mid-1970s: a shift from the wild "irrationality" of the Freudian drives to sober reflections on language and logic. In the period of *Libidinal Economy*, he develops an aesthetics based around intense affects, theorized in terms of a radical idea of libido as energy. In this period, he is interested in how works of art can affect their receivers by disrupting stable and habitual representations of reality, disruptions he associates with extremes of feeling (whether high or low). The relation between a viewer (or "client-body") and a work is understood in terms of a transmission of energies from one to another, and the transformation in the client-body this transmission effects. Sensations (of colors, timbres, volumes, and so on) are understood on a Freudian model as influxes of energy, which have the potential to affect the libidinal organization of the client-body. The art which Lyotard most strongly affirms in this period is that which has the potential to transmit the most intense affects, insofar as the work itself contains a great deal of "unbound" libidinal energy; that is, energy unconstrained by traditional rules of representation.[2]

Lyotard's shift between *Libidinal Economy* (1974) and *The Differend* (1983) appears extreme. What lies behind it? In his writings, he offers a number of clues, but arguably the most important is what can be described as a shift from *exteriority* to *interiority* in terms of a strategic stance towards the object of "critique." He expresses this last point in the essay "On the Strength of the Weak" (*Semiotext(e)* version),[3] given at the 1975 *Schizo-Culture* conference at Columbia University. Here, he gives a critical account of the so-called "schizo-culture" of which his libidinal philosophy might be said to have been a part:

> the general attempt was to stay outside the magisterial injunction and to produce, under extremely varied names, some sort of an exteriority: spontaneity, libido, drive, energy, savagery, madness, and perhaps schizo.
>
> Now, that is exactly what the magisterial position and discourse ask for. In other words, there is a trick of the magisterial discourse, of the Occidental discourse if you will, there is a ruse of that discourse, which consists precisely in requiring that we place ourselves outside of it in order to avoid it. The device is very simple, it consists in making exteriority the necessary complement of that discourse. And, I may add, a complement to be conquered, an opaque zone in which that discourse must penetrate in its turn. When one externalizes oneself in order to avoid the magisterial discourse, one is just extending that position, nourishing it.[4]

Lyotard had already tried to avoid the trap of exteriority in *Libidinal Economy* through the concept of dissimulation,[5] but he apparently remained dissatisfied with this solution. (Its language, at least, remains "exterior" to traditional "Occidental discourse".) This is how Lyotard, in 1975, now proposes to proceed:

> Thus, what we should devise is a strategy which can dispense with exteriority, which, as far as language is concerned, would not place itself outside the rules of the discourse of Truth, that is of the discourse of power, but inside those rules. And which instead of excluding itself under the name of delirium, or madness, or pathos in general, or whatever, would on the contrary, play these rules—or rather the Rule of all these rules against itself by including the so-called meta-statements in its own utterances.[6]

Lyotard takes up this strategy through the analysis of the pragmatics of narrative discourse. Hence, we can identify this shift as his "pragmatic turn."

Lyotard's uptake of narrative pragmatics is largely political in motivation, and it is not difficult to see why. As he makes plain in the passages just quoted, the move to interiority is a political response to the oft-commented ability of capitalism to incorporate apparently any and all exterior resistances (think, for example, of all the Che Guevara products now available for consumption on the world market); it is the attempt to work out a new political strategy. Yet his approach to art and art commentary also changes, a change we can also understand on the model of the move from exteriority to interiority. David Carroll's study of Lyotard in his book *Paraesthetics* helps to position this. He explains exteriority in an artistic context as follows:

> Few would deny that art has "a certain" exteriority and autonomy in relation to philosophy, history, and the socio-political sphere, that everything in art cannot be accounted for, or, is not determined, in all its aspects by these other fields. And yet the extent and importance of this exteriority is much debated: some would want to diminish it as much as possible in order to derive the essence of art from these other fields, while others would insist that the superiority, universality, transcendency, or simply critical force of art rests on it being *other*, and that this alterity should be respected and protected at all costs.[7]

Speaking of the period from *Discourse, Figure* to *Libidinal Economy*, Carroll then states that "[p]robably no critical philosopher in recent times has made more radical and sweeping claims in the name of the exteriority of art—not just to theory but to discourse in general (at least to discourse as it is defined by philosophy and linguistics)—than Jean-François Lyotard."[8] Following the turn outlined above, in the realm of art theory and commentary, Lyotard moves away from the "exteriority" of the figural and the libidinal, to the "interiority" of narrative pragmatics. This shift is, of course, a matter of degree, since in the earlier work Lyotard was always careful to complicate his analysis and to implicate discourse with the figural or the libidinal. Yet the shift remains significant, because it is one from "taking the side of the figural" *against* the structuralists and semioticians, the "partisans of language," to one in which the analysis takes place *within* the critical vocabulary and concepts of linguistic discourse.[9]

What, then, is the "pragmatics of narrative discourse" that Lyotard takes up? Most simply and commonly defined, *narratives* are accounts of events. Typically, they tie together two or more real or fictional events in a coherent story.[10] In the late 1970s, Lyotard presents narrative as the primary form of linguistic meaning, taking it to be the most important element of meaning to be analyzed, and claiming that other forms of meaningful language use, which claim not to be narrative (such as theory), are in fact reducible to narrative.

In one of Lyotard's earliest engagements with narrative,[11] he draws heavily on Gérard Genette's *Narrative Discourse*.[12] While Genette doesn't use the term "pragmatics," we can gain a clarification of Lyotard's approach to the pragmatics of narrative discourse from Genette's own clarification of terms in his introduction. Genette specifies three aspects usually included in what is meant by "narrative," as follows: *story* is "the signified or narrative content"; *narrative* he proposes to reserve for "the signifier, statement, discourse or narrative text itself"; and finally, *narrating* is the action of producing the narrative.[13] Genette then explains what it would mean to analyze narrative discourse: "Analysis of narrative discourse will thus be for me, essentially, a study of the relationships between narrative and story, between narrative and narrating, and (to the extent that they are inscribed in the narrative discourse) between story and narrating."[14] While Lyotard will define the elements of narrative to be analyzed somewhat differently, he takes up this idea of analyzing the relationships between elements of the narrative under the heading of *pragmatics*.

Lyotard gives the following definition: "Pragmatics. It means all the complicated relations that exist between a speaker and what he is talking about, between the story-teller and his listener, and between the listener and the story told by the story-teller."[15] Narrative pragmatics, then, concerns the analysis of the relations between the "instances" of the narrative, rather than of the meaning of the narrative isolated from such instances. In Lyotard's writings from this period, he posits that there are three such instances (or "poles," as he also calls them), which form what he calls *the pragmatic triangle*: addressor, addressee, and referent. (Later on, in *The Differend*, "sense" will be added as a fourth instance.)

The relations between the instances can take very different forms. For example, the addressor may address the addressee as a disciple or as an equal, the referent may be positioned as an objective reality or as an invention of the addressor, and so on. These relations are also open to permutations over time. Permutations can involve a shift in emphasis from one instance to another, transpositions from one instance to another, identification of one instance with another, prohibition of identification of one instance with another, and so on—Lyotard claims that such permutations are in principle infinite. Given the possibility of a vast array of different relations and permutations between the three instances of the pragmatic triangle, the flexibility of its application is enormous, despite involving only three terms.

In linguistics, pragmatics developed in the 1970s, being influenced by the American pragmatist philosophers and J.L. Austin's speech-act theory. The concern is to show how pragmatic context has import for semantic meaning. Yet, while remaining within the vocabulary of linguistics, Lyotard's emphasis seems rather to be the opposite: to demonstrate how what is often thought of as the *extra*-linguistic is implicated within linguistic discourse itself. In particular, for Lyotard pragmatic relations involved in linguistic contexts can be understood as relations of power. He demonstrates this in texts such as "Lessons in Paganism," where the texts of the *Nouveaux philosophes* are critiqued for their pragmatics, not their explicit semantic content. Yet, he also extends his interest in narrative pragmatics in the direction of art and art commentary, which is my concern here.

The pragmatics of art

Lyotard outlines a pragmatic approach to art and art commentary most clearly and concisely in two short texts: "Theory as Art: A Pragmatic Point of View" (1977),[16] and "Petites ruminations sur le commentaire d'art" (Short Reflections on Art Commentary) (1979).[17] This approach understands artworks on the model of, or "akin to," narratives,[18] and this, then, allows an analysis of art in terms of narrative pragmatics. To understand a work of art pragmatically is to consider it from the point of view of its *effects*, rather than of its meaning. What kinds of effects can a work of art have? First, Lyotard, in line with his earlier aesthetics, continues to insist that sensory qualities can have direct aesthetic effects on bodies, independent of semantic, cognitive, or art-historical meanings. Yet second, he also gives a description of the pragmatic effects of art in narrative terms. "Effects" can be understood in terms of the concepts of *force, work*, and *displacement*. The force of an artwork is measured by the amount of work accomplished,[19] while in turn "[t]he amount of work is measured by the displacements (*Verstellungen* and *Entstellungen*) which the work of art produces at the three poles from which it taps its energy and among which it redistributes that energy: the poles of its emission, of its reception and of its reference."[20] In other words, the poles of the three pragmatic instances: the addressor, addressee, and referent. Notably, we can see that Lyotard's formulation here continues to draw on an energetic model of the drives and their processes. This aspect will later disappear, as Lyotard becomes more skeptical towards such an energetics, seeing it as a form of metaphysics. Most obviously, artworks can have effects on viewers (addressees), on culture, and perhaps on politics. Pragmatics in the realm of art can be understood as concerning relations of *aesthetic effects* (broadly construed): relations between the artist and the work itself, either or both of which might be understood as the addressor, the viewer or audience of the work (the addressee), and the reference of the work (what it is about, or connects with in its subject matter). Third, a significant effect of art according to Lyotard is its giving rise to discussions about it, including art commentary. We will turn to this particular pragmatic effect in detail shortly.

Lyotard's pragmatics is essentially linguistic in form, and his extension of it to art depends on analogy. His pragmatic approach to art and commentary, which begins with his work on the pragmatics of narrative, also draws on linguistic notions introduced a little later, such as language games and phrases. Rather than a thoroughly worked out theory, Lyotard instead gives us various perspectives on how a pragmatic approach might be understood by drawing a number of possible analogies between linguistic and communicational models and artworks.

One such analogy Lyotard draws is between the linguistic phrases of Wittgenstein's "language games" and what he calls the "plastic phrases" of the visual arts. He writes: "Call language all the systems of signs transmitted by a support and a specific medium: pigments on bidimensional surfaces, light on volumes, imprints of photons on sensitive moving films, etc."[21] There are an enormous number of possible plastic phrases (Lyotard would have us believe they are infinite and inexhaustible), yet it is possible to group together kinds or classes of phrases, which are then analogous to Wittgenstein's language games, and which we can call "plastic games." Broadly speaking, there are languages of art which differ according to their *material* (which Lyotard defines here provisionally as *support + medium*), and within any particular "material language," there are many possible games. Inspired by a passage in the *Philosophical Investigations* which lists possible types of language games,[22] Lyotard suggests the following as a sample of possible types of "plastic games" within the "material language" of painting:

> A painting which commands
> A painting which narrates
> A painting which portrays
> A painting which questions and responds
> A painting which is on its own terms an ornament
> A painting which is on its own terms a painting
> A painting which quotes.[23]

This is no more nor less than an analogy and, as Lyotard reminds us, we must be careful to reflect on its limits while employing it.[24] First, he warns us that the plastic phrase remains different from and irreducible to the linguistic phrase. This is what he highlights when drawing attention to the *immediate somatic* effects of plastic phrases, due to their intrinsic sensorial value, outlined above, which he opposes to the *mediate* functioning of linguistic phrases within a network, the emergence of linguistic meaning through structural, differential value. And so, even in making the analogy of the plastic phrase with the linguistic phrase, Lyotard has not entirely abandoned the insistence on the differences between the sensorial and the linguistic, a main theme of *Discourse, Figure*. So why make the analogy in the first place? Lyotard's pragmatic approach to art and commentary is most fully articulated in his writings on Daniel Buren, and it is in this context that he gives his most explicit explanation.

Lyotard wrote in 1981 about Buren's two-colored striped works, which he had been making since 1965. He describes them as follows: "canvas or paper with alternating white and color vertical bands, each 8.7 cm wide. The height and width of the piece varies according to the site."[25] The pieces are produced industrially, and often destroyed after they have been exhibited. Lyotard takes this to mean that what is at stake in the works is not painterly expression, nor even the material itself other than as it is exhibited in time and space.[26] What is at stake, rather—according to Lyotard's commentary—is the questioning of the conventions of the time and space of art exhibitions themselves. Buren frequently displayed his works in "non-conventional" places, outside museums and galleries, or in unusual places inside them, and gave precise instructions regarding the time of their display. In this way, Lyotard contends, Buren draws critical attention to the way in which art is institutionally displayed. He writes:

From the point of view of a pragmatics of the site, the artistic institution consists in a subset of choices made explicitly or implicitly in the whole set of alternatives opened by the whole set of these operators: does one install the piece in the gallery or outside (or both)? Is it fixed or in motion? Is it applied to a support or floating? If it is floating, is it tied down by one or more sides, stretched flat or suspended vertically?[27]

Buren's exhibitions call viewers' attention to these institutional choices, which frequently go unnoticed and constitute a set of unconscious assumptions or rules, by choosing otherwise.

Significantly, Lyotard remarks that Buren's work functions in part by the removal of an affective relation to the viewer. In the 1981 essay "La Performance et la phrase chez Daniel Buren" (The Performance and the Phrase in Daniel Buren), he distinguishes Buren's works, considered as installations, from performances:

Performance seeks rather to produce some affects, fear, anger, desire, anxiety, hate, to move deeply; Buren's work, to provoke some phrases. What sort of phrases?[28] . . .

Buren's work would seek on the contrary to weaken the moment of affection. The commentator does not have to say what he feels, he feels little or nothing . . . The work induces principally, if not exclusively, a reflexive phrase, without the mediation of an affective participation.[29]

Lyotard argues, in short, that performance (like, he says, painting) induces affects in the viewer, which then (if she is an art commentator) provoke "second-order" phrases which take for their reference how the work made her feel. By contrast, Buren's installations produce little or no feeling in the viewer, thereby directing attention away from the work itself (which fails to move the viewer and thus to keep her attention) and causes her to reflect on the conditions for the reception of artworks as such. The phrases provoked by such installations are *reflective* phrases, which take place *without the mediation of affect*.

Lyotard justifies his use of the analogy between linguistic phrases and artistic phrases in the specific case of his analysis of Daniel Buren's works in the following way: "The DB piece, although visible and non-legible, can be called a 'phrase' because it results from simple and invariable rules of formation and linking. It is legible like a syntactic, non-semantic axiom."[30] Lyotard draws attention here to the structural composition of the work; the fact that it is composed of atomic elements with linkages between them, and that the rules for formulating these works are simple, and are structurally analogous to a syntactic axiom. This simplicity and relative invariance of the works functions to call attention to the "plastic operators" of the time-space in which the phrase is then inserted—the conventions of time and space which constitute art-institutional choices. Thus, the reduction of the work to something as "semantically thin" as a syntactic axiom allows it to question the context in which it is presented, by removing the distractions posed by feeling or by the semantic "reading" of the "meaning" of the work itself.[31]

The pragmatics of commentary

I turn now to my second consideration here, art commentary. Lyotard's pragmatic approach to art commentary is to understand it as a pragmatic effect of the work itself. Among other effects, one of the effects of art is to make people talk and write about it: to commentate on it. From a pragmatic point of view, the work is understood as the collection of its effects, and this, then, makes commentary itself a part of the work. Lyotard explains: "the work contains its commentary as a quality of an aspect of its proper pragmatic situation."[32] Since from a pragmatic point of view the artwork itself can be seen as a collection of effects, this, then, also "ranks the interpretive work among the works of contemporary art."[33]

This reading requires that Lyotard also transform the traditional understanding of theory, displacing it from that of a masterly discourse informing commentary and allowing it to tell the "truth" of art. First, he gives the following pragmatic analysis of theory as it is understood in its "traditional" sense, as a discourse of the True: the referent is in the position of authority, and is taken to speak "through" the addressor. (That is, the veracity of the discourse depends upon the adequation of the narrative and its referent.) The addressee is positioned as the disciple of the addressor, who is being prepared to take the addressor's place and speak the Truth of the referent. Lyotard emphasizes the "irreversibility" of the relations in the pragmatic triangle of traditional theory; it is a relatively rigid structure, hinged on the authority of the referent, taken to be independent of discourse (a kind of "anchorage in reality"). Typically, "art theory" and its application in commentary have been understood to have the aim of *interpreting* the artwork, where interpretation is understood as revealing a deep, intelligible truth hidden by the sensible appearance of the work.

Against this "traditional" understanding, Lyotard offers a pragmatic conception of theory *as* art. He writes: "I take the view that theories themselves are concealed narratives."[34] Moreover, he construes theory as a genre of *literature.*[35] In line with his interest in the sophists in this period, Lyotard "levels" theory with other forms of narrative, claiming that instead of having a real grounding in reality or claim to truth, what distinguishes theory from any other rhetorical discourse is simply the feeling of *conviction* it is able to produce in its listener. This feeling of conviction is what is (mis)taken by the partisans of theory as Truth. Having leveled theory to a narrative among others, and a form of rhetorical discourse among others, theory appears as an art for Lyotard, just as much as any of the other rhetorical arts. It functions pragmatically, and its value should be understood in terms of the effects it is able to produce (rather than its adequation to reality, its truth-value).

Lyotard then understands theory as having a particular pragmatic function in relation to commentary: it acts as an *operator, filter,* or *transformation group* between the work and its particular effect that we call commentary. He writes:

> If the commentary is an "effect" of the work, and if as we said the commentary is itself a work, it is necessary to consider the "theory" which guides the commentary as a filter or as an operator, sometimes complex, between the work and its effect, that is to say between the commented-on work and the work which is the commentary.[36]

An *operator* is something which acts on something else in order to transform it, to produce an effect.[37] Theory allows the passage from plastic phrases (the work) to linguistic phrases (the commentary) by *working* on the former in order to produce the latter. Theory is thus a kind of machine or device. Lyotard notes that there are at least two transformations clearly effected by the operator "theory": first, it transforms the addressee (of the artwork) into an addressor (of the commentary), and second, it transforms the current phrase (the artwork) into a quoted phrase in the art commentary.[38]

According to Lyotard, what the pragmatic approach achieves for art commentary is this: "It snatches it from the malady of being the doctor of the arts and of *telling the truth* where the arts disguise it. The commentary enters into the field of the arts, and picks up its experimental imagination. We, commentators, don't have to tell the truth about the subject of artworks, but to do work with their propositions."[39] The role of art commentary is thus not reference, but *transformation*. But how can commentary proceed in this pragmatic manner? How can we give a commentary on a work of art when we are concerned with its effects, not with its signification or meaning? Lyotard suggests at least two answers to this question, perhaps seemingly in contradiction with each other: 1. theoretical pluralism and 2. descriptions of devices. First, he proposes a radical, "permissive" theoretical pluralism with respect to art commentary. He claims that any and all theories may legitimately be applied as operators to works to produce new commentaries (including those he typically criticizes, such as the psychoanalytic and Marxist approaches). Moreover, he suggests that this work will never be exhausted, as new theories for "decoding" works may be invented without limit.[40]

Second, Lyotard gives us a more specific prescription: "works must not be taken as symptoms symbolically expressing a concealed discourse, but as attempts to state perspectives of reality. *Interpretation must in turn give way to descriptions of devices.*"[41] Pragmatic art commentary will then concern itself not with interpretation, but with *descriptions of devices*. These "devices" are what Lyotard calls *dispositifs*, or "set-ups" (as this term is generally translated). They are now no longer described by Lyotard in terms of the economy of drives, of the dammings and flows of libidinal energy, as they were in the period of *Libidinal Economy*, but of *effects* more generally. The aim of describing devices is to understand how such devices work: "not only to analyze the set-up, but to understand its efficacy. This is what the pragmatic enables."[42]

Lyotard suggests that we can identify certain "plastic games" (families or types of plastic phrases) in terms of devices, for example "the organization of pigments on the support of Brunelleschi and Alberti made in principle according to the set-up called the *construzione legittima*."[43] Moreover, this description of devices is indeed what Lyotard seems to be doing in many of his own commentaries on specific artists and artworks. For example, the descriptions of incongruous spaces in *Duchamp's TRANS/formers*,[44] the complex analysis of planes and colors in the essay "On the Constitution of Time through Colour in the Recent Works of Albert Ayme,"[45] and perhaps most clearly, since the theory of pragmatics is also worked out in these writings, the commentaries on Daniel Buren discussed above. In these works, Lyotard is not seeking to understand *what* any of these works *mean*, but *how* they *work*.

Is Lyotard contradicting himself, if he says that all theoretical approaches to art commentary are legitimate, but at the same time proscribing "truthful" interpretation and prescribing the specific approach of describing devices? The force of this apparent contradiction is ameliorated if we recall that theories are to be understood in the specific pragmatic sense that Lyotard defines, bereft of their referential, truth-functional role, and considered as pragmatic transformation groups. As such, theories give rise to "perspectives on reality," and may be understood as specialist toolkits for taking apart and analyzing the multitude of devices devised in the workshops of contemporary artists.

Conclusion: pragmatics and affect

Lyotard's pragmatic period stakes out a particular set of problems and attempted solutions in the course of his *oeuvre*. With the advent of his pragmatic approach to art and art commentary, he interrogates the move of modern art away from its traditional stakes of sensation, nature, and sensibility, and this includes affect. He turns to language, which he had previously argued was "other" to art, to investigate this changing of stakes. But it is not to the structural linguistics he had previously opposed that he now turns; it is to models of language which incorporate its frequently-overlooked conditions: it's pragmatics.

By the late 1980s, Lyotard returns to the centrality of affect, as he attempts to incorporate into his philosophy of phrases key aspects of the libidinal philosophy which had been removed from it (the body, time, space, color, art, and the unconscious, in addition to affect).[46] In essays such as 1993's "Anima Minima," affect, understood as the power of being affected by sensation, appears central to all aesthetic problematics.[47] Yet Lyotard's model of affect has now significantly changed: he is no longer working with the libidinal energetics of the Freudian drives, but with a model drawn from his work on the temporal paradox of "deferred action" (*Nachträglichkeit*) associated with unconscious affect. It is this model which informs "the affect-phrase," his supplementary attempt to account for affect in terms of the philosophy of phrases worked out in *The Differend*.[48] We can summarize, then, Lyotard's itinerary in aesthetics in the following way. The turn away from libidinal aesthetics and towards pragmatics was largely a turn away from a focus on affect, and one which allowed him to 1. pursue a strategy *internal* to the problem of the linguistic overcoding of aesthetics to which he had previously opposed an *external* resistance; 2. explore developments in contemporary art which seemed to leave behind the problematics of sensation and affect; and 3. "purify" his aesthetics of a metaphysics of energy which he increasingly considered problematic. While affect returns as central in his later aesthetics, it bears the marks of the significant theoretical displacements undergone in this itinerary. An understanding of the pragmatic phase therefore contributes to a deeper appreciation of the way affect traverses Lyotard's thought.

Notes

1   See Jean-François Lyotard, *Writings on Contemporary Art and Artists*, 6 vols., ed. Herman Parret (Leuven: Leuven University Press, 2009–13); Kiff Bamford, *Lyotard*

and the *"figural" in Performance, Art and Writing* (London and New York: Continuum, 2012); Peter W. Milne et al. (eds), *Rewriting Lyotard: Figuration, Presentation, Resistance*, special issue of *Cultural Politics* 9.2 (2013); and Graham Jones, *Lyotard Reframed* (London and New York: I.B. Tauris, 2013).

2   For an outline of the basic principles of this aesthetics, see the last chapter of *Libidinal Economy*, trans. Iain Hamilton Grant (London: Athlone, 1993), "The Economy of This Writing." For applications to various arts, see some of the essays collected in Lyotard's *Des dispositifs pulsionnels* (Paris: Union Générale d'Editions, 1973).

3   There is another paper by Lyotard published under this title, with broadly similar subject matter but substantially different content: "Sur la force des faibles," *L'Arc* 64, "Lyotard" (1976), 4–12. Trans. "On the Strength of the Weak" in *Toward the Postmodern*, eds Robert Harvey and Mark S. Roberts (Atlantic Highlands, NJ: Humanities Press, 1993).

4   Lyotard, "On the Strength of the Weak," *Semiotext(e)* (1978), 207.

5   For an account of this, see James Williams, *Lyotard and the Political* (London and New York: Routledge, 2000), Chapter 3.

6   Lyotard, "On the Strength of the Weak," 207.

7   David Carroll, *Paraesthetics* (New York and London: Routledge, 1987), 23.

8   Ibid., 24.

9   "Taking the Side of the Figural" is how Mark Sinclair translates the title of the first chapter of *Discourse, Figure* in *The Lyotard Reader and Guide*, eds Keith Crome and James Williams (Edinburgh: Edinburgh University Press, 2006).

10 See Gerald Prince, *A Dictionary of Narratology* (Aldershot: Scholar Press, 1988), 58.

11 Lyotard, "A Short Libidinal Economy of a Narrative Set-up: the Renault Corporation Relates the Death of Pierre Overney," trans. Keith Crome and Mark Sinclair in *The Lyotard Reader and Guide*. Original French publication 1973.

12 Gérard Genette, *Narrative Discourse*, trans. Jane E. Lewin (Oxford: Basil Blackwell, 1980). Originally published as "Discours du récit," part of *Figures III* (Paris: Editions du Seuil, 1972).

13 Ibid., 27.

14 Ibid., 29.

15 Lyotard, "Lessons in Paganism," trans. David Macey in *The Lyotard Reader*, ed. Andrew Benjamin (Oxford and Cambridge, MA: Basil Blackwell, 1989), 125.

16 In *Image and Code*, ed. Wendy Steiner (Ann Arbor: University of Michigan Press, 1981). This is the English translation of "Dissertation sur une inconvenance" from *Rudiments païens: Genre dissertatif* (Paris: Klincksieck, 1977).

17 Lyotard, "Petites ruminations sur le commentaire d'art," *Opus International*, 70–1 (1979), 16–17. Translations from French texts mine unless otherwise stated.

18 Lyotard, "Theory as Art," 72.

19 Ibid.

20 Ibid.

21 Lyotard, "Petites ruminations," 17.

22 Ludwig Wittgenstein, *Philosophical Investigations*, trans. G.E.M. Anscombe (Malden, MA: Blackwell, 2001), §23, 10.

23 Lyotard, "Petites ruminations," 17.

24 The specific caveats here are from "The Site" in *What to Paint?: Adami, Arakawa, Buren*, ed. Herman Parret (Leuven: Leuven University Press, 2012).

25 Lyotard, *What to Paint?*, 315.

26 Ibid., 317.

27 Ibid., 327.

28 Jean-François Lyotard, "La Performance et la phrase chez Daniel Buren," in *Performance, Text(e), Documents*, ed. Chantal Pontbriand (Montréal: Parachute, 1981) §8, 68.

29 Ibid., §11, 68.

30 Lyotard, *What to Paint?*, 335, translation modified.

31 While this analysis seems very particular to Buren, Lyotard also applies the "phrase" analogy in a number of other works of art commentary. Among others are the texts "A Game of Painting," on Henri Macheroni (1980) and "Attraction," on Jean-Luc Parant (1985). Both in *Miscellaneous Texts II: Contemporary Artists*, ed. Herman Parret (Leuven: Leuven University Press, 2012).

32 Lyotard, "Petites ruminations," 17.

33 Ibid., 16.

34 Lyotard, "Lessons in Paganism," 130.

35 Lyotard, "Theory as Art," 71.

36 Lyotard, "Petites ruminations," 17.

37 Lyotard does not define what he means by "transformation group," but presumably he is taking the term—in a rather free way—from its usage in modern algebra.

38 Lyotard, "Petites ruminations," 17.

39 Ibid.

40 See ibid., 16.

41 Lyotard, "The Unconscious as Mise-en-scène," trans. Joseph Maier in *Performance in Postmodern Culture*, eds Michel Benamou and Charles Caramello (Madison, WI: Coda Press, 1977), 98. Italics mine.

42 Lyotard, "Petites ruminations," 17.

43 Ibid.

44 Lyotard, *Duchamp's TRANS/formers*, ed. Herman Parret, trans. Ian McLeod (Leuven: Leuven University Press, 2010). Original French publication 1977. The book is composed of texts written between 1974 and 1977.

45 Lyotard, "On the Constitution of Time through Colour in the Recent Works of Albert Ayme" in *Miscellaneous Texts II: Contemporary Artists*. Original French publication 1980.

46 See Lyotard, "That Which Resists After All (an Interview with Gilbert Larochelle)," *Philosophy Today* 36.4 (1992), 402–17.

47 In *Postmodern Fables*, trans. Georges Van Den Abbeele (Minneapolis: University of Minnesota Press, 1997).

48 On the affect-phrase, see "The Affect-phrase (from a Supplement to *The Differend*)," trans. Keith Crome in *The Lyotard Reader and Guide*. For a discussion of this in relation to unconscious affect, see in particular "Emma: Between Philosophy and Psychoanalysis," trans. M. Sanders (with R. Brons and N. Martin) in *Lyotard: Philosophy, Politics and the Sublime*, ed. Hugh J. Silverman (New York and London: Routledge, 2002).

4

Anamnesis

Anne Tomiche

Anamnesis: the term appears in Lyotard's writings in the mid-1980s and it recurs until his latest texts in order to think the nature and the function of art. It is through this notion that I want to investigate Lyotard's thinking on art in its relation to Freudian psychoanalysis.[1]

One of the first and then most developed occurrences of the term concerns painting. Used in the essay written for the catalog of the Adami exhibit in Paris at the Pompidou Centre in 1985—an essay originally entitled "Anamnesis of the visible or: Candour"[2]—it is reworked and included, under the title "Anamnesis," in *What to Paint?* in 1987.[3] Four years later, a section in *Lessons on the Analytic of the Sublime* is also entitled: "Anamnesis."[4] Furthermore, the final version of a text that was first delivered in 1993, and then published twice in slightly different forms in 1995 and 1998, is included in the posthumous volume *Misère de la philosophie* under the title, "La peinture, anamnèse du visible" (Painting, anamnesis of the visible).[5] Painting is thus recurrently associated by Lyotard with anamnesis. If the term "anamnesis" is most often used in relation to painting, it also recurs in relation to other arts. In *The Inhuman*, the essay on music entitled "Obedience"[6] suggests that what is at stake in musical experimentation is "the anamnesis of the feeling of sound."[7] Another essay in the same volume, "*Logos* and *Technē*, or Telegraphy," associates *writing* with anamnesis—"writing as passing or anamnesis," in Lyotard's terms.[8] "Anamnesis of the visible," "anamnesis of the feeling of sound," "writing as anamnesis": art in all its forms is indeed associated with a movement of "anamnesis."

It might then seem paradoxical to consider the articulation between Lyotard's thinking on art and Freudian psychoanalysis—which is what I intend to do—through a notion that is not Freudian, strictly speaking. The term "anamnesis" is not, as such, one of the key Freudian concepts when it comes to issues of memory and recollection. Freud—Lyotard's Freud—is, however, very important in

Lyotard's elaboration of the notion. Indeed, his use of the term "anamnesis" does not refer to Plato's epistemological and psychological theory of knowledge as developed in the *Meno* and *Phaedo* (where Plato develops the idea that what one perceives to be learning is actually the recovery of what is in the soul from eternity). Nor does Lyotard use the term in reference to the concept of anamnesis in liturgical theology (where the memorial aspect of worship is considered not as a passive process but as one that gives access to the Paschal mystery). Lyotard associates anamnesis with psychoanalysis, and his use of the term is part of his ongoing dialog with Freudian psychoanalysis. Indeed, Freud is one of the key operators throughout Lyotard's writings, from *Discourse, Figure* up to the latest texts. Anamnesis can be seen as an operator, or rather as a "transformer" if we use the term, borrowed from Lyotard himself (i.e., from *Duchamp's TRANS/formers*), and given as the title of the volume of essays on Lyotard edited by Corinne Enaudeau, Jean-François Nordmann, Jean-Michel Salanskis, and Frédéric Worms in order to try to encompass all the facets of Lyotard's thinking with its shifts and evolutions—*Les Transformateurs Lyotard*.[9] Freud is a key transformer in Lyotard's thinking in a series of moments and movements of break or rupture: the break away from phenomenology as well as from structuralist linguistics in *Discourse, Figure*; the break away from Marxism in *Libidinal Economy*; the break away from metapsychology and the attempt to think the unconscious as a phrase from *Heidegger and "the jews"* onward ... "Anamnesis" is part of this Freudian transformer; more precisely, it is introduced after *The Differend*, that is to say, after the elaboration of the (non-linguistic) notion of the "phrase" understood as *event*, and it is part of Lyotard's attempt to phrase both the unconscious and art in terms of phrases.

So, what can it mean to associate painting, music, and writing to psychoanalytical "anamnesis?" What can it mean, not so much for psychoanalytic theory or practice (my point here is not to investigate Lyotard's relation to Freud's texts),[10] but mainly for art: what assumptions about art does it convey? Borrowing from Lyotard's own terminology, my argument will proceed in four steps in order to investigate, through anamnesis, the status of art in Lyotard's thinking: linkage, work, affect-phrase, and time.

Linkage—linking psychoanalysis and art through anamnesis

Anamnesis is to be understood as one of the operators that allow Lyotard to *link* psychoanalysis and art. The question of *linkage* is central to Lyotard's "philosophy of phrases" introduced in *The Differend*: what is at stake with the notion of "phrase" is precisely the question of linkage, and one of the canonical well-known theses of *The Differend* is that phrasing entails linking and that "to link is necessary, but how to link is not."[11]

From *Discourse, Figure* up to *Signed, Malraux* and the essays gathered in *Misère de la philosophie*, beyond the shifts undergone by Lyotard's appropriation of Freud and beyond the various names used to think art in relation to the Freudian texts (figural, infancy, affect-phrase, *phōnē* ...), what remains is Lyotard's *strategy* to *link* Freud and art (be it painting, literature, or music), his strategy to *phrase* art with Freud and Freud with art—"Freud according to Cézanne," as he titled a 1972 article on "Psychoanalysis and Painting" in the *Encyclopaedia Universalis*.[12] Indeed, from *Discourse, Figure* to "Emma" or *Malraux*, Lyotard's *phrasing* of the relation between Freudian psychoanalysis and art relies on the power of *analogy*. In *Discourse, Figure*, it is an analogy between the dream-work and the work of the "figural": the topography of the figural is analogous to the topography of the unconscious, and art operates according to the same "rules" as the dream-work. Lyotard can thus write: "the 'language' of the dream seems to be nothing more nor less than the language of art."[13] So, when Lyotard reads Freud with Cézanne—"Freud according to Cézanne"—such a reading entails elaborating an analogy between the scene of the unconscious and the space of the painting: "The artwork ... could be conceived as an energetic *analogon* to the psychic apparatus ... Such a hypothesis, if it were to be developed, would lead us to draw an 'economic aesthetics' in the sense in which Freud talked of libidinal economy."[14] In *Heidegger and "the jews"* Lyotard's reading of Freud shifts, but the analogy between art and the unconscious remains: more precisely, the analogy is between what Kant articulated under the name of the sublime and what Freud elaborated under that of primary repression. Indeed, in the opening chapter of the book, Lyotard explicitly suggests that it is useful "to dare to propose that secondary repression is to primary repression as the beautiful is to the sublime."[15] When he introduces the idea of an "anamnesis of the visible," in the section "Anamnesis" in *What to Paint?*, Lyotard suggests that the very notion requires one "to pursue the analogy between vision and the misrecognition due to desire."[16] In that sense, anamnesis is one of the analogical operators allowing Lyotard to *phrase* art with the Freudian unconscious. There is, though, a limit to such an analogy: working-through during the analytic session, the patient may work but s/he does not make a work in the sense of an *oeuvre* whereas the artist produces an *oeuvre*, an artwork. So, what does the analogy rely on?

Work—anamnesis as work; art as work

While the term "anamnesis" does not belong to Freud's main lexicon, in the psychoanalytic perspective that is Lyotard's, it is nevertheless linked to the question of recollection, more precisely to the question of different modes of recollection, as Freud elaborates it in particular in the essay "Erinnern, wiederholen und durcharbeiten,"[17] where he draws a well-known distinction between "remembering," "repeating," and "working-through" (*Durcharbeitung*). The patient, in his/her symptoms, does not *remember* what has been forgotten and repressed: s/he acts it out, and *repeats* it as an action without being aware of the fact that s/he is repeating it. Such repetition takes place through transference, not only onto the analyst but also in the patient's life. Repeating thus does not mean remembering: repetition, on the contrary, is a form of resistance to remembering. On the other hand, the analytic process consists in *working-through* such resistances. And it is to this process of *working-through* that Lyotard associates his use of the term "anamnesis," as he formulates it in *The Postmodern Explained to Children*:

> For a proper understanding of the work of modern painters, from, say, Manet to Duchamp or Barnett Newman, we would have to compare their work with anamnesis, in the sense of a psychoanalytic therapy. Just as patients try to elaborate their current problems by freely associating inconsequential details with past situations—allowing them to uncover hidden meanings in their lives and their behavior—so we can think of the work of Cézanne, Picasso, Kandinsky, Klee, Mondrian, Malevich, and finally Duchamp as a working through (*durcharbeiten*).[18]

Lyotard thus explicitly links his use of the term "anamnesis," as he applies it to the work of modern painters, to the Freudian notion of *durcharbeiten*. And again, in "La peinture, anamnèse du visible," the formulation is similar: "writing is an anamnesis of its matter, words; painting is one of colors and lines. *Writing*, be it literary or pictorial, *works through* 'language,' that is to say *through* all that has been received by it in words, colors, and lines."[19]

The German term that designates the process, *durcharbeiten*, inscribes the verb "to work" (*arbeiten*) and the preposition "through" (*durch*)—the patient works through screen memories and through transference. To associate art and anamnesis thus entails paying particular attention to the "work" inscribed in the English term "*work* of art" (and it is easier to do so in English than in French where, in the expression "*oeuvre d'art*," the meaning of the verb "*oeuvrer*"—to work—is no longer really heard in common language). It also entails linking the *work* of art to the *work* inscribed in the process of *working-through*. Here also, the French is more remote than the English from an immediate perception of the *work* in the word—in the French *"perlaboration,"* the sense of a "labor" is more remote than the "work" of the term "working-though"; furthermore, the "labor" of the *"perlaboration"* does not echo the *"oeuvre"* of the *"oeuvre d'art"* as the *work* of art can be heard to echo the *work*ing-through.

Associating the work of art, as Lyotard does through anamnesis, to the patient's working-through, raises the question of the *subject* of such anamnesis: whose anamnesis is talked about? If, in clinical practice, the subject of anamnesis can fairly easily be identified with the patient, entangled as s/he might be in a network of transferential relations, in the case of the artwork, whose work is talked about (by Lyotard, by me after Lyotard)? The work of the artist? The work of the *oeuvre*? The work of the viewer/reader/critic? It is precisely one of the stakes of Lyotard's thinking on art in terms of anamnesis to challenge the subject/ object dichotomy that governs both the discourse of philosophy and that of art in order to include in the *work* of anamnesis the subject-artist, the *oeuvre* as object as well as the viewer/reader/critic. Indeed, the work of art understood as anamnesis is not—or rather not only—the result of the efforts of a conscious subject (i.e., the artist). It is not a conscious mnesic operation of remembrance carried out by an individual subject. Describing modern painters' work as a *working-through* in *The Postmodern Explained*, Lyotard adds: "a 'working-though' (*durcharbeiten*) performed by modernity on its own meaning."[20] The passive construction makes "modernity" a subject of the working-through (but it is not an active subject, it is the passive agent) at the same time as "modernity" designates the entire sequence of painters "Cézanne, Picasso, Delaunay, Kandinsky, Klee, Mondrian, Malevich and finally Duchamp," in such a way that the subject, far from being individual, can only be thought of in collective terms. Elsewhere, in *What to Paint?*, Lyotard writes: "I would not be able to work through the anamnesis of the visible without carrying out the anamnesis of *Discourse, Figure*."[21] The philosopher (critic, reader, viewer) is here the subject of anamnesis. It is not, however, a work to be understood as Aby Warburg's *Detektivarbeit* ("detective work")—the work of the art historian put forth by Warburg to identify the Florentine portraits represented on the fresco of the Santa Trinita chapel. Lyotard's anamnesis of *Discourse, Figure* suggests that, in 1987, the 1973 book functions as a screen—in the sense of Freud's "screen memories"—in Lyotard's understanding of art. The anamnesis of *Discourse, Figure* entails working-through the screen; working-through the screen means changing the analytical paradigm according to which Lyotard understands the *work* of art.

Indeed, the emphasis placed on the *work* of art, on art as *work*, is not something that Lyotard introduces with the notion of "anamnesis." It is one of his most stable assumptions about art and it appears as early as in *Discourse, Figure* and recurs until his latest texts. However, the nature of the work that is at stake in art undergoes a shift. In the 1970s, Lyotard analyzes the dream-*work* (Freud's *Traumarbeit*) and he associates the *work* of art and the *work* of the dream. In *Discourse, Figure*, the figural *works* in, on, and against the text, in, on, and against discourse, in a way that Lyotard assimilates to the *work* of the primary processes in the dream. Hence his formulation, borrowed from Freud himself in *Die Traumdeutung*: "the dream-work does not think." And if it does not think, it is because it works: "The dream-work is not a language; it is the effect on language of the force exerted by the figural."[22] If in *Discourse, Figure* and in the 1970s Lyotard associates the *work* of art and the *work* of the dream, after *The Differend* and from the mid-1980s on, anamnesis, understood as *Durcharbeitung*, is a *work*, and art as anamnesis is thus to be thought of as *work*. In *Misère de la philosophie*, the associations between art, psychoanalysis, and work remain, as the essay "La peinture, anamnèse du visible" opens with the statement: "Painting is a struggle, a *work* in the strong sense of the term, as it is used in . . . psychoanalysis."[23] While the association between art and work remains from *Discourse, Figure* up to "La peinture, anamnèse du visible," what changes and shifts is the nature of the work at stake in art. In *Discourse, Figure*, the *work* of art is elaborated in terms of energy and forces. Hence, when Lyotard discusses, for example, two of Butor's texts dealing with the representation of the United States, one published in an issue of the journal *Réalités* (1962) entitled "L'appel des Rocheuses" (The Call of the Rockies) and an excerpt from *Illustrations* (1964) entitled "Les Montagnes Rocheuses" (The Rocky Mountains), he analyzes the textual fragments that constitute the representation of the United States in *Illustrations* as the traces of the operations of condensation and displacement working on the text of *Réalités* in order to deconstruct it: "Butor's book does not signify these operations (as does the *Traumdeutung*); rather it allows one to sense the traces they leave on the position of the constituents of discourse and on the intervals between them."[24] With *The Differend* and as Lyotard attempts to "supplement" *The Differend* with a phrasing of the notion of differend specific to art, the nature of the *work* of art shifts as it too is elaborated in terms of phrases. For, whereas the figural is to be understood in terms of *forces* at work, Lyotard's phrase cannot be said to *work* per se. Indeed, Lyotard thinks of the phrase as an *event*, as an occurrence—hence the canonical formulation of *The Differend*: "a phrase 'happens.'"[25] As such, the phrase is understood neither in energetic terms (as force), nor in linguistic terms (as communication), but as the presentation of what Lyotard calls a "universe," organized around four instances (referent, meaning, addressor, and addressee). A phrase does not "work" in order to present a universe: it just does, and the nature of its occurrence is not explained by the notion of "work." However, art as anamnesis does *work* in a sense that is not mechanistic: it works through phrases (through articulated phrases, through forms) in order to make present an event of color or of words, that has the specificity of being a "pure" presentation, an occurrence *that* happens "before" the content of the occurrence (a *quod* that happens before any *quid*). The anamnesis of *Discourse, Figure* thus consists in a shift from an emphasis placed on the deconstructive force of the figural to a phrasing of art as the working-through towards the event of presentation.

Art *works*. This is to say that art interests Lyotard insofar as it is a *process* rather than a finished product. And insofar as this process is not external to the object. In other words, Lyotard is not interested in the artwork as a cultural object, he is not interested in the work of construction of the cultural object—to study such work is the job of the art historian, it relies on a historical and sociological investigation, which is not Lyotard's main concern. Indeed, for Lyotard, "there is no history *of art* ... There is a history of cultural objects," hence the "long indictment against the history of art" in *Karel Appel. A Gesture of Colour*.[26] Of course the artwork (be it a painting or a book) is a cultural object. But art can also (and not all paintings or all books do) *work* to make present an *event* of color or of words. If the artwork is not to be assimilated to the cultural object, it is because the *work* of art is more *essential*—it is a work that opens onto an *essence* (a precarious essence, indeed, but essence nevertheless) of art, i.e. the *event* that art is. This precarious *essence* of art, Lyotard, in the texts following *The Differend*, calls "affect-phrase," "unconscious affect," or "pure affect," or else "inarticulate itself."

Affect-phrase

Anamnesis, insofar as the term designates the *work* of art, art working-through, thus opens onto what Lyotard, in the texts written after the mid-1980s, after *The Differend*,[27] calls a "pure affect," an "affect-phrase," an "inarticulate phrase," or sometimes even the "thing"—these expressions function as synonymous. It is through a reading and a rephrasing of Freud's notions of "unconscious affect" and primal repression that Lyotard elaborates the notion of affect-phrase.

For Freud, the unconscious, insofar as it is a *repressed* unconscious (that is, insofar as it is constituted by and through repression), is made of "thoughts" and "wishes," which belong to the order of representation. In the essay entitled "Repression," Freud elaborates how a drive (*Trieb*) manifests itself by means of representatives (*Triebrepräsentanten*), that consist, on the one hand, of an ideational content (*Vorstellung*, the order of word and thing representations) and, on the other hand, of a charge of affect (*Affektbetrag*), detached from this ideational content. While this idea belongs to the order of representation (*Vorstellung*), the affect is a representative of the drive (*Triebrepräsentanz*) detached from the idea, a representative that is therefore not a representation and that belongs to an order radically different from that of word and thing representations. Indeed, in "The Unconscious," published the same year as "Repression," Freud explains that repression does not bear on the drive or on its non-representational *Repräsentanz* (the affect), but on its *Vorstellungrepräsentanz*: only representations can be repressed into the unconscious.

However, in the same essay, Freud raises the question of what he paradoxically calls "unconscious affect and unconscious emotion." One would think that the very nature of emotion is to be perceived, hence to belong to consciousness. Moreover, if repression bears only on representations, then there could not be any unconscious affect or emotion. In fact, things work differently. An affect can be perceived yet remain unrecognized or misconstrued because its own ideational representative has been repressed and because the affect has attached itself to another representation of which, as far as consciousness can tell, it is the manifestation. As Freud writes, "in every instance where repression has succeeded in inhibiting the development of affects, we term those affects ... 'unconscious.'"[28] The difference between unconscious ideas and unconscious affects is thus crucial: "Unconscious ideas continue to exist after repression as actual structures in the system *Ucs*, whereas all that corresponds in that system to unconscious affects is a potential beginning which is prevented from developing."[29] The unconscious affect thus belongs to consciousness (insofar as the affect is *perceived*) while at the same time it is outside consciousness, since the representation of the original affect has been repressed and lies in the unconscious.

Lyotard's affect-phrase or inarticulate phrase corresponds to Freud's notion of "unconscious affect," and the opposition Lyotard draws between inarticulation and articulation corresponds to the opposition Freud established between *Affekt* and *Vorstellung*. Both Freud's "unconscious affect" and Lyotard's "affect-phrase" are simultaneously inside and outside consciousness, and what makes this paradoxical status possible is the fact that neither the "unconscious affect" nor the "affect-phrase" belongs to the order of representation. Through the notion of "unconscious affects," Freud opened up the possibility of a nonrepresentational unconscious. Lyotard's "affect-phrase" and his distinction between inarticulate and articulate phrases take up the possibility opened up by Freud and go further. Not only does the affect-phrase not belong to the order of representation (it is not representational), but furthermore it does not even belong to the order of delegation (the order of address and destination). In other words, it is neither a representation nor a representative. It "is there, but not for anything other than itself. This constitutes, at the same time, both its irrefutability and insufficiency as witness. The affect only 'says' one thing—that it is there—but says neither for what nor of what it bears witness. Neither when nor where."[30] What distinguishes Freud's "unconscious affect" and Lyotard's "affect-phrase," though, is that the Freudian concept of *Affekt* presupposes a quantitative theory of cathexis— indeed, the affect is defined as the subjective transposition of the quantity of energy attached to the drive. On the other hand, Lyotard's affect-phrase is defined without recourse to energetics and physics (and thus moves away from the physicist model of the *figural* in *Discourse, Figure*): it is defined as a specific type of "phrase," that is to say a phrase that happens without having destination, addressor, reference, or meaning. It is a non-signifying, non-addressing, non-addressed, and non-referenced phrase—a *quod* without any *quid*.

Anamnesis, understood as the work—the working-through—that opens onto the affect-phrase is thus a peculiar kind of work: it does not designate forces at work, nor does it designate a conscious or voluntary activity. It designates a passage—a "passibility," Lyotard writes in "Emma" or in *Lectures d'enfance*,[31] that is an openness—towards the affect-phrase. Passibility—from *patheia*—is the ability to be affected. Anamnesis thus allows us to think literature, painting, or music in terms of their capacity to affect, in terms of our ability to be affected. Not only does the "model" (however inappropriate the term may be) elaborated by Lyotard in *Discourse, Figure* to understand the artwork shift from forces to phrases, from energetics to phrastics, but furthermore, such a shift entails an opening onto a *subject* (onto subjects) who is (who are) affected. Passibility towards the affect concerns both the subject-artist (painter, musician, or writer) and the subject-viewer, listener or reader of art. And it is the very function of art to open that path. Such an opening constitutes a passage in and through time, a passage that transgresses the time of the historical present, the time of chronologies, the time framed by a *before* and an *after* in order to open onto a paradoxical time made of repetition.

Time—the time of anamnesis; the time of art

Anamnesis entails working through a paradoxical structure of time, which Lyotard associates with the temporal structure of the Freudian *Nachträglichkeit* and which he investigates on several occasions—in particular in *Heidegger and "the jews"* and in the essay "Emma," published at the same time, in 1988 and 1989. Indeed, *Heidegger and "the jews"* begins with Lyotard's reading and rewriting of the Freudian scenario of *Nachträglichkeit* as a "double blow" asymmetrical process in a temporal structure that has nothing to do with a phenomenology of consciousness. Lyotard's elaboration relies on the French translation of the German term as "*après-coup*" (literally "after the blow" or "after the shock"), in order to think the temporal structure of *Nachträglichkeit* in terms of "blows" or "shocks," that is to say in terms of affects, themselves understood as phrases. What is at stake in the temporal structure of *Nachträglichkeit* is the paradoxical relation between two times at which two shocks occur: a time that chronologically comes first, when an initial shock hits the psychic apparatus without apparently affecting it and then a time that chronologically comes second, when the psychic apparatus is affected (in the form of a symptom or a disorder) but without any apparent shock. "The first blow," Lyotard writes in *Heidegger and "the jews*," "strikes the apparatus without observable internal effect, without affecting it. It is a shock without affect. With the second blow there takes place an affect without shock."[32] The time that chronologically comes first corresponds to a shock that strikes without being registered: the affect is thus an "unconscious affect," an "inarticulate phrase"; it is present but not represented. The time that chronologically comes second corresponds to the activation of the first shock and constitutes a deferred reaction to it.

Analytic anamnesis—whether in the case of "Emma" or in that of the *Rat Man* as Lyotard reads it in "La peinture, anamnèse du visible" and in "Voix"[33]— produces a narrative organization and a chronologization of a time that is not chronological, and thus opens a path towards the first and originary blow, towards the retrieval of a time (the first blow) that was never registered because it constitutes a case of originary differend, a case of the necessarily missed encounter between articulation and an inarticulate phrase (the originary shock, identified by Freud as an "originary seduction," rephrased by Lyotard under the names of "infancy" or "sexual difference" in order to designate an originary unpreparedness of the psychic apparatus to represent and bind).

Psychoanalysis, as the process of coming to terms, through anamnesis, with this "originary" shock (i.e. with this originary unpreparedness), is explicitly associated by Lyotard with literature: art proceeds like clinical analysis as far as its temporal structure is concerned—"psychoanalysis," Lyotard writes at the end of Chapter 6 of *Heidegger and "the jews,"* "the search for lost time (*la recherche du temps perdu*), can, like literature, only be ... anamnesis."[34] Defined as "*recherche du temps perdu*"—through the relation of grammatical apposition, psychoanalysis' relation to time and literature's relation to time—to time lost—are assimilated. Proust's cycle functions as a paradigm for the literary work of anamnesis because, Lyotard explains, the *Recherche*, which is entirely structured as a search for lost time, ends but only to open, at the end, onto the time when the writing of the *Recherche* begins; furthermore, all memories and all representations are questioned as possible deceptions—"through them," Lyotard writes, "it [*La Recherche*] attempts to signal the affect of an absent 'presence' ... the thing, that writing both marks and misses."[35] Freud and Proust meet in this remembrance of things past which is the task of art—and if anamnesis is a search for lost time, it is not insofar as the time lost would be represented, or even presented, but insofar as art ensures a passage towards the essence of time lost, a "pure affect," the "pure event" of a "it happens." With Proust, though, the paradigmatic example of literary anamnesis is an example that can be read, at the level of its content (the level of its narrative), as a story about memory (the narrator's recollections) and about the history of an anamnesis (the narrator's gradual awareness of the importance of involuntary memory, that is of a memory of affects). Lyotard, however, distinguishes anamnesis and history—at least in theoretical terms. Both anamnesis and history have to do with keeping present that which is forgotten. History and memory do so by testifying to what happened, by phrasing the event, by telling *what* happened. Anamnesis, on the other hand, does not try to be faithful to what happened: "it lets itself be led by the unknown that happened then, by what is unpredictable and invisible in the event ... It explores the meanings of something that is 'present,' of a phrase from now, without concerning itself with (referential) reality, through associations said to be 'free' ... The past is not sought in order to be established."[36] Whereas history tries to testify to *what* happened (it testifies to a *quid*), anamnesis tries to testify *that* it happened (it testifies to a *quod*). Art in Lyotard's analyses is not, however, systematically devoid of content—testifying to a *quod* can also entail a *quid*: such is precisely the case of Proust's *Recherche* where remembrance is the very content of the narrative. Similarly, in the field of the visual arts, the work of Ruth Francken, from her early paintings in the 1950s and 1960s up to her work with photography and drawing at the end of the 1970s and in the early 1980s, allows Lyotard to tell *The Story of Ruth* (1983), which has to do with her specific place in the history of the twentieth century after Auschwitz, of "its time, brutal and without memory"[37] (and Lyotard is explicitly reconstructing her trajectory from the Prague Jewish community to Paris via Vienna, Oxford, New York, Venice, and Berlin). So, commenting on Ruth Francken's *Portraits* and on her large photometallic montages, Lyotard sees them as "an anamnesis of the amnesiac terror hidden by flash,"[38] an anamnesis of what is the disaster of our twentieth century. Both Proust's *Recherche* and *The Story of Ruth* are stories in which it may be difficult to separate the "it happens" (*quod*) from the "what happens" (*quid*).

It is probably easier to isolate anamnesis from the time of history in the works of such visual artists as Buren—it is an anamnesis *a minima*, Lyotard says, insofar as Buren, "by drawing attention to the site … rescues [it] from oblivion,"[39] an anamnesis *in situ* and *in tempore suo*, that obeys its own temporal rules and confronts them with the usual rules of presentation of artworks. Lyotard thus talks about an "anamnesis of art vision, performed by means of plastic situations."[40] Buren's counterpart in literary terms for Lyotard is probably Gertrude Stein. Lyotard never devoted a book nor even a full essay to Stein (as he did with Malraux, Augustine, Kafka, and Joyce, among others), but he comes back to her work at crucial places in his own: she is the only literary figure to whom he devotes a "Notice" in *The Differend* (along with Aristotle, Kant, Hegel, or Levinas). It is interesting that what he focuses on in this "Stein Notice" is the relation between writing and affect. He quotes Stein: "A sentence is not emotional, a paragraph is," and he adds: "Because the feeling or the sentiment is the linkage, the passage."[41] But if Stein's work, like Buren's, functions as an anamnesis *a minima*, it is not because of *what* Stein says: it is because of the way she questions the nature of linkages between words and between sentences. Indeed, in *What to Paint?*, Lyotard explicitly associates Buren's "anamnesis of the art vision," his anamnesis of the conditions of possibility of vision, with Gertrude Stein's: he draws a parallel between Buren's visual apparatus (which he phrases as: "color then white then color then white") and Stein's formula: "a rose is a rose is a rose is a rose."[42] If Stein's literary texts testify to the differend, it is not because they tell the paradigmatic story of the differend (that is, the Shoah), but because they work through language in order to call into question the traditional linkage between words and between sentences, the temporal linkage that relies on causality, continuity and logic. The "anamnesis of words"—which is the ultimate function Lyotard assigns to literature—testifies to the presence within articulated discourse of that which renders linkage problematic, just as the "anamnesis of the visible" testifies to apparition over appearance, testifies to the presence in the visible of an invisible upon which presentation and visibility rely. "One paints, one writes, not in order to represent or reproduce that which is present there, but in order to make one see the invisible that makes the enigma of presence possible."[43]

What is at stake—and the reason why Lyotard's texts, his readings of art and literature, his comments on painters and writers, are of interest to us, his readers who are also viewers and readers of art and literature—is neither a general aesthetics or a philosophy of art nor a theory of aesthetic judgment or a psychoanalytic theory of art, but what Lyotard himself calls "an attempt at a general poetics of the event"[44] (of color, or sound, or of language). But the term "general" may be too systematic: for what, following the term "anamnesis," we encounter in Lyotard's texts are ways to pay attention to the conditions of presentation of the work of art (more than to what it represents), ways to pay attention to the event of presentation without reducing it to a discourse *on* and about the event, ways to pay attention to the emotions and affects it testifies to— for such is, for Lyotard, the function of art.

Analysis, Freud said, is, in principle, interminable (even if it can be terminated). It is so because anamnesis is, in principle, interminable—the chain of associations is interminable, even its determination (that which could be seen as the "reason" for the chain) is part of the chain. Of course, in clinical practice, analysis can (and needs to) be terminated when anamnesis is felt to be sufficient—it is the function of the affect to signal it. In art, anamnesis—be it of the visible, of words, or of sound—is also interminable. Not in the sense that the artist would never put an end to his/her work, obviously. But in the sense that the *work* of art as anamnesis proceeds from a movement of un-doing of language, forms, linkages that *is* interminable. "The work un-works language [*désœuvre la langue*]," Lyotard writes, "... [t]he work is but a pause in the process of un-working [*désœuvrement*]."[45]

Notes

1   I would like to thank Julie Gaillard and Mark Stoholski, who organized the conference where this paper was first delivered. In turning the oral paper into this text, their help with the English translations of Lyotard's texts has been extremely precious.

2   Jean-François Lyotard, "Anamnèse du visible, ou: la franchise," in *Adami* (Paris: Collection du Musée National d'Art Moderne, Centre Georges Pompidou, 1985), 50–60. The essay has been translated as "Anamnesis of the visible or: Candour" in *The Lyotard Reader*, ed. Andrew Benjamin (Oxford and Cambridge, MA: Blackwell, 1989), 220–39.

3   Jean-François Lyotard, "L'anamnèse," in *Que Peindre?* (Paris: Éditions de la différence, 1987), 59–66; reprinted by Hermann, 2008, 95–108; translated as "Anamnesis," *Écrits sur l'art contemporain et les artistes. Writings on Contemporary Art and Artists*, vol. V: *Que peindre? Adami, Arakawa, Buren/What to Paint? Adami, Arakawa, Buren*, bilingual edition by Herman Parret (Louvain/Leuven: Presses Universitaires de Louvain/Leuven University Press, 2012), 236–55.

4   Jean-François Lyotard, "L'anamnèse," in *Leçons sur l'analytique du sublime* (Paris: Galilée, 1991), 49–52. "Anamnesis," *Lessons on the Analytic of the Sublime*, trans. Elizabeth Rottenberg (Stanford: Stanford University Press, 1994), 32–5.

5   Jean-François Lyotard, *Misère de la philosophie* (Paris: Galilée, 2000), 97–115. The version published in *Misère de la philosophie* has not been translated as such. A translation of the 1998 version (entitled "Anamnèse du visible") can be found under the title "Anamnesis of the Visible" in *Écrits sur l'art contemporain et les artistes. Writings on Contemporary Art and Artists*, vol. IVb: *Textes dispersés II: artistes contemporains/Miscellaneous Texts II: Contemporary Artists*, bilingual edition by Herman Parret (Louvain/Leuven: Presses Universitaires de Louvain/Leuven University Press, 2012), 562–93.

6   Jean-François Lyotard, "L'obédience," in *L'Inhumain* (Paris: Galilée, 1991). First delivered in 1986. Reprinted Paris: Klincksieck, 2014, 159–72. Translated by Geoffrey Bennington and Rachel Bowlby as "Obedience," in *The Inhuman* (Stanford: Stanford University Press, 1991).

7   Lyotard, *The Inhuman*, 165.

8   Ibid., 56–7: "We envisage this writing as passing or anamnesis in both writers and artists as a resistance . . . to the syntheses of breaching and scanning."

9   Corinne Enaudeau, Jean-François Nordmann, Jean-Michel Salanskis, and Frédéric Worms eds, *Les Transformateurs Lyotard* (Paris: Sens & Tonka, 2008).

10 For such an investigation, see Laurence Kahn, "*D'une lecture apathique de Freud*," in *Les Transformateurs Lyotard*, 261–76.

11 Jean-François Lyotard, *The Differend. Phrases in Dispute*, trans. G. Van Den Abbeele (Minneapolis: University of Minnesota Press, 1988), 66.

12 Jean-François Lyotard, "Psychanalyse et peinture," in *Encyclopaedia Universalis*, vol. 13 (Paris: Encyclopaedia Universalis, 1972), 745–50. Reprinted as "Freud selon Cézanne" in *Des dispositifs pulsionnels* (Paris: Christian Bourgois, 1980 [first ed. UGE, 1973]), 67–88.

13 Jean-François Lyotard, *Discourse, Figure*, trans. Antony Hudek and Mary Lydon (Minneapolis: The University of Minnesota Press, 2011), 256.

14 Lyotard, "Freud selon Cézanne," 83. Translation mine.

15 Jean-François Lyotard, *Heidegger and "the jews,"* trans. Andreas Michel and Mark Roberts (Minneapolis: University of Minnesota Press, 1990), 5.

16 Jean-François Lyotard, "Anamnesis," in *Que peindre?/What to Paint?*, 237.

17 Published in 1914 and included in Sigmund Freud's *Gesammelte Werke, Band 10: Werke aus den Jahren 1913–1917* (Frankfurt am Main: Fischer Verlag, 1946), 126–36.

18 Jean-François Lyotard, *The Postmodern Explained: Correspondence 1982–1985*, eds Julian Penafis and Morgan Thomas (Minneapolis: University of Minnesota Press, 1992), 79–80.

19 Lyotard, *Misère de la philosophie*, 103. Translation mine.

20 Lyotard, *The Postmodern Explained*, 80.

21 Lyotard, *Que peindre?/What to Paint?*, 239.

22 Lyotard, *Discourse, Figure*, 266.

23 Lyotard, "La peinture, anamnèse du visible," 99. Translation mine.

24 Lyotard, *Discourse, Figure*, 376.

25 Lyotard, *The Differend*, xii.

26 Jean-François Lyotard, *Écrits sur l'art contemporain et les artistes. Writings on Contemporary Art and Artists*, vol. I: *Karel Appel. Un geste de couleur. Karel Appel. A Gesture of Colour*, bilingual edition by Herman Parret (Louvain/Leuven: Presses Universitaires de Louvain/Leuven University Press, 2009): "long indictment against the history of art" is the title of section 14 (86–7) and the quote is on 90–1.

27 In particular, *The Inhuman, Heidegger and "the jews"* and "Emma," in *Nouvelle Revue de Psychanalyse* 39 (Spring 1989), 43–70; reprinted in *Misère de la philosophie*, 55–95. Trans. Michael Sanders et al. as "Emma: Between Philosophy and Psychoanalysis," in *Lyotard. Philosophy, Politics, and the Sublime*, ed. Hugh J. Silverman (New York and London: Routledge, 2002), 23–45.

28 Sigmund Freud, *The Standard Edition of the Complete Psychological Works of Sigmund Freud*, trans. James Strachey, vol. 14 (London: Hogarth, 1957), 178.

29 Ibid.

30 Lyotard, "Emma," *Lyotard. Philosophy, Politics, and the Sublime*, 32 (translation modified).

31 The term is used, for example, in "Emma" in order "to signal a passibility more 'archaic' than all articulation and irreducible to it" ("Emma," 44, translation modified: the English translator chose to translate the French *passibilité* by "susceptibility," which reads more easily in the sentence in English than "passibility." I nevertheless prefer to use the term "passibility": it sounds no more awkward in English than it does in French, and one can hear both *patheia* and *passage*). The term is also used in "Retour" (*Lectures d'enfance*, Paris: Galilée, 1991), to suggest that what is at stake in writing is "to bear witness to a passibility to that voice that, within man, exceeds man" ("Return upon the Return," *Towards the Postmodern*, ed. Robert Harvey and Mark S. Roberts (New Jersey and London: Humanities Press, 1993), 198, translation modified: here the French *passibilité* has been translated "liability"; for the same reasons as above, I choose "passibility").

32 Lyotard, *Heidegger and "the jews,"* 16.

33 Lyotard, *Lectures d'enfance*, 140–53. A first version of the essay published in *Lectures d'enfance* appeared, under the title "Les Voix d'une voix," in *Nouvelle Revue de psychanalyse* 62 (fall 1990). That version has been translated by Georges Van Den Abbeele, "Voices of a Voice," in *Discourse: Journal for Theoretical Studies in Media and Culture* 14, no. 1 (winter 1991–2): 126–45.

34 Lyotard, *Heidegger and "the jews,"* 20, translation modified.

35 Lyotard, *Misère de la philosophie*, 103, translation mine.

36 Lyotard, "La peinture, anamnèse du visible," *Misère de la philosophie*, 100–1.

37 Jean-François Lyotard, *L'Histoire de Ruth*, in *Écrits sur l'art contemporain et les artistes. Writings on Contemporary Art and Artists*, vol. IVb: *Textes dispersés II/ Miscellaneous Texts II*, 386–7.

38 Ibid.

39 Lyotard, *Que peindre?/What to Paint?*, 317.

40 Ibid., 343.

41 Lyotard, *The Differend*, 67.

42 Lyotard, *Que peindre?/What to Paint?*, 333–5.

43 Lyotard, "Formule charnelle," in *Misère de la philosophie*, 280. Translation mine.

44 Lyotard, "La peinture, anamnèse du visible," in *Misère de la philosophie*, 112.

45 Ibid., 103.

5

Lyotard's Gesture

Kas Saghafi

1. Following the publication of *The Differend*, Jean-François Lyotard frequently expressed his wish to publish a supplement to his "book of philosophy" that would address the "affective dimension" of the differend. In fact, his essay "The Affect-phrase" (originally titled "L'inarticulé ou le différend même"—The Inarticulate, or the Differend Itself) that appeared in the posthumous volume *Misère de la philosophie* (published in 2000) bears the subtitle "D'un supplément au *Différend*" (From a Supplement to *The Differend*). Unfortunately, Lyotard was not able to publish this envisioned text. Or so the story goes. Did he not, I'd like to ask, a little mischievously or some would say quite erroneously, write this supplement—perhaps not in the form that he had wished or that we would expect, but under different guises?

2. While all the essays collected in *Lectures d'enfance*, mainly written in the late 1980s and early 1990s, cannot be described as simply addressing the affective dimension of the differend, it can be argued that Lyotard's essays on Aristotle and Freud ("Voix"), and Kafka ("Prescription") take up the relation between *phōnē* and *logos*, inarticulate voice and articulated language, Freudian affect and presentation (*Darstellung*), first touch and the law. In addition, "Emma," in *Misère de la philosophie*, explores the relation between an other temporality and pure affectivity, or childhood. Moreover, does not Lyotard's book on Karel Appel take up the above-mentioned dimension of the differend in the relation between gesture and commentary?

3. *Karel Appel: A Gesture of Colour*, containing Lyotard's most extensive late ruminations on painting, following on from *What to Paint?*, may be said to be the aesthetic or inaesthetic component of his reflections on the differend that we are discussing. The Appel project which began around 1985, and was supposed to result in a volume for Galilée, was not published until a German edition appeared in 1998, the year of Lyotard's death.[1]

4. Art "gives to thinking [*donne à penser*]."[2] But what art gives are not "givens [*données*]" or cultural objects. For Lyotard, whose interest throughout his years of writing about art was mainly in painting, what art gives are bursts of color. "Painting is the passion of color," he was fond of saying.[3] What cannot be denied when faced with a painting is the undeniability of *this* matter. The work occurs; it happens to space-time-matter. It is, each time, an event in space-time-matter.

5. The thinking viewer incurs a debt to this work. The work makes him or her indebted by its very existence, or by what Lyotard dubs after Levinas, its "way of being [*manière d'être*]."[4] Recall that in *Totality and Infinity* Levinas explained that the I and *Autrui* ("Other") existed in two different ways. Using *façon* and *manière* (manner or way) interchangeably, Levinas wrote of the singular way of being of the Other. Here, Lyotard writes that each work has its own way of being in space, in time, and in matter, to which the thinker is indebted. The artists ask one, whether directly or indirectly, "to think the sensible singularity" of the work "presented here and now."[5]

6. The gesture that the work is is an *actus* and a *situs*.[6] As an *actus*, "as movement and passage of colors, lines, volumes or sounds, it is an upsurge [*poussée*] of matter."[7] It is also a *situs* (not a *situs* that simply takes place in a site, but one that in happening to space-time and re-orders it). But this space, this time, and this matter cannot be presupposed as already pre-existing or pre-established, since they come about as the work takes place.

7. The gesture that the work is, what Lyotard refers to as its happening, its existence, and perhaps most provocatively, its "presence," constitutes its impenetrability to thought. "Do not read me, do not understand me," Appel's work seems to proclaim.[8]

8. Lyotard candidly discusses his role as a philosopher regularly approached by artists who request that he provide an account of their work and admits to the difficulty of philosophizing about these gestures. Traditionally, philosophy has used the language of *experience* to write about these gestures. But experience in the language of the philosopher, Lyotard notes, is "predisposed to comprehension," already made for the philosopher.[9] Philosophy fashions and organizes all givens for the understanding. The concept "determines and regulates the forms of the object in order to know it."[10] Thus, the mind ends up digesting experience in order to produce a reasonable discourse. The work of art becomes a "prey" for philosophical thought.[11]

9. Accordingly, the contemporary discourse on art, the production of "theories" of objects, is in the service of their determination. While this is to a degree necessary and inevitable, the work is not *simply* a cultural object. It

overflows all determinations of its "reception" and its "production."[12] The profusion of discourses—religious, political, psychological, philosophical— which seek to objectify the work condemn it to being merely a phenomenon among other phenomena. These discourses, which are appropriate to *anthropological* givens, reduce "the force of *apparition* that the work possesses" to "the form of its *appearance*."[13]

10. "There is no history *of art* as such," Lyotard writes, but "a history of [determinable] cultural objects."[14] What the latter discourses do is to confuse art with the cultural object, artistic time with historical time. But art is not solely the expression of its time. The "astounding power" of the work is independent of periods and of contexts.[15] This is why previous pronouncements about "the death of art" and the transformation of beauty into kitsch are misguided, for they also commit the same error.

11. Rather than comprehending and making comprehensible, which have been the traditional task of the philosopher, painting now calls for "reflection." Taking Kant's writings as inspiration, Lyotard writes in favor of reflection rather than argumentation. This reflection is guided by feeling, by pain and/or pleasure on the occasion of a work—an affected thinking. The painter, who is touched by a circumstance, makes paintings out of his feeling and those who encounter them are in turn touched. Paying tribute to the work, Lyotard seeks to call into question the authority of arguments and to disturb the serene assurance of philosophical aesthetics. He writes of the latter's defection, of its forfeiture, which leave him with uncertainty and torment.[16]

12. What seems to be undeniable is matter and its "enigma."[17] Chromatic matter is given to thinking and the "work" is "a gesture of and in matter [*geste de et dans une matière*]."[18] It is as though the understanding were under assault by colors and, when faced with them, feels its "impotence."[19] A "rapture" or "astonishment," Lyotard writes, causes thinking to suspend its activity, to come to a standstill.[20]

13. A "debt of obligation" is thus incurred.[21] How is reflection to act? How could canvases with swathes of color resulting from a gesture, "the gesture of painting," be articulated?[22] The philosopher is put in the position "to reach the gesture that is the work," to translate this way of being into words and to "transcribe it in his or her own space-time-matter."[23] But how to do this? In the tone of "an account of affect [*un compte-rendu d'affect*]."[24] The affect can only be accounted for by transmitting it. Lyotard observes: "It seems to me that the philosopher who loves art must learn to carry out, on a singular work, an anamnesis of the secret gesture from which the work receives its paradox of

space-time-matter, and which touches us."[25] The work, which holds or keeps in reserve the gesture, a curve, color, range, rhythm, or tonality, can be an event. It cannot be decoded.

14. "The gesture of painting" opposes to thinking a kind of aporia. This gesture inscribes in the space-time-matter of the visible figures that stem from an entirely other space-time-matter, not abstract, but visible in an entirely other way ("*tout autrement*").[26]

15. Lyotard himself admits that "gesture is surely not a great name."[27] In *"Le Geste de Dieu" Sur un lieu de l'*Ethique *de Spinoza*, Alfonso Cariolato argues that the French term *geste* is derived from the Latin *nutus*. Signifying movement, nod or shake of one's head as a sign of assent or approbation, *nutus*, which appears in Cicero, Livy, Lucretius and others, is in turn derived from the Greek *to neuma*, to incline or tilt one's head, to command or order.[28] In Medieval Latin, *nutus* was another term for *gestus*. According to Jean-Claude Schmitt, in the Middle Ages, *gestus* gave way to *signum* and occasionally to *nutus*.[29]

In *Karel Appel*, Lyotard explains that *gestus* is the substantivized supine of the verb *gerere*, meaning "the state of 'carrying oneself,' of holding oneself in a certain way."[30] The "carrying" carries itself, intransitively. The reversal of a verb of action or of a state, *gestus* is thus "itself a gesture of language, a gesture of and in the space-time-matter of language."[31]

16. Lyotard remarks that *gestus* could be joined to *actus* and *situs*: *actus*, understood not simply as an act, but the acting where "the action will have been," and *situs*, understood not simply as a situated site, but as "the situating of which there will have been a situation."[32] It is through the gesture that art "transforms the conditions of being-there [*être-là*]," but the work, which is "the trace of this transformation," must be there in the regular presentation.[33]

17. *Gestus*, "a torsion of the time of an action or of a state," indicates that "the state *will have* appeared and persisted."[34] In this future anterior, "the state has not yet appeared at the moment of speaking," and "later on, when one tries to think of it, it no longer will be."[35] But "this torturous gesture, this *twist* [tors], must present" itself in the "space-time, where it becomes a work."[36] The gesture "has to be rendered sensible at the same time that it is a challenge to sensibility." This challenge itself is what makes art. The work, then, "will have gestured" to another time, space, and matter, to which commentary will have to link on.[37]

18. "The example of a 'deferred affect [*l'affect après-coup*],'" Lyotard writes, "reveals the necessity of the future anterior to the understanding of the aesthetic gesture."[38] Drawing an analogy with the Freudian *après-coup* (*Nachträglichkeit*— belated stroke, deferred effect, after shock, after the fact, after the event), he writes

of an event that is not marked in ordinary conscious experience or space-time. "The work, which invokes a space-time-matter different from the ordinary one, reveals, after the fact [*après-coup*], a hard before-shock or a blow before the fact [*une frappe avant-coup*] which without it would have remained unknown."[39] The work reveals "a trace of the event that had remained hidden without presentable trace before-shock [*avant coup*]."[40] The debt to a before-shock, this "delicate touch, coming, perhaps, from another time"[41] is present in a "blank [*blanche*]" affectability or a passibility.[42] This is a debt of art, or what Lyotard prefers to call, "a debt of gesture."[43] The debt can be "recalled" and the gesture of art *is* this "recall [*rappel*]."[44] Thus, Lyotard writes, "What is there will have done justice to what perhaps was, which from now on will have been there and which has never been."[45] This is the "astonishing authority" of art that is negotiated in Appel under the motif of what Lyotard refers to as *childhood*.

19. If the writer/thinker is always asked "to get across [*fasse comprendre*]" what the artist has done, he or she can only do so, Lyotard ruefully admits early on in *Karel Appel*, "in an operation . . . on the order of a crossing [*une traversée*]: decanting [*transvasement*], transcription, transposition, transition, translation and always treason."[46]

20. A stroke, a line, a swathe of color—painting's gesture—gives rise to or signals affects (*pathēmata*), affects of pain and/or pleasure. Like a timbre, an intonation or an inflection, a gesture, painting's gesture, is not articulated; it does not present a phrase universe. As Lyotard explains in "L'inarticulé ou le différend même," it is on the occasion of objects that pleasure and pain are signaled by "gestures—*The Differend* §110."[47] This gesture, however, is mute, it only signifies affections. Even though there is "a communicability of pleasure and pain," it is "without the mediation of *logos*."[48] How, then, to respond to this mute communication? To respect its mutism would be to lend it one's ear.

21. Transcription is inevitable. Transcription—or transference—is the transmission of affect. To report the affect arising from the gesture of painting is to transmit it. A report or account of the affect provoked by the work—an anamnesis of the gesture—is its transmission in a gesture in, and of, writing. But need this writing be, strictly speaking, the employment of *logos*? As Lyotard writes, *gestus* is itself "a gesture of language, a gesture of and in space-time-matter of language."[49] One can only "bear witness" to matter-color by means of this gesture.[50]

22. Transference then would be, adopting its definition in *Lectures d'enfance* while slightly modifying it, the gesture of, and in, painting "in the process of articulating itself."[51] Trans-mission, trans-lation, trans-position, trans-formation,

trans-scription, or trans-ference speak of a gesture, of writing, which is haunted, inhabited by another gesture. Even though the two gestures of painting and writing are "heterogeneous" to each other, the former can inhabit the latter, like the apparition that Lyotard often reminds us inhabits the appearance. For example, when in a dense passage, he writes: "Beauty is *and* is not sensible. It is an apparition at the heart of appearances. It is in what it promises."[52] What it promises is "the happiness of a free presentation."[53] This freedom "makes an appearance [*fait apparition*]" in beauty "without appearing itself."[54] For, what appears is only "a trace, the work."[55] Elsewhere, in "Fait pictural [Necessity of Lazarus]," a text on Albert Ayme in *Miscellaneous Texts II: Contemporary Artists*, Lyotard observes that "the work is an appearance [*apparence*] in which an apparition happens [*advient*]."[56] The gesture of writing would somehow bear the pleasure and/or pain provoked by the gesture of painting.

23. The affect can inhabit articulated language, but it is an inarticulate muteness that needs to be conjured, cajoled into articulation by writing.[57] Though, in what idiom can one express affects and the happening of painting's gesture? The writing of gesture would be an *affected writing*, a writing inhabited by affect, or the writing of gesture inhabited by the gesture of painting. This writing, then, would not take the shape of a *logos*, but rather would be a "trace of a gesture of and in language that links on or with a work of art."[58]

24. In *Flora Danica: The Secession of the Gesture in the Painting of Stig Brøgger*, Lyotard refers to Brøgger's paintings, these "pieces of painted wood" on display at the Statens Museum for Kunst in Copenhagen, as "phrases."[59] But they are phrases without referent, sense, addressor, or addressee. They can thus be likened to affect-phrases because their *inarticulation* makes them similar to feelings. Standing before these works, Lyotard writes, "I must receive some *gesture* in my thoughts (in my phrases)" that comes to encounter "the singular gesture" of these pieces.[60] However, the commentary that Brøgger's works would require, Lyotard writes, is "a commentary that questions the sense, the reference, and the address of the articulated language in which this commentary itself is articulated."[61] He refers to the *gestures* "of painting as well as writing" because each is nothing but "a way of time, space, and matter (color for painters, words for the writer) to *organize* themselves [se gérer]."[62] It should be noted that the gesture is not the form, for the form tends to "hide the gesture" that brings it about.[63] The gesture withdraws into the form, which represses it and denies it.[64]

25. Perhaps this thinking of gesture would begin to account for the kind of writing practiced by Lyotard in his later writings on contemporary artists such as Sam Francis, Pierre Skira, François Rouan, and Corinne Filippi. These texts

display Lyotard's attempt to put himself in tune with the gesture of the artistic work, "awakening the layers asleep in words and in linkages of words."[65] The gesture of writing would be the transmission of affect: it would somehow bear at once the affect, the pleasure and/or pain provoked by the gesture of painting, *and* be its transmission. This, then, would be his writing—Lyotard's gesture—a writing that feels its state of being affected.

Notes

1   The original German edition was published as *Karel Appel: Ein Farbgestus, Essays zur Kunst Karel Appels mit einer Bildauswahl des Autors*, trans. Jessica Beer (Bern/Berlin: Gachnang & Springer, 1998).

2   Jean-François Lyotard, *Karel Appel: Un geste de couleur* (Leuven: Leuven University Press, 2009), 38; trans. Vlad Ionescu and Peter W. Milne as *Karel Appel: A Gesture of Colour* (Leuven: Leuven University Press, 2009), 39. All further references are cited with page references first to the French, then to the English, of this bilingual edition. I have very occasionally silently modified the translation to reflect my reading.

3   "La peinture, anamnèse du visible," in *Textes dispersés II: artistes contemporains/ Miscellaneous Texts II: Contemporary Artists*, ed. Hermann Parret (Leuven: Leuven University Press, 2012), 585.

4   Lyotard, *Karel Appel*, 34–6/35–7.

5   Ibid, 40–1.

6   "Gesture" is a late term in Lyotard's writings. References to gesture in painting begin to appear in texts from 1991 and 1993.

7   Ibid., 40–1.

8   Ibid., 44–5.

9   Ibid., 42–3.

10 Ibid., 82–3.

11 Ibid., 36–7.

12 Ibid., 90–1.

13 Ibid.

14 Ibid.

15 Ibid., 96–7.

16 Ibid., 26–7.

17 Ibid., 34–5.

18 Ibid., translation modified.

19 Ibid., 32–3.

20 Ibid., 192–3.

21 Ibid., 56–7.

22 Ibid., 26–7.

23 Ibid., 52–3.

24 Ibid., 190–1. Following Freud, Lyotard understands affect as an excitation that cannot be represented, thus remaining "within" the apparatus as "unconscious affect." For affect in Freud, see Sigmund Freud, "Entwurf einer Psychologie," *Gesammelte Werke* (GW), vols 1–18, eds Anna Freud et al. (Frankfurt am Main: S. Fischer Verlag, 1960), Nachtr.: 387–477, translated as "Project for a Scientific Psychology" (1895), in *The Standard Edition of the Complete Works of Sigmund Freud* (SE), 24 volumes, eds James Strachey et al. (London: The Hogarth Press, 1953–74) 1: 283–397; *Drei Abhandlungen zur Sexualtheorie* in *Studienausgabe*, GW 5, 13–145, translated as *Three Essays on the Theory of Sexuality*, SE 7:135–243; "Zur Einfuhrung des Narzissmus," GW 10, 137–70, translated as "On Narcissism: An Introduction," SE 14: 73–102, and *Hemmung, Symptom und Angst,* GW 14. 113–205, translated as *Inhibitions, Symptoms, and Anxiety* (1926) in SE 20: 87–172.

25 Ibid., 194–5, 195–6.

26 Ibid., 200–1.

27 Ibid., 202–3.

28 Alfonso Cariolato, *"Le Geste de Dieu": Sur un lieu de l'*Ethique *de Spinoza* (Chatou: Editions de la Transparence, 2011). The phrase *"le geste de dieu"* is a translation of *nos ex solo Dei nutu agere* that appears in Spinoza, *Ethics,* Part II, Proposition 49, Scholium.

29 Jean-Claude Schmitt, "'*Gestus*'—'*Gesticulatio*.' Contribution à l'étude du vocabulaire latin médiéval des gestes," in *La Lexicographie du latin médiéval et ses rapports avec les recherches actuelles sur la civilisation du Moyen Age* (Paris: CNRS, 1981), 383.

30 Lyotard, *Karel Appel*, 202–3. Lyotard notes that in scholastic Latin *supinus* means "turned onto one's back." "Thus the gesture is a carrying oneself that has been turned on its back."

31 Ibid.

32 Ibid., 204–5.

33 Ibid.

34 Ibid., 202–3.

35 Ibid.

36 Ibid., 204–5.

37 Ibid.

38 Ibid., 206–7.

39 Ibid.

40 Ibid.

41 Ibid., 84–5.

42 Ibid., 210–11.

43 Ibid., 208–9.

44 Ibid., 210–11.

45 Ibid., 206–7.

46 Ibid., 38–9.

47 In "La phrase-affect (D'un supplément au *Différend*)," in *Misère de la philosophie* (Paris: Galilée, 2000), 53, translated as "The Affect-Phrase (from a Supplement to *The Differend*)," in *The Lyotard Reader and Guide*, eds James Williams and Keith Crome (New York: Columbia University Press, 2006), 109, Lyotard adds a passage about gesture as an extension of the *phōnē* to paragraph no. 13: "it will thus be necessary to extend the *phōnē* as far as *gesture*." This passage does not appear in the earlier version of the essay, "L'inarticulé ou le différend même," in *Figures et conflits rhétoriques*, eds Michel Meyer and Alain Lempereur (Brussels: Editions de l'Université de Bruxelles, 1990), 205.

48 Lyotard, "The Affect-Phrase," 108 ("La phrase-affect," 51).

49 Lyotard, *Karel Appel*, 202–3.

50 Ibid., 200–1.

51 Jean-François Lyotard, *Lectures d'enfance* (Paris: Galilée, 1991), 144.

52 Lyotard, *Karel Appel*, 204–5.

53 Ibid.

54 Ibid., 204–6, 205–7.

55 Ibid., 206–7.

56 Jean-François Lyotard, "Nécessité de Lazare," in *Textes dispersés II: artistes contemporains/Miscellaneous Texts II: Contemporary Artists* (Leuven: Leuven University Press, 2012), 350; translated by Geoffrey Bennington, Vlad Ionescu and Peter W. Milne as "Fait pictural [Necessity of Lazarus]," 351.

57 See Claire Nouvet's excellent "The Inarticulate Affect: Lyotard and Psychoanalytic Testimony," in *Minima Memoria: In the Wake of Jean-Francois Lyotard*, eds Claire Nouvet, Zrinka Stahuljak, and Kent Still (Stanford: Stanford University Press, 2007).

58 Ibid., 32–3.

59 Jean-François Lyotard, *Flora danica: La sécession du geste dans la peinture de Stig Brøgger*, in *Textes dispersés II: artistes contemporains/Miscellaneous Texts II: Contemporary Artists* (Leuven: Leuven University Press, 2012), 628; translated by Vlad Ionescu and Erica Harris as *Flora Danica: The Secession of the Gesture in the Painting of Stig Brøgger*, 629.

60 Lyotard, *Flora Danica*, 630–1.

61 Ibid.

62 Ibid.

63 Ibid., 632–3.

64 Ibid., 634–5.

65 Lyotard, *Karel Appel*, 52–4, 53–5.

6

No Place for Complacency

The Resistance of Gesture

Kiff Bamford

The challenge I address in this chapter is a fear of repetition, as I turn to a performance by an artist whose work has already provoked my own thought and writing—the Chinese-born artist based in Germany, Yingmei Duan. At a performance in a London gallery, in spite of my personal acquaintance with the artist and despite my own fears, misgivings, and hesitancy, I found space-time-matter transformed by her presence. Or perhaps it is because of this hesitancy and the unanticipated power of the gesture that I was prompted to respond in kind, mouthing manacled words to camera in the making of a video piece that attempted to link on to that gesture. The art is in the gesture, not the artist or the work, and it is the presence of the remainder that is the concern of this chapter. In what follows, I attempt to evoke the complexity of the gesture, which resists and rejects expected articulations, prompting a transference of affect. Accepted forms of communication are broken down and the codified body dismembered, as Lyotard writes: "The body doesn't belong to you."[1]

I ask you, the reader, to forgive the mode of address adopted in what follows: I am speaking to an audience at Emory University, Atlanta, USA, several of whom had attended a similar event two years previously at the University of Alberta, Canada. It is a small, intimate audience, one which you are now invited to join. Yet, I cannot but be aware of the perversity of such a set-up: for you have arrived too late. The moment is past. Can there yet be any gesture that remains? It is the task of my writing to recall that which couldn't then be written. The lecture theater is of medium size with a large, curved projection screen behind the speaker; light filters through the windows at the rear.

The last time I had the opportunity to speak about Lyotard's ideas, to a gathering of people also interested in Lyotard's ideas, was also the first time. As we know, events like this are special. On that occasion, two years ago in Edmonton, I spoke about Return and the difficulty of such an idea, according to Lyotard, when one cannot be sure that what returns is "precisely what had disappeared."[2] By virtue of its having disappeared, that which returns can only be returned as lost. In his late essay, "Return upon the Return," Lyotard's point of reference is the return of the wandering Odysseus to Ithaca, and the multiple differences when retold by James Joyce in *Ulysses*, but also implied is Freud's account of the process of reality-testing, where the importance of re-finding an object in perception is dogged by distortions and uncertainty. Lyotard writes, "[h]ow can one be sure that what returned is precisely what had disappeared? Or that what returns not only appears, but is reappearing? Our first gesture would be to challenge reality. What is past is not here, what is here is present."[3] I argued for the usefulness of this warning when approaching the area of performance art discourse: the history of those art events which are sometimes termed "live" art and which seem to define themselves through a refusal to exist beyond the time of their occurrence. Part of my paper was a video response to a performance piece by Yingmei Duan.[4] Two years later, I am still caught in the same seemingly circular problematic of not knowing how to respond. If I dare invoke the old technology of the vinyl record player, I could say I am caught in a groove, failing to progress to the next track; more generously, we could use the jazz reference and say I am caught in *the* groove and don't know how to respond. It is this latter I seek—not wanting to progress to the next track, but to really not know, to not know, again.

Thus my dilemma. I have argued that Lyotard helps to think through this problematic, not only by highlighting the question mark hovering over the return, but by drawing attention to the unpredictable nature of the event and, perhaps most importantly, the role of that which cannot be articulated, the focus of concern at this conference: affect and the affect-phrase. And yet, by arguing the case and publishing a book[5] which sets out to make very grand claims for the potential of Lyotard's writings to aid thinking-through questions of performance art and its documentation, I am at risk of becoming firmly entrenched in this particular groove. To such an extent that it becomes a well-known, well-worn trope—for me at least—and, consequently, one that runs counter to my own understanding of Lyotard, who demands the unsettling of presuppositions at every turn.

So, I will show you a video, again, not the same one as two years ago, but one which is based on the same premise—of me reacting to a performance by Yingmei Duan. At this point, I showed a video, four minutes in length, which is represented here by a single still image in black and white, of my mouth. The

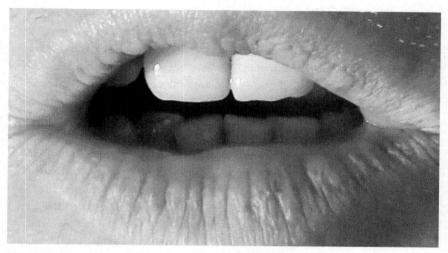

Figure 1 Kiff Bamford, *Dear Yingmei*, video, 2013, copyright of the artist

video can be viewed online[6] which gives a better sense of the color: harshly lit to emphasize the texture of the puckered skin and the bristles on the upper lip. Your screen, however, will not fill the curved, white space of the lecture theater in Atlanta, nor will it hover above the figure of the speaker whose lips had just been speaking. The deliberate sound of my reading this letter is available, however, via the online link. The sounds made by reading are the result not only of the articulations usually demanded by spoken words, the demands made of the lips and the tongue. The sounds are also touched by a deliberate concern for the visual appearance of these movements. At times, I am opening my mouth wide to create an artificially expanded orifice, to give you a sense of the performance space of which I talk: to evoke something of the unease I felt when I went to see this performance, *Happy Yingmei*. It is accompanied by another voice at times, sometimes behind, sometimes in front, of the dominant voice, not an echo but an attempt at that inner voice which runs too fast for words. It reads:

Dear Yingmei,

I enjoyed your performance very much and was pleased that you are happy—like the title of the piece: *Happy Yingmei*. I liked the small, arched entrance to the performance space through which I could see the legs of those who were already in your world (and which I waited to thin, before entering). I was wrong-footed when you left and spoke to me by name as I assumed you would be in character, but you were going for a break; so I waited, biding my time listening to the amplified sounds of the silk worms eating pungent mulberry leaves. When I did enter through the small, arched doorway into the wonderland forest with its dripping water and your welcoming face, I was wrong-footed again as you spoke to me as though we were just anywhere and you were among friends and asked me to introduce myself to the other guests. It was an intimate space: the heat increased as you asked me to talk and made me aware of the uneasiness of the situation where one is not sure how to act—whether as audience, participant or just the everyday you. But, then, you started to sing—just a note and a smile as you leant towards those in the space: one by one, (like a gift and I felt the same way I had in Manchester when you chose someone to "tour" in your performance *Naked*). This was special, and an invitation to become part—not of a piece in a theatrical sense—but of a shared zone, what Acconci calls a "field," a field of transference.

And I enjoyed that. I also enjoyed the singing: the Chinese song fitted the setting and made me relax slightly into the comfort of your role as a performer and storyteller. I enjoy it because I know how to respond: I smile. And I would have stayed longer but feared being the only one left in the space, alone with you. I didn't want the spell to be broken, for you to ask me about everyday things (yes, the children and my wife are fine, thank you . . .). That is why I left the gallery when I saw you appear later in everyday clothes ready to leave; I didn't want to abandon my memory of the girl telling stories, unfolding tasks and wishes from her pocket, a task which asked me questions about the one-child policy in China, about which I knew something, of course, but to which I had never given much thought. And now I am thinking: were you the result of the one-child policy in China? Is that why you took your parents' love for granted, but are now eager that others shouldn't do what you did, but show them love before it's too late:

"Kiss your mother's wrinkles
And your father's eyes."

I shall. And I will tell them that Yingmei told me to.
With love,
from Kiff x.

When I went to see this performance *Happy Yingmei*,[7] I went because I knew the artist and her work, but I didn't expect to write about it, for the reasons I've already indicated. I thought the situation too familiar, I'd written about a previous performance, made my own commentary and a video: to do the same for this performance would be too contrived. The form of my response, that of a letter, is a conceit. Although I did send it to her (by email), I wrote it for myself, as a way of responding to what I had experienced despite myself.

Despite myself.

I think it is here, with the notion of "despite myself" that I come close to what

Lyotard is toying with in some of the later essays including "Music, Mutic," collected in *Postmodern Fables*, and also his writings on the artist *Karel Appel: A Gesture of Colour*. In particular, I am thinking again of the idea quoted above, that "[t]he body doesn't belong to you, it is sensible only insofar as it is exposed to the other thing";[8] we are rendered helpless when subjected to that which Lyotard terms "gesture," the force in the artwork. We are rendered helpless, but also find that this body (which does not belong to us) is "forced beyond what it is and what it is able to do, beyond what we believe it is and is able to do."[9] Thus the body exceeds its boundaries and our presumptions about its function and its subservience to an individual subjectivity: the body overthrows space-time-matter and the conventions of articulated communication to receive that signal which Lyotard identifies as the affect-phrase. The body considered, then, as a physical entity capable of receiving not messages but gifts, which are not the preserve of coded communication but the underside (underneath?/below?) of language—to paraphrase the reference to Pascal Quignard which crops up through these late writings of Lyotard. The underside of language, "language beneath languages,"[10] language without direction or source—sound below language, the guttural groan, growl, wail, and the *phōnē* which Lyotard discusses in relation to the affect-phrase.[11] The *phōnē* of the affect-phrase is that left-over of the differend, the differend itself, even: bachelors spurting their love potion in the *Paysage fautif* (Faulty Landscape), coming onto black velvet, *Blue Velvet*—Denis Hopper's grunting over the white picket fences of white suburban respectability; Freddie Jones talking high speed gibberish, his animal squawking in the French quarter of New Orleans, in another David Lynch film—"Love me tender..." I am singing now, eyes closed momentarily and swaying to the rhythm of the words whose saccharin coating makes any commentary a mockery.

There will be no mourning: no morning mourning, says Bennington, says Derrida, says Lyotard, of Lyotard. No "luxuriating in the wealth of words" is permitted, only necessary failure.[12]

"*Il n'y aura pas de deuil*" (There will be no mourning), writes Jacques Derrida; "*Il n'y aura pas de deuil*," writes Lyotard, of Derrida; "*Il n'y aura pas de deuil*" says Derrida, of Lyotard, posthumously. "There will be no mourning," the phrase becomes a motif in the exchange between Lyotard and Derrida, before and after Lyotard's death. Translators and commentators, including Antony Hudek and Geoffrey Bennington, have been drawn to discuss the phrase and the context of its utterances because of their own position: writing between the words, identifying with the task that Lyotard sets himself when responding to painting, drawing, music.[13] It is his sensitivity to the matter of art that distinguishes

Lyotard as a philosopher who writes with, not on, art and artists. Discussing the problematic task of translating *Sam Francis: Lesson of Darkness*, Bennington picks up on the "[c]hance of translation" which allows the homophone of mourning/morning when discussing the different sensibilities presented by mourning and melancholia. The latter is always still there in the morning: "the work of mourning in the morning, morning mourning the night that is always its dark returning truth."[14] To respond in translation to Lyotard's night has constraints, writes Bennington, "no luxuriating in the wealth of words" is permitted, only necessary failure.[15] And yet in "The whiteness of the whale"— section thirty of *Sam Francis: Lesson of Darkness* and the pivotal point of that book for me—what Lyotard gives to us in his writing (maintained in Bennington's translation) is an example of the interweaving of the philosopher as commentator and the artist as commentator. They are brought together through their reciprocal unease with the languages they find themselves exploring—Lyotard incorporating and branching off from the words of Sam Francis—"The best way to know a thing is to eat it lick it."[16] I said "branching off from," but maybe it is more appropriate to talk of "growing out of" or "living from" or even "*vivre de*," that expression used by Emmanuel Levinas, in *Totality and Infinity*, to illuminate the relationship with objects (especially food) in the life of interiority prior to the encounter with the Other. "*Vivre de*" is translated by Gary Gutting as the wonderfully unidiomatic phrase "living off of."[17] "Living off of" is more than an extemporization on a theme, it is more an *ingestion* of a theme, one which is digested and used as a rich source for the furthering of the theme. Sam Francis' words, "[t]he best way to know a thing is to eat it lick it," become ingested by Lyotard in "The whiteness of the whale" as follows:

> You must, he says, let the thing approach and hold it firm, apply the mouth and open it to the delicious juices. *The best way to know a thing is to eat it lick it.* Lick and lap the lymphs disgorged by white to your tongue, and I'm not saying that you are going to begin to see but, if god wills it, you are perhaps going to stop looking.... Begin to receive the kiss. Not your gaze but your whole body absented, passible, gathered on your lips.[18]

Whereas in *Libidinal Economy* it was the energetics of desire as force (*puissance*) that turned the body inside out into the great libidinal skin, here in the *Lesson of Darkness*, it is the work that transforms the body, dismembers the expected organization and confuses the accepted roles of body parts: work "obliges the eye to turn into a mouth," to suckle sensations and pour sound into "the throat of our ears."[19] Thirty years earlier, Lyotard, writing in the "Gift of

Organs," sounds similar warnings; using the terminology of *Discourse, Figure*, Lyotard describes how the philosopher attempts to defeat the figural only to find that "the figure has passed into his own speech, and while he thinks he is making reason with his mouth, his words are full of eyes, his clarities full of night."[20] His tongue is full of eyes, the throat is of our ears, always mixed up, a *corps* truly *étranger*, un *cadavre exquis* (a foreign body, an exquisite corpse), and whilst I would not wish to artificially impose continuities on such a corpus, it is nice to return to the remainders which didn't make it into the Anglophone realm—the body parts of Hans Bellmer which furnished the introduction to "Energumen Capitalism," but which were, until recently, cut off in translation.[21] The affected body which knows no body and thwarts language (resists articulation), depositing only traces in the gesture waiting to be actualized within a body sensitive to sound and yet, even then, not the same. A trace is not the gesture, but a trace is made to make the gesture visible, audible, perceptible, and then it is no longer the gesture. A work—being of another space-time—doesn't allow itself to be assimilated into an archive and resists those greedy desires to ingest it into another matter-space-time-configuration, not of its making. Here is the complex inter-relationship between trace, gesture, and affect. It is the challenge to thought presented by the gesture of art which drove Lyotard to write again, and again, in response to the work as a trace of the gesture, not to translate the gesture, but to acknowledge "the impenetrability of work to thought"[22] and "the absolute *in-significance* of the gesture of which the work is the trace."[23] The gesture is specific to a particular space and time, the singularity of the event, but might not its affective impact recur again, not through the same gesture but, perhaps, initiated by an affective trace of the gesture? We can never tell if this is the same gesture as that which disappeared; how would we know? There is no sign by which it can be marked and recognized as having returned. Such an act of marking, the designation of a sign, a mark of signification, would require the articulation of the gesture and its inevitable dissolution as gesture. Gesture "resists that which can make of it a repository"[24] if it is to be a "readable record," whereas if the work, as an accumulation of traces, provokes the making anew of the gesture, then "one never finishes rendering them sensible."[25] This question of the trace and its complexity has clear parallels with current concerns in performance art practice. Prompted both by the museum, the market and aging artists—who have lived long enough to see their experimental work of the late 1960s and early 1970s become of interest to a wider audience—the issues of archiving performance and the role of re-performance have been debated and practiced for more than a decade.[26] The widely celebrated new media artist Lynn Hershman Leeson has long been working with ideas related to the archiving of a person's life, creating avatars and alter-egos, most famously that of Roberta Breitmore, 1973–8. Breitmore's stay at the Dante Hotel, San Francisco, was initially part of a site-specific installation, but became the subject of a digital recreation through a project undertaken with Stanford University, which acquired ninety boxes of her archive in 2005. In an interview related to this project, Hershman Leeson discusses the function of the archive and the importance of reinvigorating the remains, or giving new life to the materials, not to make sense of the past, but, as she puts it: "To make them live."[27] That is my intention with my performance commentaries—the hope that by linking on in a manner that responds to a residue of that which was as gesture to me, I carry something over which does not require understanding, but rather requires a disabling of the expectations and preconditions within which I work. That can only happen through a possibility.

This is at odds with the role assumed by art historians, whose analysis is too often concerned with classification and the consequent calcification of work. The fossilized remains struggle to resist that which aims at the definitive interpretation, led on by the traditions of connoisseurship on which the discipline was founded, and the market to which it is still subservient. However, because performance art practice has always had an uneasy relationship with theater, fine art, and especially art history, it means that it has attracted thinkers who resist these conventions and traditions, such as Peggy Phelan who writes of the "deeply messy narrative we call Art History."[28] For example, talking of the relationship of photographs to performance, Phelan warns of the privilege given to photographic stills which "obliterate other moments, textures, aromas and energies of the live art event itself."[29] This concern with the materiality and immateriality of remains has led to dialogues with other disciplines, such as anthropology and archaeology. It was as part of one such joint investigation that the discussion with Lynn Hershman Leeson took place, in conversation with the Stanford archaeology Professor Michael Shanks who interprets her comment "[t]o make them live" as "[t]o make them alive again. It's reincarnation, literally. You incarnate. You give them new material forms that you engage with."[30]

The idea of new material forms is significant here through a Lyotardian lens, as is the importance of matter in Lyotard's writings. In "Music, Mutic," Lyotard explicitly denies that incarnation occurs in the performance of a musical score through musical sound, what is important is "the enigma of letting appear, of letting be heard an inaudible and latent sonorous gesture."[31] Therefore, if the archive of a performance is to become "incarnate," as Shanks terms, it is not through new material forms, but rather through the immaterial gesture that the work is reignited. Consequently, the apparent "fit" between Lyotard and the concerns of performance art's history is complex. It is important not to become misdirected by the terminology of "remain" and "trace" if we are to acknowledge the importance of the work of art as event, which is neither a remembrance nor a recurrence, but an opening to that which has not yet happened. The text on the Danish painter Stig Brøgger is helpful here in its description of the artist's need to struggle against the future possibilities offered by previous work, to avoid repetition and make way for time-space-matter "to *organize* themselves [de se gérer]":[32] a gesture that exceeds what can be perceived. This is then picked up in one of the texts on the artist Bracha Lichtenberg Ettinger where a distinction is made again in relation to memory and remembrance, with an emphasis on the labor taken to keep open the passage for space-time-matter. The gesture and its affect is not the "sole result of a conscious subject, namely the painter,"[33] but is worked on to keep open the possibility of the gesture, which is "expected and ardently wished for."[34] The labor that keeps open the possibility of the gesture is likened by Lyotard to Freud's *Arbeit* (work) of *Durcharbeitung* (working-through), *perlaboration* in French. It is not working-through to remember events from the past, but a working-over which allows affects to surface, affects which have no "site or time in which they could be inscribed"[35] and are consequently unarticulated, according to conventions of memory, history and remembrance, and lie without space-time. It is important that the clinical process of working-through continues after the finding of interpretations which overcome resistances intellectually, but which fail to provide effective relief from symptoms. This necessitates a further working-through of "lived experiences," in order that the resistances are overcome affectively. It is this interminable, endless, working that writing, painting, re-writing carries out, in which "The work [*L'œuvre*] is nothing but a pause in the process of unworking [*désœuvrement*]."[36]

Is this what I want to do through my response to Yingmei Duan's performance? To work-through, not act-out? My letter to the artist describes the way I felt: that, despite myself, I had felt that something I did not expect. I misrecognized this thing and then fought to hold onto what I wrongly believed to be its source, denying the artist as the person I knew and wanting her presence to be somehow different from the "everyday you":

> I didn't want the spell to be broken, for you to ask me about everyday things (yes, the children and my wife are fine, thank you ...). That is why I left the gallery when I saw you appear later in everyday clothes ready to leave; I didn't want to abandon my memory of the girl telling stories, unfolding tasks and wishes from

her pocket, a task which asked me questions about the one-child policy in China, about which I knew something, of course, but to which I had never given much thought.

I had projected this fantasy—of the artist transformed—onto the artist whilst in her space; it occurred because I knew there was something happening and I supposed it was something that transcended the everyday. I wanted it to remain "pure," "untouched," imagining the fallacies of presence in that moment, and yet it was also a confrontation.

"Were you the result of the one-child policy?" How could I ask such a question—Yingmei Duan is the wrong generation. Similar questions were prompted soon after, however, by another Chinese artist, Ma Qiusha, in a video shown at the Chinese Arts Centre in Manchester, UK.[37] In a simple head and shoulders monologue to camera, Ma Qiusha details the pressures of her childhood, as an only child growing up in China. Showing the slightest interest in something resulted in parental investment, through classes and ill-afforded purchases, including that of an accordion which cost ten times her father's annual income and rendered her parents in perpetual debt. At the end of the monologue, the artist inserts her thumb and forefinger into her mouth and removes a razor blade, the source of her visible discomfort displayed during the telling: the physical making manifest the account being delivered. It is analogous to the situation of analysis, where the painful razor is removed through talking. Yet this is not the process Lyotard describes in the "working-through" of commentary; it is not a working-through with an end, but an interminable process without fulfilment or fruition. It is significant that the video is looped, ready to begin again. Gestures are not symptoms, nor do they allow themselves to be eaten or assimilated.[38]

Ending 1

It always makes me nervous to talk of the seemingly insignificant artistic gesture in the same terminology and frame of reference as trauma: of psychological suffering; real loss; profound moments of anxiety, fear, despair . . . to talk of this in dialogue with art seems somehow perverse, particularly when resisting a notion of catharsis or claims for art as having a restorative function. Yet here, again, Lyotard provokes us to consider the gesture of art within the very real task of bearing witness to that which cannot be presented. And the term "gesture" doesn't excuse us from the task—it is not possible to bracket off the gesture of Karel Appel or the sounds of contemporary musical composition from the non-presentable inarticulations which arise from trauma. Gesture, like affect, resists assimilation, it is a resistance to complacency. Lyotard's 1989 text "Emma" is a long discussion of Freud's account of a patient who had developed an inability to enter shops alone, which Freud links to previous incidents: being laughed at by shop assistants, aged twelve, and twice being touched genitally by a shopkeeper, aged eight. Whilst remembering Lyotard's assertion that he is approaching Freud's text as a philosopher, not an analyst, it is significant that Lyotard refers to the act of the shopkeeper as a gesture: "His gesture—weakness or perversion— testifies that the adult, just as with the child, remains at the mercy of the unexpected occasion of 'excitation.'"[39]

Pause

"Gesture," "*geste*." There is an ironic lightness when voiced on English lips. Gesture is reduced to "*geste*": "Jest"—a trifle, a mere joke, a play, a dalliance which underscores the cruelty of these profound claims. Claims made for art which open up Lyotard, and those who quote him, to accusations of romanticism. The expressionist gesture is soaked in its own history: the figure of the lone male genius; the adoration of nature; the history of the sublime, compounded for me by the history of body art and its now-clichéd litany of gestures—wounding, suffering, endurance—whose pursuit of intensity leads lazy commentators to discuss these through reference to the myth of the artist as the figure of romantic suffering, as a conduit of metaphysical forces. And yet Lyotard is aware, all too aware, of these associations and pre-empts the criticism of romanticism in "Music, Mutic," refuting claims that the artwork is expressing or translating a phobia. Lyotard has always distanced himself from the psychoanalytic reading of an artwork as a symptom and he similarly distances himself from the metaphysics which he believes Gilles Deleuze, in his later thought, to be "bathing in."[40]

Ending 2

I suck the stones in turn, then place them in one palm and make them circle one another, their surfaces rubbing together. I don't remember how many stones, but

I remember their sound, an uncomfortable grating which accompanies the final words:

> The order of *une traversée* (a traversal) is not an easy translation; the order of *une traversée* is not an easy transcription; the order of *une traversée* is not an easy transposition; the order of *une traversée* is not an easy transition: it has an unsatisfying, interminable paucity as its end, no elevation. And still, there will be no mourning: "*Il n'y aura pas de deuil.*"

Where does this leave me in my desire to comment on the gesture of performance, the gesture which excited me, despite myself? And which drove me to respond (again)—aware of the impossibility of linking on to that inarticulate phrase, except through the violation of that gesture and the affect which was there before the thought. However, despite the impossibility of the task, it remains a necessity because we urgently seek its return. We are eager for it, but do not know when or where it will arrive, or how it will come. Lips closed in a mu of mute, always speaking with pebbles in our mouths, not muttering, but muted by these pebbles. It is a Beckett ... Beckett ... Beckett-ian participation and it is a performance. But it is the stones that are stopping our voice, not we—they are the death rattle inside us all.

Then, I dropped the stones, which was a gesture too far, too obvious. I had lapsed into the rhetoric of theater and was already anticipating the need to scrabble on the floor for their return, after the presentation.

Notes

1   Jean-François Lyotard, *Postmodern Fables*, trans. Georges Van Den Abbeele (Minneapolis: University of Minnesota Press, 1993), 233.

2   Jean-François Lyotard, *Toward the Postmodern*, eds Robert Harvey and Mark S. Roberts (Amherst, NY: Humanity Books, 1993), 192.

3   Ibid.

4   See Kiff Bamford, "A Late Performance: Intimate Distance (*Yingmei Duan*)," in *Rereading Jean-François Lyotard*, eds Heidi Bickis and Rob Shields (Farnham: Ashgate, 2013), 81–95.

5   Kiff Bamford, *Lyotard and the "figural" in Performance, Art and Writing* (London: Continuum, 2012).

6   The video under discussion, titled *Dear Yingmei*, is available via this link: https://vimeo.com/64333518.

7 Performance at the Hayward Gallery, London, as part of the exhibition "Art of Change: New Directions from China," curated by Stephanie Rosenthal, which ran from September 7 to December 9, 2012. The performance by Yingmei Duan took place every day except November 12.

8 Lyotard, *Postmodern Fables*, 233.

9 Jean-François Lyotard, *Karel Appel: Un geste de couleur/A Gesture of Colour*, trans. Vlad Ionescu and Peter W. Milne (Leuven: Leuven University Press, 2009), 214.

10 Pascal Quignard, *Petits Traités vol. IV* (Paris: Maeght, 1990), quoted in Jean-François Lyotard, *Postmodern Fables*, 224.

11 Jean-François Lyotard, "The Affect-phrase (From a Supplement to *The Differend*)," trans. Keith Crome, *The Lyotard Reader and Guide*, eds Keith Crome and James Williams (Edinburgh: Edinburgh University Press, 2006).

12 Geoffrey Bennington, "Translation in the Dark," in Jean-François Lyotard, *Sam Francis: Lesson of Darkness*, trans. Geoffrey Bennington (Leuven: Leuven University Press, 2010), 222.

13 The English translation of the exchange is published as follows: Jacques Derrida, "Writing Proofs" and Jean-François Lyotard, "Translator's Notes," trans. Roland-François Lack, *Pli: Warwick Journal of Philosophy* 6 (Summer 1997), 37–57. For commentary, see: Antony Hudek, "The Affective Economy of the Lyotardian Archive," in *Rereading Jean-François Lyotard*, eds Bickis and Shields; Bennington, "Translation in the Dark."

14 Bennington, "Translation in the Dark," 220.

15 Ibid., 222.

16 Lyotard, *Sam Francis: Lesson of Darkness*, §30.

17 Gary Gutting, *Thinking the Impossible: French Philosophy Since 1960* (Oxford: Oxford University Press, 2013), 121.

18 Lyotard, *Sam Francis*, §30, original emphasis.

19 Ibid., §35.

20 Jean-François Lyotard, "Gift of Organs," in *Driftworks*, ed. Roger McKeon (New York: Semiotext(e), 1984), 87.

21 "Capitalisme énergumène" first appeared in the journal *Critique*, (Nov. 1972) no. 316, as a review of Gilles Deleuze and Félix Guattari's *L'Anti-Œdipe* (*Anti-Oedipus*) and is included in Jean-François Lyotard, *Des dispositifs pulsionnels* (Paris: UGE, 1973). The English version, *Energumen Capitalism*, translated by James Leigh (New York: Semiotext(e), 1977), omits the first three pages. This omission is restored in a new translation by Robin Mackay collected in *Accelerate: The Accelerationist Reader*, eds Robin Mackay and Armen Avanessian (Falmouth, UK: Urbanomic, 2014).

22 Lyotard, *Karel Appel*, 41.

23 Ibid., 37, original emphasis.

24 Ibid., 43.

25 Ibid., 45.

26 See the anthology *Perform, Repeat, Record*, eds Amelia Jones and Adrian Heathfield (Bristol, UK: Intellect, 2012).

27 Lynn Hershman Leeson and Michael Shanks, "Here and Now," in *Archaeologies of Presence*, eds Gabriella Giannachi, Nick Kaye, and Michael Shanks (London: Routledge, 2012), 234.

28 Peggy Phelan, *Live Art in L.A.: Performance in Southern California, 1970–1983* (London: Routledge, 2012), 11.

29 Ibid.

30 Hershman, Leeson, and Shanks, "Here and Now," 234.

31 Lyotard, *Postmodern Fables*, 220.

32 Jean-François Lyotard, "Flora Danica. The Secession of the Gesture in the painting of Stig Brøgger," trans. Vlad Ionescu and Erica Harris, in Jean-François Lyotard, *Writings on Contemporary Art and Artists, Miscellaneous Texts II: Contemporary Artists* (Leuven: Leuven University Press, 2012), 631, original emphasis.

33 Jean-François Lyotard, "Anamnesis of the Visible," trans. Couze Venn and Roy Boyne, in Jean-François Lyotard, *Writings on Contemporary Art and Artists, Miscellaneous Texts II: Contemporary Artists*, 563.

34 Ibid.

35 Ibid., 566–7, translation modified.

36 Ibid., 570–1, translation modified.

37 Solo Exhibition by Ma Qiusha ran from January 18 to March 2, 2013 at the Chinese Arts Centre, Manchester, UK (now renamed Centre for Chinese Contemporary Art). The video described is *From No.4 Pingyuanli to No.4 Tianqiaobeili*, 2007.

38 I am paraphrasing the end of section 5 in Lyotard, *Karel Appel: A Gesture of Colour*.

39 Jean-François Lyotard, "Emma," in *Lyotard: Philosophy, Politics and the Sublime*, ed. Hugh J. Silverman (London and New York: Routledge, 2001), 44.

40 Jean-François Lyotard and Richard Beardsworth, "Nietzsche and the Inhuman," *Journal of Nietzsche Studies*, 7 (1994), 96. "Deleuze believes that he avoids metaphysics; I think he's bathing in it." The context for this remark is a discussion of attitudes to Nietzsche, force and energy, Lyotard expands on his comment with reference to part 2 of Gilles Deleuze and Félix Guattari, *What is Philosophy?* (London and New York: Verso, 1994).

Section III

Affect as Figure

7

Introduction—Before Affect

Elaborating the Figural

Julie Gaillard

To reserve "the unharmonizable," "under diverse headings—work, figural, heterogeneity, dissensus, event, thing."[1] In the introduction to *The Inhuman*, Lyotard remarks, in retrospect, that it is this very reserve, this inaccessible remainder that has driven his philosophical investigation, at least since 1971, with *Discourse, Figure*.[2] This affirmed continuity does not presume, however, that these various approaches to the unharmonizable could be harmonized with one another. The thought of the figure and the figural is rooted in a Freudian economic perspective, a "metaphysics of forces,"[3] that Lyotard sets aside when he turns to the phrastic framework of *The Differend*. His thinking of affect is a way of "rephrasing the Freudian unconscious," as Anne Tomiche points out.[4] However, his elaboration of the figural lays some essential foundations for themes that keep reappearing throughout his *oeuvre*.

"From sight to vision, from the world to the phantasy"[5]

The general aim of *Discourse, Figure* is to show that what is usually regarded as a flat, legible surface constituted by oppositions (discourse), is pierced by the depth, the thickness of a difference, which is not readable, but visible (figure). Structural linguistics shows that an object, a phoneme, a letter, bears significance only in differential opposition to other objects, phonemes, and letters. This first negation, constitutive of signification, is opened up by and onto the depth of visual reference, which introduces the sensorial field within the system. Indeed, it is the sensorial space of gestures, the visible, "that makes depth or representation possible," and that, "far from being signifiable through words, spreads out on their margins as what enables them to designate." Additionally, "this expanse is the source of the words' power of expression."[6] This opening to visual reference constitutes the first incursion of the figural—understood here as the perceptual space of designation—within the space of discourse. This depth introduces, in the system of oppositions, a difference that is itself marked by a negativity. Since perception requires the object to be posited at a distance, it implies that the object is doubled with a hidden face, the "'background' slipped under the figure":[7] the complete object is always, virtually, missing. In order to articulate these two negations, which respectively shape opposition and difference, Lyotard turns to Freud. His rereading of "Negation" inflicts a torsion upon the notion of the figural, which is no longer simply understood as the incursion of the visual into the space of discourse, but as a disruption of the visual or the perceptual space of designation as well.[8]

Reality opened by desire

Freud claims that the positing of the "no" is fundamentally linked with "the interplay of the primary instinctual impulses," out of which the intellectual function of judgment emerges.[9] The first function of judgment is to attribute a property to an object, or to negate one. "Expressed in the language of the oldest—the oral—instinctual impulses," this function can be brought back to the operations of introjection into and expulsion from an entity, dubbed "pleasure-ego" (*Lust-Ich*) which rejects (spits out) "bad" elements in the outside, and introduces (eats) "good" elements.[10] The second function of judgment consists in determining the real existence of an object. In order for this "reality testing" to be possible, the opposition of the subjective and the objective must be established, the "reality-ego" (*Real-Ich*) must "[possess] the capacity to bring before the mind once more something that has once been perceived, by reproducing it as a presentation without the external object having still to be there":[11] representation is always associated with a loss. Affirmation belongs to Eros, understood as a principle of unification, while negation, "the successor to expulsion," "belongs to the instinct of destruction."[12] The constitution of reality, polarized between object and subject, is genetically articulated via the "primary instinctual impulse" of the "instinct of destruction," out of which negation emerges.

Lyotard conflates this analysis of negation and the anterior text of *Beyond the Pleasure Principle*, stating that Freud "linked the constitution of the visible, of the imaginary, and of the utterable with the use [*appropriation*] of the couplet *fort-da* [gone-there]."[13] Freud's eighteen-month-old grandson, while his mother was away, used to play a game of his own invention, which consisted in throwing a wooden reel over the edge of his curtained cot and making it reappear by pulling it by its string. The disappearance and reappearance of the wooden reel were greeted by the sounds "o-o-o-o," *fort*—according to the inference of the child's caretakers—and "*da*." For Freud, the child channeled the distress felt at the absence of the mother, regaining, through the game, an active role and phantasmatic mastery over her coming and going.[14] Lyotard equates the opposition of *fort* and *da* with that of negation and affirmation, and associates the positing of the "no," which marks the entry into language, with the opening of the referential depth of reality: "This ability to slip away while never ceasing to be is what makes the reel at the end of a string that the child throws over the edge of its bed the model of all objects, and this string, the model of all referential distance."[15] In the *fort-da* game, the child constitutes the object as something that can both be there (*da*) or not be there (*fort*). This capacity to render present an absent object through representation, that opens at the same time the fields of objectivity ("reality"), of subjectivity, and of desire (desire for the presence of the absent object), is made possible by linguistic negation.[16] The *fort-da* game opens the space of lexical oppositions which defines the linguistic system, "where the object's 'word-presentations' will take place." But because it relies on an absence, it also "sets the stage for the object's 'thing-presentations' to appear."[17] The word- and thing- presentations, which are representatives of the drive, appear within this frame of reference:

> We recognize in these two axes—respectively, of signification (opposition) and of designation (thickness)—those of articulated language. It is in the frame of reference determined by their intersection that the energy of the drives will find itself caught. This referentiality is integral to the reality principle; it is out of the question, therefore, to infer it from the "order" issued by the drives, which it represses while reality institutes itself.[18]

Negation, associated with the referential function that is constitutive of the reality principle, also inaugurates desire, defined as the representation of the drive: we witness "the transmutation of the drive into desire as it passes into language."[19] Reality (be it exterior or psychic), organized according to the two axes of signification and designation, will from then on be understood as a set-up that binds and channels energies—captures them. The opening of space by the work of desire creates a frame of reference that is not simply a visible world, but a phantasmatic stage. This opening of reality—exterior and psychic alike—represses the drives and, as we shall see, differentiates the nature of circulation of the psychic energies. All signification, all designation, relies on the "splitting in two of what was 'originally one', *infans* [infant] at the breast."[20] Any discourse, any figure, will result from this "originary" split, and will come to be inscribed within the frame of reference opened by it: "This tearing-away produces effects of distortion in discourse. A figure is lodged in the depth of our speech, operating like the matrix of these effects, attacking our words to make forms and images out of them."[21] This figure-matrix and its effects allow Lyotard to affirm a radical connivance of desire with the figural.

The work of the figural

Thus, we shift from a phenomenological space, where sight puts the object at a distance, to an "other space" opened and moved by desire: from discourse, from the figurative, to the figural. As Lyotard announces: "Simultaneously, the figure finds itself displaced: no longer simply the image of presence or of representation, but form of the *mise en scène*, form of discourse itself, and, more profoundly still, phantasmatic matrix."[22] These three levels of the figure—image, form, and matrix—will be considered based on the operations of desire in the unconscious space, and can be observed in dream and phantasy.

In Freud's economic perspective, all pleasure is a discharge of energy, all displeasure a charge. According to the pleasure principle (at least in one of its early formulations), the quantity of energy in the psychic apparatus needs to be brought back to a minimal quantity of excitation and is thus discharged via the quickest route. The energy circulates in a free, unbound way. The principle of reality, on the contrary, does not aim at annulling the tension, but at maintaining the quantities of excitation at a constant level. The energy is bound, and directed toward specific zones via a system of facilitations and barriers. Based on this distinction that opposes primary (unbound) and secondary (bound) processes, Lyotard posits a radical heterogeneity of the unconscious space of pleasure and the space of reality.[23]

The primary processes are affirmative (the unconscious knows no negation), atemporal (the unconscious knows no succession), and have no consideration for external reality, for which psychic reality is substituted. Most important for the definition of the work of the figural within images and forms is the characterization of the movement of energies, which, free and unbound, progress by displacement and/or condensation. These operations "are defined explicitly here as checking the secondary process, that is, perception, motility, and *articulated language*."[24] The operations of the unconscious transform discourse, now understood both as the readable and the visible, insofar as it is organized according to consciousness and the reality principle, making it unrecognizable. Lyotard provides detailed examples of the work of the figural, such as the rebus, the Freudian slip, the joke, the poetic deconstruction of language, or the pictural transformations operated by the avant-gardes. Within this unconscious space, each level of the figure is defined as a specific desirous operation that transgresses this usual organization, following the principle of reality and its secondary processes, of what is perceived.

The *figure-image* is that which one sees in hallucinations, dreams, paintings, or film. It "deconstructs the percept" by transgressing the lines that delimit the silhouettes of objects, and making several contours coexist. There is no "one single and reifying point of view," but several points of view, as in the works of Picasso.[25] The *figure-form* is "the figure that upholds the visible without being seen":[26] "the scenography of a performance, the framing of a photograph."[27] Geoffrey Bennington gives as examples of the form "the Euclidian geometry which organizes the space of perspectival painting, or the *Gestalt* which distributes a given configuration in terms of figure and ground."[28] The unconscious figure-form transgresses this Pythagorean and Neo-Platonic "good form." Its energetics, indifferent to the unity of the whole, produces an "anti-good form," which Lyotard exemplifies through Pollock's Action Painting. There, "energy speeds from one point of pictorial space to another, thereby preventing the eye from finding a place to rest":[29] as Bennington remarks, it presents "no hallucinated object of desire, but the movement of desire itself."[30]

Finally, there is the *figure-matrix*, which does not tolerate being placed into discourse, forms, or images, while residing in those three spaces at the same time. "The object of originary repression,"[31] it is, as Bennington stresses, "*essentially* invisible."[32] It is "difference itself."[33] This opaque notion seems to point to a utopia radically foreign to representation, testifying "that our origin is an absence of origin,"[34] while still being related to an "'originary' phantasy" which, while invisible, informs the singular works of a man[35]—two aspects whose articulation Bennington stresses as being mysterious.[36] The figure-matrix will be further elaborated with the analysis of the phantasy. This elaboration brings about yet a new displacement in the understanding of desire, aiming at removing it from any representability: the entire model of the figural will progressively be turned towards the model of the death drive.

The matrix, the figural and the death drive

While Freud, in *Beyond the Pleasure Principle*, associates the constitution of objectivity with the absence of the mother, thereby founding the chain of desire upon the negativity of a lack, Lyotard objects that "the loss of the mother is not sufficient in itself for her to be objectified,"[37] insofar as the ambivalence in relation to the breast precedes objectivation. Beneath the constitution of the object and its correlated frame of reference Lyotard posits, with the Freud of *Three Essays on the Theory of Sexuality*, a phase of autoeroticism where the infant does not constitute the breast as an object, but substitutes for it the not-yet-objectal surface of his own body. Lyotard reads in the *fort-da* game, below the entry into language, a "pulsing between eaten-introjected and spat-expelled," a pulsing which is not referred to an object and not caught in the staged succession of a return according to the principle of reality, but is a "non-cumulative and non-referred oscillating between release and tension and governed by the pleasure principle [*principe de jouissance*]."[38] This addition of the *fort-da* game to the Freudian text on negation, and of infantile sexuality to the Freudian analysis of the *fort-da* game, enables Lyotard, at the end of his meticulous analysis of the figure-matrix as "the utopia of the phantasy," to posit that the *fort-da* game *also* proceeds from the *jouissance* of the drive. The principle of reality does not simply repress the "pleasure-ego," it also "involves" it.[39] The scansion – +, *fort-da*, is admittedly marked by the subjective function that enacts the return of the mother on the phantasmatic scene opened by referential depth. However, simultaneously, it *also* proceeds from the "incompossible" coexistence of two alternate predications: presence and absence. The compulsion plays out: the object should not return, but go away. This distinction relies on the opposition introduced between pleasure and *jouissance*. Pleasure, now associated with the principle of constancy, "cannot maintain the energy level constant except by binding it," and aims at maintaining an energetic equilibrium: Eros is fully placed on the side of the secondary processes and the principle of reality. *Jouissance*, now associated with the principle of Nirvana, which aims at reducing the energy-level to zero, is linked to the death drive and placed on the side of the primary processes.[40] "*Jouissance* results from the greatest possible disparity between the charge and discharge of tension."[41] The difference between the + and the – is, then, no longer, or not only, the measureable gap between the two edges that need to be joined together: it is a radical fracture, the possibility of the zero of energy, "a void [*néant*] separating the two moments of presence,"[42] which always menaces the positive and the negative moments of being neither sublated nor saved in the unity of succession.

As Laurence Kahn shows, "the phantasy reveals itself *in fine* to be writing": Lyotard finds in the death drive a model allowing him to reserve the primary processes as something radically heterogeneous, foreign to any binding.[43] It is the death drive, reserved as this most secret, most unharmonizable layer, which transforms the images and the forms arranged by Eros on the phantasmatic or oneiric scene, which undoes, disfigures the formations of the unconscious, the word- or thing-presentations. Lyotard concludes: "[n]ow we understand that the principle of figurality that is also the principle of unbinding [*dé-jeu*] is the death drive."[44] A "utopia" which exists in the space of the figure-images, the figure-forms, in all discourse: a heterogeneity within.

From the figural to affect

When Lyotard comes back to Freud following the phrastic framework elaborated in *The Differend*, where the pragmatic axis of address is added to the axis linking sense and reference to form the definition of the phrase-universe, the death drive is abandoned, and the emphasis placed on the unconscious and originary repression which was already at stake, though not as centrally, with the figure-matrix. What remains is "the question of the transformation of silence in phrases," as Lyotard writes in "Emma."[45] This mystery, in this later essay, will be extracted from the physical metaphor of energies and thought in terms of the temporality of *Nachträglichkeit* (belatedness): Lyotard will shift from a thinking of "excitability" to a thinking of "'pure' affectability," which is its nonphysical name.[46] "Infancy" will say otherwise the silence of the "*infans* at the breast," that silence of the drive. As Anne Tomiche notes, while *Discourse, Figure* enquires about the "interlocking" (*engrènement*)[47] of the silence of the drive with articulated language, the unarticulated affect-phrase, radically heterogeneous, resists any interlocking and interrupts linkage. The emphasis will therefore shift from the work of transgression to the working-through of anamnesis.[48] Transference will also be foregrounded.[49] One could however, as Kiff Bamford suggests, recognize in the concomitance of pain and pleasure in the sublime feeling, in the suspension of the "Is it happening?," or also in the spasm of the event of color or tone, something of "the unpredictable beat of the matrix," which "blocks together what are not compossible while retaining heterogeneity."[50] One could also, following Geoffrey Bennington, observe the relation of the figure-matrix, "difference itself," and affect, "the differend itself," and their kinship with the notion of "sexual difference," foregrounded at the end of "The Affect-Phrase" and "Emma" in an attempt to elaborate a transcendental status of *infantia*, as a faculty of pleasure and pain, as a possibility foreign to adult articulation—a difference intrinsically linked to originary repression.[51] The death drive, in its link to the figure-matrix, seems to prefigure or to engender affect, in its link to sexual difference. Both are, in any case, names under which the "unharmonizable" is reserved.

Notes

1 Jean-François Lyotard, *The Inhuman: Reflections on Time*, trans. Geoffrey, Bennington and Rachel Bowlby (Stanford: Stanford University Press, 1988), 4.

2 As Kent Still shows, reserving this remainder, this "unforgettable forgotten," and inscribing it "within the forms that occlude it," also corresponds to Lyotard's call to "rewriting modernity." See the introduction to *Minima Memoria. In the Wake of Jean-François Lyotard*, eds Claire Nouvet, Kent Still, and Zrinka Stahuljak (Stanford: Stanford University Press, 2007), xviii.

3 Jean-François Lyotard, "Emma: Between Philosophy and Psychoanalysis," trans. M. Sanders (with R. Brons and N. Martin), in *Lyotard: Philosophy, Politics and the Sublime*, ed. Hugh J. Silverman (New York and London: Routledge, 2002), 34.

4 Anne Tomiche, "Rephrasing the Freudian Unconscious. Lyotard's Affect-phrase," *Diacritics. A Review of Contemporary Criticism* 24.1 (Spring 1994), 43–63.

5 Jean-François Lyotard, *Discourse, Figure*, trans. Anthony Hudek and Mary Lydon (Minneapolis: University of Minnesota Press, 2011), 15.

6 Ibid., 8.

7 Ibid., 28.

8 See Geoffrey Bennington, *Lyotard: Writing the event* (New York: Columbia University Press, 1988), 70; and Anne Tomiche, "Phrasing the Disruptiveness of the Visible in Freudian Terms: Lyotard and the Visual," in *Afterwords. Essays in memory of Jean-François Lyotard*, ed. Robert Harvey (New York: Occasional Papers of the Humanities Institute University at Stony Brook, 2000), 34.

9 Sigmund Freud, *Negation*, in *The Standard Edition of the Complete Works of Sigmund Freud* (SE), eds James Strachey et al. (London: The Hogarth Press, 1953–74), vol. XIX, 238; *Die Verneinung*, 1925, in *Gesammelte Werke* (GW), eds Anna Freud et al. (Frankfurt am Main: S. Fischer Verlag, 1960), vol. XIV, 15.

10 Ibid., SE 236/GW 13.

11 Ibid.

12 Ibid., SE 238/GW 15.

13 Lyotard, *Discourse, Figure*, 25.

14 Sigmund Freud, *Beyond the Pleasure Principle*, SE XIII, 14–15; *Jenseits des Lustprinzips*, GW XIII, 12–13.

15 Lyotard, *Discourse, Figure*, 124, translation modified.

16 Ibid., 125.

17 Ibid., 127.

18 Ibid., translation modified.

19 Ibid., 126.

20 Ibid., 127.

21 Ibid., 128.

22 Ibid., 15.

23 Ibid., 270–3.

24 Ibid., 272

25 Ibid., 274

26 Ibid., 275

27 Ibid., 268

28 Bennington, *Writing the Event*, 92.

29 Lyotard, *Discourse, Figure*, 275.

30 Bennington, *Writing the Event*, 93.

31 Lyotard, *Discourse, Figure*, 268.

32 Bennington, *Writing the Event*, 93.

33 Lyotard, *Discourse, Figure*, 275.

34 Ibid., 268.

35 Ibid., compare ibid., 276.

36 See Bennington, *Writing the Event*, 93; "Childish Things," in *Late Lyotard* (Charleston: CreateSpace, 2005), 22s; "The Same, Even, Itself . . .," in ibid., 43–64.

37 Ibid., 124.

38 Ibid.

39 Ibid., 126.

40 Ibid., 352–3.

41 Lyotard, *Discourse, Figure*, 351.

42 Ibid., 354.

43 Laurence Kahn, "D'une lecture apathique de Freud," in *Les Transformateurs Lyotard*, eds Corinne Enaudeau et al. (Paris: Sens & Tonka, 2008), 267, my translation.

44 Lyotard, *Discourse, Figure*, 355, translation modified.

45 Lyotard, "Emma," 30.

46 Ibid., 44.

47 Lyotard, *Discourse, Figure*, 115

48 See Tomiche, "Phrasing the disruptiveness," 43 s.

49 See Kahn, "D'une lecture," 267 s.

50 Kiff Bamford, *Lyotard and the "figural" in Performance, Art and Writing* (London and New York: Continuum, 2012), 163 and 162.

51 Bennington, "The Same, Even, Itself . . .," 47.

8

Following Lyotard's Lines

Affect and Figure in Guillermo Kuitca's *Acoustic Mass VI* and *Mozart Da-Ponte VIII*

Heidi Bickis

In a 1985 interview published in *Flash Art*, Lyotard unexpectedly comments on his fascination with drawing. "I feel closer to drawing than to colours" he explains, and a few sentences later: "A simple mark with a pencil and the sheet of paper splits apart, and something is as though directed somewhere else."[1] As we shall see, this brief comment offers a compelling reflection on lines and their potential affective charge. It also remains—as far as I am aware—undeveloped. In this chapter, I examine the specific relevance of this passing remark for two contemporary artworks by Argentine artist, Guillermo Kuitca: *Acoustic Mass VI* (2005) and *Mozart Da-Ponte VIII* (1997) from the series *Theatre Collages* (2005) and *Puro Teatro* (1995–7) respectively. My purpose is not to elaborate on the philosophical implications of Lyotard's comment about "a simple mark." Nor do I intend to speculate on what he might have written had he developed this thought further. Both tasks are for another paper. Rather, my goal is to mobilize this very provocative remark about the line towards my own engagements with art and, by extension, expand on Lyotard's comment through the lens of Kuitca's collage and painting. In particular, I aim to elaborate on the implicit gesture towards a relationship between line, movement, and affect that is further underscored by the distinctive lines in *Acoustic Mass VI* and *Mozart Da-Ponte VIII*.

In *Theatre Collages* and *Puro Teatro*, Kuitca explores the space of the audience through altered reproductions, painterly transcriptions, and collages of seating plans borrowed from various Western auditoria. *Acoustic Mass VI* (180.3 × 180.3 cm) is a collage based on the Old Vic in London, England, and *Mozart Da-Ponte VIII* (190.5 × 228.6 cm) is a painting of the Royal Opera House, also in London.

Lines are a crucial component of each piece. Not only is the theme diagrammatic and architectural, but Kuitca's aesthetic interventions are directed at the plans' straight, standardized, and neatly traced lines. The distortions of the linear form in the painting and collage have a unique effect. In each work, "something is as though directed somewhere else."[2] I develop this claim by examining the lines of the painting and collage through the lens of Lyotard's "The Line and the Letter" in *Discourse, Figure.* As I shall argue, the lines of a seating plan can be likened to what Lyotard describes as discursive, whereas the lines in Kuitca's auditoria are closer to the figural.[3] The former code the space of the auditorium and, by extension, bodies, thereby ensuring orientation and bodily containment. By contrast, the figural lines create distortions and transgressions and, in turn, compel a feeling of disorientation and bodily disindividuation. With reference to *Acoustic Mass VI* and *Mozart Da-Ponte VIII*, then, Lyotard's remark describes a feeling that is strongly linked to a bodily movement. This feeling, I contend, can be likened to Lyotard's concept of the affect-phrase. It is a kind of affect-*movement*. Similar to the affect-phrase, an affect-movement is disruptive and unarticulated. It signals a suspension of the discourses that keep bodies and spaces in line. In the face of *Acoustic Mass VI* and *Mozart Da-Ponte VIII*, viewers are compelled to momentarily inhabit an unnamed elsewhere, a kind of spatial and bodily otherness. Thus, the affect-phrase might be elaborated beyond linguistic practices and, specifically, with reference to spatial practices and bodily movements. The term affect-*movement* aims to introduce one possible development along these lines.

Engaging auditoria: Guillermo Kuitca's *Acoustic Mass VI* and *Mozart Da-Ponte VIII*

As Kuitca explains, the initial idea for *Puro Teatro* and *Theatre Collages* came to him during a visit to London, England:

> In London in 1994, I went to get tickets to see *Der Rosenkavalier* at Covent Garden, and not only did I get tickets, but I discovered the kind of seating chart they have in the box offices to show ticket holders their location. It's a seating plan seen from the stage, which, rather than showing how one would see, shows how one would be seen. . . . I have always had this insistent vision of a kind of big stage, with something of the Baroque idea of the world as a stage. But that vision now turned and placed me—or the audience—on stage, so as to look from the other side.[4]

Compelled by this observation, Kuitca began to use seating charts from a range of opera and theater auditoria as the basis for a diverse collection of paintings, collages, and works on paper. Many of the pieces from *Puro Teatro*, for example, are photocopies of plans that have been altered by the addition of words, colors, and various markings. Other works, such as *Mozart Da-Ponte VIII*, are paintings of seating plans that have been similarly modified. By contrast, the plans in *Theatre Collages*—as indicated by the series title—are composed of paper lines and squares pasted onto large pieces of colored paper. Here, rather greater alterations have been made: some auditoria seem to explode across the paper and, in others, such as *Acoustic Mass VI*, the paper lines appear to blend together, reducing the space to a mass of black lines.

Importantly, then, Kuitca's interest is not in this or that specific theater, but the generic space of the audience as it plays out in different buildings. As theorist and critic Andreas Huyssen emphasizes, "[t]he point is not to focus on the identity of the theater, but on the ways the diagram [in *Puro Teatro*] is colored, inscribed, modified by the hand of the painter."[5] Indeed, referential aberration is key. Although each work is, to varying degrees, recognizable as a seating plan, the reference is tenuous. Critic Gabriela Speranza describes the relation as "allusive": "Allusion undoes the analogy as soon as it has proposed it; resemblance is mocked and bypassed, but not erased. Allusion is a kind of 'yes . . . but.'"[6]

This quality is clearly evident in *Acoustic Mass VI* and *Mozart Da-Ponte VIII*. In the latter, Kuitca transcribed London's Royal Opera House onto the canvas with oil and graphite. Although a visual of a seating plan is apparent, it is distorted. The lines vary in weight and thickness (unlike an actual plan's standardized lines) and some do not connect, or they bend out of place leaving small holes in the "seats" that are visualized in an actual plan as contained squares. Additionally, in places, there are extra seats and rows layered on top of each other, and some rows fall outside the frame. Smudges—possibly from the hand of the artist—dirty the surface. Instead of a clean image, the plan presented vibrates with an excess produced as an effect of the distinctive lines. *Acoustic Mass VI* is a collage based on the plan for the Old Vic, also in London. Here the seating plan is distorted further. The square seat is created by black paper lines pieced together but, throughout, there are gaps where the lines do not join together. The square is thus dismantled and the semblance of a row or seat no longer holds. Moreover, both works offer some sense of spatial depth that is missing from the flat, horizontal/top-view of actual plans. These plans are richly textured and, insofar as the lines unravel the clean articulation of the auditorium space—a point I develop below—they are resonant with affect.

Figure 2 Guillermo Kuitca, *Acoustic Mass VI* (The Old Vic), 2005, mixed media on paper, 71 × 71 inches (180.3 × 180.3 cm) sheet, 74¼ × 74¼ inches (188.6 × 188.6 cm) frame, © 2015 Guillermo Kuitca, Courtesy Sperone Westwater, New York.

Crucial to this allusive quality are the distinctive lines in both *Acoustic Mass VI* and *Mozart Da-Ponte VIII*. Lines are a central thematic of Kuitca's work, the "protagonists" of many drawings, paintings, and collages.[7] Indeed, although he identifies foremost as a painter, the cartographic and architectural motif firmly grounds his work in drawing. As critic Douglas Dreishpoon asserts: "After 1990 and beginning with *The Tablada Suite*, drawing—fine colored plumes of pastel and dramatic bleeds—has entered and reentered [Kuitca's] painting process: as diagrammatic element, as accent and mark, as linear articulations and numerical notation, as a way to enrich and intensify the painted image."[8] Kuitca also emphasizes this quality of his work: "My painting today . . . is diagrammatic, and even its theme is absolutely shared with drawing. The world of my paintings is almost borrowed from a world made on paper, previously drawn."[9] The particular significance of the lines in *Acoustic Mass VI* and *Mozart Da-Ponte VIII* becomes clear by turning to Lyotard's reflections in "The Line and the Letter." Simply put, the lines in the collage and painting are not the lines of a seating plan. The latter, I contend, belong to what Lyotard describes as discourse, whereas the former are closer to the figural.

Lines, discourse, and the figural: Lyotard's "The Line and the Letter"

Discourse and figure are the central motifs in Lyotard's early work *Discourse, Figure*. In this dense and philosophically diverse text—it includes considerations of structural linguistics, phenomenology, psychoanalysis, aesthetics, among other subjects—Lyotard elaborates on the distinction and complex relationship between these two terms. Discourse broadly refers to any system of meaning that organizes and codes an object or concept according to an invariant set of oppositions. The exemplary case Lyotard considers is Saussurean linguistics.[10] According to this model, language operates on a flat space in which meaning is derived simply by comparing words and letters. "Cow," for instance, is distinguished by its dissimilarity to "horse." The relationship between the word and the animal is arbitrary. There is no cowness to the word cow. Importantly, discourse also encompasses visual representational practices such as linear perspective. As Readings explains, "the geometricization of perspective" also operates discursively insofar as it "determines the visibility of objects as their relation to other objects on the spatial grid of the perspective plane."[11] Discourse, then, "designates the regularity of any coding system that is readable and so abides by the communicative function of language."[12]

The figural is more difficult to define. In fact, it eludes the kind of determination a definition prescribes. Crucially, it is not the opposite of discourse. Rather, the figural is resistant to discourse and marks an otherness that cannot be reduced to representation or signification. It exceeds the capacity of the code. To borrow again from Readings, "the figural opens discourse to a radical heterogeneity, a singularity, a difference which cannot be rationalized or subsumed within the rule of representation."[13] There is always an excess to anything that might be said, painted, or otherwise represented about an object. As Lyotard writes in the opening chapter of *Discourse, Figure*, any discourse "is not only signification and rationality but expression and affect."[14]

The relevant section for my engagements with Kuitca's auditoria is "The Line and the Letter," a reflection on discourse and figure with specific reference to the line. The chapter is foremost a study of the contrasting lines in the work and aesthetic theory of two contemporaneous artists, Paul Klee and André Lhote. In addition to furthering the primarily philosophical themes of *Discourse, Figure*, "The Line and the Letter" foregrounds the complexity, variability, and multidimensionality of what is ostensibly a simple component of an artistic gesture. Indeed, through the lens of discourse and figure, the line gains a greater depth and nuance.

At the center of Lyotard's reflections is the line's ambiguity, a theme to which he returns in a later essay, "It's as if a line . . ." (1988). A line oscillates between the figural and the discursive; it both resists and lends itself to the work of discourse. Lyotard begins with the example of the letter and Saussurean linguistics. The latter model contends that a letter such as *T* is identifiable based on its opposition to other letters. *T* is not *N* and so on. The actual fact of a horizontal and vertical line as the support for either letter is ignored. In this case, the line "enables writing" or "script": "the verticals, curves, downstrokes, horizontals, and angles [are] stripped of their plastic meaning and count only as constituting distinctive features of the scripted signifiers."[15] There is no need to slow the eye down and attend carefully to the line in the letter. The reader does not *see*, but "merely scans the written signals."[16] All that takes place is straightforward recognition. Line as line is effaced insofar as its plasticity—weight, thickness, curvature, and so on— is silenced and suppressed.

The discursivity of the line is also evident beyond the linguistic gesture. Consider, for instance, the outline of an object in a painting. This "revealing line" renders an object recognizable by "'giv[ing]' shape' to a body, a face, an action, where there is only bare surface."[17] As noted above, the use of perspective and other geometric techniques in visual art also function discursively. The latter are "regulating lines" that geometricize the space or object in order to make it intelligible. Lyotard borrows these descriptors from Lhote for whom the drawn line's primary function is signification. According to Lyotard, Lhote emphasizes "the relations between the elements of the tracing" and, by extension, suggests that "the curve, the vertical, the oblique or intervals that they could determine" have no plastic value.[18] His method of drawing thus resembles linguistics. As Lyotard summarizes, for Lhote, the line's role in painting is "to reduce the diverse, the singular, and the deformed to the universality of geometric form."[19]

For Klee, by contrast, the line has a very different role. According to Lyotard, Klee's line "records neither the signifiers of a discourse nor the outlines of a silhouette; it is the trace of a condensing, displacing, figuring, elaborating energy, with no regard for the recognizable."[20] The latter describes a particular figural form, the figure-matrix, and can be distinguished from two other forms, the figure-image and the figure-form.[21] Each one names a unique mode of resistance to, and transgression of, a discursive structure in the realm of the visual. The figure-image "is the *transgression of the contour* [*tracé révélateur*]."[22] Here, "the object of deconstruction" is the line that delineates an object.[23] Lyotard offers Picasso's *Étude de nu* (Study of a Nude) (1941) as an exemplary case. In this drawing, the body of a woman sleeping is made visible by multiple outlines; Lyotard notes "the coexistence of several silhouettes."[24] As a result, the drawing "allows a single body to display several positions in a single place and time."[25] Whereas the figure-image involves the "transgression of the object," the figure-form resists form itself.[26] Evident in Jackson Pollock's action painting, the latter includes no outlines at all. It is an "anti-good form" or " 'bad form.' "[27] As Lyotard describes with reference to Pollock's work: "[the] plastic screen [is] entirely covered by chromatic runs; absence of all line construction, of all tracing even; . . . indeed, elimination of all recognizable figure."[28]

In contrast to the figure-image and figure-form, the figure-matrix "remain[s] unseen . . . it is no more visible than it is legible."[29] This articulation of the figural foregrounds Lyotard's engagement with Freudian psychoanalysis in the second half of *Discourse, Figure* and, in particular, his consideration of the figure with reference to dreams, desire, and the "unconscious space."[30] With Klee's work, for instance, one does not simply encounter the deconstruction of an outline or a bad form, but the workings of desire. As Bamford explains, "[t]he figure-matrix is invisible and troubles both the visual and discourse equally; it is the force of desire that is unbound, manifest everywhere and destroys established orders through its energetics."[31] Indeed, for Lyotard, Klee's picture "bears all the traces of desire's own processes: displacements, deviations, reversals, unity of opposites, and disregard for time and reality. Klee's interworld is not an imaginary world: it is the displayed workshop of primary process."[32]

A line, then, also resists representation and signification. It can make "visible" an otherness or excess that cannot be reduced to discourse. In such instances, a line is closer to the figural. As Lyotard maintains, the line is figural "when, by her or his artifice, the painter or drawer places it in a configuration in which its value cannot yield to an activity of recognition."[33] This unrecognizable line is, in a sense, visible. Its plasticity—texture, weight, thickness, direction of contour, and so on—is foregrounded and the eye and body are compelled to attend to the energy of the graphic form. Thus, rather than reading, I *see* this line. Additionally, beyond transgressions of form and object, a line might also bear traces of the workings of desire. Indeed, Lyotard reinforces this point with reference to Italian artist Valerio Adami in the essay "It's as if a line . . ." He writes: "line is inhabited by a desire, it has a desire's infinite power . . . it is proliferous in its potential cues."[34] This emphasis on desire might be shifted to a language of affect. A line is inhabited by affect, and resonates with an unrepresentable excess and potential. It pulses, vibrates, elongates and swirls. Additionally, this affect or energetics *affects* the space of its inscription and the viewing bodies who encounter it. The energy of graphic form directs away from signification, slows the eye down and, as I elaborate below, becomes the occasion for a feeling.

The seating plan: discursive lines and figural transgressions

Through a Lyotardian lens, the seating plan and its artistic rendering in *Acoustic Mass VI* and *Mozart Da-Ponte VIII* acquire an added layer of significance and complexity. A plan is a drawing or diagram that provides a top or horizontal view of an object or a space. It also visually describes how things are, or will be, arranged. Thus, in a seating plan, the auditorium is presented as a flattened, two-dimensional space and shows what appears to be both a top (i.e. as if from the ceiling) and horizontal view (i.e. as if from the stage). The depth, scale, size, and other qualitative aspects of this space are missing. Although seating plans vary from auditorium to auditorium, in general, they visually describe the space using a "language" of lines, rectangles, and squares. In turn, the auditorium is conceptualized as a series of self-contained boxes, neatly arranged one alongside the other, in which a person will be housed. A plan, like a chart or diagram, is also informational. It provides details about relations and arrangements, in other words, how things fit together. The famous London Underground map designed by Henry C. Beck is a good example. The map shows how the railway lines are connected, not how they are actually shaped or the distances between them.[35] It is topological, insofar as it focuses "on connections."[36] Similarly, a seating plan functions as a kind of map. By providing information about a set of spatial relationships, it enables audience members to navigate and locate themselves in the space.

As a diagrammatic form, a seating plan is composed of a configuration of lines. Indeed, *The Oxford Encyclopedic English Dictionary* defines diagram as: "a drawing showing the general scheme or outline of an object and its parts; a graphic representation of the course or results of an action or process; a figure made of lines used in proving a theorem, etc."[37] Thus, the seating plan's descriptive and informational capacity stems in great part from the straight and neatly traced lines that delineate and organize the space. In other words, a plan codes the auditorium in order to make it recognizable and intelligible. These lines function discursively; they reveal and regulate. I *read* a plan, rather than *see* it.[38] Moreover, the lines' plasticity is silenced in favor of the good form and "language" of the plan.

This spatial discourse has crucial implications for bodies. As feminist geographer Kathleen Kirby shows, visual representations (i.e. productions) of space also imply ideas about subjects and, by extension, bodies. The Enlightenment individual, for instance, is "inextricably tied" to the concept of space produced by Enlightenment cartography. As Kirby explains, "the 'individual' might be pictured as a closed circle: its smooth contours ensure its clear division from its location, as well as assuring its internal coherence and consistency."[39] In this case, the body is implicated insofar as it is absent. The subject mapped is disembodied. Similarly, we might consider how bodies are implied in a seating plan. Indeed, as the history of Western theater performance and architecture shows, seating arrangements enact changing practices of gathering informed by various hierarchies. Historically, differential sections often conveyed a kind of body (e.g. lower class, marginal) and, in some cases, a specific body (e.g. the king's body).[40] Despite the apparent democratization of contemporary seating, not only do cost differences highlight the persistence of hierarchies, but plans continue to convey a particular bodily form.

The modern auditorium seat, visualized graphically by the square, can be likened to an individual architectural enclosure. It acts as a mobile form of private property within the public space of the theater and contains the discrete, individual and "civilized" body.[41] As architectural theorist Catherine Ingraham asserts, the linearity of modern architecture—in which the diagrammatic plan can be included—is "marshaled against the possibility of catastrophe and the loss of orientation in the world—a loss that [is] related to the disruption of certain proprieties."[42] Architecture, then, alongside "[c]lothing, mores, laws, social structures, [and] statistics ... attempt[s] to keep the body going in a straight and decorous line."[43] Thus, the organization of the audience space as pictured in a seating plan is similar to other spatializations that divide, hierarchize, and individuate bodies. It can be likened to the city that, as Elizabeth Grosz contends, "geographically divid[e]s and defin[es] the particular social positions and locations occupied by individuals and groups" and becomes "the [role] and means by which bodies are individuated to become subjects."[44] To this end, a seating plan contributes to the rationalized, standardized, contained, and individualized body of modernity and, equally, serves to reproduce ideologies of private property and ownership.[45] Importantly, then, the discursive function of the seating plan and its lines extends well beyond the coding of the auditorium space. These lines also regulate and reveal a discrete bodily outline, even if bodies remain unseen in the plan itself. Here, by ensuring orientation and bodily containment, discourse serves to keep things *in line*.

Kuitca's auditoria, however, deviate from this discourse on space and bodies. The paper and painted lines in *Acoustic Mass VI* and *Mozart Da-Ponte VIII* trouble intelligibility and recognition. Indeed, they are closer to the side of the figural. In each work, line is disconnected from the various forms of the plan— seat, row, rectangle, square, space—and its plasticity is foregrounded. *Mozart Da-Ponte VIII*, for instance, appears somewhat blurry, as if out of focus. Upon closer viewing, this quality clearly stems from the transgression of the contour. The lines are layered, vary in thickness and weight, and fall outside the diagram's borders, distorting any possibility of a clean outline. The squares and rectangles also remain incomplete; the lines do not always adjoin to produce a discrete form. For instance, moving from the corner on the left where a small section of seats and rows are clearly articulated, I come to the main body of stalls: 1, 2, 3, 4, 5, etc. It is hard to read these numbers and once I arrive farther along the row, another series of seats crosses over the one I have been following. Is this also 1, 2, 3, 4? It is not legible. As I move from row to row, it is the same: numbered seats, one after another. At times, neatly traced and at others, they are blurred slightly by a thicker or repeated line, or by the layering of additional rows that cross over the top. Some of the rows seem to fall out of the diagram-painting, as if they had been squeezed out. Similarly, the paper lines in *Acoustic Mass VI* upset the plan's contained geometric organization. Here, the diagram disintegrates into lines. From the first "row," the increasing thickness of the layers of paper lines effaces any outline and only a mass of black lines remains. The eye is thus compelled to slow down as it stumbles across unrecognizable traces. The lack of delineation creates a subtle chaos on the way to anti-form.

Kuitca's lines, then, neither regulate nor reveal; they do not signify or outline an object. Recognition is triggered but forestalled. Crucially, I *see* these lines. They do not refer my eye "to a system of connotation."[46] The allusive seating plans in Kuitca's collage and painting compel "thought to abandon" its security and certainty in signification.[47] The plan thus no longer functions as a plan. Its informational and navigational capacity is disrupted. Without clear markers that carve the space into cleanly divided seats and rows, I cannot place myself in this space. Similar to Kuitca's maps, these plans "put the spectator into spatial and temporal limbo."[48] They confront viewers with what Kuitca describes as "the unknown" and "a sense of the abyss of the blank canvas."[49] What information these plans offer—if any—is not obvious.

By extension, the discourse on bodies is also undermined. In *Acoustic Mass VI* and *Mozart Da-Ponte VIII*, the bodies conveyed by the square seats are piled one on top of another. They seep outside the boundary of the square seat, blend together and fall outside the diagram's boundaries. The outline no longer holds strong and the individuated, contained, and civilized body unravels. Whereas a seating plan keeps things *in line*, the various modes of the figural in Kuitca's auditoria move things out of line and, "something is as though directed somewhere else."[50]

Affect, movement, and "as though directed somewhere else"

This directing elsewhere and movement out of line signals the trace of an affect. Lyotard engages with the question of affect by elaborating on his philosophy of phrases developed in *The Differend*. As he asks in "The Affect-phrase (From a Supplement to *The Differend*)": "Is feeling a phrase?"[51] He answers in the affirmative. A sentiment is a particular kind of phrase, what he calls an "affect-phrase." Unlike a phrase which is articulated insofar as it presents "a universe"— that is, has an addressor, addressee, sense, and referent—an affect-phrase remains unarticulated. It is addressed to no one and from no one.[52] Moreover, whereas a phrase is a foundation for discourse, "within the order of discourse the affect-phrase is inopportune, unseemly, and even disquieting."[53] Affect is, therefore, disruptive. In a later echo of the figural, it undermines various representational practices from verbal articulations to the formation of the ego. As Lyotard argues in "Emma," "the childhood [affect-phrase] brings no guarantee of personal identity . . . it rather imposes upon the supposed identity a denial."[54] Moreover, affect potentially encompasses a range of unarticulated phrases such as silence, a gesture, or an unvoiced sound.

Through the lens of Kuitca's collage and painting, the "as though directed somewhere else" can be likened to something like an affect-phrase. It signals a disquiet in, and a suspension of, a spatial and bodily discourse. Moreover, it remains unarticulated—how might I put into words this sense of movement, of an elsewhere, of a not being here nor there? "One cannot find the words, etc."[55] In addition, the notion of a directing elsewhere—in particular with reference to

Kuitca's auditoria—strongly implies a movement. Here affect and movement are not easily disentangled. The lack of articulation can be construed in part as a matter of orientation. Missing is a set of spatial coordinates: "'One cannot find [the place], etc.'" Importantly, the movement is not to somewhere. There is no redirection that would simply reground and reorient. Nor am I explicitly moved or directed to move by a something or someone. The poles of addressor and addressee are missing. A movement happens. It involves a shifting and skewing that interrupts the supposed discreteness of bodies and space. "I" am caught up in this directing elsewhere and thus compelled to inhabit, however briefly, this place of neither here nor there, up nor down. The lines in *Acoustic Mass VI* and *Mozart Da-Ponte VIII* are thus "an occasion"[56]—to borrow from Lyotard—for a movement-affect. By creating openings in the diagrammatic code, the figural lines skew the space and the implied bodies. As a result, a shifting elsewhere happens, and an otherness shimmers in the excess and vibrancy of the lines in Kuitca's plans.

Lyotard wrote prolifically about art. His *oeuvre* includes an abundance of commentaries about specific artists and his works of philosophy contain multiple references to artworks and artists. Both offer a rich resource for scholars engaging with visual art, whether the approach is philosophical, historical, sociological, or critical. Additionally, these varied writings serve as an invitation or even provocation[57] to "linger with" art and attend to its unique experiments with color, space, form, and line.[58] This chapter has sought to respond to this call and, in particular, to engage with the line, an area of Lyotard's writings on art that remains underexplored. Kuitca's *Acoustic Mass VI* and *Mozart Da-Ponte VIII* provided a lens through which to consider Lyotard's brief remarks about "a simple mark" and Lyotard's reflections on lines in "The Line and the Letter" in turn offered a means to examine the distinct work of the lines in the collage and painting. With this creative reading, the chapter has demonstrated how Lyotard might be mobilized as part of ongoing practices of commentary on, and reflection with, art. In particular, it foregrounded the possibilities of attending to the lines in visual art and examining their unique affective dynamic.

Notes

1   Bernard Blistène and Jean-François Lyotard, "A Conversation with Jean-François Lyotard," *Flash Art*, March 1985, 34.

2   Ibid.

3 Jean-François Lyotard, *Discourse, Figure*, trans. Antony Hudek and Mary Lydon (Minneapolis: University of Minnesota Press, 2011).

4 Graciela Speranza and Guillermo Kuitca, "Conversations with Guillermo Kuitca," in *Guillermo Kuitca: Everything* (London: Scala Publishers, 2009), 78.

5 Andreas Huyssen, "Guillermo Kuitca: Painter of Space," in *Guillermo Kuitca: Everything* (London: Scala Publishers, 2009), 28.

6 Speranza and Kuitca, "Conversations," 80.

7 Rosanna Albertini and Guillermo Kuitca, "Guillermo Kuitca: Body of Painting: Abstraction According to Kuitca," *Art Press*, 249 (1999), 32.

8 Douglas Dreishpoon, "Sometimes Walking is Enough," in *Guillermo Kuitca: Everything* (London: Scala Publishers, 2009), 45.

9 Guillermo Kuitca, cited in ibid.

10 Lyotard, *Discourse, Figure*. See in particular the chapters titled "Linguistic Sign?" (72–89) and "Effect of Thickness in the System" (90–102).

11 Bill Readings, *Introducing Lyotard: Art and Politics* (London: Routledge, 1991), 4.

12 Vlad Ionescu, "Figural Aesthetics: Lyotard, Valéry, Deleuze," *Cultural Politics* 9.2 (2013), 144.

13 Readings, *Introducing Lyotard*, 4.

14 Lyotard, *Discourse, Figure*, 10; Geoffrey Bennington, "Go Figure," *Parrhesia* 12 (2011): 37.

15 Lyotard, *Discourse, Figure*, 210.

16 Ibid., 211.

17 Ibid., 231.

18 Ibid., 215.

19 Ibid., 218.

20 Ibid., 232.

21 Ibid. See "Desire's Complicity with the Figural," 268–76.

22 Ibid., 274.

23 Ibid.

24 Ibid.

25 Ibid., 275.

26 Ibid., 276.

27 Ibid., 275.

28 Ibid.

29 Ibid.

30 Ibid., 274. See also in *Discourse, Figure*, "The Dream-Work Does Not Think."

31 Kiff Bamford, *Lyotard and the "figural" in Performance, Art and Writing* (London: Continuum, 2012), 22.

32 Ibid., 232.

33 Ibid., 213.

34 Jean-François Lyotard, "It's as if a line . . ." trans. Mary Lydon, *Contemporary Literature* 29.3 (1988), 457–82.

35 Fred Dubery and John Willats, *Perspective and Other Drawing Systems* (London: Herbert Press, 1983), 10–11; Rob Shields, *Spatial Questions: Cultural Topologies and Social Spatialisation* (London: Sage, 2013), 103.

36 Ibid., "Beck's Tube map shows the relationships between stations in a network: each station is a circle on a colored line that represents one routing. All the routes are smoothed out, the detail of actual twists and turns underground is omitted in the schematic style."

37 Judy Pearsall and Bill Trumble, *The Oxford Encyclopedic English Dictionary*, 3rd edition (Oxford: Oxford University Press, 1996), 393.

38 Lyotard, *Discourse, Figure*. See pp. 205–13 from "The Line and the Letter."

39 Kathleen Kirby, "RE: Mapping Subjectivity: Cartographic Vision and the Limits of Politics," in *Bodyspace: Destabilizing Geographies of Gender and Sexuality*, ed. Nancy Duncan (New York: Routledge, 1996), 45.

40 Marvin Carlson, *Places of Performance: The Semiotics of Theatre Architecture* (Ithaca, NY: Cornell University Press, 1989), 149. Carlson points to this bodily demarcation in a description of the spatial organization of late eighteenth-century European theater houses:

> The prince in his loggia (later the central royal box), the lesser aristocracy seated near the prince in slightly less favorable locations, and the general public standing or seated in the orchestra or pit below. Later, when a more distinct class of merchants, clerks, and professional men developed, especially in England, these claimed the pit as their territory, while footmen, grooms, and other such marginal members of society were relegated to rows of benches in the remote and uncomfortable area above the boxes, the galleries or paradise.
>
> Very frequently these divisions were so arranged that although all spectators shared the same auditorium, there was little or no actual overlapping of social spaces.

41 Norbert Elias, *The Civilizing Process*, 2nd edition (Oxford: Blackwell, 2000); Chris Shilling, *The Body and Social Theory* (London: Sage, 2012).

42 Catherine Ingraham, *Architecture and The Burdens of Linearity* (New Haven, CT: Yale University Press, 1998), 61.

43 Ibid., 54.

44 Elizabeth Grosz, "Bodies-Cities," in *Sexuality and Space*, ed. B. Colomina (New York: Princeton Architectural Press, 1992), 250.

45 Shields, *Spatial Questions*, 95–7.

46 Lyotard, *Discourse, Figure*, 213.

47 Ibid.

48 Huyssen, "Painter of Space," 24.

49 Matias Duville and Guillermo Kuitca, "Guillermo Kuitca," trans. Margaret Carson, *Bomb* 106 (2009): 52.

50 Blistène, "A Conversation."

51 Jean-François Lyotard, "The Affect-phrase (From a Supplement to *The Differend*)," trans. Keith Crome in *The Lyotard Reader and Guide*, eds Keith Crome and James Williams (New York: Columbia Press: 2006), 104.

52 Ibid.

53 Ibid., 106.

54 Jean-François Lyotard, "Emma: Between Philosophy and Psychoanalysis," trans. Michael Sanders, et al. in *Lyotard: Philosophy, Politics, and The Sublime*, ed. Hugh J. Silverman (New York and London: Routledge, 2002), 40.

55 Lyotard, "Affect-phrase," 104.

56 Jean-François Lyotard, *Karl Appel: Un geste de couleur/Karel Appel: A Gesture of Colour*, trans. Peter W. Milne and Vlad Ionescu (Leuven: Leuven University Press, 2009), 193.

57 Kiff Bamford, "A Late Performance: Intimate Distance (Yingmei Duan)," in *Rereading Lyotard: Essays on His Later Works*, eds Heidi Bickis and Rob Shields (London: Ashgate, 2013), 81.

58 Lyotard, *Karl Appel*, 193.

9

Philip Guston's Piles

Jana V. Schmidt

I.

Philip Guston's paintings often present us with a side view of the scene. Their expanse positions the onlooker sideways not only in relation to the painting's subject—which is often literally on its side, like the cyclopean eyeballs of *Cabal* (1977)—but via our distance from the canvas. In Guston's late "bad" paintings from the 1970s,[1] we are held almost always at approximately the same distance, which allows us to see the scene in its entirety, and thereby places us off to the side (the only side Guston grants). Sidelined in this manner, the viewer is urged into a curious position, in which an intimate knowledge of the scene—illicit glimpses of cellars (*The Pit*), skeletons in closets hidden by half-open doors in dimly-lit rooms (*Dark Room*)—coincides with a calculated distance, holding her at arm's length.

In one of Guston's most well-known paintings, *The Street* (1977), the confrontation of two piles of arms, trashcan lids, and hoofed legs stages a back alley persiflage of epic heroism. But the painting also reads as a bastardization of Duchampian freeze-frame technique—trashcan lids are lifted a myriad times as urban masses march—which exhibits its technical "failure" rather blatantly. When he abandoned the painterly mastery and quasi-religious sublimity of Abstract Expressionism in the late 1960s, Guston began to seek out failure, freely exhibiting what form casts aside by baring countless layers of underpainting beneath a purposefully crude touch. The declarative badness of the 70s canvases was offensive because it stultified expectations of increasing refinement (or "purity," as Guston called it) to pronounce art a "wonderful ruin."[2] What Guston said about Alberto Giacometti in 1974 can therefore also be applied to his own late project: "a most profound failure ... in the sense that what he wanted to achieve was impossible to achieve."[3] Guston's failure is, however, above all else his subjects' failure. Enveloped in an air of melancholy belatedness, his subjects appear as if cast aside and muted by an unnamed event to which they cannot attest. What takes form *aside from failure* is what I therefore take to be the question that guides Guston's inquiry.[4]

The supposedly conspiring heads of Guston's late painting *Cabal*, for example, constitute such a muted subject: ten large one-eyed bulbs form a pile in a vermillion sea. They are outlined in white against a bluish black horizon, but they have no bodies, no opacity or weight. None of the heads face us. In fact, they seem to avoid our gaze, looking upward and sideways, down into the sea, or closing their eyes with long spidery lashes. Some of the shadowy outlines of these tumbling eyeballs are only raised from the background by a dotted line and the ear-shape of a "C," as if echoing the painting's title by initial. Lost at sea, the ten cabalists look infinitely sad, and though perhaps appealing to a higher (or lower) divinity, they appear to tell neither of hearing nor of seeing. Rather than scheming, the cabalists hover in the kind of imposed isolation and impotence that is characteristic of nightmares or traumatic states.

Hovering, as Guston calls the ideal state of the artist, names precisely the condition of the dreaming subject in relation to the form or *figure*,[5] which Jean-François Lyotard in *Discourse, Figure*, his neglected study of painting, perspective, and desire, describes as "a spatial manifestation that linguistic space cannot incorporate without being shaken, an exteriority it cannot internalize as *signification*."[6] For Lyotard, the figure describes an interruptive force closely related to the effect of desire on discourse as it distorts representation and meaning. Figure therefore names an intermediate space between language and image, signification and designation, which challenges the "sovereignty" of both the visual and the discursive realms. The "connivance of desire with the figural" lies in the transgression of a "text" (shreds of memories in the dream, say) on whose *disfiguration* desire *feeds*.[7] That is why Lyotard's notion of the figure helps us realize that Guston's late paintings are not "writings on the wall" depicting signs or symbols to be deciphered. The critical emphasis in much of Guston scholarship on his "alphabet," signifying chains, metaphor versus metonymy, and "figure of speech" is therefore misleading.[8] Guston's late works are not *figurative* but *figural*, figures.

According to Lyotard's definition, figure must be understood as what is *marginal* to the order of discourse; figure is "over there, like what it designates in a horizon: sight on the edge of discourse."[9] The figural therefore operates both from within discourse as the form it takes *and* from without as that which is to be seen and perceived without ever being absorbed by language. In several ways,

Lyotard associates the figure with the spatial dimension of designation—as depth, expanse, and gesture—that makes representation and meaning possible in the first place. What he points to in his critique of structuralist linguistic theory is thus an excess of meaning which signification cannot encompass fully. "There exists another, figural space" Lyotard writes. "It is desire's own space."[10] Lyotard is quick to qualify that we are not to think of the figure as desire's fulfillment, though. Rather than dialectical catharsis or the gratification of a wish, the figure (and desire through it) operates negatively; its "critical function" lies in the deconstruction of a script or writing, in the way that Sigmund Freud proposes the dream treats "the text as if it were material."[11]

In Freud's conception, the "dream-work" is the "non-linguistic" process by which the dream lends a "new form" to everyday memories (the "text" of the dream) by censoring, that is displacing and condensing, them. The apparent meaning of any dream is therefore as misleading as the surface appearance of the rebus, the small picture-puzzle Freud takes to be emblematic of the dream's labor of plastic disfiguration. Perhaps most important for any discussion of painting through a Lyotardian "figural" lens is the observation that the figure is not "arbitrary" like the sign; rather, it bears a relationship to the body of the viewer, "positions" her, and effects a "bodily synergy."[12] Such a relation is not a matter of harmonious fusion but pertains to the way in which desire "distorts" even the very elements subject to signification (here we might think of how Billie Holiday sings the last notes of "Solitude" off-key because the emotion of the song requires it).

While the line "is always caught between the two contradictory demands"[13] of signification and its plasticity, letter and shape, the figure complicates recognition and thus confronts us with what Lyotard identifies as a cultural insensitivity in the West to non-signification and "plastic space," including a refusal of the "slowness required by the figural."[14] With his model of painting as a desirous surface, Lyotard also turns his back on the privileging of representation in Western art since the Renaissance and thereby follows modernist painters like Paul Klee and Guston in their emphasis on the materiality of art. In the end, Lyotard's aim is not to drive a wedge between line and letter but to show how both open onto the horizon of the other. He seeks to disclose how discourse, while smoothing over the bumps of the figural to yield signification, does not antecede an "originally" figurative meaning. Rather, the genuine insight of Freud's interpretation of the rebus, for Lyotard, is that "[t]he figural is immediately present in the context; the figural is always already there. The textual is already there in the core-figure."[15] This is precisely because line and letter are inseparable and, in the rebus as in the dream, stand in for each other in a constant movement of "exchange." "Desire does not manipulate an intelligible text in order to disguise it ... we never have anything but a worked over text, a mixture of the readable and the visible."[16]

For the question of the image, and for painting in particular, this means that seeing is deeply enmeshed with both desire and repression. An insight that resonates as particularly true to the experience of looking at painting is Lyotard's claim that some paintings block desire's fulfillment *"for the simple reason that these forms refuse to be ignored."*[17] What we cannot see in painting is its original fantasy. Nevertheless, the working of desire is articulated in the invisible "*Ur*"-figure or "figure-matrix" which, while immediately repressed, also always already violates discourse (and representation) from within. Thus, for Lyotard, the figure as figure-matrix returns, as Mary Lydon notes, to the dumbness and fracturedness of the pre-constituted self, the state of "infancy" of the individual in which seeing is a kind of overly literal or "abstract" event without unity. *Discourse, Figure* thus follows a tension in Lyotard's thinking between the attempt to write "[w]hatever does not permit itself to be written, in writing,"[18] hence doing away with the last vestige of representation, and the persistent indebtedness to looking. Representation, though often featured in Lyotard's discussion as a hindrance to seeing, nevertheless remains a necessary obstacle, not unlike the "elbow room" required by designation. In this regard, Lyotard's use of Freudian dream-analysis, particularly the processes of condensation and displacement, posits an important counter-model to representation which yet appears to be not entirely divorced from representational means. However, rather than being mimetic or repetitively depicting something external to the work, the "critical artwork" bears the "traces of pure difference ... exhibiting *condensation itself* as process."[19] Philip Guston's piles, which populate the canvases of his last two decades with such astonishing frequency that one might call the "pile-up" (the title of one of his last drawings) his overarching subject, are such condensations. In obstinately illegible ways, these paintings self-consciously distort text and reference. With obsessive persistence, they show us condensation, rendering material *as figure* a concentration of affect on which Guston could not gain perspective. These are "forms, which touch and bump and overlap each other, strain to separate themselves, yet cannot exist without one another. While they strive to become independent, a condition of delirium persists, as if these forms desire to configure other combinations of themselves. What a restless and startling state for forms to be in!"[20]

Even a cursory glance at *Red Cloth* (1976)[21] must register its monumental frontality. In the manner of a frontispiece illustration of a title banner, two hands hold up a red cloth to present a pyramid-shaped pile of interlinked legs and shoe

Figure 3 Philip Guston, *Red Cloth*, 1976, oil on canvas, 78 × 105½ in (198.1 × 268 cm), Brooklyn Museum, © The Estate of Philip Guston.

heels stacked in alternating layers. Rather than merely a backdrop for the pile, the cloth, which appears to be folded in half, has been lifted and presents what it covered. With a sort of exclamation mark—the light bulb in the center—the picture shows the moment of unveiling: there it is! Its first effect is gloomy and vaguely oppressive, as if confronting us with a sight no one really asked to see. The image's crowdedness, the fact that Guston left no "open" spaces between the legs, as he frequently did, adds to its stifling appearance. Since the viewer is positioned *before* the pyramid, that is, at its bottom, the *sacral* air of standing below an altar so familiar in worldly monuments is echoed here. As soon as we ask whose monument this is, however, the absurd pathos of the lifting gesture tilts the entire scene from hallowed sublimity to bathos. As is often the case with Guston, the viewer is coaxed into a posture of anticipation—of the grandness and elevation attached to painting, of its *monumentality*—only to see this anticipation flung *on its side*, belly up with the "crapola,"[22] as Guston called his pasty mounds of junk and fleshy parts. At the same time, with its play on hide-and-seek, crap and sublimity, *Red Cloth* also offers an allegory of the artwork itself; its gesture of presentation within presentation is a kind of *mise-en-abîme* that comments on painting as what makes appear and conceals. Thus, Guston's piles riff on the vertiginous possibilities of *Schein* (appearance, semblance); they expose the thing itself *and its obstacle.* As we saw above, painting's failure is never far from Guston's mind.

II.

A former student of Philip Guston, the painter Robert Bordo, tells a story about growing up Jewish in Montreal in the 1950s: "The war was the only cultural signifier of our identity" he remembers. Though his family belonged to the local Temple, Bordo's precariously upper-middle-class parents were immensely conflicted about their Jewishness. As immigrants of the second generation they were obliged to maintain their attachment to the community, but for the Bordos, being Jewish meant antisemitism, Auschwitz, and pogroms, topics about which the family talked frequently. He was four or five when Bordo's nanny—a token not of wealth but of a working mother—took him on an outing on the city bus. Montreal was then a city of "unassimilated" immigrant neighborhoods who led a difficult existence under Quebec's Catholic pro-fascist government. When Robert and his nanny passed through the Jewish part of the Main, a major boulevard and center of Yiddish culture, a bleak Salvation Army store with two large windows awakened his curiosity. Each of the store's barren displays was taken up by a large bin filled with donated shoes. Pointing at the store, the small boy proclaimed to his astonished nanny: "Auschwitz shoe store."[23]

Piles, ruins, carcasses, stacked legs and shoes, excess and bodies as waste— these motifs certainly allude to the great disaster of the twentieth century.[24] Yet, Bordo's memory of the stacked shoes suggests that a pile is not merely a leftover, not just waste, but a way of categorizing objects. As the noun's older meaning of pier, pillar, and monument indicates, piles are human-made, horizontal accumulations in which object is stacked upon object. In this way, Guston's pile paintings often separate objects in piles, as if to hint at a systematic accumulation process.

But is "Auschwitz" what these paintings congeal, what they strive to displace while also figuring it? The art historian Bryan Wolf reads Guston's *Ancient Wall* (1976) as a palimpsestic writing in which "something that is different, or perhaps disturbing, to the larger economy of the painting"[25] is buried and returns. He asserts that the "unspeakable" subject of Guston's late work is not the Holocaust, but witnessing as the "haunting" of his work, a subject which makes the palimpsest, as the "machinery" of memory, its necessary and adequate form. Yet, if witnessing is crucial to Guston, *Ancient Wall*, with its jumble of limbs "on the wall," does of course also mock the ominous notion of a "writing on the wall" and, like *Red Cloth*, is eminently flat. Neither of these paintings is representational in a referential sense; their space is, as Lyotard writes, "that of an object, not a text."[26] Though they are figurative—a category which, Lyotard suggests, has no bearing on post-representational art—they cannot be read, but only seen. Rather than a palimpsestic layering of texts, Guston's figures perform a slippage which proves the association of figuration and image with stasis, and its contrast with the supposed flexibility of the signifier, to be false. Figuration, in Guston, is not the retrieval or recognition of form, but the constant motility of figures negotiated on the material surface of the picture; figures that appear on the stark Morandiesque horizon line like puppets in a shadow play.

One of these recurring sliding forms is that of the heel, which, barring the rest of the shoe, became a permanent feature of the many piles Guston was to paint until his death in 1980. The heel, as visible in *Red Cloth*, is not only the rear part of a shoe sole (the partition in two halves can be seen in *The Coat* (1977), *Sleeping* (1977), and, already almost as a separate heel, in *Division* (1975)), but is a form that may also be a lid (*Monument* (1976)), hoof (*To J.S.* (1977)), horseshoe (*Rock* (1978)), or the parted hair of Guston's wife Musa (*Black Sea* (1977)). In the latter painting, a rounded structure of brick and nails is planted in a greenish-black sea. According to Guston's iconography, the divided upper arch of this giant horseshoe resembling parted hair beckons to his wife, whose forehead appears in other paintings.[27] In a companion piece from the same year, *Calm Sea*, the partition on the arch is gone and the entire composition is now doused in blood red. What looked like two bricks at the bottom of the structure in *Black Sea* has now been replaced by a thin nail-studded layer. Crucially, neither arch, in *Calm Sea* or *Black Sea*, opens onto the sky beyond; the "horseshoes" are opaque, exposing an inner chamber "filled" with short pink brushstrokes rather than a hollow revealing the "other side."

Guston first consciously saw the photos of the liberation of the concentration camps taken by Allied photographers two or three years after the end of the war. "This was in 1946 or 1947, after the films of the concentration camps started coming back, and photos and stories."[28] They "started coming back," says Guston, as if the photos returned to the US in a sort of latency loop. In a way, that's just what they did. Though liberation photos had appeared in magazines (such as Margaret Bourke-White's Buchenwald photos in *Life Magazine*) and newspapers as early as May 1945, documentary film footage was shown in lurid movie theater newsreels "for only a few days"[29] that same spring. After this brief exposure, a dormancy period seems to have ensued. In the mid to late 1940s, films and photos were shown again in documentaries, newsreels, and public affairs television.[30] In 1947, an English version of the Soviet film *Nuremberg Trials* was released in the US,[31] which very clearly noted the "crime against the Jews" and showed footage from liberated camps.[32] Accordingly, in his registering of the return of the images, we may sense Guston's shock: to see them two years after the fact—and in some ways several years late to "the event"—complicates responding, since the "innocence" of first sight was unavailable. Traumatic in its deferred action, the camp footage may have really hit Guston the second time around, leaving him a "witness" only to deferral itself. In Dore Ashton's account of her friend's reaction, Guston began to think about the conditions of figuring the Holocaust. "Guston recalls that they [he and a fellow painter] had seen films about the concentration camps. 'Much of our talk was about the holocaust and how to allegorize it.' ... Guston 'was searching for *the plastic condition, where the compressed forms and spaces themselves expressed my feeling about the holocaust.*'"[33]

During the same period, he painted *Tormentors* (1947–8) and *Porch II* (1947), abstracting the shapes of his earlier realist, mural-influenced paintings.[34] In *Tormentors*, some of the most iconic shapes of his late work are explored in thin white outlines, as if tentatively gaining form. Traced against a black background, the triangular or rounded, dotted and seamed figures appear to grow in and out of each other. At the painting's center, a hood and, prominently, a horseshoe shape levitate side by side. Both the large delta-shaped hoods and the half-oval in the middle bear the same dotted marks of stitching and nails that became firm parts of Guston's late repertoire of forms. Though entirely "abstract," the stitched triangle already foreshadows the hooded figures whose adventures Guston playfully imagined in the late 1960s while the menacing title implies that we are seeing an image of torture, perhaps from the perspective of the perpetrator.[35] Again with the perpetrators in mind, we can see that *Tormentors* first conceives that troublesome figure of the horseshoe/heel which unites the shoe with the oven. Ovens, those half-oval brick structures with studded metal sides and an inner, hermetic cavity, are what is in fact pictured here. Just such ovens, those of Buchenwald, Auschwitz, and Treblinka, became the unanimous symbol (and "secret") of human depravity in the postwar years. ("History's Most Shocking Record!" reads the caption of a newsreel from 1945, followed by a close-up of a Buchenwald crematorium oven, the doors of which open to show dust and bones.)

Yet, it is of course false to read the ovens of Auschwitz as the key to Guston's ambiguous figures in *Calm Sea* and *Black Sea*. Though they look like the ovens from the early documentary films, Guston's "ovens" appear in their full *unclarity*;[36] that is, by merging with other figures in fantasy, these ovens figure affective relations, turning shoes into ovens, heels into monuments, and form into a repetition of the displaced object of designation ("You're painting a shoe; you start painting the sole, and it turns into a moon; you start painting the moon, and it turns into a piece of bread").[37] With Lyotard, we might therefore call the late paintings "critical images" in so far as they perform a reversal (*retournement*): "The critical reversal on the other hand does not reinstate ... instead what it repeats are the operations that make this figure possible among others."[38] Rather than subjecting figure to text and unconscious to conscious, what this reversal "wants" is "to keep open the space in which the order of discourse and of acts enclose themselves."[39] Instead of repeating the "text" (say, by painting an image of a crematorium oven), this reversal lies in the production of "unsightliness"; an unsightliness which is generated by the affect of disfiguration and condensation. Thus, Guston's "slip of image," his condensation figure of the heel/oven repeats the operations of the "*mobled*" object it designates.[40] This object is not "the Holocaust" as a name which founds the historical unity it purports to capture,[41] but a muddled relationship to the representation and meaning of the event. As figures, the late works cathect form affectively and thereby resist symbolic exemplarity, which is to say that the oven is not the original shape or meaning of these paintings—and many others which exhibit the same figure—but that the figure has *already begun to move on*.

Guston continued to paint "compressed forms and spaces [which] themselves expressed [his] feeling about the holocaust" after 1947. Or rather, he *returned* to figuring affect more overtly with his "political turn" in the late 1960s. What he began to politicize is, as Harold Rosenberg recognized, the role of art itself: "It might be argued that finding art problematical is itself a form of political thinking, in that it considers the kind of society which makes art difficult to practice and value."[42] Guston rendered art and art-making problematic in countless ways by not only questioning the value of adding yet more images, but also by invoking the artist as perpetrator (in *The Studio* (1969), for example) and the artwork as a cover-up or obstacle to the truth. Not coincidentally, a critical view of art's role might thus go hand in hand with a consideration of art's relationship to nationalism, racism, and genocidal violence. In *Calm Sea*, the red arch painting referred to above, undertakes this labor on several levels beyond its allusion to the ovens. In referencing Johann Wolfgang von Goethe's poem "Calm Sea" (*Meeresstille*), intoned by both Ludwig van Beethoven and Felix Mendelssohn as "Calm Sea and Prosperous Voyage," Guston evokes the history of Jewish emancipation in Germany as the fantasy of an assimilation by art (or *Kultur*, of which the Mendelssohns were a prominent symbol) which failed,[43] thus obviating the happy ending of the two-poem overture. No land is ever reached. "Calm Sea" ends on a bitter realization: "Terrifying deathly stillness! / And in the uncanny distance / Not a wave moves."[44]

The problem of art as deception also occupied Guston more directly in relation to the murder of European Jewry. In a conversation with Morton Feldman from 1968, Guston mentions that he read Jean-François Steiner's "documentary novel" *Treblinka* (1966) and found it extraordinary for its mention of *trompe l'œil*. To numb "the incredulity of the tormentors" as well as the fear of the victims, Guston summarizes, *trompe l'œil* painting was employed by the Nazis, who eagerly installed a false railroad station, including painted ticket windows, plants, "and a potbellied stove" in the Treblinka death camp.[45] Though Feldman is clearly unwilling to see a connection, Guston singles out the artist's responsibility "to unnumb yourself, to see it totally and to bear witness" not only to the conditions at Treblinka, but to the entanglement of art with corporate capitalism today.[46] Transposing the image of the camouflaged death camp into the present, Guston challenges us, not merely in words but visually, in his paintings, to consider form political(ly) and as incessantly morphing in and out of other, "older" forms (perhaps in the way Walter Benjamin speaks of the allegorical image as "petrified unrest").[47] Similarly, Guston's piles ask us to see waste as what remains, "the leftover (the waste, the unanticipated and unwanted consequence) of an ordering bustle of the past."[48] Guston's figures are, however, not merely what remains (waste) but what *exceeds*: figures and piles that order the pieces of a shipwreck they could not but witness as absence. The artist's paradoxical responsibility hence lies in the doomed task of witnessing "a disaster that consisted in a radical failure of witnessing, an event to which the witness had no access, since its very catastrophic and unprecedented nature as event was to make the witness absent: absent to the very presence of the event; present in, but not to, what was taking place."[49] In this sense, we might define figure as what remains in excess of failure, a *more-than*-failure which names in particular the surplus of a failure to witness.

Certainly, Guston's relationship to his own Jewishness plays a role here. In the 1930s, the young painter changed his name from Goldstein to the French-sounding Guston. In this respect, and with respect to the "missed encounter" with the Holocaust, Guston's piles are "overdetermined" conglomerates of the messy relation to and between guilt, anger and fear, repression and the return of the repressed. As the dreamer is subjected to the nightmare, the event of attempted genocide sidelined those who were forced into passive viewership and whose full realization of what had taken place, in 1946 and 1947, came as a retrospective rupture. Guston's subsequent concern with figuring "the plastic condition, where the compressed forms and spaces themselves expressed my feeling about the holocaust" discovered its means in the slippage of the figure. Thus, rather than erecting monuments to the dead, Guston's late figures morph constantly in and out of designation. In flux, as shoe and oven, heel and hair part, these moving images portray the present as alive with the forms of the past. As our desire to see the Holocaust and to see it "fulfilled" by representation is thwarted by these piles, and perspectival realism is parodied leaving us with matter itself, fleshiness and piling, we are positioned sideways, subjected to remaining *on the side* rather than "empowered" to witness head-on. Guston's kind of witnessing thus subjects us, even from afar, from *not* witnessing, to an intimacy with our projection. *Schein* and subject all at once, Guston's piles picture the failure of witnessing the event and yet still figure that we receive more than we can perceive.

Notes

1   Bad painting is a term that Guston coined for himself with a cheeky story of the artist's freedom to offend taste, whether political or aesthetic, which suggests that for Guston *bad painting* is *literary painting*: "Isaac Babel gave a lovely, ironic speech to the Soviet Writers Union. It was 1934. He ended his talk with the following remark: 'The party and the government have given us everything, but have deprived us of one privilege. A very important privilege, comrades, has been taken away from you. That of writing badly.'" Philip Guston, *Philip Guston: Collected Writings, Lectures, and Conversations* (Berkeley: University of California Press, 2011), 280.

2   Guston, *Collected Writings*, 295.

3   Ibid., 249.

4   See Shoshana Felman, "Crisis of Witnessing: Albert Camus' Postwar Writings," *Cardozo Studies in Law and Literature* 3.2 (Autumn 1991): 197–242.

5   Right before his death in 1980, Guston, who was one of the most articulate and intelligent artists of his generation, defines art for us in a way that resonates with Lyotard's use of Freudian dream analysis: "All art is a kind of hallucination, but hallucination with work. Or dreaming with your eyes open." Guston, *Collected Writings*, 298.

6   Jean-François Lyotard, *Discourse, Figure*, trans. Anthony Hudek and Mary Lydon (Minneapolis: University of Minnesota Press, 2011), 7.

7   Lyotard, "The Connivances of Desire with the Figural," *Driftworks*, ed. Roger McKeon (New York: Semiotext(e), 1984), 57–68. This text corresponds to the chapter "Desire's Complicity with the Figural" in *Discourse, Figure*, but the term connivance as in the original French subheading "Connivences du désir avec le figural" resonates specifically as the (secret) conspiracy of desire and figure. In my reading of the conniving heads of *Cabal*, I can only hint at the dimension of conniving at, of suffering, in the sense of overlooking a wrong.

8   Guston emphasizes that his images exceed signification. Prompted by his friend, the poet Clark Coolidge, while looking at a painting of a tangle of legs, *Monument* (1976), Guston exclaims: "It has nothing to do with feet and legs. Nothing." In the film, Guston also gives us a hint as to what it *is* about. Speaking about an unfinished canvas in his studio, he reveals why he painted over what was there before: "The painting was too much of a painting. . . . I hadn't experienced enough on it." Guston's choice of words—to experience *on* it—suggests that his is a sensual, experiential, and desirous activity more than it is a matter of exposing language's functioning. In *Philip Guston, A Life Lived*, directed by Michael Blackwood, New York: Blackwood Productions, 2010. For the semiotic argument on Guston, see Harry Cooper, "Recognizing Guston (In Four Slips)," *October* 99 (Winter 2002): 96–129, also reprinted in Joanna Weber, *Philip Guston: A New Alphabet, the Late Transition* and Robert Slifkin, *Out of Time: Philip Guston and the Refiguration of Postwar American Art* (Berkeley: University of California Press, 2013). Though Guston did call his paintings allegories, his understanding of allegory—based on a review by Charles Rosen of Walter Benjamin's *The Origin of German Tragic Drama*—was of art as ruin and opaque, meaning-denying image-object.

9   Lyotard, *Discourse*, 7.

10 Ibid., 129.

11 Ibid., 235.

12 Ibid., 206.

13 Ibid., 210.

14 Ibid., 212.

15 Ibid., 267.

16 Ibid.

17 Ibid., 357, Lyotard's italics.

18 Lyotard, *Lectures d'enfance*, cited in Mary Lydon, "Veduta on *Discours, figure*," *Yale French Studies* 99 (2001), 25.

19 Lyotard, *Discourse*, 385–6.

20 Guston, *Collected Writings*, 280.

21 I want to thank the Brooklyn Museum and Marguerite Vigliante for granting me precious one-on-one time with *Red Cloth* and the lithograph *Untitled (Room)* (1980).

22 Philip Roth, *Shop Talk: A Writer and His Colleagues and Their Work* (New York: Houghton Mifflin, 2001), 135.

23 I am indebted to Robert Bordo not only for sharing his story but for his generosity as a thinker of painting. The wealth of his knowledge and the nuance of his observations introduced me to painting as a mode of thinking in its own right, though never separate from concerns of subject and meaning.

24 *Deluge*, the title of three different paintings, and the profusion of overflowing seas in Guston recall Klaus Theweleit's theory of (fascist) male subjectivity beset by the constant threat of femi-communist red floods. Unlike the German *freikorps* men, however, Guston does not fear the flood; it has already happened. See Theweleit, *Male Fantasies: Volume I: Women, Floods, Bodies, History* (Minneapolis: University of Minnesota Press, 1987).

25 Bryan Wolf, "Between the Lines: Philip Guston, the Holocaust and 'Bad Painting'" (forthcoming), 6.

26 Lyotard, *Discourse*, 264.

27 Guston confirms this association in the film *Philip Guston, A Life Lived*. The forlorn mood of *Black Sea*, the impression it gives of having reached a "dead end," combines with the knowledge of the geographical location of Guston's reported place of heritage, Odessa on the Black Sea (from which his parents escaped the pogroms), and his wife's stroke in 1977.

28 Guston, *Collected Writings*, 151.

29 Jeffrey Shandler, *While America Watches: Televising the Holocaust* (New York and Oxford: Oxford University Press, 1999), 18.

30 Ibid., 2.

31 John J. Michalczyk, *Filming the End of the Holocaust: Allied Documentaries, Nuremberg and the Liberation of the Concentration Camps* (London and New York: Bloomsbury, 2014), 150.

32 Other images and stories that appeared two and three years after the end of the war include David Bernstein, "Europe's Jews: Summer, 1947. A Firsthand Report by an American Observer" in *Commentary* (August 1947): 101–9; a number of TV documentaries which showed liberation footage, including "Placing the Displaced" (1948), "UN Casebook: Genocide Convention" (1949), episode 22 of "Crusade in Europe" (1949); an article from September 1948 in *Time* magazine discussed Gisella Perl's work as an abortion doctor in Auschwitz (her book *I Was a Doctor at Auschwitz* also appeared in 1948). This is a cursory and spotty list but it allows a guess as to what an American in 1947–8 could have known about the attempted genocide of Jewish and Romani people.

33 My emphasis. Philip Guston, cited in Dore Ashton, *A Critical Study of Philip Guston* (Berkeley: University of California Press, 1990), 74, http://ark.cdlib.org/ark:/13030/ft4x0nb2f0/. Ashton's book was first published in 1976.

34 Many commentators have seen *Porch II* as the most overt "Holocaust painting" in Guston's oeuvre. Bryan Wolf puts it most succinctly: "*Porch No. 2* is a painting about denial, complicity, and guilt. It marks both Guston's need to bear witness and his sense of separation from the very events that haunt him." Wolf, "Between," 14.

35 These "hoodlums" first appeared in Guston's political murals and drawings of the 1930s. They unmistakably depict the grisly costume of the Ku Klux Klan whose terror Guston protested. His later paintings of hooded men driving, painting, or discussing art use this still recognizable form in a more subtly ironic gesture that pursues the image's complicity with the mask and its status as both object and obstruction.

36 "To will a new form is unacceptable, because will builds distortion. Desire, too, is incomplete and arbitrary. These strategies, however intimate they might become, must especially be removed to clear the way for something else—*a condition somewhat unclear*, but which in retrospect becomes a very precise act. This 'thing' is recognized only as it comes into existence. It resists analysis." Guston, "Faith, Hope, and Impossibility," in *Collected Writings*, 53,4 (my emphasis). Though Guston speaks of removing desire here, I think what he means is not *purity* (against which he railed on several occasions) but a distancing from willed attachment which would degrade the work's autonomy.

37 Philip Guston, quoted in Bill Berkson, "The New Gustons," *Art News* 69.6 (October 1970): 44–7.

38 Lyotard, *Discourse*, 385.

39 Ibid., 384.

40 Lyotard uses Shakespeare's slip of the tongue of the "*mobled* queen" in Hamlet to show how the slip retraces the operations of desire in the play, specifically the Oedipal desire for the "displaced and condensed mother." See Lyotard, *Discourse*, 388.

41 Alexander Garcia-Düttmann, *The Memory of Thought: An Essay on Heidegger and Adorno* (New York and London: Continuum, 2002), 1.

42 Harold Rosenberg, "Liberation from Detachment: Philip Guston," in *The De-Definition of Art* (Chicago: University of Chicago Press, 1972), 139.

43 For a short history of the idea of assimilation, see Hannah Arendt, "Original Assimilation: An Epilogue to the One Hundredth Anniversary of Rahel Varnhagen's Death," in *The Jewish Writings* (New York: Schocken, 2007): 22–8 and "Antisemitism," in *The Jewish Writings* (New York: Schocken, 2007), 46–122.

44 Peter Mercer-Taylor, *The Cambridge Companion to Mendelssohn* (Cambridge: Cambridge University Press, 2004), 99. David Kaufmann notes a similar play with historical reference in the triptych *Red Sea, The Swell*, and *Blue Light*, all from 1975, in which Guston renders Bernardino Luini's *The Crossing of the Red Sea* more disastrous by leaving out the shores of Canaan from which the Israelites watch the drowning of the pharaoh's army. "By literalizing the sea, he secularizes the painting,

and by eliminating the promise of redemption, he universalizes its disaster. He turned a localized miracle into a catastrophe as general as Noah's flood." Kaufmann, *Telling Stories: Philip Guston's Later Works* (Berkeley: University of California Press, 2010), 48.

45 Guston, *Collected Writings*, 80.

46 Ibid., 81. Guston cites a newspaper clipping on "Los Angeles Museum to Put Artists Inside Plants" championing a new program for developing "new art forms in new media."

47 Walter Benjamin, "Central Park," trans. Lloyd Spencer, *New German Critique* 34 (winter 1985), 40.

48 Zygmunt Bauman, *Wasted Lives: Modernity and Its Outcasts* (Cambridge: Polity, 2004), 15.

49 Felman, "Crisis," 230–1.

Section IV

Affect and the Sublime in the Age of New Technologies

10

Gods, Angels, and Puppets

Lyotard's Lessons on Listening

Kirsten Locke

For Lyotard, music would always testify to the darkness of sound, to the shadows cast by the audible incisions into an inaudible abyss. As an art form, music comes a distant third to the two other colossi—painting and literature—that absorbed most of his powers of critique. Yet, he applied the same attentive, listening eye to music. The few essays he devoted solely to this art form exhibit the same attention to detail as those that belong to the realms of colors and words. With painting, literature, and music, Lyotard was interested in what was "at stake" in the evanescence of matter. In music, the sonic affective landscape is analyzed as intricately, and tightly interwoven into a constellation of time, sound, space, and silence.

In relation to matter, Lyotard spent his energies exposing what it was about a reading of Beckett that made us forget the clumsiness of words, where abstract formulations in painted color could communicate unspeakable truths, and how music could make us forget audibility. Music asserts a fragile authority over the other forms of art in the explicit link to listening, which held a privileged potency in Lyotard's analytic arsenal. Listening is not just the domain of ears and, indeed, as an organ that is always physically open, sometimes even ears can falter.

Eyes listen. Eyes soak up timbre and search for the harmony of the physical. Lyotard's re-writing of the Kantian "*Sensus Communis*"[1] as a common sense heard as a *chorus* communicable to all is inverted and thrown into the dark subterranean strata of music in the essay entitled "Music, Mutic,"[2] where a "mute" death rattle exposes us all as writhing, sonically-starved beasts. By the time of encroaching darkness in *Soundproof Room*,[3] listening is something that the artwork promulgates by cleaving open the strident scream of timeless, haunting death, where color testifies to blindness and music testifies to deafness.

This chapter explores music and the type of listening Lyotard considered contemporary music, and its deep link with technology, to expose. As an art of time, this analysis of music involves a discussion of repetition: new technologies, even in Lyotard's lifetime, were able to exactly record a performance. Yet, Lyotard will skew this relationship to time as repetition by insisting on the singularity of musical time as that which escapes inscription and archiving. Lyotard wants us to get as close as possible to the genesis of sound itself where musical affect is always unrepeatable, unknowable, and inaudible. Technology is heavily implicated in this explosion of sound in time and space; it is needed, but it must be surpassed, "revealing a destination which in any case exceeds the scope of techno-scientific research envisaged technically, yet thanks to which [an] obedience [to sound] is revealed."[4] Here is the search for a type of listening found only, but not *necessarily*, in music.

The following discussion concentrates on two essays that deal explicitly with listening and affective receptivity through music. In these essays, "God and the Puppet,"[5] and "Obedience,"[6] Lyotard dedicated himself to the task of understanding the affective potentiality held in music in an age challenged and stimulated by technological developments in the musical domain. These two essays show Lyotard unleashing an array of metaphorical props that will be set upon different sound stages to expose a destination of listening that turns back on itself: gods of sound, wooden puppets or marionettes controlled by wires, and celestial angels capable of hearing heavenly music that is out of this world. Kant looms large in these texts, but Lyotard's use of marionettes and mystical angels would have been horrifying to Kant, who started writing his *Critiques* in part to fend off the influence of Swedenborg's conversations with angels.[7] Lyotard forces Kant to fold back on himself, from First *Critique* to Third *Critique*, sprinkling a dusting of sublime gold dust over the puppets and angels on the way to turn their inanimate or outer-worldly passivity into the very qualities receptive to (inhuman) artistic vibrancy and richness. The following discussion helps explain what Lyotard was looking, or *listening*, for in music, and in writing about music as providing lessons on the art of listening. Primarily, the following discussion explores Lyotard's concern to extend the inaudible affect of music through utilizing contemporary technologies in the creation of new sounds. The first part of the chapter deals with the affective dimension of music within the analysis of "God and the Puppet." This is then developed toward an analysis of the extension of the inaudible in music through a focus on the essay "Obedience." Throughout both sections there is a focus on ways to find new possibilities in sonic landscapes to enhance listening toward a deeper engagement with musical affect.

Musical sublime presence

The idea of there being a musical presence, "a pure, punctual presence,"[8] ties into the "mutic" dimension of music as the inaudible breath or lament that inhabits music. Presence is developed further in the essay "God and the Puppet"[9] as that which escapes any subjective synthesis and repetition. As in the more poetic rendering of presence in "Music, Mutic," musical presence is described here as the nuance and timbre that inhabits the musical performance, which can only be felt *negatively* as a sign that surpasses the binding powers of a mind to synthesize data. Sound as pure matter is the presence in music, and must be utterly unfamiliar and unrecognizable to the synthesizing powers of the mind. "A nuance in its actuality, its here-and-now of that time, can exercise on a given mind," Lyotard goes on to explain, "not only the effect of a formal pleasure, which is something quite different, but the power of a loss."[10] The contemporaneousness of musical perception as nuance and affect, and the loss that Lyotard speaks of, is of the *subject*; subjectivity has to be suppressed or surpassed. The pure matter of sound as nuance can only reach the subject "at the cost of surpassing, or 'sub-passing,' its capacity for synthetic activity,"[11] Lyotard continues. The subject, to perceive musical nuance as affect, must lose its *self*.

And yet, Lyotard insists the loss and trauma of subjectivity is rehabilitated within an absence that, as it "breaks the mind,"[12] simultaneously affects it, causing both pain (through the loss of the subject's powers to synthesize) and joy (through the ability to be "seized" by musical nuance). The presence of musical matter that is felt through the subject's absence recalls very strongly the pain and jubilation that Kant ascribes to the feeling of the sublime. "The delight in the sublime does not so much involve positive pleasure as admiration or respect,"[13] Kant tells us. As such, it "merits the name of a negative pleasure."[14] The presence Lyotard is embracing in music is analogous to the shimmering of meaning described as a process of retreat and advance in the sublime experience articulated by Kant. This Kantian account of the sublime involves the mind's failure to grasp an awesome object, which instead leaves it scrambling and grappling in the realms of the imagination to compensate for the lack of cognitive data. What is awakened in this failure, says Lyotard, is "magnitude, force, quantity in its purest state, a 'presence' that exceeds what imaginative thought can grasp at once in a form."[15] Lyotard remains with this Kantian sublime, but emphasizes the zero-sum dimension between subjectivity and musical matter, turning further to the Epicurean logic of death to explain musical presence through absence as the feeling of the sublime. Musical matter, in its occurrence as timbre or nuance in sound, has the same finality as death: "if it's there, I'm not there; so long as I'm there, it's not there."[16] Lyotard explains: "In recalling the Epicurus text, I do not mean to dramatize things—they do not need it. But I do so at least in order to get across the idea that if, among these "things," there is one which does not tolerate repetition, it is death, it is matter."[17] Death and matter are the impossible qualities that cannot be repeated, following Epicurean logic, simply because the subject can never know death and can never understand matter because it must be absent from both. However, Lyotard adds to this logic a twist by stating that the reason why matter as affect cannot be understood cognitively or conceptually is because it is not *inscribed* on a surface, whether that surface is a mind or any other support capable of what Lyotard defines as a process of archiving information. Here we have the echoes of Lyotard's Kafkaesque prescriptive apparatus of torture in the essay "Prescription."[18] The ethical impetus turns into one where the artistic act must continue to search for that which escapes inscription insofar as it exceeds determination and prescription.[19] This, for Lyotard, is what the musical performance must reach for as a kind of writing that must escape and exceed the apparatus. Lyotard continues: "This is what writing—including musical writing— is looking for: what is not inscribed. . . . But first of all *outside any support*."[20]

"Divine automatism" as pure perception

If Lyotard places music within the sentiment of the sublime, he also focuses attention onto music as an experience of time as non-chronological or non-diachronic. From this stance, a move is made to empty subjectivity of any agency and to free the musical from subjective representation. Consciousness, as the privileged center of reference, is decimated in this critique, and, with it, the locus of the musical genius as the focal point in the history of Western music. However, it is not just the genius that suffers. Lyotard's analysis forces a rethinking of the relationship between music and the experience of music as perceived sound. This critique of subject-centered rationality in music involves a new subjectivity that takes as its beginning point a lack of mastery over sound. This is a subjectivity, sublime in origin, that is borne through negation and deprivation, but which is the more richly complex and fully endowed to perceive *because* of this deprivation. Rather than consciousness as the nexus in which musical sounds are perceived within differences from each other, Lyotard talks of a Bergsonian pure perception in which sounds, as (im)material objects, differ from each other independently of the subject-centered significations. Music must be made to be inhuman, and must be shifted to a para-human dimension, if it is to become a properly human experience. This is the ultimate paradox of the inhuman quality that art aspires to, and which signals the darkly ironic meaning behind the title "God" and the "Puppet."

(God/sound) + (puppets/ humans) = music as divine automatism

Lyotard will shortly draw specifically on Bergson's theory of duration to position musical perception as aspiring to a pure mechanistic process freed from all intentionality. However, as is so often the case, to help explain and prime the philosophical, Lyotard turns to literary fiction. In this case, the object of reference is the nineteenth-century German poet and novelist Heinrich von Kleist (1777–1811) and his short story *On the Marionette Theatre*.[21] This time, however, Lyotard's muse appears to have read the same philosophical texts, and Kleist's story is the result, according to Nikolchina,[22] of a radical re-reading of Kant's *Critique of Practical Reason*. In his story, Kleist's narrator is told of the mechanistic movement of the marionette puppets played as street theater to the milling crowds, and the grace they exemplify in their dance movements. Controlled by a machinist who pulls the strings, the puppets display in their empty intentionality a gracefulness that only God could hope to emulate. Humans, the narrator tells us, with their knowing minds and busy thoughts, sully their movements with their ragged determinations and intentions. Even the most exquisite dancer would fall short of the grace these puppets epitomize as inanimate matter, their otherwise inert limbs obeying only the pull of gravity and the twitch of the machinist. Lyotard sides with Kleist against this version of Kant, who ridicules the pervading mysticism of his time and the fabulous stories of those who thought they could experience *noumena* directly so that "God and eternity with their awful majesty would stand unceasingly before our eyes."[23] Kant then brings in the analogy of the marionettes in derogatory fashion, maintaining this type of belief reduces men to mere puppets "prepared and wound up by the Supreme Artist."[24] Kant continues his stinging critique: "Self-consciousness would indeed make him a thinking automaton; but the consciousness of his own spontaneity would be mere delusion if this were mistaken for freedom."[25] Further, Kant draws poetry into the foray (at least in Kleist's view) by pointing out that if there is such a thing as direct contact with the thing-in-itself (that sits between the external world and internal experience of that world), then all art is a puppet-show where "everything would gesticulate well, but there would be no life in the figures."[26] Instead, the puppets are simply the automatons of God's divine will. Kleist's story, celebrating the divine automatism of the puppets, can be read both as a protest against Kant's critique and reinstatement of the primacy of the artist.

Unequivocal as he is with Kleist's literary project, Lyotard, however, reads the empty intentionality of the puppets through the lens of the later Kant of the Third *Critique*, and the supreme gracefulness of their movements as an analogy of the human experience of the sublime. Emptied of the powers to synthesize, the sublime experience "is an experience of the *being* of time rather than of the *passing* of time."[27] The mechanism that the puppets obey is akin to the suppression of subjectivity that must be induced in relation to the sensation of time characterized by the sublime. Lyotard amalgamates this reading of the sublime with the musical experience: music must render the subject a puppet that responds to the external stimuli of sound exclusively so that the subject can feel musical time directly. Kant might have been against mysticism, but his notion of the sublime turns the empty agency of the marionettes into the supreme inhuman model to tap into what is unrepeatable to the musical experience. Only the renunciation of subjectivity morphed into "divine automatism" in the sublime experience can allow music *as presence* to emerge.

The god of sound

However, Lyotard never mentions the machinist who pulls the strings initiating movement in the puppets. In his study of Adorno and Lyotard, de la Fuente[28] attributes Lyotard's essay to a movement toward a negative-theology that situates the analysis as theologically inspired and closely related to Adorno's negative-dialectical formulation of music. The idea of there being a musical presence does sound theological, but when positioned as an occurrence within the sublime, this presence is borne of negation and nothingness. There is no chance of a Hegelian synthesis, even if it is couched in a negative dialectic, when Lyotard positions sound as emerging from the great void and abyss of Kant's *nothingness*. Kant does not let you *knowingly* touch the Thing, but he does give you *no*-thing in return, "an absence, a void, an empty place, the place of nothing"[29] that Lyotard supplants with a god made of inaudible music. The puppets are not only deprived of agency and intentionality, but are also pulled upwards by the inaudible promise in music in order for music's sound to "fall" and be heard. Lyotard evokes the machinist as the horizon of potentiality in music of which the manifold, as the possibility to all music, is sound.

This leads to a central paradox: why is this horizon of music, its manifold, inaudible? The puppets need to be shifted to the background and the horizon of sonic possibility needs to be shifted to the foreground for this to be understood. Lyotard places two poles to mark the extremities in this horizon of sound. At one extremity is sound conceived as *minimal*, the other extremity involves sound as *excess*. In fact, these two poles will serve Lyotard's analysis of the differing approaches to musical composition in contemporary music. These poles are given the qualities of a monad as conceptualized by the German philosopher Gottfried Leibniz. At the excessive extreme to this manifold of sound is Leibniz's rich monad that is able to incorporate every sound of the world and every potential sound. This god of sonic overabundance holds power over what Lyotard calls the "music of the spheres."[30] This rich monad, as god, "hears all the sounds in the world, the so-called real world, but also of the other possible worlds, in the same instant."[31] Leibniz's god of sound is in possession of the best possible sound worlds ever conceived, or about to be conceived. In unabashed optimism, this god offers the best possible combination of sounds at any given moment. This deluge of sound renders, according to Lyotard, the god of sound *intemporal*, in that this "celestial" music suffers from an excess of synthesizing, and music is thus rendered inaudible through the overabundance of sound. "All the beatings of what we spread out in what we would call the sound-history of the world are received as in a single chord, which has neither beginning nor end, since it is limited by no other possible sound,"[32] Lyotard explains.

At the other extreme, Lyotard utilizes Leibniz's naked monad, this time positioned as the god who can only absorb a single beat of sound at once. This is where Bergson, having read Leibniz (and Kant) closely, formulates his idea of instant duration. The analogy that Lyotard makes to illustrate this minimal god of sound is with the surface of a billiard ball. Here, the billiard ball can only perceive sound by one shock at a time, and because of its hard and shiny surface, no shock can be inscribed. "Its hardness and polish were conceived and realized precisely to prevent any impression being or remaining marked on it,"[33] Lyotard explains. If sound—as a series of vibratory shocks—can only be perceived one wave at a time, the billiard ball is incapable of remembering any other shock and can only perceive sound as a non-sound. This lack of retaining a remembrance of past shocks to constitute musical sound enables a forgetting of repetition. What the billiard ball "lacks in order to be able to forget is the capacity for synthesizing in a single pinch or grasp (or intuition, to talk in Kant's language) two—at least two—successive shocks."[34] Bergson's theory of duration, exemplified by the billiard ball, ensures the automatic preservation of the past and the present *in the same instant*.

Music and grace

It is time for the marionettes to resume their dancing. The god that Lyotard is referring to in his title is a god that incorporates both minimal and excessive approaches to sound. The grace of the puppets that Kleist introduced is achieved through both of these poles of sound, because both approaches free the mind from "diachrony, from all task of synthesis."[35] It is a *grace* that derives from "the sufficiency of the all in one, according to God, or the one in all and for all according to mechanics."[36] Lyotard wants us to be open to music in the way the puppets are open to the fateful certainty of their movements as inanimate matter. Rather than attaching stories and meaning to music, Lyotard instead wants us to get lost in the pure perception of music, as a "pure act"[37] before the birth of consciousness. However, music itself has to aspire to this grace too, "and this is why God and the [puppet] have no 'quality,' since quality is power."[38] Instead, music must emulate the emptiness of the puppets through incorporating the extremities of sound as inanimate matter. This also means that music must aspire to forget repetition just as the limbs of the puppets forget each movement in order to move with the spontaneous and pure grace that Lyotard (and Kleist) describe. Sound needs to be thought of in its singularity, not as a series of sounds put to use to communicate a musical message. Lyotard elaborates this minimalist message in the following:

> We are a long way from the god, the god has exploded, galaxies of resonances flee the *templum sanctum* (where the initial sound sounds) at high speed. No doubt they sing, linking such diverse frequencies, pitches and durations. But what cannot be equaled or repeated does not reside in linkings. It hides and offers itself in every atom of sound, perhaps.[39]

Listening as "obedience": wrestling with the angels

Lyotard continues the analysis of music as affect in the essay "Obedience."[40] Any attempt at art, for Lyotard, meant entering into a state of deprivation, of struggle, of withdrawal from the external to the pull of the internal battle that would have to be raged against the known into the unknown. However, this struggle never guaranteed anything (and certainly not salvation). This unknown (or the Kantian void of nothingness mentioned above) was often to involve the analogy of angels. In the sensorial universe explored in Augustine's confessions, Lyotard utilizes the biblical figure of the angel as a pure annunciation that conveys no message outside the "message" of its own occurrence.[41] When writing on the sublime in Newman's paintings, Lyotard names the paintings themselves as angels, as annunciations that "speak" without words or viable modes of communication, yet still affect and move the observer.[42] In Lyotard's usage, art entails a struggle with angels, and the best you can hope for is to come out limping and damaged. Total victory was and must remain always impossible and you never, *ever*, come out unscathed. In relation to music, Lyotard posits sound, or rather the temporal blowing up of sound, as that which composers must go into battle for. This battle that must be fought with music entails wrestling the temporal explosion of sound, the "ungraspable instant [of] its flight and … wait"[43] *away* from the domain of the angels. Contemporary music, such as that of Edgard Varèse, exposes this struggle as the quality in music that is now at stake for Lyotard, as the "feeling of occurrence, which all contemporary music has in common."[44] This *feeling of occurrence* in music opens a further discussion on exactly what Lyotard means by the notion of obedience, and the wrestling of sound away from the angels.

Lyotard places his angels in the zone of the sonic occurrence, and he draws on the Swedish mystic Emmanuel Swedenborg's transcriptions of conversations with angels to evoke the type of listening that contemporary music needs to capture. This is an interesting juxtaposition of old-world mysticism with the metallic techno-scientific interface of the late twentieth century (and beyond) that Lyotard creates. Both the conversations with angels and the technologically developed worlds evoke the inhuman otherworldly context that Lyotard is striving for in this depiction of music, and both worlds are complicit in re-thinking what music can *do*. Lyotard describes how, in one of his conversations, Swedenborg writes of the deities in charge of hearing, whose purpose is to act as conduit between sound and thought "in simple Obedience … which do not reason to see if a thing is thus … whence they can be called Obediences."[45] Unadorned with ulterior motives, these spirits are passively open to receiving sound in the same way as the puppets, as inanimate matter, are open to unfettered movement. Because of their passivity to hearing sound, these spirits or "angels" enjoy a type of music that is out of this world in its purity and beauty before passing it along to the mind's ear of "man" where it must lose some of its evanescence if its destination is understanding. This is what interests Lyotard, and what Swedenborg articulates with such unabashed mystical logic: that these angels of listening seem to have a direct line to sound which is passed between them as "the correspondence between spirits,"[46] and that "man knows nothing, and wants to know nothing, of this dependence of the ear on the spirit, of this taking hostage of hearing by the beyond of the body."[47]

Of course Lyotard's "beyond of the body" is not the realm of angels, but it is the realm of artificial or synthetic sound opened by computerization that stretches and extends the audible as the "radically unthought"[48] of sound, as "the unthought of the ear, something inaudible."[49] Angels or computers, it does not matter which, are the "beyond" of the body and what we can sense, and, for Lyotard, both exhibit the qualities of listening as an obedience to sound that is inhuman in origin and reaches towards the artistically inhuman in execution. Lyotard's treatise on the warfare of sound describes the battle in musical sound that must be fought through the new technologies to constitute new sounds. The angelic listening that holds dominion over sound before it reaches the mind must be exposed in contemporary music so human ears can supplant the angels, and we can experience the first explosion of sound. Lyotard concedes that Swedenborg's rendition of transcendental music might be a little too fantastical, but continues:

> On the other hand one can understand him to be designating precisely the essential features of what there is to be "liberated" in sound, and in particular the essential features of what music aided by contemporary technologies is trying to free in sound, its authority, the belonging of the spirit to the temporal blowing-up involved in the "being now" of the heard sound.[50]

The sound-feeling

Sound's authority, as the realm that Swedenborg's angels have control over, is exposed through extending the inaudible as the creation of new sounds, with the use of contemporary technology. This is the composer's artistic task: "It is about extending the concept of the inaudible and the means of bearing witness to this,"[51] Lyotard urges, and a necessary part of this process involves the working of computerized and digitalized technologies. However, Lyotard highlights two approaches composers can take in order for sound to be exposed. The first approach is one taken by John Cage, whose compositional pathway involves the use of sound as it is, to "let sound be."[52] Not only are the bustling sounds of New York traffic put to use in the famous 4'33, but also the audience's silence plays a central tenet in the work of music. The second approach is the opposite of this, when both organic and synthesized sounds are combined and structured with rapid repetitions and more complex configurations. Lyotard names this "the Boulez tendency."[53] Either approach has the same aim for Lyotard, as both approaches open a zone for listening as *obedience* through either "a minimalism of the very complex,"[54] or a heightened complexity of the minimal or "poor."[55] What such music produces in the listener, however, is a sound-feeling that places the mortal ear precisely in the position of Swedenborg's angels. In both approaches, the opening up of this inaudible space in sound aims "to return the ear to listening."[56] Lyotard continues:

> There is no music, especially not as *Tonkunst* [musical art], without the enigma of this *Darstellung* [presentation], immediately transcribed into feeling before any objectivation and therefore, in a sense, before any "audition," in a sound-feeling which is perhaps the most elementary presence *of* time or *to* time, the "poorest" degree or state (although it is not a state) of being-time: *Durchlaufen* [passing through].[57]

The sound-feeling, as an obedience to sound, is one in which the weave that "mutes listening is undone."[58] Lyotard's point is that the contrapuntal affect of music, with its differences in timbres, tones, and musical forms, covers over the zone of the first emergence of sound as its explosion into being, and the aim is to recover or reassert the primacy of this space through new technological developments in the production of sound. When describing his entry into post-war American society on a quest to find new sounds, Varèse was quoted as saying: "I became a sort of diabolical Parsifal ... on a quest for a bomb to explode."[59] Avant-garde composers such as Varèse blow apart the walls of the traditional forms or frames of the Western musical tradition by concentrating instead on sound and extending the inaudible within sound. The musical frame as a container for the sound in traditional Western music constructs is to be viewed with incredulity because even in such contexts, even "in this frame, even in the case of the greatest—Bach, Beethoven, Mozart—(the musical frame) can remain empty inside."[60] But Varèse and others like him also blow apart the walls of an anthropological construct of listening, where they wrestle the temporality of sound away from the angels, and return it instead back "to the marvel of the sound-event alone."[61] This is the passivity of and to sound that is needed in order for music in its current context to still provide the means to affect and excite. The walls of the body as sound and flesh need to fall if obedience to the art of sound can be accomplished. "With these walls, a whole anthropology of sound falls."[62] Lyotard explains: the obedience revealed for a moment in *Tonkunst* (with or within new technology) means that we (who, we?) are due to the donation of the event. This request is ontological, as it were; no one is asking us anything.[63]

Conclusion

Like the change in destination of listening, the processes promised by Lyotard—the working through of his thought as a working through of music—involve lessons in bearing witness to music. Getting rid of the mind to respond automatically to sound, getting rid of the human to produce the sound needed to respond, getting rid of the "angels" to listen to this sound, are the lessons that Lyotard tries to teach. In his writing on music, Lyotard pulverizes the musical form and dismantles the scaffolding of the body of the musical object. With anthropological walls dismantled, what we have left is only sound as matter, and not even sound comes out unscathed. Music must now be placed in a position that exposes sound to be tapped into directly, without form, without meaning. This is the automatism to music that Lyotard evokes through the puppets, an automatism that is able to respond directly and obediently to music as matter, as a mode of listening that is both primordial and mechanistic. The art of sound has significance in the stretching of sound toward the inaudible as an endless quest, aided by technology, made necessary *because* of technology. Reaching to the beyond of sound is all that is left in music if it is to escape the rule of performativity that anticipates the beyond in the present. Music can be performed through computerized technologies, but not in the communicational and pragmatic *manner* of a computer because what it is that is *musical* escapes archiving. Will we ever hear what the angels hear? Maybe not, but the struggle is what keeps on promising the possibility, and that is precisely what art is about: the promise of the impossible in the possible.

Notes

1 Jean-François Lyotard, "*Sensus Communis,*" trans. Marian Hobson and Geoffrey Bennington, in *Judging Lyotard,* ed. Andrew Benjamin (London: Routledge, 1992), 1–25.

2 Jean-François Lyotard, "Music, Mutic," in *Postmodern Fables,* trans. Georges Van Den Abbeele (Minneapolis: University of Minnesota Press, 1997), 217–34.

3 Jean-François Lyotard, *Soundproof Room: Malraux's Anti-Aesthetics,* trans. Robert Harvey (Stanford: Stanford University Press, 2001).

4 Jean-François Lyotard, "Obedience," in *The Inhuman: Reflections on Time,* trans. Geoffrey Bennington and Rachel Bowlby (Stanford: Stanford University Press, 1991), 165–81.

5 Lyotard, "God and the Puppet," in *The Inhuman: Reflections on Time*, trans. Geoffrey Bennington and Rachel Bowlby (Stanford: Stanford University Press, 1991), 153–64.

6 Lyotard, "Obedience."

7 Miglena Nikolchina, "It Always Gives Watching: The Nothing and the Parahuman in Rilke's Duino Elegies," *Filozofski Vestnik*, XXVI(2) (2005), 161–71.

8 Lyotard, "God and the Puppet," 156.

9 Ibid.

10 Ibid.

11 Ibid.

12 Ibid.

13 Immanuel Kant, *Critique of Judgment*, trans. Werner S. Pluhar (Indianapolis: Hackett, 2002) 98/KUK 245.

14 Ibid.

15 Jean-François Lyotard, *Lessons on the Analytic of the Sublime*, trans. Elizabeth Rottenberg (Stanford: Stanford University Press, 1994), 53.

16 Lyotard, "God and the Puppet," 157.

17 Ibid.

18 Jean-François Lyotard, "Prescription," in *Toward the Postmodern*, trans. Christopher Fynsk, eds Robert Harvey and Mark S. Roberts (New York: Humanity Books, 1999), 176–91.

19 Kirsten Locke, "Lyotard's Infancy: A Debt that Persists," *Postmodern Culture* 23 (2012).

20 Lyotard, "God and the Puppet," 158.

21 Heinrich von Kleist, "On the Marionette Theatre," trans. Thomas G. Neumiller, *The Drama Review: TDR* 16.3 (1972), 22–6.

22 Nikolchina, "Watching," 162.

23 Immanuel Kant, *Critique of Practical Reason*, trans. Werner S. Pluhar (Indianapolis: Hackett, 2002), 185/KPV 146.

24 Ibid., 101.

25 Ibid.

26 Kant cited in Nikolchina, "Watching," 163.

27 Temenuga Trifonova, "A Nonhuman Eye: Deleuze on Cinema," *SubStance* 33.2 (2004), 149.

28 Eduardo de la Fuente, "Music as Negative Theology," *Thesis Eleven* 56 (1999), 57–79.

29 Nikolchina, "Watching," 164.

30 Lyotard, "God and the Puppet," 162.

31 Ibid.

32 Ibid.

33 Ibid.

34 Ibid.

35 Lyotard, "God and the Puppet," 163.

36 Ibid.

37 Ibid.

38 Ibid.

39 Ibid., 164.

40 Lyotard, "Obedience."

41 Jean-François Lyotard, *The Confession of Augustine*, trans. R. Beardsworth (Stanford: Stanford University Press, 2000).

42 Jean-François Lyotard, "Newman: The Instant" in *The Inhuman*.

43 Lyotard, "Obedience," 176.

44 Ibid.

45 Ibid., 178.

46 Ibid.

47 Ibid.

48 Ibid., 172.

49 Ibid.

50 Ibid., 179.

51 Lyotard, "Music and Postmodernity," *New Formations* 66 (2009), 37.

52 Lyotard, "Obedience," 177.

53 Ibid.

54 Ibid.

55 Ibid.

56 Ibid.

57 Ibid., 176.

58 Ibid.

59 Igor Toronyi-Lalic, "Edgard Varèse Dropped Bombs on the 20th Century," *Times Online*, last modified April 9, 2010, http://www.thetimes.co.uk/tto/arts/music/classical/article2470662.ece.

60 Lyotard, "Obedience," 179.

61 Ibid., 177.

62 Ibid., 180–1.

63 Ibid.

11

Autoaffection and Lyotard's Cinematic Sublime

Erin Obodiac

The 2011 publication of Jean-François Lyotard's *Miscellaneous Texts I: Aesthetics and Theory of Art* and *Miscellaneous Texts II: Contemporary Artists* confirms that Lyotard was a philosopher preoccupied with painting, and that unlike Walter Benjamin, who wrote extensively on media technologies, or Gilles Deleuze, author of *Cinema I: the movement-image* and *Cinema II: the time-image*, Lyotard's writings on film, apart from the brief works "Acinema" and "Idée d'un film souverain" (Idea of a Sovereign Film), never fully developed.[1] This sparsity is even more surprising if we consider that Lyotard himself belonged in the 1970s to a film collective and tried his own hand at experimental filmmaking: *L'Autre Scène* (The Other Scene), *Mau Gillette*, and *Tribune sans tribun* (Tribune without a Tribune).[2]

Although it appears that Lyotard's forays into the cinematic sphere were short-lived and left barely a trace in his writings on aesthetics and art theory, as we shall see, we might nevertheless discern an affinity between "Acinema" and *Lessons on the Analytic of the Sublime*, Lyotard's definitive text on Kant's *Critique of Judgment*. In his explication of the Kantian sublime, Lyotard provocatively states that there is an "affinity of aesthetic sublimes with an era of technique."[3] Both the Kantian sublime and Heidegger's name for the essence of technology (*Ge-stell*: Enframing) concern a subreptive use of, in Kant's case, the imagination's failure to answer in full to reason's unreasonable demand to present the totality of nature in one intuition, and, in Heidegger's case, a denaturing employment of poietic being or *physis* (nature) in the service of an instrumental causality. The affinity between *Ge-stell* and the sublime should come as no surprise since, as the third *Critique* progresses, the "faculty" or "power" (*Vermögen*) to cognize *a priori* must be understood as *technē* (technics). Judgment is, after all, Urteils*kraft*, i.e. power (ability), technical craft. Kant says as much: "I shall call technical the power of judgment."[4] Likening the workings of aesthetic reflective judgment to a technical prosthesis[5] or machinic apparatus is licensed by a remark Lyotard makes in "Idée d'un film souverain." In this late conference paper (1995), which revisits some of the questions from his 1973 essay "Acinema," Lyotard writes, "[t]he camera works here in the manner of the Kantian *Zusammennehmung* [a gathering or holding together]."[6] Lyotard compares the synthetic act of comprehension, which constitutes temporality and movement, with cinematography. If, as we shall see, the acinema concerns immobilization and excess mobilization—in effect, "*a-temporalité*" (atemporality) or "*la stase atemporelle*" (atemporal stasis)[7]—which interrupt and suspend the synthetic act of comprehension, then the acinema operates in the manner of a cinematic sublime. Before turning to the affinity between the sublime and the acinema, let us more generally consider the manner—and unexpectedly this will concern affect, specifically autoaffection—in which aesthetic reflective judgment is prosthetic, technical, and even machinic.

In *Lessons on the Analytic of the Sublime*, Lyotard follows Kant in emphasizing that aesthetic reflective judgment is a *feeling* (*Gefühl*) of pleasure or displeasure. As early as paragraph one of the third *Critique*, Kant writes that, in judgments of taste:

> presentation is referred only to the subject, namely, to its feeling of life—under the name feeling of pleasure and displeasure—and this forms the basis of a very special power of discriminating and judging. This power does not contribute anything to cognition, but merely compares the given presentation in the subject with the entire presentational power, of which the mind [*Gemüt*] becomes conscious, when it feels its own state.[8]

Lyotard also discusses autoaffection when he notes, quoting Kant, that it is again *feeling* that orients thinking, that orientation is based on the capacity "to feel a difference within my own subject, namely, that between my right and left hands."[9] Lyotard further stresses that feeling traverses *all* thinking, even thoughts concerning the Ideas of reason. Instead of a *cogito ergo sum* (I think therefore I am), we have a *feeling*, yet the subject or substrate of thought is not a substance: "If there is a substrate in Kantian thought, it exists as the regulative Idea, for the substrate is the supersensible about which we have no knowledge."[10] Although inaccessible to knowledge, thought's supersensible substrate is nevertheless pointed to by the feeling of the sublime. As a pointing, however, this feeling is peculiarly detached from a subject, and Lyotard observes that Kant manages to write about aesthetic reflective judgment without a subject: "little mention is made of a subject."[11] Even when he is discussing pleasure, Lyotard makes sure not to imply a reified subject, but instead describes a facultative set of relations:

Kant's analysis of the beautiful "prevents pleasure from being attributed to a subject."[12] And, repeatedly, Lyotard indicates that with the judgment of the sublime "the most elementary conditions (the synthesis of time) for the synthesis of a *Selbst* [self] are lacking here."[13] He continues: "Yet this failing does not in the least prevent the feeling of the sublime from being a feeling, that is, a 'sensation' by which a thought, reflective in this case, is made aware of its state."[14] Although we have feeling without a subject (no inner sense as a synthesis of time), nevertheless there is a kind of subjectivity (a feeling by which thought is made aware of its state), what we might call the *autoaffection* of thought. On the one hand, as an aesthetic reflective judgment, this feeling is what Lyotard calls "tautegorical"[15]—a kind of identity of form and content—yet, on the other hand, this feeling concerns aesthetic reflective (dis)pleasure, not the self-identity of a Cartesian *cogito*. That this (dis)pleasure is not to be attributed to the subject— least of all the body—yet serves to make thought aware of its own state, prompts the question of its status or "location."

If the feeling of (dis)pleasure in the judgment of the sublime points to thought's supersensible substrate, and if Kant calls "technical" the power of judgment, is the autoaffection of thought a kind of technical prosthesis? In "Stelarc and the Chimera: Kant's Critique of Prosthetic Judgment," Howard Caygill argues that although Kant was able to elaborate judgment as technics, he relegated its source to the supersensible, rather than making it an organization of matter: "The uncanny source of organization was invisible to Kant because of his historically limited understanding of technology: while considering the concept of the technic of judgment as a source of organization, he was not able to align this with existing technology."[16] If Kant understands judgment as technics, with what existing technology might *we* align the judgment of the sublime? If we venture to re-read the workings of the sublime as those of a technical apparatus, can thought's vocation remain immaterial?

Lyotard himself somewhat heads in this direction in his essay "Can Thought Go On Without A Body?" In the "HE" section of this text, Lyotard considers the relation between thought and the living being as well as between thought and materiality. In a rejection of the sublimity of thought, the HE character states that thought depends on living being and living beings depend on the life of the solar system.[17] Because the HE character connects thought to the material conditions of life, and because everything is a morphogenesis of matter, there is also no distinction between life and technology: "You know—technology wasn't invented by us humans. Rather, the other way around. As anthropologists and biologists admit, even the simplest life forms, infusoria (tiny algae synthesized by light at the edges of tidepools a few million years ago) are already technical devices."[18] And the human being is merely the most complex of these technical devices:

> What's true is that this human being is omnivorous when dealing with information because it has a regulating system (codes and rules of processing) that's more differentiated and a storage capacity for its memory that's greater than those of other living beings. Most of all: it's equipped with a symbolic system that's both arbitrary (in semantics and syntax), letting it be less dependent on an immediate environment, and also "recursive" (Hofstadter), allowing it to take into account (above and beyond raw data) the way it has of processing such data. That is, itself.[19]

The HE character continues this parody of cognitive science and its dilemmas. The division between mind and body is transposed onto the distinction between software and hardware.[20] On the one hand, this reconfiguring of the mind-body problematic as software-hardware acknowledges that thinking must have a material basis, that its substrate entails matter, yet it still participates in the fantasy that medium doesn't matter, i.e. that thinking can inhabit any container or life-support system. Even if logic and other symbolic systems are supremely adaptable to digital technics—they are in themselves binary systems—embodied mind is an analogue system. The HE character explains:

> Our disappointment in these organs of "bodiless thought" comes from the fact that they operate on binary logic ... But as Dreyfus argues, human thought doesn't think in binary mode ... Which is why it's appropriate to take the body as model in the manufacture and programming of artificial intelligence if it's intended that artificial intelligence not be limited to the ability to reason logically.[21]

It seems that human thought cannot be reduced to the informatics of binary digital systems.

At first, we might liken what is at stake here with Lyotard's emphasis on aesthetic reflective judgment as a *feeling*. We might presume that feeling is an aspect of embodied mind. Judgment as a *feeling* of pleasure and displeasure would have to be connected to body. We must recall, however, that with aesthetic reflective judgment, the feeling of pleasure is not connected to the sensory or material charms of bodies—that would be mere agreeableness—but to the form of the object. The pleasure of the beautiful is an autoaffection of thought: it concerns the free-play of the faculties upon the occasion of the form. And yet, with the judgment of the beautiful, Kant does not entirely detach thought from a metaphysics of life. In the "General Comment" at the end of the Analytic of the Sublime, Kant, in a departure from the Cartesian *cogito* and a return to Epicurus, states that:

> in the absence of feeling of the bodily organ, life is merely consciousness of our existence, and not a feeling of being well or unwell, i.e. of the furtherance or inhibition of the vital forces; for the mind [*Gemüt*] taken by itself is wholly life (the very principle of life), whereas any obstacles or furtherance must be sought outside it and yet still within man himself, and hence in connection with the body.[22]

As both inside and outside, the feeling of pleasure and displeasure prosthetically links the mind's system of autoaffection—a kind of self-isolated mind taken as the principle of "life" itself—to the living body. This is not entirely unexpected if we agree with Kant that the conditions of possibility of appearance issue from the mind's own structures of time and space: the feeling of pleasure cinematically projects the life of the mind onto the life of the body. Yet, the HE character from "Can Thought Go On Without A Body?" has already become suspicious of this so-called life of the mind. The question here is: in what manner does thought's autoaffection, its feeling of its own condition, relate to a feeling of life? This is, according to Kant, what aesthetic pleasure performs: the pleasure felt in the judgment of the beautiful concerns the quickening, the enlivening, the animation of the faculties in their free play. The judgment of the beautiful is "directly attended with a furtherance of a feeling of life."[23] It would seem that the judgment of the beautiful belongs to a residual vitalism in Kant's philosophy, as Lyotard himself notes.[24] Yet, even if the beautiful is still attached to a certain metaphysics of life, the sublime signals a departure from it.

Although Lyotard stresses that judgment is a feeling (of pleasure and displeasure), we might disconnect the "feeling" of the sublime from the living body—human or otherwise—even though Kant makes reference to a life of the mind that is animated or quickened in the judgment of the beautiful. In contemporary robotics, the feedback loop of sensor and sensation generates a kind of technical autoaffection, a technics of feeling, yet the circuit between a phototropic sensor and the light that it senses does not engender the kind of feeling that Kant has in mind with aesthetic reflective judgment. Nonetheless, if we take judgment as technical prosthesis, which Kant himself suggests that we do, then what kind of feeling is the feeling of judgment exactly? We have seen that Kant addresses this immediately in the opening paragraph of his third

Critique: "under the name feeling of pleasure and displeasure," the power of judgment refers presentation to "the entire presentational power, of which the mind becomes conscious when it feels its own state."[25] For the contemporary reader, autoaffection—thought feeling its own state—sounds like a recursive apparatus, a feedback loop. If we subreptively discard Kant's invocation of the supersensible and think only in terms of a material basis for thought, a kind of machinic systems theory of judgment might come to the fore. I would like to suggest that aesthetic reflective judgment finds a kind of counterpart in the cinematic apparatus if thinking is understood as, to quote Lyotard, a "complex technical device."[26] If the judgment of the sublime is already a kind of technics or prosthesis of thought—the imagination "gains an extension [*Erweiterung*] and a might greater than that which it sacrifices [*aufopfert*]"[27]—its analogue might be what Lyotard calls the "acinema."

Before turning to the essay "Acinema," we will briefly see in what manner there is a cinematic principle already at work in Kant's sublime. The analytic of the sublime's discussion of synthesis, composition, and comprehension (*Zusammensetzung* and *Zussamenfassung*) bears on the question of the synthesis of the "before" and "after" in cinema: in the montage, in the sequence of frames (24 fps), which simulates movement, and the sequence of shots, which produces a narrative or a concept through movement. The apprehension of these movements is synthesis, and temporal synthesis is essential to the constitution of movement. For Kant, synthesis is essential to any apprehension of phenomena. Lyotard writes, "successive synthesis is the *a priori* condition of 'apprehension' even of phenomena . . . The text insists: only 'through successive synthesis of part to part in [the process of] its apprehension [*in der Apprehension*]' can the phenomenon 'come to be known.'"[28] As with Kantian temporality, the synthesis of before and after is constitutive of movement in cinema, yet this synthesis must also negotiate a certain passing, a synthetic passage. The movement must also be a temporal and spatial passage. Discussing the mathematical sublime, Lyotard notes the necessity of both synthesis and passage:

> the successive composition of the apprehension of the phenomenon as extensive magnitude demands syntheses of apprehension and reproduction. The first consists in containing (*erhalten*) the manifold "in a single moment" (*als in einem Augenblick*) in such a way that the "run-through" [*par-cours*] or the "trans-currance" (*das Durchlaufen*) is "held together" by a single take, so to speak, the *Zusammennehmung*. Obviously there is only flux, a passage of the manifold, if there is succession, and the latter requires the simultaneous for its constitution. The current flows only in the "hold" of what does not flow.[29]

In short, succession not only requires a passage of "stills," but also a synthesis, a spatio-temporal frame, for this passage, a "single take" if we follow the cinematic metaphor: recall that Lyotard tells us that the camera operates in the manner of a *Zusammennehmung*. With cinematic movement, succession requires both a retention (reproduction) and a disappearing of the previous images (apprehensions); composition, as Kant defined it, synthesizes the sequence and retains the previous ones in a kind of comprehension. Of aesthetic comprehension, Lyotard writes, "[r]eproduction allows a unit apprehended earlier, thus actually absent, to be kept present in thought. This synthesis of retention is the doing of the imagination. And 'composition' necessarily includes it."[30] The mnemotechnics of composition and comprehension can be likened to that of a cinematic apparatus. The question will be: what, then, is the moment of the sublime for this apparatus?

Kant tells us that the imagination can compose (*Zusammensetzung*) syntheses *ad infinitum*. Yet the imagination is overwhelmed when it is asked to "'comprehend' [*Zussamenfassung*] in a glance what it 'composes' 'successively.'"[31] The imagination's failure to comprehend simultaneously the entire sequence is the negative moment in the feeling of the sublime as a mathematical synthesis. The simultaneous grasp of the time series (*Zeitfolge*) destroys time, and time is, for Kant, the inner sense. The synthesis of the before-after dyad, which constitutes time as the inner sense of the transcendental subject, suffers a catastrophe in attempting to synthesize an infinite sequence in the mathematical sublime. When the cinematic apparatus "assembles at once all past events ... without placing in succession, but by co-presenting them in a virtual simultaneity,"[32] we have a kind of machinic analogue of what is attempted in the sublime. Lyotard notes, however, that although the experience of the mathematical sublime puts in jeopardy the inner sense as constituted by time, an autoaffection nevertheless persists in aesthetic reflective judgment: "however disastrous it may be for inner sense, the 'regression' demanded of the imagination is nonetheless declared to be 'subjectively' felt and felt as *zweckwidrig* [contrapurposive], as contravening the finality of the faculty of presentation."[33] Despite the collapse of the inner sense as a synthesis of time, a certain kind of subjectivity, a feeling without a subject, is in play, and Lyotard, on this ground, suggests that the sublime does not belong to a philosophy of the subject. More importantly for our purposes, would be whether or not, with the sublime, thought is detached from animation and the so-called "life" of the mind. The sublime could be thought as a kind of *inanimation*, an interruption of the synthesis of the before/after series, and, hence, in cinema, the movement of the image.[34] The annihilation of serial time, the movement of the image in cinema, might engender a form of suspended animation, a still life.

Aesthetic delight provides animation (*Belebung*) for thought. That the feeling of the beautiful is an "animating" bears on the question of animation and movement in cinema since it is movement—even its uncanny simulacrum—that is taken as a sign of life. For the life of the mind, the pleasure of aesthetic reflective judgment sets in motion, quickens, enlivens. Lyotard identifies a symptomatic vitalism in Kant's text concerning the nature of this animation:

> representation is then "referred wholly to the subject, and what is more to its feeling of life [*seines Lebensgefühl*]—under the name of the feeling of pleasure or displeasure." As in any doctrine (or metaphysic) of energy, pleasure is made a metaphor for the vital force of the "subject" and displeasure for the reduction of this force. The principle that increases this force is called *Geist*, which Philonenko translates as soul [*âme*] because its function is precisely to animate: the life vein of thinking.[35]

As a principle of animation, aesthetic pleasure increases the life force: we recall that this pleasure is not the agreeableness that the body feels, but the formal attunement and free play of the faculties of mind, a feeling of its own condition when a given representation is compared to the capacity of representation as a whole. The somewhat phantasmatic and intermedial site of this autoaffection engenders an uncanny interface, neither inside nor outside, and we might wonder what kind of life is being named in this enlivening. Kant tells us that "of itself alone, the mind [*Gemüt*] is wholly life (the very principle of life), whereas any obstacles or furtherance must be sought outside it and yet still within man himself."[36] We might say, using Mark Hansen's concept,[37] that there is here a kind of *introjection of technics*, whereby aesthetic pleasure shows itself as a constitutive prosthesis, both outside and "in the human itself." Aesthetic pleasure seems to be the prosthetic interface between mere life, perhaps the life of the body or animality, and what Kant calls mind, the life principle itself. And just as animation or movement is conventionally taken as a sign of life, aesthetic pleasure—which is both inside and outside the human being—becomes a sign of human life, is the prosthesis of human life, is human life as prosthesis. It appears that a technical prosthesis is what configures the "feeling of life," which is not, to follow Kant, "merely consciousness of one's existence," neither *cogito*, nor *sum*, but well-being, "the feeling of well-being."[38] Although aesthetic pleasure signals the morphogenesis of something vital for thought, i.e. that the feeling of life is exceptional, that life, in aesthetic reflective judgment, is exceptional, it remains unclear what life—life as technical prosthesis—actually is. Why is the energetics of a technical prosthesis still called life?

What we do know is that with the aesthetic reflective feeling of the sublime, the animation at work in the beautiful somewhat dies out, as it were. With the sublime, the imagination's proliferation of forms reaches its end, its limit: "The concept places itself out of reach of all presentation: the imagination founders, inanimate."[39] This inanimation, this stilling of movement and life, is theorized in a specifically technological context in Lyotard's essay "Acinema."

For cinema, animation refers directly to its constitutive principle: to movement, or the movement of the image. In the essay "Acinema," Lyotard is interested in what immobilization and the excess of mobilization might mean as an art or technics of cinema: "the acinema, we have said, would be situated at the two poles of the cinema taken as a writing of movements: thus, extreme immobilization and extreme mobilization. It is only for *thought* that these two modes are incompatible."[40] Of Lyotard's term "acinema," Jean-Michel Durafour writes:

> this acinema will cover the two polar tendencies of experimental cinema: *extreme mobilization* (the flashes of Paul Sharits and Tony Conrad, the permanent decenterings with Snow, the polychrome fulgurances of Kubelka or Lye, the molecular and nebulous matter of Jordan Belson)—*where, according to ordinary perception, it should be appeased* (the perception class of "objects" and motionless locations); *extreme immobilization* (the long static shots on static figures with Warhol) *where, according to the same ordinary perception, it should move* (man is animated).[41]

Although molecules might move (in space or in an experimental animated film), Durafour underscores the association between the life of the human being and movement, i.e., animation. Yet, although with the beautiful the free-play of the faculties is felt as a "furtherance of life" or the vital forces, with the sublime these forces experience a *Hemmung*, a hemming in, and then an *Ergießung*, a gushing forth. The two moments—*Ergießung* and *Hemmung*—could be mapped onto the two poles of the acinema, its two inanimations (extreme mobilization and immobilization), what Lyotard calls "a figural aesthetic of the 'much too much' that defies the concept, and an abstract or minimal aesthetic of the 'almost nothing' that defies form";[42] in short, an art or technics of the sublime, an acinema of the sublime, as the excess of motion and immobilization. At once formless and an unlimited profusion of forms, at once motionless and an unlimited frenzy of movement, this distribution informs both the sublime and the acinema.

The question of the figural—not as representation, but as *presence*—is central to the sublime (without-figure, the disaster of figures) and the acinema. Yet, presence of *what* is a lingering question. For Kant's analytic of the sublime, it is perhaps the pointing to the supersensible, or thought's supersensible vocation, that is "present." For the acinema, however, it may very well be the presence of the nonhuman, the operations of the machinic apparatus. Durafour suggests that the human being is somewhat absent in this scene and that the human "no longer intervenes in the process of the genesis of the image henceforth governed by the sole laws of physics and chemistry."[43] Following Lyotard's "The Unconscious as Mise-en-Scène," Durafour writes of Michael Snow's film *La Région centrale* (The Central Region), that it "is exemplary of a deanthropomorphizing abstract acinema."[44] It presents nonhuman (geologic, planetary, cosmic) temporalities; the film recounts, says Lyotard, "a story about horizons or forests, or the substance of the earth, or the clouds in the sky."[45] Although these temporalities decenter the human, everything nonhuman is not necessarily equivalent. This is one reason why in comparing "the perceptual data produced by the set-up of *La Région Centrale* and the psychic mechanism of the unconscious,"[46] Lyotard nevertheless does not equate, says Durafour, "the cinematographic machinery of Snow and the psychic machinery of Freud."[47] I would like to heed this observation when comparing Lyotard's analysis of the Kantian sublime with his own concept of the acinema: although there may be proximities here, the two "apparatuses" are distinct.

From the outset of "Acinema," from the essay's first sentence, Lyotard designates cinematography as "the inscription of movement, a writing with movement, a writing with movements."[48] With cinema, we are dealing, as it turns out, with a kind of *graphesis*[49] (*graphein*: "to write, to draw"), with inscription and writing—which we shouldn't equate—but which we might differentiate in the phrases "inscription *of* movement" and "writing *with* movement." The latter is, perhaps, a kind of media form: using movement to write, movement is the medium of the writing. On the other hand, with "the inscription of movement," we have the inscribing of movement itself, movement's inscription: cinema involves both the inscription of and the writing with movement.

In "Acinema," however, Lyotard is specifically interested in cinematography as the writing of *immobility* and the writing of the *excess* of movement. What he calls "acinema" is a kind of negative *Darstellung*, a negative presentation, of what should, by definition, exceed cinema: the "otherwise" of movement, i.e. immobility and the blur of excess motion. If cinema is characterized by a throng or crowd of all kinds of movements—from movements within the shot, to the movements of the frame and lens, to the sequencing of frames and the montage, and the spatio-temporality of the narration—Lyotard insists that the essence of conventional cinematic technique involves *eliminating* possible movements. He writes, "image, sequence, and film must be constituted at the price of these exclusions . . . If no movements are picked out we will accept what is fortuitous, dirty, confused, unsteady, unclear, poorly framed, overexposed . . . A scene from elsewhere, representing nothing identifiable, has been added . . . an undecidable scene."[50] From a throng of all kinds of possible movements, the without-use or without-purpose must be eliminated. Lyotard explains what is at stake aesthetically and politically with this elimination: conventional cinema is concerned with a regime of order, the order of the whole, order in movements, and the movement of order. He notes, "[w]riting with movements—cinematography—is thus conceived and practiced as an incessant organizing of movements . . . The so-called impression of reality is a real oppression of orders."[51] Lyotard compares movement in cinema with the object in political economy, the movement of exchange and substitution. An object is valuable, he writes, "only insofar as it is exchangeable against other objects . . . Therefore, to be valuable the object must move: proceed from other objects ('production' in the narrow sense) and disappear, but on condition that its disappearance *makes room for still other objects*."[52] All movements in conventional cinema must belong to the movement of production; they must be productive. Any movement that is not productive, which exhibits what Lyotard calls "a simple *sterile difference*"[53] is subject to elimination, to the "enforcement of the nihilism of movements."[54] We will see that what Lyotard calls "acinema" disrupts and interrupts all manner of production, from life, to thought, to capital. The sterility of the acinema in its singularity and its without-interest shares an affinity with the autoaffection of aesthetic reflective judgment.

Lyotard writes of the difference concerning sterile movement in a sub-section entitled "Pyrotechnics." Sterile movements don't fit the (narrative) norm of "the synthesis of good movement,"[55] which is understood as productive. He writes, for instance, that:

> A match once struck is consumed. If you use the match to light the gas that heats the water for the coffee which keeps you alert on your way to work, the consumption is not sterile, for it is a movement belonging to the circuit of capital: merchandise/match—merchandise-labor power—money-wages—merchandise-match. But when a child strikes the match *to see* what happens—just for the fun of it—he enjoys the movement itself.[56]

The experimental nature of the "see what happens" or the "just for the fun of it" is characteristic of aesthetic reflective pleasure, which happens without precedent and apart from any law of return. This enjoyment of "the movement itself"—and the movement of a flame is one of Kant's examples of the beautiful—stands as a singularity outside the sequence of conceptual production and interest, which are requirements of aesthetic reflective judgment. The child who strikes a match just for the fun of it "enjoys the movement itself . . . enjoys these sterile differences leading nowhere, these uncompensated losses . . . Intense enjoyment and sexual pleasure (*la jouissance*), insofar as they give rise to perversion and not solely to propagation, are distinguished by this sterility."[57]

Lyotard's figure of sterile movement, a figure associated with reproductive barrenness, employs both the vitalist tradition that takes movement as a sign of life and the aesthetic as a feeling of animation. What Lyotard calls "the motion of pleasure as such"[58] would, as sterile, stand outside a certain conception of life, or perhaps points to that life Kant names the autoaffection of thought: the quickening, the animating, at work in aesthetic reflective judgment. Although Lyotard doesn't name the aesthetic here, he does suggest that:

> In lighting the match the child . . . if he is assuredly an artist by producing a simulacrum, he is one most of all because the simulacrum is not an object or worth valued for another object . . . It is thus that Adorno said the only truly great art is the making of fireworks: pyrotechnics would simulate perfectly the sterile consumption of energies in *jouissance*.[59]

Movement outside the circuit of production—sterile motion—would share in this pyrotechnics. Lyotard sees two possibilities for "a cinematographic object, conforming to the pyrotechnical imperative . . . immobility and excessive movement. In letting itself be drawn toward these antipodes the cinema insensibly ceases to be an ordering force; it produces true, that is, vain, simulacrums, blissful intensities, instead of productive/consumable objects."[60] Immobility and excessive movement, like the pyrotechnics of a match struck for the pleasure of the movement itself, short-circuits the organization of capital, its movement of return, and might also name the acinema of the sublime. Although Lyotard provides examples for immobilization and the excess of mobility through special effects from the 1970 movie *Joe*—the cascading of superimposed sequential images presenting the murder of a hippie-girl's boyfriend by her father, and a freeze-frame of the girl, murdered, again, by her father—he cautions that these two arrhythmias, "while they may upset representational order, clouding for a few seconds the celluloid's necessary transparency (which is that order's condition) . . . do not fail to suit the narrative order."[61] In that film, the sterility of immobility and excess movement is reinscribed within the movement of narrative and capital. A movie also from 1970, like *Two-Lane Blacktop* (Monte Hellman), however, perhaps does otherwise. The film ends with a pyrotechnics of celluloid: in an excess of mobility—a high-speed drag race—the driver, the automobile, and the film itself all come to an end, immobilized forever in a pyrotechnical *jouissance*.[62]

Notes

1 Jean-François Lyotard, "Acinema," in *The Lyotard Reader*, trans. Paisley N. Livingston (Oxford: Blackwell, 1989). "Idée d'un film souverain," in *Misère de la philosophie* (Paris: Galilée, 2000).

2 Copies of these films are available for screening through *Cinédoc: Paris Films Coop*: www.cinedoc.org/EN/collection/fiche-auteur.asp?id=63.

3 Jean-François Lyotard, *Lessons on the Analytic of the Sublime*, trans. Elizabeth Rottenberg (Stanford: Stanford University Press, 1994), 70.

4 Immanuel Kant, *Kritik der Urteilskraft* 280/*Critique of Judgment*, trans. Werner S. Pluhar (Indianapolis: Hackett Publishing, 1987), 390.

5 In "Stelarc and the Chimera: Kant's Critique of Prosthetic Judgment," *Art Journal* 56.1 (Spring 1997), 46–51, Howard Caygill suggests that contemporary artist Stelarc's robotic prostheses help us understand the power of judgment as a technical prosthesis. Lyotard's "Acinema" could help us see Kant's technics of judgment in a new light just as well.

6 Lyotard, "Idée d'un film souverain," 217.

7 Ibid.

8 Kant, KUK 204/*Critique of Judgment*, 44, translation modified.

9 Lyotard, *Lessons*, 7, quoting Kant, "What is Orientation in Thinking?," in *Kant's Political Writings*, ed. H. S. Reiss (Cambridge: Cambridge University Press, 1970), 238.

10 Lyotard, *Lessons*, 13.

11 Ibid., 14.

12 Ibid., 16.

13 Ibid., 23.

14 Ibid.

15 Lyotard, *Lessons*, 12.

16 Caygill, "Prosthetic Judgment," 7.

17 Jean-François Lyotard, "Can Thought Go On Without A Body?," in *The Inhuman: Reflections on Time*, trans. Rachel Bowlby and Geoffrey Bennington (Stanford: Stanford University Press, 1992), this essay in particular trans. Bruce Boone and Lee Hildreth, 9: "what's finished or finite has to be perpetuated in our thought if it's to be thought as finished. Now this is true of limits belonging to thought. But after the

sun's death there won't be a thought to know that its death took place ... it will be too late to understand that your passionate, endless questioning always depends on a 'life of the mind' that will have been nothing else than a covert form of earthly life."

18 Ibid., 12.

19 Ibid.

20 Ibid., 13: "philosophy is possible only because the material ensemble called 'man' is endowed with very sophisticated software ... So the problem of the technological sciences can be stated as: how to provide this software with a hardware that is independent of the conditions of life on earth."

21 Ibid., 13.

22 Kant, KUK 277–8/*Critique of Judgment*, 139.

23 Ibid., 244/98, translation modified.

24 Lyotard, *Lessons*, 61: "pleasure is made a metaphor for the vital force ... The reader might be struck by this abrupt recourse to vitalism."

25 Kant, KUK 204/*Critique of Judgment*, 44.

26 Lyotard, *The Inhuman*, 13.

27 Kant, KUK 269/*Critique of Judgment*, 129, as quoted in Lyotard, *Lessons,* 188 and following that translation.

28 Lyotard, *Lessons,* 105, quoting Immanuel Kant, *Kritik der Reinen Vernunft*, B 218/*Critique of Pure Reason,* trans. Werner S. Pluhar (Indianapolis: Hackett, 1996), 247. The translation here follows that given in the *Lessons*.

29 Ibid. The embedded quote is from Kant, *KRV* A 131–2/*Critique of Pure Reason,* 204–5. The translation here follows that given in the *Lessons*.

30 Ibid., 106.

31 Ibid., 109.

32 Lyotard, "Idée d'un film souverain," 217.

33 Lyotard, *Lessons*, 144.

34 Lyotard, "Idée d'un Film Souverain," 217: the cinematic *Zusammennehmung* "assembles at once all past events ... without placing in succession, but by co-presenting them in a virtual simultaneity."

35 Lyotard, *Lessons*, 61, Kant, KUK 204/*Critique of Judgment* 204, translation following the *Lessons*.

36 Kant, KUK 278/*Critique of Judgment*, 139.

37 Mark Hansen, *Bodies in Code: Interfaces With Digital Media* (New York: Routledge, 2006).

38 Kant, KUK 278/*Critique of Judgment,* 139, translation modified.

39 Lyotard, *Lessons*, 76.

40 Lyotard, "Acinema," 356.

41 Jean-Michel Durafour, *Jean-François Lyotard: questions au cinéma* (Paris: Presses Universitaires de France, 2009), 23, translation mine.

42 Lyotard, *Lessons*, 76.

43 Durafour, *Questions au cinéma*, 100.

44 Ibid., 58.

45 Ibid., 60, quoting Lyotard, "The Unconscious as Mise-en-Scène" in *Performance and Postmodern Culture*, eds Michel Benamou and Charles Caramello (Milwaukee: University of Wisconsin-Milwaukee, 1977), 97, translation modified.

46 Ibid., 59.

47 Ibid.

48 Lyotard, "Acinema," 169.

49 Marie-Rose Logan, "Graphesis. . ." in *Yale French Studies* 52, *Graphesis: Perspectives in Literature and Philosophy* (1975), 4–15. In her introduction to this issue, Logan writes of the neologism *graphesis* that it "de-scribes the action of writing as it actualizes itself within the text independently of the notion of intentionality" (12).

50 Lyotard, "Acinema," 169.

51 Ibid., 170.

52 Ibid.

53 Ibid.

54 Ibid.

55 Ibid., 174.

56 Ibid., 170–1. One wonders if Lyotard's example of the *allumette* is an allusion to Yoko Ono's 1965 experimental film, *One* (Fluxus Films). The motion of striking, igniting, burning, and extinguishing the match are intensified through slow motion: www.youtube.com/watch?v=cTTtKsv_JD0.

57 Ibid., 171.

58 Ibid.

59 Ibid.

60 Ibid., 172.

61 Ibid., 174.

62 Just for the fun of it, to see what happens, for the pleasure of the movement itself, we might end with the final scene from *Two Lane Blacktop*: www.youtube.com/watch?v=0BVHFuQDFkk.

Section V

Affect in Postmodern Politics

12

A New Kind of Sublime

Lyotard's Affect-Phrase and the "*Begebenheit* of Our Time"

Peter Milne

It is possible to identify a certain tension in Lyotard between politics and what might loosely be called "aesthetics," a tension that can even be said to traverse the diversity of texts signed under this name. On the one hand, the aesthetic—including the work of art and the affect with which it will (potentially) come to be associated—is not to be reduced to politics. This is as much the case for the "figural" or "libidinal" Lyotard as it is for the Lyotard of *The Differend* or *Karel Appel*. Art, for example, or the "gesture" that it might be said to in some way perform,[1] is not to be subordinated to political ends and owes politics nothing, whether this is couched in the language of resistance to ideology or theory, or in terms of a "turning away" from narrative, discourse, or commentary. Nonetheless, this very language of resistance hints, on the other hand, at how the aesthetic is never without a certain import or even "lesson" for thinking, including political thinking. This becomes even more pronounced in the work on the sublime, that aesthetic (or perhaps, more properly, "anaesthetic") which introduces the affect into thinking on art.[2] The affect elicits thought, but thought must adjust itself to the affect, attempt to think what has not yet been thought. It is elicited, then, at the site of the differend, the possibility of which, at least for the Lyotard of the book of that name, is politics.[3]

One might suggest, then, that the affect comes to provide a link or perhaps a "passage" between the otherwise heterogeneous realms of aesthetics and politics. What I should like to do here is to examine whether and in what way this might be said to be the case, in the context of a specifically political invocation of that affect known as the sublime: Lyotard's reading of Kantian enthusiasm. But the question is double-edged. On the one hand, my interest is in what this discussion of enthusiasm, which Kant considers a mode of the sublime, might tell us about the possible "political" implications of this aesthetic, and of the affect more generally. But on the other, there remains the further problem of whether whatever conclusions we might draw would still hold in light of what he will come to say about the affect-phrase, and the project of "supplementation" of *The Differend* with which much of the work of the 1980s and 1990s can be associated. The two parts of this chapter reflect this double problem.

I.

Lyotard begins the little book on *Enthusiasm* by drawing an analogy between philosophy and what in this work is called "the political" (*le politique*).[4] This analogy holds, however, only if philosophy is understood not as doctrine but as "critical" in the Kantian sense. Doctrine is guided by the idea of a system. The doctrinal "phrase," to use the language of this text, is a phrase that is already legitimated; its claims to validity have already been judged. In this sense, it comes "after" critique. By contrast, it is precisely the claims to validity of any "systematic phrase" (cognitive, ethical, juridical, and so on) that the critical philosopher must judge.

This means that such a philosopher must judge without the comfort or guidance of the system's rules, which cannot be presupposed if the judgment is to be truly "critical." If Kant rather famously refers to critique as the work of a judge, then this judge cannot be a magistrate. The critical judge does not have recourse to an "established and irrefutable law," since such a law is precisely what has yet to be legitimated. Judgment here must proceed case by case. It is thus reflective (*reflektierend*) rather than determinative (*bestimmend*), to use the distinction from the third *Critique* that is so important to Lyotard's reading of Kant: it judges in the absence of any established rule or law, in the absence of any universal. This model comes from the Introduction to Kant's work, where judgment is described as that faculty (*Vermögen*) which mediates the "gulf" or "abyss" (*Kluft*) between the domain of the concept of nature (as the sensible) and that of the concept of freedom (as the supersensible).[5] As Lyotard puts it, judgment "appears in this text as the power of 'passages' [*Übergänge*] between the faculties."[6] It has no domain (*Gebiet*) of objects over which it legislates,[7] but it nonetheless "makes possible the transition" from the thinking that operates in accordance with the principle of one faculty to the thinking that operates in accordance with the principles of the other.[8] In the idiom of *Enthusiasm*, judgment is said to intervene "already and necessarily every time it is a question of saying that 'this is the case' to validate a phrase, hence for presenting an object allowing this validation."⁹

But let us note that if Kant places judgment between the faculties of understanding and reason, he also associates this power with "another ordering of our powers of representation," one that appears to be "of still greater importance" than that of the kinship between "the family of faculties of cognition."¹⁰ These are the "powers of the soul" (*Seelenvermögen* or *Fähigkeiten*). Judgment is here associated with the feeling of pleasure and displeasure, situated in its turn between the faculty of cognition (*Erkenntnisvermögen*) and that of desire (*Begehrungsvermögen*).¹¹ Lyotard will draw out this distinction in the *Lessons on the Analytic of the Sublime*: "'logically' reflection is called judgment, but 'psychologically' [in quotations, since the term is improper here from a technical point of view] it is *nothing but the feeling of pleasure and displeasure.*"¹² At least in this later work, then, reflection is in part affect—and nothing else but affect. It thus seems to have important links to what elsewhere Lyotard calls the affect-phrase. And it would appear that "aesthetics," as this is understood in Kant's third *Critique*, is the term that designates reflective judgment insofar as it is related to this pure feeling of pleasure and displeasure,¹³ a claim that is at the very least not explicit in *Enthusiasm*.

Kant, at any rate, is clear that the feeling he calls "enthusiasm" (*Enthusiasmus*) is a mode of the sublime.¹⁴ We recall the argument: though in no way an advocate of revolution, Kant sees the enthusiasm for events like the French Revolution by those spectators who are not directly involved to be a "sign" of the progress of the human race towards the better.¹⁵ Such a claim cannot be the object of a cognitive phrase, since cognition, in Kant, requires the intuition of objects corresponding to such claims, and one cannot have an intuition of progress. One can, of course, intuit historical phenomena—the problem lies in synthesizing these phenomena into a series that would make claims not only about their connection throughout the past and into the present, but on into the future. What is needed is a "passage" from, in this case, the empirical historical phenomena to the Idea of progress such that what Lyotard calls the "historico-political" object can be phrased—a responsibility that Lyotard, at any rate, gives to reflection. Given that the referent for such a phrase lies in "a part of human history that is yet to come," it will be necessary to change phrase families, seeking in human experience "not an intuitive datum (a *Gegebenes*) ... but what Kant calls a *Begebenheit*," an "occurrence" or an "event," one that would not simply validate a descriptive phrase but might indicate, *hinweisen* (though not prove, *beweisen*), that human beings are capable of being both cause and author of their own progress.¹⁶

Of course, one should be careful not to confuse the historical event with the event that is the *Begebenheit*. What is at issue in Kant's text is not the revolution itself, but the "mode of thinking" (*Denkungsart*) of the spectators, which publicly (*öffentlich*) betrays itself when it is a matter of great historical happenings, revealing humanity's common moral disposition.[17] The moral character that is here revealed not only allows us to hope for human progress, but indeed is already that progress insofar as it is a measure of human moral development toward a cosmopolitan Idea.

This feeling of *Enthusiasmus* is linked by Kant to aesthetics because such a "sign" reveals, as Lyotard puts it, that the "sense" of history "does not take place solely on the stage of history ... but also in the feelings of obscure and distant spectators ... who watch and hear" the deeds and misdeeds that take place there.[18] This is also why it is a modality of the sublime feeling. For what is sublime in Kant is not the object (or event) that occasions the feeling, but the Ideas of reason that are "provoked and called to mind" by the failure of imagination to present the given in sensible form.[19] The "destination" (*Bestimmung*) of the subject is revealed in this feeling, in its striving to "bring itself into accord with the Ideas of reason" in the face of this formlessness.[20] The "joy" (*joie*) of the sublime, at least in Lyotard's parlance, is in the revealing of this destination, "which is to supply a presentation for the unpresentable, and therefore, with regard to Ideas, to exceed everything that can be presented."[21] In enthusiasm, the failure to present the full force of the event makes the imagination feel the "elimination of the limits of sensibility," out of which a "merely negative" presentation of the infinite is possible, one "which nevertheless expands the soul."[22]

Enthusiasm nonetheless remains "an *Affekt*, a strong affection," blind and with no "satisfaction" (*Wohlgefallen*) of reason.[23] It has no ethical validity, attached as it is to a kind of motivating pathos.[24] Its "passage" is in fact only ever in the process of coming to pass, "a kind of agitation in place," in Lyotard's words.[25] Says Kant: the imagination "finds nothing beyond the sensible to which it can attach itself."[26] What validity it contains is only aesthetic; it is "an energetic sign,"[27] "a tension of the *Denkungsart* on the occasion of an object that is almost pure disorder."[28] This sign of history could only be found on the side of the audience, in part because the actors of this drama are caught up in the interests and passions of empirical events and thus cannot be "disinterested." But further, in the taking up of a position (*Teilnehmung*) by this disinterested spectatorship, the sublime feeling is "spread out onto every scene on every national stage, and potentially at least ... is immediately universal."[29] Enthusiasm may be an aesthetic feeling, then, but it nonetheless has a cosmopolitan potential, and the revolutionaries' action could extend beyond the national stage, to "the federation of states in a project for peace, which then concerns the whole of humanity."[30] In this sense, we might note that enthusiasm, as Kant describes it, remains part of a thoroughly modern project.

This universality is of course always "in abeyance,"[31] a reference to the *sensus communis* that is a component of all aesthetic reflection and that is governed by the logic of the "as-if" that dominates the third *Critique*. Nonetheless, it is this "Idea of community"[32] that allows for the aesthetic sensibility of the sublime to act as an index of humanity's moral progress, for in the case of sublime feeling (and as opposed to that of the beautiful) the communicability in question is not dependent on a community of sensibility or imagination, but one of practical reason, ethics: "The addressee must be made to understand here that the measurelessness of size and might in nature is as nothing compared to our moral destination, freedom."[33] The feeling of the sublime requires a susceptibility to Ideas that is in turn the result of culture; the "extreme sublime" that enthusiasm is indicates that that culture is very far advanced, since it signals a susceptibility to ideas of civil and even international peace.[34] Not just any "aesthetic phrase," then, can display humanity's constant progressing towards the future.[35]

I cannot here do justice to Kant's description of enthusiasm, nor to Lyotard's careful and detailed reading of it. But we can see that this aesthetic affect seems to entail a kind of "transference" into the socio-historical phrase. Clearly, Lyotard will not follow the moral-historical teleology that structures Kant's text, but he does suggest in *Enthusiasm* that "the Kantian political" is "as close as can be to what we understand today, crassly, as the political."[36] In part, this has to do with the need to judge reflectively—i.e., "critically"—in order to respect the heterogeneity of different phrase families.[37] Kant's critical judge provides an Ideal of sorts for thought in the wake of *The Differend*. But further, this appears, at least in this text, to remain importantly linked to the role that affect may play as a "sign of history." If there is a *Begebenheit* of our time, Lyotard associates this event with a very particular affect, "the feeling of a fissure in [the] great deliberative political core" inherited from modern (and indeed, Kantian) politics.[38] This *Begebenheit* thus has nothing to do with the enthusiasm with which Kant is concerned. It marks, rather, "what has been called postmodernity to designate our time,"[39] which Lyotard elsewhere associates with Habermas's techno-science and Heidegger's *Gestell*.[40] The feeling of this fissure is not enthusiasm, and if it is sublime, it would have to be "a new kind of sublime, one even more paradoxical than that of enthusiasm, in which not only the irremediable gap between an Idea and whatever presents itself in order to 'realize' it would be felt, but also the gap between various phrase families and their respective legitimate presentations."[41] Lyotard refers to this as a "highly cultivated communitarian sense" and its occasions have names like Auschwitz, Budapest 1956, Kolyma, and "1968." Judgment is "liberated" by each of these "abysses," at exactly the moment when it becomes necessary to "judge without criteria in order to feel them."[42] Lyotard even seems to suggest that this is the sign of a kind of "progress," "the beginning of the infinity of heterogeneous finalities."[43] For this *Begebenheit* is awoken not by the Idea of an end, "but by the Idea of several ends, or even by Ideas of heterogeneous ends."[44] It thus has obvious resonances with what might be called, "crassly," the "political" of our time. And, as affect, it appears to remain a kind of "common sense"—if the "postmodern condition," for instance, can be said to result from this type of "common sensibility." This latter, indeed, may be precisely the question.

II.

Such, at any rate, is the argument in this text written "in conformity with the spirit" of *The Differend*. But it is true that Lyotard felt the need to "supplement" the latter book in several texts that followed, not least the short text on the "affect-phrase."[45] The description of the affect here would appear to be slightly different from that of enthusiasm and the feeling of "fissure" that is said to be occasioned by the *Begebenheit* of our time. The affect-phrase is not articulated; it not only avoids linkages, but seems capable of nothing else than interrupting them; it does not give rise to a genre and cannot be argued.[46] It is thus what Lyotard in the *Lessons* would call "tautegorical": it "is at once an affective state (pleasure or pain) and the sign of this state."[47] Indeed, it is associated with aesthetic feeling and with Freudian affect, a sentiment whose time is only ever now, with no guarantee that it ever repeats itself, since it cannot be identified and localized in any chronology.[48] How to situate the *Denkungsart* of enthusiasm or the sentiment of a fissure in the deliberative political core *vis-à-vis* this silent affect-phrase? Does *Enthusiasm* also need "supplementing" in this respect? If the work on the affect-phrase can be seen as marking a "transition" in Lyotard from a philosophy of phrases to a thinking of affect, does the inability to phrase or link on to the affect undermine the "affinity" between the critical and the "politico-historical" that Lyotard invokes at the outset of *Enthusiasm*? Is it still possible to transition from the affect to a "sociohistorical phrase"? Indeed, can the affect still be "shared" or even "common," a *Begebenheit* of our time"?

These questions would be on a par with the suspicions of Jacques Rancière, who sees Lyotard's "late" recourse to the affect (and the sublime most specifically) as evidence that he has surrendered politics for a kind of immemorial and ethical "law of the Other." Rancière's criticisms have in part to do with what he takes to be a separation in Lyotard between aesthetics and politics, an ill-advised divide that Rancière sees himself as attempting to remedy.[49] It's still possible to see the "political" import of art or aesthetics more generally in earlier texts like the "Critical Function of the Work of Art," where Lyotard explicitly speaks of art's "lesson for politics."[50] But what might be "political" in the anaesthetics of the sublime? Lyotard suggests that the sublime is the most "modern" of aesthetics, but that it also contains the seeds of the dissolution of aesthetics itself.[51] We can see an explicitly political invocation of the sublime in *Enthusiasm*, but is it not also possible to see the sublime—and the affect more generally—as containing, in turn, the seeds of dissolution of the "political"?

I have addressed Rancière's criticisms of Lyotard elsewhere and I won't repeat those disagreements here.[52] But perhaps I might use the occasion this controversy affords to outline another possible reading of the shift to the affect in Lyotard's thinking. In a few brief but fascinating passages with which he begins a text from 1991 on the subject of "music and postmodernity," Lyotard re-situates the "postmodern," twelve years after the publication of *The Postmodern Condition*, in language that is much closer to that which characterizes the writings on affect.[53] He now describes the earlier work as an attempt to understand an event, "something that supervenes, that comes out of nowhere."[54] Like all events taken in this sense, this event was still nothing; it had no explanation and could not even be named. Those who were affected by it were not ready for it, could not place it in a system of signification or identify it. Nonetheless, for such an event to occur (*advenir*) "it must touch some 'surface' where it leaves its trace: a consciousness, an unconsciousness, individual or collective."[55] Perhaps it even had to invent the surface upon which to leave its "trace of strangeness" and thus, like all events, to await its signification only ever after, once it had already passed and even before it was clear *what* (*quid*) it was.

The event in question in *The Postmodern Condition* is one that "touched developed societies" at the end of the 1970s. Lyotard is clear that he thought of this event as "western," affecting that part of the human world that "'invents' the Idea of emancipation" and then tries to realize it, an attempt that itself "rests on the principle that history is the record of the progress of freedom in human space and time."[56] The name "grand narratives" was given to the various philosophies of history that have been guided by this principle, narratives that served to "legitimate, in the name of progress, the benefits and detriments [*bienfaits et méfaits*] that the West has bestowed upon itself and the world throughout the centuries."[57] That such narratives have, in Lyotard's view, ceased to be credible is very well known. But here, some years after both the event and the initial attempt to think it, this loss of faith in grand narratives is linked more clearly to what Lyotard calls "capitalist development" and to its techno-scientific methodology or logic. Capitalism appears to be its own grand narrative, and certainly the promise of emancipation (and more recently, the continual invocation of the exercise of a certain inviolable individual "freedom") is central to capitalist politico-economic discourse. But this promise is an illusion. Capitalist development has no necessary connection to the progress of freedom,[58] and therefore has only a superficial resemblance to the grand narratives of emancipation. Development is rather a question of fine-tuning systems in the name of better performance. It "operates without finality," good or bad, right or wrong, the only good it recognizes being "the improvement of performances" itself.[59] Human freedom is not, in fact, its goal—indeed, this freedom can easily and readily be compromised in the name of the smooth running of the system, which operates according to its own logic and refuses to recognize the legitimacy of what Lyotard would here call other "genres" of discourse.[60] Capitalist development, then, is not a project of emancipation, but a program in the service of ever-increasing performance. The "postmodern condition," in its turn, is the condition human beings find themselves in when they are caught in the process of capitalist development, a process which "simultaneously develops their powers and demands their enslavement."[61]

Transferred into the language of *Enthusiasm*, the *Begebenheit*, the event that "delivers itself" to the developed societies of the late 1970s under the name of "postmodernity," would appear to be affective. It leaves the trace of its arrival in the form of a feeling on some "surface" of the collective unconscious of the "West." But if we are to take the language of affect seriously, this feeling cannot yet be of anything specific, since it escapes signification. It comes in undue and improper form, as without-form—the very modality of the sublime, and of the affect as Lyotard comes to describe it. The feeling of a "fissure" in the core of deliberative politics, on the other hand, is perhaps more specific, an attempt to give form to this feeling. The affect-phrase does not present a phrase universe; it signals only one sense, as we have seen: pleasure and/or pain. It not only can but must await a kind of transcription[62] or even "transference"[63] into the discourse of *logos*, wait to be situated in the universe of an articulated phrase. And as we have also already seen, this cannot be a process of what Lyotard calls "linking" or "linking on" (enchaîner): discourse or logos can meet with the affect-phrase, the inarticulate voice that Lyotard, following Aristotle, also calls phōnē—but logos and phōnē do not link. The affect does not obey the law of logos; the inarticulate can only be "wronged" (tort, which would include the jurisprudential sense) by articulation.[64] Instead their meeting is characterized by that lack of a common rule of judgment that Lyotard calls a differend.[65]

But perhaps it is precisely such differends that are in play here. The occasions for the "highly cultivated communitarian sense" that is the Begebenheit of our time have names, let us recall, like Auschwitz, Budapest 1956, and Kolyma, although Lyotard will also speak of the "resistance" of the "multiplicity of worlds of names" and of the "insurmountable diversity of cultures" that challenge Eurocentric narratives of modernity.[66] Each opens an "abyss" in modernity's organizing narratives—in the Idea of human rights, for instance, or of universal human history. They thus "liberate judgment" from these narratives; but in so doing, they also create the need to be judged, without these narratives providing the rules by which to do so. We recall that this means the need to judge them "in order to feel them,"[67] although perhaps by the time of "The Affect-phrase" and the Lessons we might say that judging them in some sense is to feel them, or that judging them comes out of the feeling they produce—feelings not confined by any narrative, or perhaps better, the feeling of the opening of a "fissure" in the narratives or other frameworks that condition the experience of the world.

We return, then, to the realm of reflection, that form of critical judging that is analogous to the political. In the Lessons, Lyotard's understanding of reflection does seem to have been "supplemented": here it is described as having a tautegorical aspect, that is, one of pure feeling. But such a feeling must in turn be given expression in articulated phrases (phrases, perhaps, like "the feeling of a fissure in the deliberative political core"). If it is true that in the earlier book Lyotard still insists that "one cannot not link on" and that "to establish the rule, one must link on,"[68] he also ends that text by suggesting that "reflective responsibility" today might consist in "discerning, respecting, and making respected differends, in establishing the incommensurability of the transcendental exigencies proper to heterogeneous phrase families, and in finding other languages for what cannot be expressed within existing languages."[69] The differend between logos and phōnē appears even here, then, to be respected by the critical judge, who nonetheless must find an idiom to accommodate what as yet has no place in signification.

By the time of the Lessons, this kind of task is given to the second operation that Lyotard identifies in Kantian reflection: its "heuristic" function. In addition to being pure feeling or affect, that is, "tautegorical," reflection also functions as a kind of guiding operation, a "principle of subjective discrimination"[70] that allows thought to orient itself out of this feeling. Reflection, as Clemens-Carl Härle puts it, is thus at once and inseparably both an affective state and a noetic act.[71] Perhaps we could say that the need to find a "passage" from affect to language does not change in the later work, even if the feeling that must be given a place is now more explicitly conceived of as turning away from discourse or knowledge, as refusing this linking. The affect may be "untranslatable" and always "outside" of the articulated phrase, as Lyotard puts it elsewhere.[72] In this sense, it remains outside of "doctrine." But it continues to call for judgment, even in the absence of the rule required to do so. This is the Kantian reflective judgment, as we have seen, but now perhaps we would have to see it as reflection in its heuristic function, regulating "without a rule of regulation," discriminating and assembling by analogy.[73]

Strictly speaking, this would mean a move beyond the aesthetic, since the aesthetic judgment, at least according to the Lyotard of the *Lessons*, is reflective judgment in its "purest" form, stripped of all teleology and even of the heuristic function itself.[74] In this latter text Lyotard will therefore put politics aside. Nonetheless, the "little known" object of historico-political judgment remains a paradigm of the "anamnesic tone" of Kantian critical philosophy, of the *Critique*'s indebtedness to reflection in both its tautegorical and heuristic functions.[75] What's more, if the affect is to open itself to the "promise" of communicability, it would appear to be able to do so only through a heuristic.[76]

It is true that, taken as a "crisis" of space and time as the forms of givenness, the aesthetic judgment known as the sublime gives no hope of community— neither of the "faculties" nor of individuals. It thus has no cosmopolitan prospects. It is "a sudden blazing, and without future."[77] Indeed, the sublime signals "the withdrawal of a community of feeling" and thus questions the very foundations of the political community itself, at least insofar as this community is capable of progress.[78] The sublime is the occasion not only of a break of the harmonious relation between mind and world, but of a break also between the event and the "subject" that one would have to hesitate to say "undergoes" it.[79]

The sublime is thus associated with anxiety created by this loss of forms, an anxiety that produces several possible responses, including the attempt to neutralize such events through calculation (which Lyotard calls "techno-science"). This response would not be unrelated to the "modern" or nostalgic response to the anxiety of the "lack of reality of reality" in "What is the Postmodern?"[80] But this is not the only possible response to the sublime. One might instead resist nostalgia and melancholy and affirm the opening it announces, along with the attending need to question "reality" anew. The suspension of forms of the sublime opens a space for artistic experimentation and inquiry, but it also allows us to "wage war" on techno-science because it undermines the latter logic's tendency to totalize.[81] This would surely be in keeping with what Lyotard will come to say about the "inhuman" debt to which each mind is subject through the affect—and of the resistance that this first "inhuman" offers to that other inhuman, techno-scientific or capitalist development, "which takes away the hope of an alternative to the system."[82] For the Lyotard of *The Inhuman*, indeed, this resistance might just be politics "today."

Given that they are not addressed, the vocalizations of the *phōnē*, it's true, would not seem able to produce a community of addressees and addressors.[83] But there is the possibility of a kind of "communicability or transitivity of affects without expectation of a return."[84] Such a communicability would not exactly be "communication." But the voice must find a way to be heard. The affect is transitive: it shifts and travels; it can be "shared." It can even be "transmitted," but only through an Idea in the Kantian sense, that is, an Idea that exceeds what can be presented in sensibility.[85] If the "*Begebenheit* of our time" is in part an affect linked, however loosely or vaguely, with the feeling of a shift from something like the Kantian *sensus communis* to the loss of unity in multiplicity and diversity, this suggests that the community's foundations have come into question—and are open to question. What will make such a feeling "sublime"? Perhaps an Idea that attempts to be "adequate" to this loss or lack of due form, a way to think of political bodies (in multiple senses) in the plural, as precisely not "common."

The political, for the Lyotard of *Enthusiasm*, is no longer a question of political doctrine.[86] Rather, it must be "critical": reflective, discriminating, responsive to the singular or particular. And if reflection is at least in part "tautegorical," affective, it is also "heuristic," able to discern, guide, and orient while also leaving room for "hesitation."[87] The affect is the occasion for thought, but reflection is not only affective: it also discriminates among heterogeneous phrase families and allows for passages between them. What's more, these passages must still include the addressees and addressors of these phrases.[88] Such is the "communitarian sense" of the third *Critique*, both its necessity and its contingency.[89] While Lyotard will drop the teleology of progress to be found there, and will insist on the necessity, "today," of bearing patient witness to what he calls "differends," he nonetheless wishes to remain faithful, at least in *Enthusiasm*, to a certain Kantian "trace of freedom": the aptitude to propose (new) ends. This may mean going beyond what is properly "aesthetic" in the

Kantian analysis. But it would remain faithful, in turn, to Lyotard's insistence that thinking orients itself according to a feeling.

Notes

1   Jean-François Lyotard, *Karel Appel: A Gesture of Colour*, trans. Vlad Ionescu and Peter W. Milne (Leuven: Leuven University Press, 2009).

2   Jean-François Lyotard, *The Inhuman: Reflections on Time*, trans. Geoffrey Bennington and Rachel Bowlby (Stanford: Stanford University Press, 1991), 97.

3   Jean-François Lyotard, *The Differend: Phrases in Dispute*, trans. Georges Van Den Abbeele (Minneapolis: University of Minnesota Press, 1988), 138, §190.

4   Jean-François Lyotard, *Enthusiasm: The Kantian Critique of History*, trans. Georges Van Den Abbeele (Stanford: Stanford University Press, 2009), xvii. For a discussion of the distinction in French between politics (*la politique*) and the political (*le politique*), see Van Den Abbeele's "Translator's Preface," ix–x.

5   Immanuel Kant, *Critique of the Power of Judgment*, trans. Paul Guyer and Eric Matthews (Cambridge: Cambridge University Press, 2000), 63/5: 175–6. Hereafter cited as KUK. As with all references to Kant, I will quote first the page number of the translation followed by the standard German Academy pagination.

6   Lyotard, *Enthusiasm*, 12.

7   Kant, KUK, 64/5: 177.

8   Ibid., 63/5: 176.

9   Lyotard, *Enthusiasm*, 11.

10 Kant, KUK, 64/5: 177.

11 Ibid., 64–5/5: 177–8.

12 Jean-François Lyotard, *Lessons on the Analytic of the Sublime*, trans. Elizabeth Rottenberg (Stanford: Stanford University Press, 1994), 4, my italics.

13 Ibid., 9.

14 Kant, KUK, 154/5: 272.

15 Immanuel Kant, *The Conflict of the Faculties*, trans. Mary J. Gregor and Robert Anchor, in *Religion and Rational Theology*, eds Allen W. Wood and George di Giovanni (Cambridge: Cambridge University Press, 1996), 301–2/7: 85. Cf. *Enthusiasm*, 26 ff.

16 Lyotard, *Enthusiasm*, 26.

17 Kant, *Conflict*, 302/7: 85; see also *Enthusiasm*, 28.

18 Lyotard, *Enthusiasm*, 29.

19 Kant, KUK, 129/5: 245.

20 Lyotard, *Enthusiasm*, 29.

21 Ibid., 30.

22 Kant, KUK, 156/5: 274.

23 Lyotard, *Enthusiasm*, 31; see Kant, KUK, 154/5: 272.

24 Lyotard, *Enthusiasm*, 32.

25 Ibid.

26 Kant, KUK, 156/5: 274.

27 Lyotard, *Enthusiasm*, 32.

28 Ibid., 33.

29 Ibid., 34.

30 Ibid.

31 Ibid.

32 Ibid., 36.

33 Ibid., 37.

34 Ibid., 39; see KUK, § 83.

35 Lyotard, *Enthusiasm*, 39.

36 Ibid., 61.

37 "Now, if we inventory the phrase families put into play in deliberative political functioning, we cannot help but find again all the ones Kant isolates and mixes together in the historico-political writings." Ibid., 62.

38 Ibid., 63.

39 Ibid.

40 See, for instance, the interview "What to Paint?" and the essay, "Argumentation and Presentation: The Foundation Crisis," both of which can be found in *Rewriting Lyotard: Figuration, Presentation, Resistance, Cultural Politics* 9.2 (2013), 212–8 and 117–43 respectively.

41 Lyotard, *Enthusiasm*, 63.

42 Ibid.

43 Ibid., 63–4.

44 Ibid., 63.

45 Originally delivered as a lecture under the title "L'inarticulé ou le différend même" and later published as "La phrase-affect: d'un supplément au *Différend*." See Jean-François Lyotard, "The Affect-phrase (From a Supplement to *The Differend*)," trans. Keith Crome, in *The Lyotard Reader and Guide*, eds Keith Crome and James Williams (New York: Columbia University Press, 2006), 104–10.

46 Ibid., 105.

47 Ibid.

48 Ibid., 106.

49 See, for example, Jacques Rancière, *Aesthetics and its Discontents*, trans. S. Corcoran (Cambridge: Polity, 2009); and *The Politics of Aesthetics*, trans. G. Rockhill (New York: Continuum, 2004).

50 Jean-François Lyotard, "Notes on the Critical Function of the Work of Art," trans. Susan Hanson, in *Driftworks*, ed. Roger McKeon (New York: Semiotext(e), 1984),

69–83. I discuss this "political lesson" in an essay called "Lyotard's 'Critical' 'Aesthetics'," *Rereading Jean-François Lyotard: Essays on His Later Works*, eds Heidi Bickis and Rob Shields (Farnham, UK: Ashgate, 2013), 189–207.

51 Cf. Lyotard, *Lessons*, 54.

52 See Peter Milne, "Sensibility and the Law: On Rancière's Reading of Lyotard," *Symposium: Canadian Journal of Continental Philosophy* 15.2 (2011), 95–119.

53 Jean-François Lyotard, "The Inaudible: Music and Postmodernity," trans. D. Bennett, in *Miscellaneous Texts I: Aesthetics and Theory of Art* (Leuven: Leuven University Press, 2012), 200–23.

54 Ibid., 201.

55 Ibid.

56 Ibid.

57 Ibid., 202–3.

58 Ibid., 203.

59 Ibid.

60 To take a relatively recent example, one need only consider the plight of Bangladeshi textile workers, whose "freedom to earn" is continually invoked at the same time that they are subject to the worst working (and living) conditions. But examples of this are everywhere.

61 Lyotard, "The Inaudible," 203.

62 Lyotard, "The Affect-Phrase," 106.

63 Ibid., 109.

64 Ibid.

65 Ibid. For the definition of a differend, see Lyotard, *The Differend*, xi.

66 See Jean-François Lyotard, "Universal History and Cultural Differences," trans. David Macey, in *The Lyotard Reader*, ed. Andrew Benjamin (Oxford and Cambridge: Blackwell, 1989), 319.

67 Lyotard, *Enthusiasm*, 63.

68 Ibid., 65.

69 Ibid., 67, translation modified.

70 Lyotard, *Lessons*, 40.

71 Clemens-Carl Härle, "Tautégories. Lyotard lecteur de Kant," *Les transformateurs Lyotard*, ed. Corinne Enaudeau et al. (Paris: Sens & Tonka, 2008), 51.

72 Jean-François Lyotard, "Emma: Between Philosophy and Psychoanalysis," trans. Michael Sanders et al., in *Lyotard: Philosophy, Politics, and the Sublime*, ed. Hugh J. Silverman (New York and London: Routledge, 2002), 40.

73 Ibid., 28.

74 Lyotard, *Lessons*, 6.

75 Ibid., 33.

76 Ibid., 47–8.

77 Ibid., 55.

78 Lyotard, "Argumentation and Presentation," 136.

79 See *Lessons*, Chapter 5 and "Emma."

80 I slightly modify the translation of the title. See Jean-François Lyotard, "Answering the Question: What is Postmodernism," trans. Régis Durand, in *The Postmodern Condition: A Report on Knowledge* (Minneapolis: University of Minnesota Press, 1984), 79–81. I make a similar argument to the one that follows in my "Exceeding the Given: Rewriting Lyotard's Aesthetics," published as the Introduction to the volume of *Cultural Politics* cited above. See 112–13.

81 Lyotard, "What is Postmodernism," 82.

82 Lyotard, *The Inhuman*, 7.

83 Lyotard, "The Affect-phrase," 110.

84 Ibid.

85 Lyotard, "Argumentation and Presentation," 131.

86 Lyotard, *Enthusiasm*, xviii.

87 Lyotard, *Lessons*, 31.

88 Lyotard, *Enthusiasm*, 65.

89 Ibid.

13

Lyotard on Affect and Media

Or the Postmodern-Version 2.0 Explained by Orwell's *1984*

Kent Still

Affect "resists" thought, defying articulation. As for thought, especially what passes for philosophical thought, it "resists" affect: rejecting pathos as not worthy of study, or else treating it as an object of study like any other. Let's postulate, instead, that taking affect as the referent of philosophical discourse requires, at a minimum, testifying to that mutual resistance. Such is the task undertaken by Jean-François Lyotard's later works. Not merely describing the resistance between affect and thought, they *enact* it—throwing his earlier works into question, as if rendering an account of affect required questioning any pre-established conceptual apparatus. "The Affect-Phrase" is a case in point: its rewriting of *The Differend* in light of that mutual resistance, what Lyotard once called "*le différend même*" (the differend itself), having received much attention.[1]

Less attention, however, has been devoted to Lyotard's other discussion of the "*différend même.*" In "Examen oral" (Oral Exam),[2] an interview with Niels Brügger, Lyotard offered an especially provocative reformulation of the "*différend même,*" this time as a critical reassessment of *The Postmodern Condition*, one phrased in an Orwellian idiom, recasting "performativity" as Big Brother (figurehead of Orwell's dystopia), and "paralogy" in the guise of Winston Smith (*1984*'s ill-fated protagonist).[3] What follows is an elaboration of Lyotard's rewriting of Orwell's *1984* as a postmodern fable, emphasizing the intersection of techno-scientific development, political power and affect.

A brief user's guide to the postmodern 2.0

While its remarks about "incredulity towards metanarratives" have received more press,[4] *The Postmodern Condition* (let's call it the "1.0 version" of the "postmodern") offered competing—and apparently contradictory—characterizations of postmodernity:

1. "*Performativity*," for Lyotard, is a matter of *efficiency*, the optimization of a system's performance: minimization of input and maximization of output.[5]
2. "*Paralogy*" consists in *dissensus*,[6] designating, ambiguously, both the conflicts between incommensurable practices, and the process of questioning the rules of those practices, a questioning that may give rise to emergent practices, equally incommensurate to their predecessors.[7]

Performativity and paralogy, then, seem incompatible. "Postmodernity" is the intersection of incommensurable practices; the "performativity criterion," however, holds them all to a single standard of measure: optimal efficiency. Yet, despite that tension, *The Postmodern Condition* linked the two, arguing that paralogy increases performativity.

Alas, 1.0 versions tend to be "buggy"—and, if I'm not mistaken, it was that quasi-dialectical intertwining of paralogy and performativity that "bugged" Lyotard the most. All of Lyotard's subsequent works will have contested its subordination of paralogy to performativity.[8] Works such as *The Postmodern Explained to Children* and *Postmodern Fables* were not "sequels," but "reboots"—rewritings, questioning the earlier version's rules, deleting some, reformulating others. Let's call it "the *postmodern-version 2.0*," the serial rewriting of *The Postmodern Condition* throughout Lyotard's subsequent works.

The Differend, for instance, introduced key terms (e.g., "differend," "litigation," and "wrong") that provide a concise criticism of *The Postmodern Condition*'s argument:

> As distinguished from a litigation, a differend would be a case of conflict, between (at least) two parties, that cannot be equitably resolved for lack of a rule of judgment applicable to both arguments. One side's legitimacy does not imply the other's lack of legitimacy. However, applying a single rule of judgment to both in order to settle their differend as though it were merely a litigation would wrong (at least) one of them (and both of them if neither side admits this rule). . . . A wrong results from the fact that the rules of the genre of discourse by which one judges are not those of the judged genre or genres of discourse.[9]

The Postmodern Condition "litigated" the "differend" between performativity and paralogy, because its case for paralogy—that it be supported, since it increases performativity—was formulated in the discourse of performativity. The problem, then, is *not* that *The Postmodern Condition* was *wrong* (in the sense of being inaccurate).[10] Paralogy does increase performativity. The problem is that it subordinated paralogy to performativity, thereby *wronging* any use of reason other than instrumental rationality.

But, be it its "bug" or its most commercially viable "feature," the 1.0 thesis that dissensus increases efficiency is not simply deleted in the 2.0 version. It is rewritten: acknowledging that paralogy and performativity may—on occasion—overlap and yield emancipatory effects, but contesting any false equivalence between the two. In sum, the 2.0 version supplements that thesis with the task of bearing witness to how dissensus, even when furthering efficiency, remains subordinated to the performativity criterion.

Consider the repeal of the "Don't Ask, Don't Tell" policy (the US military's ban on homosexuality). While occasioning edifying rhetoric, taking the repeal of that discriminatory policy as the result of considerations of "justice" requires criminal levels of naïveté. Its emancipatory effects notwithstanding, it was clearly undertaken for maximal efficiency—and an efficient military is not equivalent to justice. Thus, even when the aspirations of the partisans of justice are realized, efficiency trumps justice. No doubt, such litigation is preferable to a discriminatory and inefficient policy; however, it obscures a differend, evidenced by other discriminatory practices, no less unjust, but not yet recognized as inefficient. Emancipation arrives hand in hand with an even greater emphasis on efficiency, occluding differends for the sake of *development*.

"Development," in other words, is the 2.0 version of performativity, a term chosen to prohibit any confusion with the "progress" that Modernity promised techno-scientific advancements would deliver. Instead, techno-scientific complexification increases disparities between "developed" and "less developed" nations—and between classes within nations. As Lyotard explained, "[h]umanity is divided into two parts. One faces the challenge of complexity, the other that ancient and terrible challenge of its own survival. This is perhaps the most important aspect of the failure of the modern project—a project, need I remind you, once applied in principle to the whole of humanity."[11] Development asserts itself as an end in itself, human emancipation being an occasional means to that end. Hence it is "no longer possible to call development progress."[12]

As for "paralogy," it takes on multiple reformulations, which are not synonymous, intensifying instead its ambiguity in *The Postmodern Condition*: 1) the *static* analysis of conflicts between established language games, and 2) the *dynamic* process of questioning the rules of existing language games, adopting new rules, giving rise to emergent language games. In *The Differend*, the former are differends between genres of discourse, the latter *performed* by its definitions of "*philosophy*" (tasked with questioning the rules of its discourse)[13] and "*politics*" (not one discourse amongst others, but the intersection of conflicting discourses).[14] After *The Differend*, more reformulations follow—"*rewriting*,"[15] "*anamnesis*,"[16] and "*reflexive writing*"[17]—which not only describe but *enact* that process: "The Affect-Phrase" and "Emma" attesting to *The Differend*'s exclusion of psychoanalysis, and *What To Paint?* to its exclusion of the "figural."[18]

Lyotard's rewriting of *1984* provides perhaps the most effective introduction to the postmodern-version 2.0, since it brings together those multiple rewritings of paralogy, situating them within the political problematic concerning performativity. Consider "Examen oral," which begins with a discussion of "The Affect Phrase," but concludes with a strikingly different and decidedly strident reformulation of the "differend itself"—performativity is recast as "the inhuman of Big Brother, of development,"[19] and paralogy as "the resistance of Winston against Big Brother," which "consisted precisely in taking refuge in a corner of his cell and writing, doing his anamnesis."[20] Admittedly, that rewriting is as problematic as it is provocative. Though Big Brother remains a resonant reference in discussions of the "War on Terror," cyber-surveillance and torture, Winston Smith is largely forgotten—no doubt, because his political resistance to Big Brother is ineffective. Some may rush, then, to take Lyotard's citation of Winston's journal as a model of resistance as a confession, a guilty plea to the accusation that postmodernism abandons hope of changing the world, a de facto acceptance of the status quo. Yet, *contra* such criticisms, Lyotard's turn to pathos is not a retreat from the *polis*, providing instead important insights into political power's use of media to mobilize affect.[21]

Winston's journal and anamnesis: paralogy 2.0

Winston's journal is an unlikely model of paralogy. Granted, *1984* initially presents Winston as its hero, the Cartesian model of modern man, secluding himself in a makeshift study, questioning what he has been taught, writing daily meditations—at least, until one reads what Winston actually inscribes in a "small but childish handwriting," eventually "shedding first its capital letters and finally even its full stops."[22] Winston, then, is revealed not as a figure of political resistance, but psychoanalytical resistance, not recognizing that his own thought is already programmed:

> Last night to the flicks. All war films. One very good one of a ship full of refugees being bombed somewhere in the Mediterranean. Audience much amused by shots of a great huge fat man trying to swim away with a helicopter after him. first you saw him wallowing along in the water like a porpoise, then you saw him through the helicopters gunsights, then he was full of holes and the sea round him turned pink and he sank as suddenly as though the holes had let in the water. Audience shouting with laughter.[23]

The apparent Cartesian beginning is, instead, a parody, a damning reminder that no *epoché* or reduction of one's operative beliefs is ever complete.

What else would one expect from Orwell (*né* Eric Blair)? His novels elaborate his attempt to free himself from his own cultural upbringing in intensely emotional terms.[24] And, with Winston's journal, he undertook the uncomfortable task of revealing the disavowed prejudices lurking within one's own culture, hence also one's own psyche:

> then you saw a lifeboat full of children with a helicopter hovering over it. there was a middleaged woman might have been a jewess sitting up in the bow with a little boy about three years old in her arms. little boy screaming with fright and hiding his head between her breasts as if he was trying to burrow right into her and the woman putting her arms around him and comforting him although she was blue with fright herself. all the time covering him up as much as possible as if she thought her arms could keep the bullets off him. then the helicopter planted a 20 kilo bomb in among them terrific flash and the boat went all to matchwood.[25]

This passage dramatizes Orwell's *dictum*: "Autobiography is only to be trusted when it reveals something disgraceful. A man who gives a good account of himself is probably lying, since any life when viewed from the inside is simply a series of defeats. However, even the most flagrantly dishonest book ... can without intending it give a true picture of its author."[26] For Orwell, celebrating Nazism's defeat and criticizing Stalinism was not sufficient; the post-World War II West had to recognize its own fascistic tendencies. In Winston's journal, Orwell attempted to reveal them, not as explicit theses, but culturally sedimented assumptions.

Case in point—Winston does not view the film as a fictional spectacle: "*then there was a wonderful shot of a childs arm going up up up right up into the air a helicopter with a camera in its nose must have followed it up.*"[27] Here is none of what Husserl, a century ago, called the "neutrality modification"—exemplified by consciousness of depicted scenes, a mode of intentionality not positing the existence of its intentional object.[28] New millennial readers may greet Winston's credulousness with incredulity; however, rejecting such credulity as unbelievable would repeat the repression that greeted *1984*'s publication, by ignoring its attention to the post-World War II West's fascistic tendencies, reading it solely as an attack on Stalinism. Fictions can—and do—have real effects.[29] Just ask Saddam Hussein, whom nearly seventy percent of Americans, in a 2003 poll, believed—erroneously—to have been involved in the 9/11 attacks.[30]

Unlike his protagonist, Orwell was an incisive critic of culture and media, as evidenced by the passage beginning with the cut in visual perspective, and continuing to the end of the entry. It functions as a *mise-en-scène*, a zoom-out, extending beyond the screen, bringing the theater into view, and revealing the mechanism responsible:

> *and there was a lot of applause from the party seats but a woman down in the prole part of the house started kicking up a fuss and shouting they didnt oughter of showed it not in front of the kids they didnt it aint right not in front of the kids it aint until the police turned her turned her out I dont suppose anything happened to her nobody cares what the proles say typical prole reaction they never* –[31]

Unlike Michael Snow's *The Central Region*,[32] the mechanism here is not simply technological, but cultural and psychoanalytical: Winston, rebellious intentions notwithstanding, identifies with the Party/film's perspective, consenting to the silencing of dissent. Though famous for its warning that "BIG BROTHER IS WATCHING YOU," *1984* reveals that Winston already views the world through the eyes of Big Brother—his thought shaped by the maintenance of political power via media's mobilization of affect.

Claude Lefort emphasized this aspect of *1984* in his important essay on Orwell, "The Interposed Body."[33] For both Lefort and Lyotard, *1984* is not a theoretical critique of totalitarianism, but a literary work endeavoring "to make it felt."[34] Via Winston's journal, "the world of consummate bureaucracy is delivered to Orwell's reader burdened by mundane worries, reduced to the frame of a subjective life that will never take in the totality, infiltrated by daydreams, dreams, and phantasms, in other words, by the most singular formations of the unconscious."[35] The reference here to "the unconscious" is pivotal, for *1984* is as much about psychoanalytical resistance as political resistance.

Discourse, Figure contested Lacan's thesis that the unconscious is structured like a language,[36] demonstrating that the unconscious is heterogeneous: discursive and figural, signifying and non-signifying. "Gloss on Resistance" (one of *Discourse, Figure*'s earliest reboots) defines "phantasm" as "the idiom that speaks itself in the idiom I speak. It speaks more softly than I do. It wants to say something that I do not want to say, and something that I do not say."[37] Between what I want to say and what—despite my intentions—nevertheless speaks itself in what I say (even if that "speaking" consists merely of lapses and unacknowledged biases), there is a differend, not between genres of discourse, but between discourse and what *Discourse, Figure* called the "figure-matrix," a differend manifested in Winston's journal, which he only discovers by writing.

In Winston's first entry, the image of the anonymous woman in the lifeboat, protecting a young boy, was not authorized importance. Belatedly, that figure reappears in a dream: this time as Winston's mother, holding his younger sister, in "a sinking ship,"[38] with Winston, as in the film's perspective, looking down from above. Though he had not earlier (watching the staging of killings in the name of his nation),[39] Winston now feels guilt: "they were down there *because* he was up here."[40] But it is only in a later dream that Winston connects the two: "The dream had been comprehended by—indeed, in some sense it had consisted in—a gesture of the arm made by his mother, and made again by the Jewish woman he had seen on the news film, trying to shelter the small boy from the bullets."[41] That second dream reawakens the repressed memory of the last time he saw his mother, reassuringly holding his sister, a memory he "deliberately pushed out of his consciousness over many years."[42] Winston's identification with that film's first-person shooter perspective results, then, not merely from a visual perspective, but a two-fold resistance, rejecting responsibility for his complicity as a citizen, and abandoning his family—a resistance "blocking together" the political and the psychoanalytical, *koinē* and *idiom*, to which we will return.[43]

Through his reflective, free-floating writing not subordinated to a particular end, Winston practices "*anamnesis*." Originally a Greek term, rendered by Plato's English translators as "recollection," Lyotard used it instead to characterize Freud's account of "*working through*" (*durcharbeiten*). For both Freud and Lyotard, what must be worked through is precisely *resistance*: operating anonymously, unbeknownst, coming to one's attention only through the very process of working through it. As Freud puts it, "one must allow the patient time to become more conversant with this resistance, with which he has now become acquainted, to *work through* it, to overcome it, by continuing, in defiance of it, the analytic work according to the fundamental rule of analysis."[44] But, paradoxically, the "fundamental rule of analysis" demands *free association*: one learns to follow that rule by *failing* to do so, thereby becoming acquainted with one's resistance to breaking the tacit rules governing one's behavior, aware of the pre-given concepts one habitually applies to events, and one's own self-censoring. In that regard, Winston's journal is indeed *exemplary*, dramatizing his failure to confront his psychoanalytical resistance.

To be fair, though Winston at first unknowingly sees the world through Big Brother's eyes, unaware of how he is governed by cultural rules operating in tandem with his own psychoanalytical resistance, his subsequent entries begin to elaborate the initial stages of an anamnesis. Winston's journal, perhaps, might be regarded as paralogical—unsuccessful to be sure, but still dramatizing the labor of working through resistance. Granted, the dynamics of personal analysis differs from *The Postmodern Condition*'s account of the invention of paralogic practices; they are, however, analogous, because both work through resistance.[45] Artistic experimentation, for instance, involves a paralogic questioning: "One after another, the presuppositions implied by the exercise of the craft are subjected to trial and contestation: local color, linear perspective, the rendering of color values, the frame, ... the medium, ... place of exhibition, and many others ... are plastically questioned by the various avant-gardes."[46] Artworks, then, are not merely a symptom of the artist's unconscious, but the result of an anamnesis of the presuppositions of a particular medium and artistic tradition: "What is important to Van Gogh when he applies paint to the canvas is to work the past of painting," to work through "a tradition which is given," in order "to say something else."[47] As Lyotard phrased it:

> Rembrandt, Vermeer, Van Gogh, etc., they are all able to say something that was not known and which had never been marked. So, a work of anamnesis, but one which works on the matter itself. It is the same thing for a writer: his or her relation to language is an anamnesis of language in that language can always say more than what it actually says.[48]

Here one works through resistance, posed not by a patient's repression, but culturally sedimented practices: "The adversary and accomplice of writing, its Big Brother ... is language: by this I mean not only the mother tongue but the whole inheritance of words, phrases, and works that we call literary culture. One writes against language, but necessarily with it. To say what it already knows how to say is not writing."[49] Artists and writers work through the resistance their own education poses, the practices of beloved past masters, their Big Brothers, which must be worked through in order to say something that has not been said before.

Ever attentive to heterogeneity, Lyotard insisted that psychoanalysis is only analogous to artistic anamnesis. The "unconscious" of artistic mediums and traditions consists primarily of cultural practices, whereas Winston must work through his own secondary repression (his last encounter with his family—the source of his musophobia, functioning as a screen memory), and primal repression (since he was unprepared for his childhood traumas). Still, the analogy is stronger than Lyotard explicitly acknowledged, since Winston's own resistance works in symbiosis with culturally sedimented practices. Neither merely psychoanalytic nor artistic, that anamnesis is a matter of politics.

The two minutes hate: or the affect-phrase 2.0

Orwell's "Two Minutes Hate" depicts televised propaganda mobilizing public affect, appealing to nationalism and xenophobia (hence also racist and ethnic stereotypes), stirring fear and loathing directed at the Party's enemies, and love and gratitude for Big Brother. No need to detail its relevance for contemporary political campaigns or news coverage of the so-called "War on Terror." Let us consider, instead, whether Orwell's account is at odds with Lyotard's insistence upon the *non-referentiality* of affect.

"The affect-phrase is at once an affective state (pleasure or pain) and the sign of this state."[50] The referentiality characteristic of articulated phrases (a sense referring to a referent) is missing here, since the affect-phrase does not refer to anything else (or, if there is referentiality, it never fails, since the affect-phrase is at once both sign and referent). This is not to deny that articulated phrases can take affect as their referent. Lovers, writers, and psychoanalytic analysands, for instance, can go on and on about their feelings. Lyotard articulated the dynamic of how articulated phrases can nevertheless take affect as their referent, and how they can even endow it with a referent. In such a "transcription" of affect, the affect may be determined in various ways: e.g., as a sentiment causally produced by a particular referent, or intentionally directed at a particular addressee, etc.[51] As Claire Nouvet has made clear, Lyotard designated such determinations "sentimental meaning," thereby distinguishing them from affect in its inarticulate and indeterminate state.[52]

The latter, however, was Lyotard's primary interest, hence his attention to the Kantian sublime and Freud's "unconscious affect." But Lyotard's emphasis differs from other philosophical approaches. For instance, phenomenology, which describes affect as an act of intentional directedness, may seem more equipped to explain the Two Minutes Hate's mobilization of affect toward a determinate target, and, for that matter, Winston's resistance to that manipulation, which also consists in redirection (transference): "It was even possible, at moments, to switch one's hatred this way or that by a voluntary act."[53] The question, then, is: does Lyotard's emphasis on the non-referentiality of affect render him incapable of accounting for propaganda's mobilization of affect?

The answer is that, if it is possible to mobilize affect and—further still— transfer it toward a target of one's choosing, it is precisely because that affect is not related to any particular target in the first place. That transference is, instead, the result of the construction of sentimental meanings that occlude affect's inherent indeterminacy. Such, indeed, is the lesson of Orwell's account of the Two Minutes Hate: "the rage that one felt was an abstract, undirected emotion," which is why it "could be switched from one subject to another like a blowtorch."[54]

Here "abstract" means "indeterminate"—unrelated to specific referents. Beware of interpretations rarifying that affect, rendering it ethereal. The affect driving Emma out of the store, resulting in her phobia of all stores, may be indeterminate; it does, however, disrupt her life, driving her to Dr. Freud's couch. And the indeterminate affect permeating the atmosphere after 9/11, like an omnipresent cloud, its redirection toward a determinate—albeit unrelated— target, in the lead-up to the invasion of Iraq, had all too tangible consequences. Far from ethereal, that "abstract" affect—I suggest—is what Lyotard called "the extreme real."[55]

That indeterminate affect—more precisely, its mobilization and its transference to an unrelated referent—is also the motor driving much of *1984*'s plot. It explains the dynamic of Winston's resistance to the Two Minutes Hate: "Winston's hatred was not turned against Goldstein [the Party's nominal enemy] at all, but, on the contrary, Big Brother."[56] Yet, while no longer accepting the perspective depicted in mediatized propaganda, Winston merely repeats the same tactic. And that repetition—attesting to a lack of anamnesis—exemplifies his character flaws: "Winston succeeded in transferring his hatred from the face on the screen to the dark haired girl behind him."[57] What's more, the details of Winston's subsequent phantasy about raping and murdering Julia (the dark haired girl behind him during the Two Minutes Hate)—i.e., shooting her "full of arrows like Saint Sebastian"[58]—should be lost on Winston, given the Party's eradication of such cultural allusions. Whether or not such details provide evidence of Orwell's misogyny, Winston's conflicted feelings for Julia—and Katherine, his estranged wife (the subject of another murder phantasy)—are (also) instances of *1984*'s central motif: the transformation of free floating anxiety into extreme feelings directed at unrelated targets, love and hate. The Two Minutes Hate, for instance, directs hate at the Party's enemies, and love at

Big Brother. Even Winston's torture serves dual ends: betraying Julia, and declaring allegiance to Big Brother. Accordingly, *1984*'s last line—"He loved Big Brother"—is not surprising; it follows the dynamic operative above: mobilizing an indeterminate affect, channeling it to determinate—but conflicting— extremes, transferring those sentimental meanings toward capricious targets.

Here political propaganda works in tandem with the darkest reaches of Winston's psyche, his figure-matrix: "As Lefort points out in elaborating this zone where the private and the public overlap, Orwell's narrative reveals that the exercise of domination is only total when it enters into symbiosis with the singular passions of those that it oppresses."[59] And it is in this highly qualified sense—i.e., that political power is only *total* when it can put affect to work for its own ends—that Lyotard described (albeit hesitatingly) performative hegemony as totalitarian.

Big Brother and development: performativity 2.0

Recasting performativity as Big Brother may be the most troubling aspect of Lyotard's rewriting of Orwell's *1984*, seemingly at odds with my user's guide to the postmodern 2.0—specifically, its claim that performativity has emancipatory effects, albeit localized, and always for the sake of greater efficiency. And that characterization of performativity as seeking a *total* mobilization certainly troubled Lyotard, whose frequent hesitation on this issue is summarized in what follows.

Obviously, it is absurd to characterize what Lyotard called the System (a term inherited from the Habermas-Luhman debate, though retaining, for Lyotard, a distinctly '68 accent) as "totalitarian"—at least as this term is used to describe Stalinism, etc. Even in "Examen oral," Lyotard noted that, despite attesting to the post-World War II West's fascistic tendencies, *1984* was largely "an extrapolation of Stalinism," hence somewhat "naïve"—at least, "for us today," though "not at all naïve for that time."[60] This is not to deny that innumerable pretenders to the throne of Stalinist strongman remain, infesting the zones running an outdated version of the System. Nor is it to deny that, much as Winston repeated the tactics of the Two Minutes Hate, even so-called "developed nations" have proven themselves willing to resort to the Stalinist playbook, employing torture and electronic surveillance. It is to insist that, despite such shameful exceptions, the System does have emancipatory effects, because emancipatory movements put pressure on it to abandon culturally sedimented practices that are no longer efficient, favoring instead increasingly complex and more efficient practices. Accordingly, Lyotard conceded, "the current system should not be represented as it was fifty years ago, as an overwhelming totalitarianism reminiscent of Orwell's Big Brother: it is far more subtle and complex."[61]

Those differences, however, did not prevent Lyotard, in "Examen oral," from insisting, "we are in a certain fashion in a totalitarian society, in the sense that it claims from us indeed the maximum expenditure of energy in order to make complexification work."[62] Granted, later texts seem to retract that claim. But, for each retraction, there is a corresponding insistence that, as in Orwell's depiction of a totalitarian dystopia, the System is driven to put everything—affect even—to work. For example, though "The Intimacy of Terror," one of Lyotard's *Postmodern Fables*, conceded, "it's not that the system is totalitarian,"[63] it also noted:

> In 1920, a little after the defeat of the German Empire, Ernst Jünger evaluated the Allied success in these cynically thermodynamic terms: a community of citizens who believe themselves free is better suited for a "total mobilization" than the hierarchical social body of Wilhelm II's subjects. This diagnostic was verified by the outcome of the Second World War and by that of the Cold War.[64]

In sum, Lyotard remained committed to the thesis that there is an extremely qualified sense in which the System may be characterized as "totalitarian," insofar as it seeks to mobilize every source of energy—including affect—in order to optimize its performance.

That notion of "total mobilization" was central to Lyotard's account of what he called the "metaphysics of forces":

> (W)hat Habermas calls *techno-science*, what I myself have attempted, in the name of provocation, to call the *postmodern*, is the realization of metaphysics in everyday life. Metaphysics is a general physics, where one thinks everything in terms of the harnessing of energy, of total mobilization, of the setting-to-work of energies, be they physical, cosmological, human . . .[65]

"True metaphysics," according to that argument, "has never been a metaphysics of the subject (we have been quite mistaken in this regard), but a metaphysics of forces."[66] Yet, though avoiding the terminology of the metaphysics of forces when elaborating paralogy and affect (resisting Freud's attempt, in the *Project*, to describe affect in thermodynamic terms, treating affect instead as a "phrase," while nevertheless emphasizing its difference from articulated phrases), when discussing the System, Lyotard himself employed such "cynically" thermodynamic terminology, differentiating totalitarianism—characterized (in thermodynamic terms) as a "closed" (relatively isolated) system—from the contemporary System, which is more efficient, because it is "open."

That distinction is exemplified by the fate of dissensus—regarded, for millennia, as a threat to political order—in each. Totalitarianism tried to eradicate it; the System uses it to optimize its performance:

> The System's real mode of functioning henceforth entails programs that are not just directed toward optimizing what exists but also are venture programs, research efforts just "to see," which generate more complexity and make room for more "flexible" institutions.... The task of criticism is precisely to pinpoint and denounce every failure of the System, and critiques of whatever nature they may be are demanded by the System in order to carry out this charge more efficiently.[67]

Criticisms of the system's failure are central to the system's functioning, because they "open" it to new practices, increasing its efficiency. Accordingly, Lyotard emphasized that paralogic discourses are, to relative degrees, exempted from immediate relation to the performativity criterion, on the grounds that they may eventually contribute to greater efficiency (the extent to which this remains the case in the age of "austerity" is—I would add—an important question). One condition, however, must be fulfilled: paralogy enhances performativity as long as differends are treated as litigations. This treatment ensures that criticism does not lead to "revolutions," only to "revisions" of the system.

1984 dramatizes such reincorporation of dissensus: "what Orwell's text says is that it is precisely by using the notes of the diary of this poor Winston that he will be vanquished."[68] Here, Lyotard refers to a pivotal plot point: the Thought Police provided Winston with his journal, and will later utilize it during his interrogation.

It may be tempting to interpret that plot point as a parable about the popular reception of *The Postmodern Condition*, which silenced its alarms about performative hegemony, generating the misguided meme of Lyotard as championing all things postmodern. That interpretation is made more tempting still by *The Postmodern Condition*'s cryptic reference to *1984*, which quoted O'Brien (a member of the Thought Police, characterized by Lyotard as "the bureaucrat"—a functionary of the System): "We are not content with negative obedience, not even with the most abject submission. When finally you do surrender to us, it must be of your own free will."[69] It is as if incredulity toward the Enlightenment, Marxism, etc. is not yet abject enough: the System, instead, requires redressing dissensus in the guise of belief in—and freely given consent to—performativity as the primary criterion of societal self-regulation.

Such an interpretation, however, occludes the fact that, as early as *The Postmodern Condition*, what interested Lyotard in Orwell's *1984* was the suggestion that political power must control affect, as if any truly efficient system had to mobilize even that immeasurable—hence least breachable—source of resistance (in all senses): affect.

In media res: the differend itself-version 2.0

Whereas "The Affect-Phrase" concerned the conflict between affect and discourse, "the differend itself-version 2.0" emphasized the conflict between technological development and affect. Both, admittedly, lead to criticisms of Lyotard for setting up un-deconstructed oppositions.[70] Allow me to conclude by contesting that criticism.

Consider, for instance, the conflict between performativity and paralogy: while they do indeed follow different rules and have divergent stakes, it is also true that, in the cold electric light of the megalopolis, they are constantly comingled, blocked together. If it is imperative to distinguish them, it is precisely because the System blurs them, blocking them together in such a way that paralogy is occluded, even as it is exploited.

Lyotard's rewriting of Orwell's *1984*, however, also dramatizes the conflict between what *The Inhuman* called the "inhuman" of development and the "inhuman" of affect (characterized as "inhuman" due to its resistance to articulated discourse, long taken as humanity's defining characteristic).[71] That conflict seems more extreme than that between performativity and paralogy, a suspicion seemingly confirmed by Lyotard's claim that:

> there is something within that system that it cannot, in principle *deal with* [traiter]. Something that a system must by virtue of its nature, overlook. And if history ... is not simply a tale of development, the result of an automatic process of selection by trial and error, this is because "something intractable" is hidden and remains lodged at the secret heart of everything that fits into the system, something that cannot fail to make things happen in it [*d'y faire événement*].[72]

Affect seems to be that intractable remainder, exceeding the System's control, while nevertheless making "things happen" within it.

Here, however, it is important to note that Lyotard identified multiple sources of resistance to the System: "the Thing" and "the Law" (or "the Voice"). The Thing designates affect and its resistance of all kinds (political, psychoanalytical, etc.); the Voice designates the ethical injunction: "Be just!"[73] And, as attested by Winston's resistance to the Two Minutes Hate's mobilization of affect, not every affective resistance to the System is just.

In addition, I would emphasize—perhaps going beyond what Lyotard explicitly said—that, if the "inhuman" of development must be dissociated from the "inhuman" of affect,[74] it is because they are blocked together. Like an old couple, they resist each other, but can also be complicit with each other. Orwell's *1984* demonstrates that affect can indeed be made complicit with the demands of performativity: Winston's psychoanalytic resistance working in symbiosis with Big Brother's mobilization of affect. Indeed, what makes Winston's journal so important is the way it stages that the "two inhumans" are blocked together with the political practices of what passes for "humanity."

Consider Lyotard's later formulation of the postmodern transformation of politics: "By post-modern, I intend the immediate effects on everyday life and politics today of technological or scientific development, obliging humanity to adapt to all the instruments and 'prostheses.' Politics itself becomes the art of making development bearable to humanity, because at times development is anything but bearable."[75] If development is at times unbearable, it is *not* because technology is totalitarian. Granted, Winston's writing facilitates the Thought Police's eradication of his political resistance; however, it is precisely writing that allows Winston to begin to work through his affective resistance. If techno-scientific development is at times unbearable, is it not at least in part because its emphasis on acceleration allows little time for anamnesis?

Dissociating the two inhumans, then, "does not mean shutting ourselves away in ivory towers or turning our backs on the new forms of expression bestowed on us by contemporary science and technology."[76] It requires embracing those new forms to undertake an anamnesis of one's own affective resistance, while also taking into consideration the demands of justice.

Of course, there's no giant reset button, only an ongoing rewriting, following multiple lines of resistance. It remains necessary to remind the System—through whatever medium available (the ballot box, the picket-line, online, etc.)—that injustice is inefficient, and that the transformation of differends into litigations is, ultimately, better for business. But it also remains necessary to bear witness to the differends that remain. Both tasks require anamnesis, the labor of working through affective resistance, in order to say what has not yet been said.

Notes

1   Jean-François Lyotard, "The Affect-Phrase," trans. Keith Crome, in *The Lyotard Reader and Guide*, eds Keith Crome and James Williams (New York: Columbia University Press, 2006), 104–10. That essay was originally titled "L'inarticulé ou le différend même," in *Figures et conflits rhétoriques*, eds Michel Meyer and Alain Lempereur (Brussels: University of Brussels, 1990), 201–7.

2   Niels Brügger, "Examen oral: Entretien avec Jean François Lyotard," in *Lyotard, les déplacements philosophiques* (Brussels: De Boeck-Wesmael, 1993), 137–53; all translations mine.

3   See Brügger, "Examen oral," 151–3.

4   Jean-François Lyotard, *The Postmodern Condition*, trans. Geoff Bennington and Brian Massumi (Minneapolis: University of Minnesota Press, 1984), xxiv.

5   See ibid., 41–53.

6   See ibid., 53–67.

7   Given its traditional philosophical usage (a logically illegitimate inference), Lyotard's neologistic use of the term "paralogy" to designate different—and conflicting—uses of reason is itself an act of dissensus.

8   Even apparent exceptions are related; see Dolorès Lyotard, "Perpetual Letter," trans. Rob Shields, in *Rereading Jean-François Lyotard*, eds Heidi Bickis and Rob Shields (Surrey: Ashgate, 2013), 69–71; see also Stephen Barker, "The Weight of Writing,'" in *Rereading Jean-François Lyotard*, 55–68, esp. 65–7.

9   Jean-François Lyotard, *The Differend*, trans. Georges Van Den Abeele (Minneapolis: University Press, 1988), xi.

10 Here I extend Geoffrey Bennington's explication of the term "wrong"; see *Lyotard: Writing the Event* (New York: Columbia University Press, 1988), 136.

11 Jean-François Lyotard, *The Postmodern Explained*, trans. and ed. Julian Pefanis et al. (Minneapolis: University of Minnesota Press, 1992), 79.

12 Ibid., 78.

13 See Lyotard, *The Differend*, esp. 60–1.

14 Ibid., esp. 138.

15 See especially Jean-François Lyotard, *The Inhuman*, trans. Geoffrey Bennington and Rachel Bowlby (Minneapolis: University of Minnesota Press), 24–35. See also Kent Still, "Introduction: Minima Memoria," in *Minima Memoria: In the Wake of Jean-François Lyotard*, eds Claire Nouvet, Zrinka Stahuljak, and Kent Still (Stanford: Stanford University Press, 2006), xi–xxiv, esp. xv–xviii.

16 See especially Jean-François Lyotard, "Anamnesis of The Visible 2," trans. John Ronan, *Qui Parle* 11.2 (1999), 21–36.

17 See especially Jean-François Lyotard, *Postmodern Fables*, trans. Georges Van Den Abbeele (Minneapolis: University of Minnesota Press, 1997), 24, 32, 81, 95, 101, 119, 136–8, 147, 203.

18 Regarding the return of the figural, see Jacob Rogozinski, "Lyotard: le différend, la présence," in *Témoigner du différend* (Paris: Osiris, 1989), 61–79; Geoffrey Bennington, "Childish Things," in *Minima Memoria*, 197–217, and "The Same, Even, Itself . . .," in *Late Lyotard* (Lexington: Createspace, 2005), 43–64; and Anne Tomiche, "Phrasing the Disruptiveness of the Visible in Freudian Terms: Lyotard and the Visual," in *Afterwords: Essays in Memory of Jean-François Lyotard*, ed. Robert Harvey (Plainview: William Charles Printing, 2000), 3–28. See also Antony Hudek, "Seeing through *Discourse, Figure*," *Parrhesia* 12 (2011), accessed July 14, 2015, http:// parrhesiajournal.org/parrhesia12/parrhesia12_hudek.pdf.

19 Brügger, "Examen oral," 152.

20 Ibid.

21 By contrast, Gérald Sfez argues that the "second philosophy of the differend" is characterized not only by an "increasingly critical attention to postmodernity," but also by both an "eclipse of the political" and a corresponding attention to affect; see Gérald Sfez, "The Writings of the Differend," trans. Kent Still, in *Minima Memoria*: 86–105, here 89 and 90. See also Gérald Sfez, *Jean-François Lyotard: La faculté d'une phrase* (Paris: Galilée, 2000).

22 George Orwell, *1984* (New York: Signet, 1961), 8.

23 Ibid., 8.

24 See Ben Highmore, "Bitter after Taste: Affect, Food and Social Aesthetics," in *The Affect Theory Reader*, eds Melissa Gregg and Gregory Seigworth (Durham, NC: Duke University Press, 2000), 118–37.

25 Orwell, *1984*, 8–9.

26 George Orwell, *Dickens, Dali and Others* (Cornwall, NY: Cornwall Press, 1946), 170.

27 Orwell, *1984*, 9.

28 See Edmund Husserl, *Ideas pertaining to a Pure Phenomenology and to a Phenomenological Philosophy: First Book*, trans. F. Kersten (Dordrecht: Kluwer Academic Publishers, 1982), 257–9.

29 See Jean-François Lyotard, "The Unconscious as Mise-en-scène," trans. Joseph Maier, in *Performance In Postmodern Culture*, eds Michel Benamou and Charles Caramello (Madison: Coda Press, 1977), 87–98.

30 See http://usatoday30.usatoday.com/news/washington/2003-09-06-poll-iraq_x.htm.

31 Orwell, *1984*, 9.

32 See Lyotard, "The Unconscious as Mise-en-scène," esp. 95–8.

33 Claude Lefort, "The Interposed Body," in *Writing: The Political Test*, trans. and ed. David Ames Curtis (Durham, NC: Duke University Press, 2000), 1–19.

34 Lyotard, *The Postmodern Explained*, 89.

35 Ibid., 88.

36 See Jean-François Lyotard, *Discourse, Figure*, trans. Antony Hudek and Mary Lydon (Minneapolis: University of Minnesota Press, 2011), 233–67.

37 Lyotard, *The Postmodern Explained*, 93; translation modified.

38 Orwell, *1984*, 29.

39 Judith Butler, "Contingent Foundations: Feminism and the Question of 'Postmodernism,'" in *Feminists Theorize the Political*, eds Judith Butler and Joan W. Scott (New York: Routledge, 1992), 3–21, esp. 7–12.

40 Orwell, *1984*, 29.

41 Ibid., 160.

42 Ibid.

43 For elaboration of Lyotard's use of "blocking together," see Bill Readings, *Introducing Lyotard: Art and Politics* (New York: Routledge, 1991), xxx, 23–8, 50–62.

44 Sigmund Freud, "Remembering, Repeating and Working-Through," in *The Standard Edition of the Complete Psychological Works of Sigmund Freud*, trans. James Strachey et al. (London: The Hogarth Press, 1958), vol. XII, 155.

45 See also Anne Tomiche, "Anamnesis," in this volume.

46 Lyotard, *The Inhuman*, 124.

47 Richard Beardsworth, "Freud, Energy and Chance: A Conversation with Jean-François Lyotard," *Tekhnema: Journal of Philosophy and Technology* 5 (1999), accessed July 14, 2015, http://tekhnema.free.fr/5Beardsworth.html.

48 Ibid.

49 Lyotard, *The Postmodern Explained*, 89.

50 Lyotard, "The Affect-Phrase," 105–6. See also Jean-François Lyotard, *Lessons on the Analytic of the Sublime*, trans. Elizabeth Rottenberg (Stanford: Stanford University Press, 1994), 8–15. See also Claire Nouvet, "The Inarticulate Affect," in *Minima Memoria*, 106–22.

51 Lyotard, "The Affect-Phrase," 106.

52 Jean-François Lyotard, "Emma," trans. Michael Sanders, in *Lyotard: Philosophy, Politics and the Sublime*, ed. Hugh J. Silverman (New York: Routledge, 2002), 32. See also Claire Nouvet, "For 'Emma,'" in this volume.

53 Orwell, *1984*, 15.

54 Ibid., 14.

55 See Jean-François Lyotard, "L'extrême réel: Entretien avec Gérald Sfez," *Rue Descartes* 12–13 (1995), 200–4.

56 Orwell, *1984*, 14.

57 Ibid., 15.

58 Ibid.

59 Lyotard, *The Postmodern Explained*, 88–9.

60 Brügger, "Examen oral," 151.

61 Jean-François Lyotard, "Resistances: A Conversation," *European Journal of Psychoanalysis*, 2 (1995–6), accessed July 14, 2015, www.psychomedia.it/jep/number2/lyotard.htm.

62 Brügger, "Examen oral," 152. See also Jean-François Lyotard, "Avis de déluge," in *Des dispositifs pulsionnels* (Paris: Galilée, 1993), 9–15, esp. 14.

63 Lyotard, *Postmodern Fables*, 204.

64 Ibid, 201.

65 Jean-François Lyotard, "What to Paint?," trans. Kent Still and Peter Milne, *Cultural Politics* 9.2 (2013), 212–18, here 217.

66 Ibid.

67 Lyotard, *Postmodern Fables*, 70.

68 Brügger, "Examen oral," 152.

69 Orwell, *1984*, 258; cited in Lyotard, *The Postmodern Condition*, 101–12, n. 222.

70 Richard Beardsworth formulates what is perhaps the most sophisticated articulation of this criticism, especially with regard to Lyotard's account of the "two inhumans"; see Beardsworth, "Freud, Energy and Chance: A Conversation with Jean-François Lyotard."

71 See Lyotard, *The Inhuman*, 1–7. See also Beardsworth, "Freud, Energy and Chance: A Conversation with Jean-François Lyotard."

72 Jean-François Lyotard, *Political Writings*, trans. Bill Readings and Kevin Paul Geiman (Minneapolis: University of Minnesota Press, 1993), 166–7.

73 See Lyotard, "Anamnesis of the Visible 2;" see also Elisabeth Weber, "Before the Law, After the Law: An Interview with Jean-François Lyotard," trans Perry Bennett, *Qui Parle* 11.2 (1999), 37–57.

74 See Lyotard, *The Inhuman*, 2.

75 Lyotard, "Resistances;" see also Beardsworth, "Freud, Energy and Chance: A Conversation with Jean-François Lyotard."

76 Lyotard, *The Postmodern Explained*, 97.

Section VI

Affect and the Task of Thinking

14

The Task of Thinking (in) The Postmodern Space of "The Zone"

Julie Gaillard

"Cities must be entered by way of the suburbs [*faubourgs*]."[1] With this laconic statement, Jean-François Lyotard opens "The Zone," a text originally presented at a conference entitled "Le philosophe dans la cité" (The Philosopher in the City) in 1992, and collected in *Postmodern Fables* in a section titled "Verbiages." Under the guise of this trivial observation about a geographic necessity, he lodges a radical critique of the edifice of philosophy. Or rather, he exposes in full sight the principle of a disruption that has always inhabited it. The French term *"cité"* refers to the Greek *polis*, the assembly of the citizens, the Republic which Plato ordained to be ruled by the philosopher, and founded on the gesture of an exclusion: that of slaves, metics, criminals, women, and poets. The statement, "cities must be entered by way of the suburbs," is a commonplace, but one that overthrows the arrogance of philosophy. It not only suggests that philosophy is constituted through the forgetting of Being, as Heidegger claimed when he located the root of Western nihilism in Plato's metaphysics,[2] but also through a concomitant act of repression, whereby its Other is also forgotten—an other that can either be remembered and represented, or forever be foreclosed in reaches analogous to "what Lacan called the Thing, and Freud the unconscious affect, which never let themselves be presented":[3] immemorial, unrepresentable, intractable.

Today, "you no longer *enter* into the megalopolis."[4] The limits of the *logos* are overcome by techno-science, which downgrades progress into development, and spreads the old suburbs into a planetary "zone," understood as the inhabitable surface constituted by the passage of messages, with no inside, no outside, no other—perfecting the foreclosure of the intractable, the forgetting of forgetting. In this megalopolitan space, which, as we shall see, Lyotard characterizes as "aesthetic," the philosopher can no longer be king. His task, ridiculous and urgent, is to join the lament of the poets of the zone, who know that "we no longer live anywhere,"[5] and bear witness to the fact that the absolute is lacking: he shall enter the philosophical citadel by way of the zone, the ghetto of poetry.

The present text engages with the "manner" in which Lyotard draws together the nihilism of the inhabitable megalopolis with a thinking of repression, and ascribes to writing, in a gesture which performs its very prescription, the task of "bearing witness to the fact that there is something left behind [*qu'il y a du reste*]."[6] "The Zone" is designed to resist interpretative unfolding, to loose its reader by cutting threads that are woven again later, interwoven unto confusion. Lyotard condenses—sometimes behind one single word—thoughts that have been developed throughout the various periods of his *oeuvre*; his thought progresses through metaphors and ellipses, analogies and paralogies, allusions and collusions. I hope at least to make one point clear: in order to effectively contribute to an elaboration of what it poses as the task of thinking, the "verbiage" that Lyotard claims for himself has to exceed and overcome in advance the boundaries of a reading that would pretend to achieve a totalizing perspective.

Nihilism and its perspectives

From *Discourse, Figure* onward, Lyotard liked to repeat that perspective corresponds to a logocentric, egocentric organization of space and thought, while "we are the products of the Cézannian and Freudian revolution."[7] "The Zone" also relies on the assumption of such a communication between modes of organization of thought, of the visible, of communities. The city and philosophy do not simply correspond through a relation of inclusion or causality. "Philosophy is not in the city, it is the city in the process of thinking, and the city is the agitation of thought that seeks its habitat even though it has lost it, it has lost nature."[8] The city and philosophy correspond to the attempt of the West to dwell as a community. This installation occurs through an unending negotiation of the limit between inside and outside. The suburb ensures a peripheral reserve where the center will take the "ingredients" and reject the "leftovers" of its constitution.[9] A dynamic is established between exteriority and interiority—of the city, of philosophy—which Lyotard, as early as 1976 in "Expédient dans la décadence" (Expedient in Decadence), associated with the movement of nihilism.[10] After Nietzsche, Lyotard claims that the West is characterized by what he calls a "pathetic nihilism," which destroys values only to replace them with other values, in an obstinate recurrence of the belief in the finality of a meaning. Accordingly, the space of the metropolis is constituted by what Lyotard identifies in "The Zone" as a ceaseless oscillation between "critical housecleaning and metaphysical repolluting"[11]—i.e. between the need to perpetually reinvestigate the organization of the community and the tendency to secure the dwelling by a thinking, pertaining to metaphysics, of the foundations (such as Nature, God, or Man) and of the ends (such as progress, emancipation, or happiness). The *logos* that founds the *polis*, a hegemonic discourse that claims to be founded on truth, corresponds to a perspectival structuring of space: the modern city, like an Italian theater, is organized centrally for the eye of the prince. The city, like the Cartesian method, is built anew on a ground cleared of undesirable residues, which are eliminated, rejected outside, and forgotten. Any minority perspective, which might affirm the existence of another space that knows no center, will be inscribed within the imperial space as a tension originating from the periphery, and interpreted as a dialectical moment destined to be reintegrated within the imperial discourse. Modern philosophy, critical in nature, appoints itself the "head," organizing the suburbs as a reserve of negativity that will be made to serve relative to "the unity, the totality and the finality of a Meaning."[12] As Lyotard claims in "The Zone," while the modern philosopher attempts to found the dwelling of the West by "reasoning (with) the endemic nihilism," he actually both deploys and conceals it at the very same time.[13]

To this pathetic nihilism, which defines the space of the metropolis, Lyotard opposes an "active nihilism" that welcomes the fact that nothing has value. He abdicates for his own discourse the value of theory aiming at the truth, and surrenders the efficacy of negativity upon which critique bases its pedagogical function of conviction, understood as destruction of the false.[14] Lyotard opposes to this unique perspective the affirmation, positive and with no efficacy, of multiple perspectives, and associates the invention of prose poetry in France with the retreat of logocentrism. Amongst other famous prose poets, he chooses Max Jacob, a friend of the cubist painters, to give a definition of the genre, for "[his 'cubism'] is one of the most rigorous signs that nihilism, the one from the zone, has made in literature."[15] Cubism emancipated painting from the unicity of the point of view. The place of the viewer is not inscribed in the painting anymore, for all angles of an object are equally represented, and the angles of observation are multiplied accordingly. The relation between subject and object shifts; the whole perception of space—of reality—is called into question. Accordingly, in Max Jacob's *The Dice Cup* (1916), there is no guiding unity anymore, but only "various facets and sketches."[16] Additionally, the composition of this collection is as random as the results of a game of dice. The author has organized his own disappearance, and left authorship in the hands of fate and probabilities. In the prose poem, Lyotard reads the disappearance of the rational organization of the given by the subject for the subject. "The work is girded by its distance from everything, from the author, from the subject, from any sources."[17] Max Jacob marks literature with the sign of active nihilism by dissolving logic, causality, subjectivity, objectivity, beauty, and truth—producing a nothingness of relation which resists dialectics.

This multi-perspectival, inhabitable chaos seems to correspond to the space of the megalopolis. "Zone" is also the title of the introductory poem of Guillaume Apollinaire's collection *Alcools* (1913). The poem unfolds as a contemplative wandering in a world overwhelmed by the development of technology and the flux of information, and its last words compare the sun to a decapitated head. The megalopolis has lost its head, that is, the centrality of its foundational values. The technologies of communication allow for a reticular configuration of space, that knows no center. Phenomena of tentacular suburban sprawling and conurbanization, forming the zone, correspond to this cybernetic form of spacing. The houses of "residential zones" are not dwellings (*habitats*), but cockpits (*habitacles*), nodes emitting and receiving data.[18] By "outsourcing," as it were, the management of its installation, now entrusted to techno-science, the West gives birth to a new form of space, one that is no longer organized by a subject for a subject according to a logical perspective, but is organized by the machine so as to optimize the circulation of messages—a circulation where humans are no longer necessary agents, but contingent objects. In this pattern, the old downtowns are no longer the dynamic space where the *polis* reinvents itself, but ossified, museumized places, and, as such, registrable as quanta of information. The megalopolis is not the simple extension of suburban space at the edges of the city: it suppresses the distinction between inside and outside, swallowing the city itself. "If the *Urbs* [city] becomes the *Orbs* [entire surface of the globe] and if the zone becomes a whole city, then the megalopolis has no outside. And consequently, no inside."[19]

Lyotard sees this evolution as partaking of the movement of the nihilism of the West. "With the megalopolis, what the West realizes and diffuses is its nihilism. It is called development."[20] However, the nihilism at stake in the megalopolis is not the active nihilism of cubism, which creates realities through the affirmative power of its perspectives. The system fulfills pathetic nihilism because it restores the faith in the supreme value of techno-science, and binds "truth" to a process of verification pertaining to a form of operativity based on the "prevision by an exact control of the variables."[21] The reference here is not so much Nietzsche's nihilism, but rather its Heideggerian reexamination, through the notion of *Ge-stell* (enframing), understood as the essence of technology, which, in the age of the world picture, worsens and accomplishes the forgetting of Being. As Ashley Woodward notes,

> the essence of technology consists in the setting up of a fixed framework or perspective through which beings are disclosed, which predetermines the ways in which they are disclosed.... Through the perspective of *Ge-stell*, beings are revealed as potential energy that may be stored and put to use according to the calculations and plans of willing subjects.[22]

This perspective tending towards hegemony, all beings, including human beings, fall under the perspective of *Ge-stell*. After Heidegger, Lyotard shows that the "zone" spreads itself as an awesome power of treating, and hence neutralizing, events. This treatment is no longer controlled by man, but by the machine. As Lyotard writes in "*Domus* and the Megalopolis," "the control is no longer territorialized or historicized. It is computerized. There is a process of complexification, they say, which is initiated and desired by no-one, no self, not even that of humanity."[23] The critical metropolis used to treat and control the disturbances emanating from the suburbs through a dialectical process. Now, the treatment of disturbances is managed by computers. The gigantic memory of the West is the very source of its power, since the mass of data allows for improved accuracy in provisional calculation, which increases the regulation of events by anticipating their occurrence. Man's installation, his technological enterprise of domination of nature, backfires and evicts him from his position of master of the system.

Nihilism, thus spread, gives birth to "a philosophy of being-together-in-the-world wholly other than the metaphysics of metropolises."[24] This mode is no longer critical, but aesthetic. In this space defined by the mere passage of information, where nothing has value, Lyotard states that value is relegated to the manner of presentation. "As for existence, the megalopolis lives itself [*se vit*] aesthetically."[25] Simultaneously, philosophy itself seems to be struck by a similar process of aesthetization. The movement of nihilism compels thought to adopt a new genre of discourse, and switches from "the method" to "a manner." This aesthetization at stake in philosophy, however, does not proceed from the same motive as the aesthetization of the megalopolis. "The monster of conurbanization encounters postmodern philosophy at the point of a generalized aesthetics. And it's on this point that they fail to meet."[26]

The postmodern philosopher can no longer be "in" the city, whose features his thought would elaborate. The "zone" is the product of the system, not of thought. His task will be to resist the pathetic nihilism of the zone by setting against it an active nihilism. "In the aestheticizing megalopolis, philosophy is found, or rather lost, in the position of being on guard against or having regard to the nothingness that is the absolute."[27] "The absolute" is an "empty name" that designates the locus, unlocatable, of an excess.[28] The rest of this chapter is devoted, through an investigation of the psychoanalytic references interspersed on the surface of "The Zone," to a consideration of the possible links between this "nothingness that is the absolute" and the "unconscious affect." In *Heidegger and "the jews"* Lyotard elaborates a reading of primary repression that leads him, as we shall see, to postulate that affect is linked to "sexual difference," which, he claims, "plays in the thought (in the psychic apparatus) of the (European) Occident this role of an immanent terror, not identified as such, unrepresentable, of an unconscious affect and of a medically incurable misery."[29] The West, defined by this movement of nihilism in its two manifestations (critical and aesthetic), would be inhabited and moved by this immanent and immemorial terror.

The suburb and the *après-coup* (*Nachträglichkeit*, belatedness)

Lyotard posits an analogy between the city and the psyche, stating that "[t]he suburb is the permanent *après-coup* of the inquiry led by the Western soul on the subject of the community and inhabitable space-time."[30]

The mechanism of the *après-coup*, defined after Freud's *Project for a Scientific Psychology*, is the pivot that allows Lyotard to postulate the aforementioned immanent terror. The *après-coup* implies "a double blow that is constitutively asymmetrical."[31] A first event strikes the psychic apparatus, whose intensity is so excessive that it cannot be assimilated by the system perception-consciousness. The shock cannot be recorded, but it cannot be repressed either (although Freud names this *Urverdrängung* (primary repression)), for, in order to be repressed, something would have needed to be inscribed in the first place, as a word- or thing-representation. The affect is not an object localizable in the topology of the psyche (although Freud names it "unconscious affect"). "I imagine the effect of the shock, the unconscious affect, to be like a cloud of energy particles that are not subject to serial laws, that are not organized into sets that can be thought in terms of words and images, that do not experience any attraction at all."[32] The first "blow" leaves a formless, imperceptible trace, which Lyotard describes as "outside the scene"[33] (*hors-scène*), offstage: it is "a shock without affect."[34] Not perceived, this trace left by the initial shock remains absolutely foreign to representation, as dispersed, diffuse, inert. The second "blow" consists in the sudden surfacing of an affect that cannot apparently be ascribed to any shock:

> Anxiety crushes me, I flee, but nothing had really happened. The energy dispersed in the affective cloud condenses, gets organized, brings on an action, commands a flight without a "real" motive. And it is this flight, the feeling that accompanies it, which informs consciousness *that* there is something, without being able to tell *what* it is. It indicates the *quod* but not the *quid*. The essence of the event: that *there is* "comes before" *what* there is.[35]

Chronologically, the affect condensed during the second "blow" happens "before" the "initial" shock which has "caused" it. This achronic temporality of the unconscious affect operates contra temporalizing consciousness. It undoes diachrony, interrupts it. Anamnesis will attempt to account for this unsettling achrony within a narrative organization, to "[represent] a presence without representation," to "[stage] the obscene."[36] Lyotard adds that this decision to organize the events according to a diachronic succession is "the historical decision in itself. This decision occults what motivates it, and it is made for this reason."[37] This intolerable and unfathomable excess is reinserted within the temporal succession which articulates a past, a present and a future. Its initial violence, its monstrosity for consciousness, is canceled out, *forgotten*, by the very fact that it is "treated," i.e. that a "reason" has linked the first and the second blow.

Lyotard reminds us that Freud looks for such a "reason" in many directions. Indeed, "it is necessary to 'explain' that there might (have) be(en) this stranger in the house, and to find a 'reason' for his clandestine entry and unnoticed stay."[38] This quest seems to always lead to the assumption of a "scene." However, "whatever the invoked scene might be, in the night of time, of the individual or of the species," this scene "has not taken place," "has not had a stage," "has not even *been*, because it is not representable."[39] The soul is exceeded through and by affect, because of its fundamental unpreparedness, which Lyotard calls its *infancy*. The unrepresentable event is represented as a scene or as an object on the screen of adult consciousness, which by definition masks and misses it. The "remembering" of the scene implies the forgetting of the immemorial affect, which cannot be remembered, but neither forgotten, for it has never been inscribed. It remains with representation, *within* it, in an irreducible differend. In an attempt to avoid the instantiation on such "scenes," Lyotard, after Freud, dubs "sexual difference"[40] this differend between infancy and adulthood, and defines it as the "constitutive infirmity of the soul."[41]

If it is true that the *après-coup* sets in motion the process of anamnesis, of the search for the "reasons" of this unpresentable presence, then, according to the operative collusion of the suburb and the *après-coup* in "The Zone," the suburb would trouble the city with an affect that cannot be attributed to any apparent cause, thereby setting in motion the investigation of the metropolis into the "reasons" of what worries it. The suburb contains the castaways from the *polis* that can be remembered because they have been repressed, forgotten. "Zone" of secondary repression, it would also be the occasion for an anxiety that would signal that an immemorial exteriority lies dormant inside the dwelling. In keeping with this analogy, the modern philosopher would be placed in the position of the analyst, listening to the symptoms of the metropolis, reconstructing their etiology, and ascribing the localization of "scenes" ordered within the diachrony of a causal logic.

The analysis of nihilism may encounter the Freudian hypothesis of primary repression. The West would be steered backwards, and constituted as investigation, as philosophy—*historia, philosophia*—towards its constitutive lack of an object and lack of origin. It would organize and build the objects of its habitable world as placeholders, representatives, of this lacking object, which is lacking only insofar as it has never been present, inscribed. The metropolis "seeks its habitat even though it has lost it, it has lost nature."[42] Isn't nature such an originary scene, reconstructed, "*après-coup*," as the mythical object of a lost origin? It seems that, in the hypothesis of a pathetic nihilism, as in the Freudian hypothesis, the enterprise of "critical housecleaning" is followed by a "metaphysical re-polluting." Just as Freud is led to postulate "scenes" of an "origin" for the unconscious affect, the investigation of the Western soul, attempting to provide "reasons" for the discontent here called, by way of a shortcut, "the suburb," is led to the assumption of origins and ends which are all facades masking the very thing that they pretend to name. This masking pertains to what Lyotard dubs a "foreclosure," understood in the Lacanian sense of a radical exclusion outside of any symbolic or representational order. And because "past things are remembered ahead,"[43] as we are reminded in "*Domus* and the Megalopolis," the search for origins communicates with the search for a destination. Elsewhere in *The Inhuman*, Lyotard evokes a "foreclosure of ends," which "has been dressed up in all sort of disguises: destination of man, progress, enlightenment, emancipation, happiness."[44] By bringing together a thinking of nihilism and a thinking of the psyche, Lyotard seems to suggest that the "values" that orient the constitution of communities could be understood as representations standing for the unreachable otherness whose foreclosure preempts their constitution.

The critique determines the objects that the community will adopt or reject as values. This is a metaphysical program, which, assuredly, conceals the immanent terror, while maintaining, however, an element of alterity in excess within the dwelling of the community—ultimately, under the form of "Man," last "object" of faith. "The final consignment of humanism is: Man is Man only by what exceeds him."[45] The modern "objects" still carried the trace of an intractable excess which resisted conscious grasp. With the eviction of Man from his central position of foundation of the given, nihilism takes away the last "object" whose value could be held as absolute. The megalopolis is still marked by what Lyotard calls a "metaphysics of development," yet development is not attached to an Idea that it would set as its finality.[46] The value, which cannot be attached to any object, is now borne by the style of presentation. The object is indifferent, it does not stand for anything else, it does not present itself as the placeholder for an outside in excess. This defines the "cultural" panorama of the aestheticizing megalopolis.

"Cultural politics"

Lyotard defines culture as "a means in a strategy."[47] In the metropolis, cultural politics aims at turning around the negativity of the suburb into a positive force. The consciousness of the oppressed has to be liberated, so that they can liberate themselves in reality. Unlike children, who assimilate culture and realize it in their lives when they grow up, for the adults to whom it is addressed, pedagogy remains a matter of belief. Lyotard takes the example of the cultural politics of German Social Democracy at the turn of the twentieth century, "a stepchild of the *aufklärer* [Enlightenment] project."[48] World War I, the great economic crisis of the 1920s and Nazism wipe out the communities of enlightened citizens that this cultural politics believed to have instituted: "This is a sign that democracy has not been assimilated"[49]—that conviction didn't "take." And if Nazi cultural politics, at the end of European nihilism, is capable of relaying the politics of the social-democrats, this shows that the pedagogical model of the Enlightenment and its perversion share a common resource, which is not rational, but libidinal:

> When nihilism unleashes its violence, the masses lose their head. The lost head is called the unconscious. Nazi cultural politics target the unconscious in order to tap its energy. The point is to inculcate into this people in distress the fable of

its originary destiny, that of saving Europe from its nihilist decadence.... The community is "reconstituted" by climbing onto the stage where heroic figures are offered for its wild transference.... Political art is "culture", and "culture" is the art of directing the transference.[50]

"Transference" should not primarily be understood here within the phrastic framework of essays such as "the Affect-Phrase,"[51] as the forcing of affect in a structure of address (although this framing of the notion will also be mobilized in "The Zone"), but still within a libidinal framework, as a harnessing of fluxes. The acephalous community, deprived of an origin and a destination, deprived of a means of regulating and channeling its unconscious energies, finds itself in a position similar to that of the child *infans* (unspeaking), prior to the formation of the psychic apparatus. Already in 1973, in "Acinema," Lyotard compared the formation of the ego, described by Lacan in his text on the mirror stage, and the formation of the social body before the specular surface offered to its gaze.[52] The little man libidinally cathects, and then assumes the image of himself that he perceives in the mirror as if it were the image of an other. Simultaneously, the drives are fended off and rejected into the Id, as a forever unreachable and unrepresentable remainder—foreclosed. Similarly, Lyotard claims that communities are created through the assumption by the social body of the image that a scenic set-up offers like a mirror to their view—the screen of the film, the stage of the theater, or any specular surface presented by a cultural object. Transference, in this narrow sense, is understood as the libidinal cathexis of the specular surface offered to the identificatory contemplation of the social body. This constitution of a unity is also "imaginary" in the sense of a lure, for it constitutes property, interiority, and reality, via an identification to an exterior image. The perversion of culture would consist, at times when the social body has "lost its head," to manipulate the mirror that will allow the recovery of its unity by identification. With Nazi theater, through the mythical reenactment of a fantasized ethnical and political origin by heroic figures on a stage, the people embrace the myth that returns it to its communal unity and provides it with the fantasmatic domination of its causes and ends. The price is known. Lyotard suggests that Nazi cultural politics reveals, in turn, all pedagogic or revolutionary projects as tapping into the same libidinal resources as propaganda. After Auschwitz, the philosopher should renounce "the project of revolutionizing, of converting the other through reading and the look."[53]

Now Lyotard claims that, far from having disappeared with Nazism, this seduction by means of culture is precisely what is at stake in the aestheticizing megalopolis. More generally, "directing the transference" comes down to prescribing to the fluxes of unconscious energies the locus that they will cathect, by producing figures which will "provoke [*(se) donner à*] love or hate."[54] These figures, in the megalopolis, no longer aim at manipulating a desire "of justice, equality, or destiny," but rather of "development."[55] The competitive multiplicity of the media offers a surface perfectly organized to channel these energies while projecting the fallacious appearance of pluralism and critique. Objects have to be "interesting," i.e. offer, through their style, a surface where libidinal energies are attracted. "Style is where transference takes place."[56] This surface responds to a "demand" of the individuals, which Lyotard identifies as "the demand for security or protection (against the anxiety of dereliction)."[57] The "imaginary" surface of media saturates space with figures offered to the transference of the individuals, multiplying the occasions for identification and/or seduction. This "lowering of all signs into the imaginary of management" also worsens the "foreclosing of desire."[58] Lyotard leans on Adorno to evoke what he describes, in *Heidegger and "the jews,"* as "this industrial devastation of the intimate, this placing outside, in media . . . of the concerns of representation, of the (industrial) work of providing unconscious energies with representatives on which they will come to fix themselves, this transfer of the dreamwork, of the symptom, to 'cultural' work."[59] In the aestheticizing zone, the libidinal energies are not directed on a stage opened inside the psyche, but on the exterior signs that the media offer to their investment. The very task of producing representations, which in the psychic apparatus is linked to secondary repression, is outsourced as well. Organized so as to treat the event "in real time," the aestheticizing megalopolis reduces "despair" to "a disorder to correct," prevents it from ever being heard as "the sign of an irremediable lack"[60]—it neutralizes the absolute under the gigantic memory of the signs, perfecting the forgetting of forgetting. Additionally, the constant mobilization of the forces drains the psychic apparatus, leading to an anesthesia: only "sensational" sensations, important quantities of information, are perceived. The cultural reality of the megalopolis is marked by an anesthesia that reinforces amnesia.

The phrasophile philosopher

The task of the philosopher is to set against this aesthetics of the megalopolis another aesthetics, which doesn't fall within "the imaginary of demand," but within "the real of desire."[61] In order to do so, s/he must develop a sensibility which is "impassive before the seductions of the aestheticizing megalopolis, but affected by what they conceal in displaying it: the mute lament that the absolute is lacking."[62] S/he inherits from modernism the task of thinking the enigma of an excess constitutive of the humanity of Man. "Within the aesthetic frame imposed on [thought] by contemporary nihilism, this enigma must be thought of as the 'presence' through which the absolute (which is what has no relation) makes its sign [*fait signe*] in forms (which are relation)."[63] To "cultural reality," Lyotard opposes "the *artistic*," which, as gesture, tone, or pitch, traverses the forms of culture, transcends them, "while," however, "inhabiting them."[64] Lyotard, comparing this opposition of the cultural and the artistic to that of the Lacanian "imaginary" and "real," also suggests its analogy with the Kantian opposition of the beautiful and the sublime.

This new shortcut in the argumentation seems to build upon a foundational remark that guides *Heidegger and "the jews"* where Lyotard proposes, in order to account for the forgetting that thwarts all representation, to "read side by side, though scrupulously respecting their immense differences, the Kantian text on aesthetics and the Freudian text on metapsychology, i.e., the work that, all in all, Jacques Lacan has begun. More precisely, to dare to propose that secondary repression is to primary repression as the beautiful is to the sublime."[65] In addition to providing the framework that will allow for doing away with a metaphysics of forces, this new productive analogy provides Lyotard with the pivot which allows him to postulate a certain modality of the apparition of the Thing within forms, under the name of the absolute, when the closure of representation organizes its foreclosure. In the sublime, just as in the *après-coup*, there is an excess that overwhelms and dispossesses all the boundaries of consciousness and of the syntheses of the mind:

> In the sublime feeling, the imagination is also completely unable to collect the absolute (in largeness, in intensity) in order to represent it, and this means that the sublime is not localizable in time. But something, at least, remains there, ignored by imagination, spread in the mind as both pleasure and pain—something Burke called terror, precisely, terror of "there is nothing," which threatens without making itself known, which does not "realize" itself.[66]

The absolute escapes any synthesis, any representation. In the sublime feeling, the "power of representing" ceases to constitute time as a flux. *Aisthēsis* (perception), which depends upon the syntheses of time, is made ineffective. However, the sublime feeling implies a "spasm," an apparition out of time, which combines pleasure and pain—a combination which, in "The Zone," Lyotard associates with "a sorrow felt before the inconsistency of every object," accompanied by "the exaltation of thought passing beyond the bounds of what may be presented."[67] The sublime feeling appears where it is not expected, "as an event on the occasion of the presentation of a phenomenon."[68] It therefore becomes the privileged lever of an an-aesthetic resistance against the foreclosure of the absolute by the aestheticizing and anesthetizing megalopolis.

The absolute only signals itself by this sign made in silence, beyond the reach of any semiotics and any phenomenology. "[T]o make a silent sign":[69] this is what Lyotard calls "*phrazein*, to phrase."[70] With the mention of this silent "phrase," Lyotard cracks open yet another intratextual window, which completes the circle of the notions disseminated in the text, and precipitates "nothingness," "the absolute," "the real of desire"—notions developed in very different frameworks and times—into the crucible of the "affect-phrase," which he defines in the eponymous essay: a phrase with no referent and no meaning, which doesn't come from anyone and is in no way addressed. Foreign to articulation, it still signals itself as an affective state.[71] "[T]he nothingness that is the absolute"[72] phrases in silence. Therefore, Lyotard "imagine[s] the philosopher in the megalopolis being given over to phrasophilia."[73] This *philia* is no longer a love of wisdom, but a "desire" of the absolute, a passion for its phrase—if passion implies, as Lyotard states in *Heidegger and "the jews,"* a pathos, an insensitive passibility, an anesthesia that thwarts *aisthēsis*, "that leaves the soul open to an affection more 'archaic' than the givens of nature."[74] But what will be the mode of this *phrasophilia*? How can one welcome and bear witness to the affect-phrase? As Claire Nouvet points out:

> Words will also necessarily betray the muteness of the affect by articulating that which intractably resists articulation.... The affect is indeed "no-thing" insofar as it negates—that is, annihilates—all the poles of the articulated phrase. The affect says "nothing": no meaning, no referent, no addressor, no addressee. One owes words, and lots of them, to the mute nothing of the affect. One says a lot to try to say "nothing." And one will never manage to say nothing. The testimony is doomed to fail.[75]

If the forms constitutively conceal anything that would exceed them, if affect, if the absolute, is radically heterogeneous to any representation, how will writing (art, literature, philosophy) bear witness to this silent phrase that it is bound to mask? As Lyotard states in *Heidegger and "the jews,"* "[w]hat art can do is bear witness not to the sublime, but to this aporia of art and to its pain. It does not say the unsayable, but says that it cannot say it."[76]

The phrase of poetry is melancholic: its lament articulates the fact that "we no longer live anywhere," while silently signaling the absent presence, the present absence of the absolute. The prose poem is not sublime, for there is no sublime object, just a sublime feeling that may or may not occur on the occasion of the forms. However, the artistic in the forms is the mark of a desire whose "object" is the absolute. This mark is made by "the gesture of the work [which] *signs* the ever unfulfilled desire."[77] This desire partakes of the "real," foreign to the symbolic or representational order. As such, it cannot be of a subject for an object, cannot be articulated according to the poles of address or reference, and yet it drives a gesture which will transmit the silent phrase through and beyond the forms.

The cubism of Max Jacob, who "wants the nothingness of relation,"[78] doesn't merely attest to the nihilism of the zone: it also provides Lyotard with an example of this work of desire in the forms. Jacob defines the artwork through the distinction of two traits: "style" and "situation." "You know a work has style by the fact that it gives the sensation of being closed; you know it is situated by the little shock you receive or else by the surrounding margin."[79] The impression that the work is closed allows for its consideration *as* an object. As we have seen, "style is where transference takes place."[80] By multiplying the facets of the object and the angles of observation, the cubist style troubles the transference: its surface is like a faceted mirror-ball, which unsettles the unity of the perceiving body. As for the "situation," it "impugns author, motif, public and forms."[81] The work negates the pragmatic axes of address and reference, further troubling the perception of the object. The combination of "style" and "situation" prevents seduction by surrounding itself with a distance partly pertaining to the Brechtian "distancing effect":[82] the imaginary surface of the work is revealed to be a lure. However, style and situation do not simply mark negatively the place of an absence by intentionally arranging the forms and stifling the addressor's transference. As Lyotard will note in *Soundproof Room*, their combination transmits to the work the force of stupor emitted in the instant of horror, in the spasm where the artist, brought back to a larval state reminiscent of infancy, hallucinates his own nothingness and the terror that "there is nothing."[83] "Style" and "situation" inform the forms with the stamp of this stupor whose force is communicated to the work, which may in turn—or may not—transmit it to the reader. Maybe the reader will receive a "shock"; maybe s/he will only coldly contemplate the "surrounding margins" of the work, staying on their exterior limit, without being seized and dispossessed by the silent signal of the absolute.

If phrasophilia is this bearing witness to the silent phrase by which the absolute signals itself, such as the "orphaned work" of the suburb performs, then

"The Zone" itself is a demonstration of its author "being given over to phrasophilia." The text itself proceeds from the active nihilism of cubism. The multitude of facets and sketches condensed into one space propose a parody of philosophical systematicity. The reader, searching for the unitary and totalizing horizon of a meaning, attempting to approach the text by one of its sides, feels its consistency crumbling and resisting the grasp.[84] The text deposes the affect of conviction, the seduction of academics. Its arc is constantly muddled by the work of the desire that drives writing and crushes forms and perspectives together, giving them their distinctive folds. "The Zone," in its very form, mimics the multiperspectival, inhuman chaos of the system, built on the ruins of the humanist philosophical city, where the speed of the passage of information quantitatively exceeds man's perception and understanding. But its gesture simultaneously attests to the forgotten "presence" of another inhuman: that of the constitutive misery of the soul, in excess of all representation. After all, it is in an essay on cubist painters that Apollinaire states: "Artists are men who want to become inhuman."[85] If *phrazein* appears at the end of the text, seemingly abandoning us on its edge, maybe it is also that "things past are remembered ahead": "The Zone," like *In Search for Lost Time*, completes the revolution of its orb and communicates to the reader—but in a mutic communication—the shock whose impulsion, "bearing witness to the fact that there is something left behind," will awaken her own investigation.

Notes

1 Jean-François Lyotard, "The Zone," in *Postmodern Fables*, trans. Georges Van Den Abbeele (Minneapolis and London: University of Minnesota Press, 1997), 17.

2 On Heidegger's reframing of Nietzsche's nihilism as an ontological question, and its import for Lyotard's formulation of postmodernity, see Ashley Woodward's *Nihilism in Postmodernity. Lyotard, Baudrillard, Vattimo* (Aurora: The Davies Group, 2009), 54, as well as James Williams, *Lyotard and the Political* (London, New York: Routledge, 2000), 54 s.

3 Jean-François Lyotard, "Rewriting Modernity," in *The Inhuman: Reflections on Time*, trans. Geoffrey Bennington and Rachel Bowlby (Stanford: Stanford University Press, 1988), 33.

4 Lyotard, "The Zone," 21.

5 Ibid., 17, translation modified.

6 Ibid., 32.

7 See *Discourse, Figure*, trans. Anthony Hudek and Mary Lydon (Minneapolis and London: University of Minnesota Press, 2011), section "The new space of philosophy," 175 s.

8 Ibid., 19, translation modified.

9 See ibid.

10 Jean-François Lyotard, "Expédient dans la décadence," in *Rudiments Païens. Genre Dissertatif* (Paris: Union Générale d'Editions, 1977). Translations mine.

11 Lyotard, "The Zone," 20.

12 Lyotard, "Expédient," 119.

13 See Lyotard, "The Zone," 24.

14 Lyotard, "Expédient," 118.

15 Lyotard, "The Zone," 22.

16 Ibid., translation modified.

17 Ibid., 18.

18 Ibid., 21–2, translation modified.

19 Ibid., 21

20 Ibid., 22

21 Lyotard, "Expédient," 125.

22 Woodward, *Postmodernity and Nihilism*, 62.

23 Jean-François Lyotard, "*Domus* and the Megalopolis," in *The Inhuman*, 199.

24 Lyotard, "The Zone," 21, translation modified.

25 Ibid., 22, translation modified.

26 Ibid., translation modified.

27 Ibid., 30.

28 Ibid., 29. On this exteriority whose occultation underlays the activity of thinking, see Geoffrey Bennington, "Opening Up," in *Rewriting Lyotard: Figuration, Presentation, Resistance, Cultural Politics* 9.2 (2013), 205.

29 Jean-François Lyotard, *Heidegger and "the jews,"* trans. Andreas Michel and Mark Roberts (Minneapolis and London: University of Minnesota Press, 1990), 21.

30 Lyotard, "The Zone," 19.

31 Lyotard, *Heidegger*, 15.

32 Ibid.

33 Ibid.

34 Ibid.,16.

35 Ibid.

36 Ibid.

37 Ibid.

38 Ibid., 17.

39 Ibid., 19.

40 Ibid., 19.

41 Ibid., 17.

42 Lyotard, "The Zone," 19, translation modified.

43 Lyotard, "*Domus*," 198.

44 Lyotard, "*Logos* and *Technē*, or Telegraphy" in *The Inhuman*, 54.

45 Lyotard, "The Zone," 28.

46 Jean-François Lyotard, "Introduction: About the Human," in *The Inhuman*, 7.

47 Lyotard, "Zone," 25.

48 Ibid., 26.

49 Ibid.

50 Ibid.

51 Jean-François Lyotard, "The Affect-phrase (From a Supplement to *The Differend*)," trans. Keith Crome, in *The Lyotard Reader and Guide*, eds Keith Crome and James Williams (New York: Columbia University Press, 2006), 104–10.

52 "Acinema," trans. Paisley N. Livingston in collaboration with the author, in Philip Rosen (ed.), *Narrative, Apparatus, Ideology. A Film Theory Reader* (New York: Columbia University Press, 1986), sections "The Instance of Identification" and "Directing: Putting In, and Out, of Scene," 353 s.

53 Lyotard, *Heidegger*, 37.

54 Lyotard, "The Zone," 30, translation modified.

55 Ibid., 27.

56 Ibid.

57 Ibid., 28.

58 Ibid., 31.

59 Lyotard, *Heidegger*, 48.

60 Lyotard, "The Zone," 31.

61 Ibid., 29.

62 Ibid., 31, translation modified. See also Dolorès Lyotard's characterization of Lyotard's philosophy as "migrating writing," in "L' écriture Migrante de Jean-François Lyotard," in *Contemporary French and Francophone Studies* 18 (2014), esp. 28.

63 Ibid.

64 Ibid., 29.

65 Lyotard, *Heidegger*, 5.

66 Ibid., 32.

67 Lyotard, "The Zone," 29, translation modified.

68 Ibid.

69 Ibid., 30.

70 Ibid.

71 Lyotard, "Affect-Phrase," 105.

72 Lyotard, "The Zone," 30.

73 Ibid.

74 Lyotard, *Heidegger*, 45.

75 Claire Nouvet, "The Inarticulate Affect. Lyotard and Psychoanalytic Testimony," in *Minima Memoria. In the Wake of Jean-François Lyotard*, eds Claire Nouvet, Kent Still, and Zrinka Stahuljak (Stanford: Stanford University Press, 2007), 120–1.

76 Lyotard, *Heidegger*, 47.

77 Lyotard, "The Zone," 29, translation modified.

78 Ibid., 22.

79 Max Jacob, quoted in ibid., 18.

80 Ibid., 27.

81 Ibid., 22.

82 Ibid.

83 See Jean-François Lyotard, *Soundproof Room. Malraux's Anti-Aesthetics*, trans. Robert Harvey (Stanford: Stanford University Press, 2001), 96.

84 On the analogy of Lyotard's writing with cubist painting and its import for an approach to the "unforgettable," see Kent Still, introduction to *Minima Memoria*, eds Claire Nouvet, Kent Still and Zrinka Stahuljak, xx s.

85 Lyotard, *The Inhuman*, 5.

15

Coups de Grâce

Mark Stoholski

To begin with a citation: "Attested, suffering and the indomitable are as if already destroyed. I mean that in witnessing, one also exterminates. The witness is a traitor."[1] These lines, the closing words of *The Inhuman*, bear upon the difficulty of witnessing to affect, in speech, in writing, in any mode of articulated discourse. In spite of the most noble intentions, in striving to bear witness, one will have wronged affect yet again, always. The task that Lyotard explicitly sets himself in his last writings is that of attesting to the debt to affect, even as it remains unattestable by articulated discourse. There is necessarily a double bind here, the product of articulated discourse's differend with inarticulate affect. One must take seriously the challenge that Lyotard poses with this statement. In attempting to bear witness to affect, one inevitably wrongs it. And yet the phrase refuses any simple reading. "The witness is a traitor" is not a canonical dictum issued from one of the *auctores* (authorities) of philosophy, to be received, repeated, and perhaps critiqued. To take it thus would be not to have heard what is there said. Should one lend credence to the witness who reports that witnesses are traitors? The statement belies its own authority.

In its form, the statement "the witness is a traitor" recalls the famed "Liar's Paradox" attributed to Eubulides of Megara, which Lyotard analyzes in his 1976 essay "On the Strength of the Weak." There he borrows Cicero's articulation of the paradox: "if you say that you lie and you say so truly, then you lie." The converse is also the case: "if you say that you lie and you are lying, you do so truly."[2] The paradox arises where the statement takes itself as its own referent; if the statement that declares itself to be false is false, it is true. If it is true, then it is false. The difficulty presented here is not, for the logician, insurmountable. Lyotard invokes Russell's proposed dissolution, where the statement "I lie" is decomposed into two distinct operators: "(I say truly that) I lie." Taken thus, the two clauses are set into distinct groups and treated independently. The first of these, the simple assertion, "I lie" is assigned to a category of statements that refer to objects. The "I say truly that" is relegated to a second class that takes as its referent statements that belong to the first type. These domains of reference are declared via axiom; statements of the first class must take objects as reference, and the second, statements about objects. The paradox is thus apparently dissolved; statements are forbidden to take themselves in reference. Lyotard nonetheless identifies a problem that lies in the imposition of this axiomatic division. The statement of the axiom must either belong to the class of statements that refer to other statements, in which case the paradox reasserts itself at the order of metalanguage—it would be a statement referring to a statement about statements, thus disobeying itself—or it belongs to a third class that could only be shored up with reference to a fourth, inflicting an infinite regress. Lyotard comments:

> All of this is not very serious. One could create a meta-axiom in order to arrest this regression, acknowledging simply that truth-values can in fact only be fixed under the condition of this axiom. But in a sense it is quite serious. What happens to their authority if it is not fashioned after an order that is prior to it, if, instead, it decrees itself?[3]

The danger for the logician is that without fixed, authoritative axioms, one risks anarchy. "The Strength of the Weak" celebrates this not as an end, but as a means by which minor discourses might come to assert themselves against those which are dominant. This anarchy is that which Lyotard affirmed in his "pagan" period as a means of a potential political resistance to master discourses; the rules by which these discourses operated could always be themselves made objects of play and their authority thus reversed. It is undoubtedly not the same anarchy that is characteristic of affect in the later writings, insofar as "pagan" anarchy yet relates to the domain of the practical, to politics and to ethics. The anarchy that emerges as characteristic of affect maintains no relation to the possible; it is unable to acknowledge any rule, even as reversed. Nonetheless, it is significant that the later work on affect sees the return of a gesture where argumentation undercuts itself and reveals the authority it purports to wield as fractured. Lyotard well remains an *auctor*, but one who will have exauthorized himself, will have presented his witness in a certain bad faith. This is not a flaw; the question of affect allows no alternative. The logical bad faith, manifest in the declaration that the witness is a traitor, is itself a gesture. It betrays itself in order to indicate, through this very betrayal, something of affect and its work upon articulated discourse.

Lyotard's late writings on affect will have, after a fashion, attempted to say nothing. The writings on affect strain to allow the unrepresentable "nothing" that signals the presence of affect to be heard. Inevitably, he will not have said this nothing in a "pure," "immediate" state, as if this could be imagined. The task of witnessing to affect precisely demands that one not dispense with the established discourses that have attempted to treat it—whether it be philosophy, psychoanalysis, literature, the visual arts, or any of the others that are invoked in his writings. That means that one will have continued to evoke the authorities, but precisely in that mode in which Lyotard sets himself with the paradox on witnessing; authority must be denuded if the suppression of affect is to be unworked. It must be allowed to retain its claims while these claims are shown to be troubled by what escapes them. Lyotard opens his essay "Mainmise" on this note:

> I am only going to make a few observations. The place from where they will have been made, I cannot well designate. It is not, I presume, the place of knowledge, of supposed knowledge. For of that which I speak, I *know* nothing. Not anything from that love of knowledge or wisdom with which the Greeks have inoculated us under the name of philosophy. For it seems to me that I, like many others, have only ever loved what would not let itself be known or mastered.[4]

Philosophy, as he here represents it, is a received discourse, administered by a tradition that claims classical Greece as its point of origin; with it, its inheritors have been inoculated against what cannot be represented or known. Philosophy presents a potential danger; it might serve to ground the question, in a certain sense, declaring thinkable what remains outside the bounds of thought, what cannot be linked. The unrepresentable does not belong to philosophy, which remains a discourse, even if it poses as its highest value an *epikeina tēs ousias*, a "beyond being." This claim would assert a kind of mastery over the nothing to which Lyotard refers, forcing it to become a term, a value, even if an ultimate one. Secured with a term that lies beyond argumentation, but which is the possession of a few, mastery is asserted with the name of the love of wisdom: "the friends of wisdom—Plato and Aristotle—seek to establish masterful accounts, to fix a non-referable reference, to determine a term that escapes relation and dominates all relations," he writes.[5] Lyotard rejects this position of mastery; affect is what cannot be mastered. All the same, it is not a matter of dismissing philosophy out of hand; only a rival position of mastery could authorize this. It is rather a matter of taking up philosophy against the grain, where the security provided by an imagined final term does not avail itself. The emphasis is no longer on this or that doctrine, but on the trace that it may well indicate. Of affect there is no trace; nevertheless, the discourses that have served to inoculate against it may yet indicate something of it, however minimally. Scarring, after an injection performed upon a child.

Such an approach to philosophy is no longer the self-assured project of Plato, but it remains a work of love. As Lyotard indicates in the passage quoted above, this antithetical love makes no claim as to knowing its object. It is not able to name it with any singular magistral name, even that of the ineffable. As he continues, "[p]erhaps it is not even a place. In any case, not a familiar locale. And not a utopia either. I would rather accord it the privilege of the real. Let us leave in suspense its name, its etiquette."[6] He does name it after a fashion, here designating it the real, one of many names under which affect will pass in the later writings, but offers these names only as placeholders. They indicate what cannot be named with any confidence, what cannot be transformed into a concept; where it intervenes, one is at a loss. There is a risk here; the argumentation might well turn along Socratic lines, where authority is claimed on the basis of knowing one's relative lack of knowledge. This danger cannot be avoided. Nonetheless, Lyotard's writing attempts to resist this assimilation, deciding upon the name of "the real," here a borrowed one, stripped of its specificity, deployed in full awareness of its weakness. He decides upon a name for that affective nothing, proceeding with it without attempting to apologize for this decision. It will have been a wrong—articulating it can only wrong the inarticulate—but it marks the point where a decision must be rendered if one is not to ignore the issue entirely. He does not announce anything; as Kent Still notes, his writing performs its exposure.[7] He styles weakness within his argumentation; the love that is here declared cannot serve as basis for a genre of discourse. The position of philosophy becomes otherwise; it is no longer exactly a discipline, or a genre of discourse. It becomes a mode of writing. The "sybilline" writing of Nietzsche or the late Heidegger is, Lyotard claims, still too assured in its prophetic mode, but:

> Wittgenstein, Gertrude Stein, Joyce or Duchamp seem like better "philosophical" minds than Nietzsche or Heidegger—by better, I mean more apt to take into consideration the exitless nothing that the West gives birth to in the first quarter of the twentieth century, and by "philosophical," I mean, if it is true that philosophizing is an affair of "style," what Paul Valéry concludes, in his very classically French way, in *Leonardo and Philosophy*.[8]

A philosopher, but then two (perhaps three or four) writers of literature, and a visual artist: philosophy becomes an affair of style insofar as in writing, thinking, or art, it finds itself already overtaken by that "exitless nothing" that emerges in the wake of the abeyance of faith in those "grand narratives" that Lyotard diagnoses in *The Postmodern Condition*. Philosophy finds itself in a position where it will have nothing any longer to say. It discovers that it always will have had nothing to say. What remains is style, the matter of tone, rhythm, plastic form: in short, the aesthetic, such as it reveals one's affectability, exterior to any discourse that might be articulated. This does not provide means to escape this "nothing." One plunges headlong into it, to show one's self as already affected by what lies outside of any accounting. All that one can do is to struggle to at least provide a glimpse of the suppressed affective nothing.

This approach remains a betrayal of philosophy as it is traditionally construed. Yet love and this betrayal are not contraries. In the final pages of *The Inhuman*, some paragraphs before Lyotard declares the witness a traitor, love appears as sedition, masking a certain bad faith:

> Solitude is *seditio*. Love is *seditio*. All love is criminal. It has no concern for the regulation of services, places, moments. And the solitude of the adolescent in the *domus* is seditious because it bears the whole order of nature and culture in the suspense of its melancholy. In the secrecy of his bedroom, he inscribes upon nothing, on the intimate surface of his diary, the idea of another house, of the vanity of any house. Like Orwell's Winston, he inscribes the drama of his incapacity before the law. Like Kafka. And lovers do not even have anything to tell. They are committed to *deixis*: this, now, yesterday, you. Committed to presence, deprived of representation.[9]

Love, as it is here depicted, is a species of sedition. It demands that one become apathetic to a certain extent. One must turn a deaf ear to the imperatives that demand that one perform, whether they are social, disciplinary, or any other. Yet, as Lyotard notes, this love is solitary, it entails no relation to another. It occurs in the suspension of every imperative that might bear down. It is sedition, but it is not self-serving, nor does it neutralize the law. Rather, one betrays one's self as being incapable before the law, as always having been incapable before the law. This writing is moved by something else, the presence of an affect that no articulated imperative can master, an affect that continues to impose itself and to demand its own account. One betrays what one was supposed to have kept hidden away, one's infancy, and thereby confesses that one was never quite the rational animal that the law presumes of its addressees. Not that this buys any respite—the law will not yield on this question. *Infantia*, infancy, is inevitably interpreted as *infamia*, infamy.[10] The double bind remains: one betrays the law, thus rendering one's self infamous, in order to betray something of one's affectedness. Insofar as this betrayal does not depart the domain of articulation, it will yet disserve affect, no matter how ostensibly subversive. All that the gesture may aim for is to indicate something of the affect that remains unaccounted, unaccountable.

To attest to affect, then, involves dispensing with notions of accountability, of ends allegedly necessary. To bear witness to that which speaks nothing, one does not address a testimony. The diary of the adolescent that Lyotard depicts in the passage addresses itself to no one, it addresses only its solitude, bought at the price of an affected ignorance of every legitimated end. Attempting to bespeak the presence of affect, it speaks in deictics, at the limit of representation. It signals presence without defining it. This, here, now; in writing, one addresses no one, yet poses one's self as responding to one's own affectedness. It is not "I" who writes, who assumes the position of the author. It is the event, the disturbance that affect is, unaccountably writing itself. Hence the necessary distancing from imperatives: at the level of writing or of the voice, before the grammarian intervenes, *sed itio* (going away) is *se ditio* (dominion from itself). One must go away, depart from the canons of the law if the event is to obtain of its own domain. This is, strictly speaking, impossible. Affect will have remained improprious. Thus the task emerges as interminable, it knows no progress. One must undertake it again, once more; as Claire Nouvet writes, "Writers ... know this debt that cannot be acquitted once and for all, but which can only be endlessly acknowledged in writing."[11] This interminable task of writing that bears no result is anathema to the regime of performativity. It is a "waste of time," offering no return. In this, at least, it is a labor of love.

Commenting on Lyotard's "hypobiography" of Malraux, *Signed, Malraux*, Philippe Bonnefis remarks, "[n]o doubt our fables, our beautiful fables, pretty tales of our childhood, need rewriting. Need being subjected, one after the other, to the hypocritique of infamy, from which it alone appears that they, as numerous as they are, draw the authority that they continue to exercise over grown-ups, even before they grew up."[12] The labor of criticism takes over the examination of works, renders judgments upon them, discovers in them what they meant to say or what they said without saying. If one should hear a note of hypocrisy echoed in the work of "hypocritique," this is not at all unwarranted; be it a labor of love, the differend remains, turning against what remains unsaid in any attempt to say it. This is not at all an excuse to be done with criticism, to replace it with a cheap cataloguing of aesthetic forms and their particular effects, such that they might serve as commodities, economic or cultural. Not that this could necessarily be avoided entirely. In one sense, it belongs to the work of this hypocritique that before we came to read the fables, they were already read to us, or read for us. They were organized into canons, transformed into received ideas before we were there to receive them. The proper names of writers become those of *auctores*, tokens passed around and ensuring passage towards legitimation. This is not the entirety of reading, of course, but such is the ground on which the cultural imperative to read is enshrined; few commence otherwise. All the same, it remains that our fables need rewriting; not because they might be found unworthy according to this or that criterion, but because they have not yet been written, those who wrote were never quite the *auctores* that they are taken to be. Underneath the vested authority with which they parade, they remain naked; they too were and are afflicted by something infantile that does not depart their works. It is the place of literature, as Lyotard construes it, to incline to affect, to be animated by it. In so doing, the author is exauthorized. Seized by the muteness of affect, he or she bears no authority, is no authority with regard to what is written. This sort of writing does not pertain to whatever dictum. It is a matter of the aesthetic that appears alongside but at a distance from signification, a question of style. "Style invents forms to capture the unheard-of," Lyotard writes; it attempts to give voice to the silence of affect, attempts to force a passage for the impossible.[13] What cannot be written, what cannot be named, nonetheless sounds off in writing. What is written is traversed by a presence that it cannot encompass; affect unsettles every account that articulated discourse might offer. The debt to affect remains unsettled, and thus one takes to writing again, as if it might finally be brought to term in articulation. The presumption will have wronged affect; nonetheless, this presumption serves to indicate the hold that affect asserts over infancy. One undertakes this labor all the same, out of a certain love, a love for the works that moved one in one's childhood and that continue to do so. It is fidelity surpassing what appears on the page; it gives itself to what remains unwritten upon pages. Out of this fidelity, one takes to write again, for the sake of the unwritten. It is a gesture worthy of Eubulides: one aims to write the unwritable, as it manifests itself in what has already been written. And if this is hypocritical, a betrayal of good sense, for all that it is no less love. It is not as if love has been ever known for its obedience to dictates.

The love that manifests in writing is not simple. Nor is it without its conflicts. Lyotard remarks that:

> There is a hatred of literature in the writer, of art in the painter: it is the love of what art and literature reveils by representing it, and which it is therefore

necessary to present again, to re-present, and veil anew. One tries to listen to and make heard the secret affection, the one that says nothing, one expends oneself, one exhausts oneself.[14]

It is not surprising that writing, as a work of love, should be hated by the writer. The task of presenting a witness to one's infantile affectability is interminable, forever unaccomplished, a source of frustration without end. The debt cannot be acquitted, the affect will have been wronged once more, and one will have shown one's self unworthy of the task. One must expend all of one's means in an attempt to gesture to the affect that lies beyond their reach. Utterly exhausted, one is nonetheless doomed to a certain failure; writing is "always badly formulated, however, by the mere fact of its being formulated,"[15] Lyotard remarks. Rhetorical skill, the art of figures, avails nothing:

> How can one make felt the presence of the nonrepresented unconscious, if one limits oneself to the manipulation of "figures," made to persuade, and which can only be representational compromises where presence is figured and thus misunderstood? *Aisthēsis* can only repress the truth of pathos (which is not pathetic) like the splendor of the church represses the presence of Jesus in the heart. Counter-Reformation, Jansenism, movement toward poverty in an effort to approach unfathomable misery. It is not Jesus' beauty that makes him true. He cannot even be approached through the senses; his incarnation is not his presence in the world, it is our tears sprung from joy. Thus sublime, an insensible affection, a sensible presence in the heart only. How can the affection be present in the pulpit if the preacher only speaks of it? It is not for him to make cry. One cries according to grace.[16]

What there is of the presence of affect does not give itself through forms, through any possible articulation. It appears in the tears of one utterly abandoned, tears manifesting the presence of affect. This is neither an articulated response, nor is it the result of calculation. The weeping itself is grace. It is a tautegorical signal, as Lyotard puts it in "The Affect-Phrase," both the signal of the state of being affected and this state itself.[17] It is necessary not to take the theological framing here at face value—Christian discourse being no less apt than any other to escape necessarily wronging the inarticulate—but nonetheless the inflection that Lyotard gives to this grace, in aligning it with Jansenism, is significant. It is not that of the Jesuit, for whom sufficient grace has been provided to all, such that they can obey the commandments. Neither is it that of the Lutheran, secure in faith despite the impossibility of obeying them. Rather, following Pascal, the commandments are impossible to obey; nonetheless it may happen that one may, on occasion, act justly. Yet this justice is not rote adherence to the law as it is written; the inability to obey the commandments might well entail the inability to interpret them correctly. This justice gestures to something else, to the debt to the unwritten. This is grace: what is impossible happens, without ceasing to be impossible.[18] The act of grace can only appear as a transgression of all possibles, where the impossible delivers a *coup de grâce* to the table of calculation upon which possibilities are inscribed. In its wake, there is only a body or a soul unmastered, given over to weeping convulsions. For Pascal as for Lyotard, it remains unaccountable; as impossible, this fleeting instant cannot serve as a foundation upon which new calculations might be proffered. It belongs neither to the reason, nor to the understanding, but to the heart, which Lyotard was to place aside the Kantian sentiment of the beautiful and the sublime, at the level of affectability.[19]

Literature—which would include philosophy, if we are to take seriously Lyotard's appraisal—attends to this grace. It does not will it, much less effect it. Grace, after all, might not be granted one who prays earnestly.[20] Grace is indifferent to whatever desire one might impose upon it, or impute to it. One might say that it demands indifference of the writer, but this is not precisely the case. Apathy and solitude are perhaps necessary if one is to attend to its silent passings, but grace itself asks nothing. As Anne Tomiche notes, Lyotard depicts literature as "a witnessing to the 'presence,' in the interior of articulated discourse, of non-articulation, of that which renders linkage problematic."[21] This presence passes silently in writing, showing itself only where the seams of articulation begin to come undone, where language does not signify, but signs itself affected. Lyotard depicts it thus:

> It is notable that the grace of the word, which seems to come all of its own, is suspect and must be placed under suspicion in the name of that which comes with the word, in the adornment of the word. Here also one would like to restitute to the thing that comes its exact candor. Its nudity. One insists on respecting a frankness, to make thought in its nascent stage broach the travesty of its inscription in language.[22]

The word moved by grace, he notes, appears to come of its own accord, without regard to what it may mean. It has no regard for the demands of the linkage of phrases. This is only a suspension of the law, not its abolition. This interruption does not prevent a return, one that regards the moment of grace as suspect. To honor this act of grace, Lyotard argues, is to acknowledge the resistance that it mounts to its inevitable capture by articulated discourse. For the law cannot comprehend the impossible befalling of grace as such. The word will be interrogated, for certainly it meant to say something. Interpretations will be offered, argumentation introduced, the act of grace thereby forgotten. One thus attempts to restore to the act of grace its candor, the naked state in which it means nothing, shows nothing save the nothing of affect. Only thus does thought own up to its own infancy, to the affect that set it in motion. Hence the interest in the paradoxes of Eubulides, the sophists, or even Pascal; the "absurdities" that they inflict upon the word force sense into retreat, while leaving the word its capacity to move the hearer, whether with wonder or pain. One might fault these figures for yet relying upon argumentation, however subverted. This is the case, but the differend cannot be overcome; what is offered to the affect remains articulation. One will not have ceased colluding with the *auctores*.

The term "grace" permeates Lyotard's later writings; it is nonetheless surprising that, in his last work, he turns to the Doctor of Grace himself, Augustine of Hippo. Turns, or rather returns, if one is not to ignore those works that preceded; one will not have forgotten the staunch criticisms launched in Lyotard's earlier writings.[23] Gone is the moralizing theologian; what Lyotard discovers is an Augustine not yet or no longer an *auctor*, much less an august one. This is the confessant Augustine, setting himself in a work that does not belong to the philosophical, theological, or rhetorical genres; as Lyotard writes:

> The *Confessions* are not of this vein: neither a plea whose end would be mastered and fixed by the virile intellect, caused with defending or refuting what is called for; nor a philosophical treatise, where the path would trace itself by conceptual discrimination between this and that, sensible/intelligible, soul/body, reason/ imagination. The confession does not divide, to the contrary: a crack stripes in zigzag all that offers itself to writing, to the grand despite of the *animus* [intellect], whose binary clarity is humiliated. The cut here has no place, has no time. The here-and-now, durations, places, lives and the I present themselves cracked, or rather, crack entirely, crackle themselves like a glass under a blow.[24]

The *Confessions*—*The Confessions of Augustine* of Lyotard—manifests a stricken writing. Philosophy, rhetoric, and theology are not cast aside, but appear here at the point of their disintegration, albeit one that remains unaccomplished. They have not collapsed, but show themselves to be riven by the presence of an affect that does not and cannot avail itself of their ends. Argumentation is brought to a halt. Distinctions may no longer be authorized and articulated. What shows forth is a writing that exposes itself as affected; it breaks with articulation, and thus from any particular placing in space or in time. Affect appears as a *coup de grâce* visited upon the *auctor*, overthrowing his every possible means, dispossessing him without return. There is no result here; the destruction remains unaccomplished. Nor is there a salvific recovery where the confessant is returned to himself anew. The ground of the discourses that one uses to articulate one's self gives way to the anarchic presence of affect. Writing occupies itself with this fissure: Lyotard writes, "it is in the minimal interstice of the cracking that the *stylus* styles itself, in the reciprocal fault of the enigma and of manifestation."[25] This styling, which is not Augustine's own, but the work of the stylus itself, is set to work by the impossible befalling of grace—it is moved by what it can neither master nor know. It gives forms, it writes and will have written, but only to display itself as riven, where the work of linkage has come undone.

Lyotard, it must be emphasized, does not follow the sainted doctor in sacralizing what remains outside the grasp of articulation, much less in divinizing it. Nor does he allow the text to pass without judgment; taking upon himself the role of the *advocatus diaboli* (devil's advocate), he accuses Augustine of having yet confessed in bad faith:

> He hears clearly the "Arise you who sleep," that Paul shouted to the Ephesians, but he could not get up. *Much better, were it for me, to give myself up to thy charity than to give myself over to my own covetousness, but notwithstanding the former course pleased me and convinced me, yet this latter seized me and held me confined.* Two attractions, two twin appetites, of near equal force, what does it take for one to prevail over the other? A nuance, an accent, a child humming an old tune? Who would speak of transcendence here when divine grace is placed on the same rank as a charm? . . . But evil is to desire the good just as one desires evil.[26]

Does Augustine here betray himself, as Lyotard asks, by placing divine love on the same plane as carnal pleasure? The line is one that Lyotard himself follows throughout his work on the *Confessions*, where divine grace is aligned with questions of seduction, of affectability, of a desire that has been stirred up through the senses in the wake of the impossible imposition of an absolute affect. The course of the *Confessions*, however incomplete the text may be, traces this arc, discovers it in Augustine. In short, the argument is thus: the desire for the divine is positioned in such a way that it exists within the same economy of pleasure and of phantasy that the saint attributes to his sordid phantasies. The supposed distinction between the Christian love that calls itself *caritas* and erotic love is, at best, incoherent—the moments that are intended to reveal this transcendent love remain obstinately material, this-worldly, aesthetic. The grace that reveals him as affected does not belong to any transcendence; it is ascribed to nuance, a shade of color, or the pitch of a child's tune. In these he discovers the ordeal of the absolute, evoked by those aesthetic experiences that denude him, deprive him of the means to articulate them. This is so; it is fine hypocritique. One can still hear Lyotard playing the part of the virile intellect that he had attempted to rule out—judging the validity of Augustine's attempted distinction, finding it wanting as such, and sketching out the consequences of what the text, in his reading, presents. Lyotard argues with and through the *Confessions*, a text which, if he is to be taken at face value, does not lend itself to argument. The moralist of one stripe or another will declare this a perversion and either recoil in horror, or rejoice in it, as is his or her wont. This is to miss the point. This is not a matter of fidelity, whether to a given orthodoxy or to its inverse, which remains an orthodoxy. These positions presume a firm foundation. But the passing of affect is always unfounded.

What emerges remains an act of grace, one that flies in the face of the precept that grace exists to serve the law, or that it is to serve as the governing term of the law. This is not to foreclose the event of grace, impossible though it might be. Philosophical argumentation too retains its role—argument might yet be mustered to deliver the *coup de grâce* to argumentation. The goal is not that Lyotard's argument, or any other, should be acknowledged as triumphant and become received opinion—it is to divest theory of its supposed position of mastery, to show that it yet bears with it the infantile affectability that it would deny. This is to say that Lyotard's argument is indeed in bad faith, but only the pious would remain able to condemn him for this. Argumentation is made to serve the purposes of betrayal, not one that is self-serving, but which aims towards immobilizing argumentation, if only for a moment, that something of grace might yet show through. To attest, in spite of every attempt to call it before the tribunal, that affect yet remains. Such a gesture is inevitably treasonous; the law cannot admit of grace, that there might be a limit to its means. Through one means or another it will reassert itself, declare its right, find reason for the occurrence and thereby domesticate it. Accounts will need to be settled, the disruption made to serve the law as an example. But all the same, a gesture that calls to a *coup de grâce* may yet remain an act of grace.

Notes

1 Jean-François Lyotard, *The Inhuman: Reflections on Time*, trans. Geoffrey Bennington and Rachel Bowlby (Minneapolis: University of Minnesota Press, 1991), 204.

2 Jean-François Lyotard, *Toward the Postmodern*, eds Robert Harvey and Mark S. Roberts (Atlantic Highlands, NJ: Humanities Books, 1993), 66–7.

3 Ibid., 57.

4 Jean-François Lyotard and Eberhart Gruber, *The Hyphen: Between Judaism and Christianity*, trans. Pascale-Anne Brault and Michael Naas (Atlantic Highlands, NJ: Humanities Books, 1993), 1, translation modified.

5 Lyotard, *Toward the Postmodern*, 63.

6 Lyotard, *The Hyphen*, 1.

7 Kent Still, introduction to *Minima Memoria: In the Wake of Jean-François Lyotard*, eds Claire Nouvet, Zrinka Stahuljak, and Kent Still (Stanford: Stanford University Press, 2007), xii.

8 Lyotard, *Postmodern Fables*, trans. Georges Van Den Abbeele (Minneapolis: University of Minnesota Press, 1997), 23, translation modified.

9 Lyotard, *The Inhuman*, 201, translation modified.

10 Jean-François Lyotard, *Soundproof Room: Malraux's Anti-Aesthetics*, trans. Robert Harvey (Stanford: Stanford University Press, 2001), 28.

11 Claire Nouvet, "The Inarticulate Affect: Lyotard and Psychoanalytic Testimony," in Claire Nouvet et al., *Minima Memoria*, 121.

12 Philippe Bonnefis, "Passages of the Maya," in ibid., 170–1.

13 Lyotard, *Soundproof Room*, 99.

14 Jean-François Lyotard, *Heidegger and the "jews,"* trans. Andreas Michel and Mark Roberts (Minneapolis: University of Minnesota Press, 1990), 34, translation modified.

15 Lyotard, *Postmodern Fables*, 158.

16 Lyotard, *Heidegger*, 34–5, translation modified.

17 Jean-François Lyotard, "The Affect-Phrase," in *The Lyotard Reader and Guide*, eds Keith Crome and James Williams (New York: Columbia University Press, 2006), 105.

18 See the first of Pascal's *Provinciales*, in *Oeuvres complètes*, vol. 1, ed. Michel de Guerin (Paris: Gallimard, 2000), 589–97.

19 Lyotard, *The Hyphen*, 3.

20 Pascal, *Provinciales*, 596.

21 Anne Tomiche, "Le canon littéraire de Jean-François Lyotard," in *Les Transformateurs Lyotard*, eds Corinne Enaudeau et al. (Paris: Sens & Tonka 2008), 114, my translation.

22 Lyotard, *Postmodern Fables*, 157.

23 Jean-François Lyotard, *Libidinal Economy*, trans. Iain Hamilton Grant (London: Athlone, 1993), 6–11.

24 Jean-François Lyotard, *The Confession of Augustine*, trans. Richard Beardsworth (Stanford: Stanford University Press, 2000), 48, translation modified.

25 Ibid., 50, translation modified.

26 Ibid., 22.

16

Impious Thinking

An Interview with Geoffrey Bennington

Mark Stoholski and Julie Gaillard

I. The turn to the affect-phrase

Mark Stoholski: *I'd like to begin with your text, "The Same, Even, Itself . . .," and your remarks concerning the place of the differend in Lyotard's thought following "The Affect-Phrase." As you note, this later text, Lyotard's supplement to* The Differend, *marks a key transformation of the notion of the differend. The introduction of the Freudian notion of affect and its link to the temporality of* Nachträglichkeit *(belatedness) inflicts a certain violence upon the notion of the differend. If one thought that one had a fairly stable notion of what it was, "the differend itself" (as the original title of "The Affect-Phrase" had it) will henceforth fail to ever, well, be itself.[1] Lyotard had previously attempted to account for the question of sentiment via Kant and Aristotle, who remain important interlocutors. But, as you note, when Freud enters the picture, bringing with him the question of sexual difference, this move threatens to collapse the distinction between the transcendental and the anthropological, and perhaps the problematic of affect threatens to escape the grasp of the philosophical genre. The problem of the "differend itself," and of affect, troubles those cases of differend described in the earlier work. What are the consequences of the introduction of the question of affect for the notion of the differend, and for Lyotard's work more generally? And how does the intrusion of this question trouble the genre of philosophy?*

Geoffrey Bennington: "Affect" has of course become a fashionable theme for philosophical and other reflection in recent years, though I am not sure if there is any direct line between Lyotard's late investigations and what has ensued in that field. I think it's important to see that this question is not merely "introduced" by

Lyotard as though he were simply turning to a new area of study or making a radical break with what came before (apparent breaks and new departures in his thought are always more complex than they might appear at first sight): the question of affect emerges *directly* from the problematic of the differend, and does so in a way that I think is better captured by the title "The Inarticulate: or, The Differend Itself" than by "The Affect-Phrase." Of course, there were already places in *The Differend* where the central concept of the *phrase* (phrase or sentence) was being pushed to certain limits: one of these ways (that I'll mention only briefly here) is in the strange configurations that emerge when the response to the question (for example): "Is everything that is, a phrase?," consists in saying something like, "that was a phrase of the interrogative regime," which seems to imply a kind of analytic philosophy stance (what we say and how we say it is the best evidence for working on ontological questions).[2] The other way, which is more pertinent to your question, I think, is the oblique recognition of phrases that are maybe not quite or not just phrases: so, for example (and not just any example, given what is to come), in the first of the Kant notices, the transcription of the Transcendental Aesthetic into the phrase talk of *The Differend* wants to transcribe the "language" of "matter" "spoken" by the unknown addressor of the "matter phrase," and, in so doing, is driven several times to describe this phrase as a "quasi-phrase," without that "quasi-" ever being thematized in the book. One senses Lyotard's hesitation around this term, as though he were reluctant to open any kind of breach in the general phrase-talk on which he's staked so much ("that there is a phrase is indubitable" being the starting-point for the whole enterprise):[3] but here we find, for example, "not one phrase (or quasi-phrase) but two," "two phrases or quasi-phrases."[4] And it is no accident that the same Notice describes this "matter phrase" (or "quasi-phrase") as "sentimental": it is not focused on a referent, it has a "conative" function. And in a couple of other places too, this unthematized notion of a "quasi-phrase" occurs in similarly "sentimental" contexts: once in the third Kant notice about the "feeling" alleged by the critical watchman in the exercise of reflective judgment,[5] and once in the Plato notice where he says that the epideictic genre of rhetoric "leans rather towards poetics," and goes on: "It is a matter of arousing in the addressee not phrases but those quasi-phrases, which are silent feelings. If phrases took place, they would sooner or later remove the equivocation from the pathos and dissipate the charm."[6] (It might also be worth pursuing the role of the prefix "quasi-" throughout the book, especially in the lengthy analyses of the "quasi-fact" of obligation and of "quasi-deictics," i.e. names or nouns.) It seems clear in retrospect (though it was not at all clear in 1983, to this reader at least), that these "quasi-phrases" are already evidence that the universal applicability of phrase-talk (what I have sometimes called "the language-game game")[7] is in some doubt—and it is obviously no accident that in all of these cases Lyotard talks about feeling, sentiment and/or silence. As sentiment and silence are part of the very definition of the differend "itself," then the "quasi-phrase" is already anticipating a certain general collapse of articulation (i.e. of the ability to map phrases onto their universes) and, after the fact, the strange sea-change that seems to happen in the "transitional" text now known as "The Affect-Phrase." So "affect" emerges from the very problematic of the differend itself, before Freud explicitly re-enters the picture: the suspicion might be that Lyotard has a certain "return to Freud" as an attempt to address the issues that *The Differend* certainly brought into some kind of focus, but could arguably not be addressed with the strict terms of the book itself. Lyotard himself regularly referred to the need for a "supplement" to the book (as signaled by the published subtitle of the affect-phrase piece), no doubt, as often around this time, with a nod towards Derrida.

You are right that all this gets still more complicated once Freud *does* explicitly re-enter the picture in the later texts, and it does seem as though the proper name "Freud" stands for a complication in the relations between philosophy and other "humanistic" disciplines, and might perhaps prompt a re-read of the very severe criticisms of anthropocentrism to be found in *The Differend* a propos of Kant and Wittgenstein. To state this quickly now (but I think we'll be coming back to it), once "infancy" emerges as a figure for the differend "itself," and once that infancy is apparently irreducibly marked by sexual difference—however that comes to be formulated—then what might have appeared to be the "anthropological" issue of sex takes on, at the very least, a "quasi-" transcendental importance. When Lyotard ends the affect-phrase text with a call to elaborate the transcendental status of *infantia* (infancy), he opens the transcendental to the "anthropological" in a way that perhaps also programs the otherwise extremely surprising turn to writing a biography of Malraux.

II. Sexual difference

MS: *Lyotard's engagement with sexual difference, in "The Affect-Phrase" and the texts surrounding it, centers on the notion of affect, as Freud articulates it in the* Project for a Scientific Psychology *and the metapsychological paper on the unconscious. While he is drawing from Freud, the formulation seems to be Lyotard's own. This approach to the question allows Lyotard to reframe the problem in terms of the difference between inarticulate "infantile" sexuality and articulation, which* *he associates with genital sexuality. Yet, as you note in "Childish Things," this understanding of sexual difference stands aside another, which continues to see the difference in terms of that between the sexes (I'm thinking of your analyses of the works on Malraux, and the essay on Hannah Arendt). How do you take the relation between these two models, which may not contradict, but certainly stand in tension with one another? And what does the notion of sexual difference do for Lyotard, that the late works so often invoke it as an impossible supplement?*

GB: I think there is definite hesitation in Lyotard around this question, or perhaps a progression, though I think it might be more complicated still than a question of "two models." The question of sexual difference is recurrent in Lyotard, from a very interesting passage in *Discourse, Figure*, where he approvingly quotes Marx's critique of Hegel and the idea that male and female are not in a dialecticalizable opposition, but that there is in sexual difference a relation to an "outside" (another figure of the "mute exteriority" we will be talking more about) which introduces something non-human into human sex.[8] And this is a passage he refers to again much later, in an interview with Gérald Sfez published in a special issue of *Rue Descartes*,[9] I think, as an instance of "the intractable," the "extreme real" which then enters into the series of non-synonymous terms that all seem to gesture toward the exteriority we are turning around (figure, the unpresentable, infancy, affect, etc.). This early interest in sexual difference runs through the "libidinal" and "pagan" work too (remember the very interesting essay that was translated as "One of the Things at Stake in Women's Struggles")[10] before becoming linked to the infancy thematics in the later period. Here, there is sometimes a fairly insistent narrowing of the broader focus that links infancy to the general exteriority figured, for example, by the "touch" of the aesthetic, so that, as you mention, the essay on infancy and Arendt explicitly refers infancy to the "event" of castration, "[t]he event of sexed reproduction in the history of living beings. And in individual ontogenesis, the echo of sexual difference, which is the event whose savagery the entire life of the individual is taken up with 'sorting out [*régler*].'"[11] On this reading, infancy is no longer a general name for a primary passivity, but a very specific determination of any such passivity: if we are indebted to the irretrievable past of infancy, this is no longer just to do with the structure of events in general, in their intrinsic *Nachträglichkeit*, but very specifically to do with *this* event. And I suppose that's why he can sometimes align sexual difference and ontological difference. As this theme moves into the very late work (the Malraux biography and the posthumous Augustine book, but already in "Emma" in a slightly different way), it becomes murkier still: here what he often calls "the sexual" (I really don't know if he was reading Laplanche) is often related to figures that are quite violent and disturbing, involving scenes of what we would easily think of as child-abuse (Claire Nouvet has a terrific reading of this in "Emma") and other forms of violation, up to and including anal rape, which is a recurrent figure in the Malraux work (Malraux's own obsession with this figure does not entirely explain the way Lyotard mobilizes it, or so it seems to me), and again with respect to Augustine. This development in its own *nachträglich* (belated) way then also might motivate a re-reading of *Libidinal Economy* (I refer to some examples in "Childish Things").[12] Again, this could be seen as a striking way of presenting the thought that events cannot be thought of as presenting themselves politely against a horizon of expectation, and might therefore be said to befall me by surprise, from behind (this would again be quite close to a Derridean way of thinking), but Lyotard is very insistent in relating this to these ambiguous sexual figures which do indeed seem to be pushing beyond or before the specific articulations of castration and the "official" Freudian versions of sexual difference, with the dorsal perspective of the "from behind" complicating the distribution of the sexes here. This is a point where the early characterization of the "matrix-figure" does indeed seem (first, with respect to Malraux or Augustine, who seem to function as Lyotard's stand-ins for some of these developments, stand-ins he exploits by his very extensive use of free indirect discourse, but then also to Lyotard himself) to combine the two elements the relationship of which I had long ago in *Writing the Event* criticized Lyotard for not clarifying sufficiently in *Discourse, Figure*: namely the *general* sense whereby this is the level of the figure that lines up with our "mute exteriority," and the apparently singular sense in which it is a kind of idiomatic signature of an *oeuvre*.[13] I confess that this aspect of late Lyotard remains quite mysterious to me, and that I do not really know how to construe the interrelations of (auto-) biographical and philosophical here—but I do think that this very late work is pushing quite hard at the limits of our usual ways of thinking about these matters, and that this unsettling introduction of a singularly Lyotardian auto-biographical dimension into the philosophical has perhaps not been sufficiently read.

III. Reflective judgment and politics

MS: *One of the most striking features of the texts that immediately precede* The Differend—Enthusiasm, *and* Just Gaming, *most notably—is the way Lyotard reframes the Kantian motif of reflective judgment. By putting Kant into relation* *with Aristotle and Levinas, Lyotard strips away the specificity that the aesthetic has in the Kantian corpus; judging without criteria becomes a central feature not only of ethics, but of politics as well. As you argue in "Political Animals," Lyotard maintains an interest in politics in his later works, even if it is a politics that resists any determinate program. He perhaps emphasizes it less immediately once the inarticulate and infancy enter the picture, but this is only a difference in tone. Nonetheless, this turn seems to alter the picture somewhat; it is as if we were asked, in our passages across the archipelago of language games, to turn an ear also to the murmur of the waves, which cannot be shut out. Is there a transformation of reflective judgment with the introduction of an intransigent, affected infancy and its* Nachträglich *temporality? And, if so, how does it impact a notion of politics?*

GB: You are quite right to point to judgment as a crux of Lyotard's work from the beginning of the 80s—the rather extraordinary Cerisy conference devoted to Lyotard in 1982 was quite pertinently entitled "Comment Juger? (How to Judge?),"[14] and the *Just Gaming* thematic of judging in the absence of criteria was a major concern of all the participants. This might lead to all sorts of confusions once Lyotard looks for support to the Kant of the reflective judgment, so it's important to see that, in so doing, he is pushing Kant to the limit of anything recognizable as "Kantianism"—for example, by making of the exercise of the reflective judgment a presupposition of any cognition at all (however determinative its judgments may appear to be in Kant's official presentation), and by taking very seriously the thought that in Kant's system judgment is a rigorously "critical" activity that has no "doctrinal" counterpart in the projected system of metaphysics Kant thought he was preparing. (My own view of this is that this rigorously critical status of the reflective judgment in fact disturbs Kant's "official" notion of critique itself: critique is supposed to be there to prepare the ground for the doctrinal edifice of the metaphysics to come; but if the most critical example of critique is something that does not have a doctrine to look forward to, then it contests the very teleological schema that determines the official concept of critique—and therefore, I would want to argue, all other teleological concepts in Kant.) Kant himself famously claims that the aesthetic judgment is the essential part of the third *Critique*, but I think it is going to follow from Lyotard's radical sense of the reflective judgment that the sense of the "aesthetic" here (however interested Lyotard genuinely was in aesthetics) must be the very general (an)aesthetics we have been talking about. And once that is true, then there is no problem in thinking that one salient place in which this importance of the reflective judgment shows up is in politics. "Everything is political if politics is the possibility of the differend on the occasion of the slightest linkage" is one way to formulate that thought.[15] Your excellent question suggests that nonetheless something changes here once infancy and its associated concepts enter the picture. I'm sure you are right about this: the "archipelago" image in *The Differend* to which you refer does clearly raise an issue as to the ocean in which the archipelago is found. This was the subject of an early objection by Jean-Luc Nancy, who wanted to align the question with the Heideggerian "question of being," and is subsequently the object of some good-humored banter also involving Philippe Lacoue-Labarthe about whether that ocean should be thought of as indeed "*la mer*" (the sea) or "*la mère*" (the mother), and Lyotard is not entirely consistent about his answer to that question. Either way, there's a "murmur," as you call it, which might be the *phōnē* in every *logos*, so long as we remember that *phōnē*, with which Lyotard plays fairly fast and loose in the affect-phrase text (if we bother to go back and check the Aristotle), is also explicitly referred to as *mute*.[16] This sits uncomfortably with any programmatic view of politics (I imagine Lyotard rolling his eyes at some recent attempts to revive the idea of communism), but once we accept that there is no *logos* without a *phōnē* it both represses and always fails to repress (my jokey version of this at the end of "Political Animals" is to say that *logos* is always somewhat *phoney*),[17] then one possible, and I think quite promising, line to follow would take on the connotations of sophistry and rhetoric that "phoney *logos*" entails, and develop from that a generalized politics of resistance that would be much less susceptible to the ambient self-righteousness, or "piety," to use Lyotard's term, than much political discourse today.

MS: *What role would the politics of resistance play, then, relative to the manifestations of the "phoney" logos" that are marked in many of Lyotard's texts? I think, in particular, of* Libidinal Economy—*a text that he himself would come to resist somewhat in his later years—and his comments upon the status of its writing in* Just Gaming. *There he mentions that it is entirely rhetoric, perhaps in the epideictic mode that you mentioned above; as he describes it "it works entirely at the level of persuasion, of the old Peithō [Persuasion], and even if the turns employed were not controlled . . . nevertheless it is certain that the 'calculated' (but uncontrolled) effect was certainly not that of a pedagogy, nor that of a dialectic; it was much more poetic, more literary, but in a somewhat odd sense of the term."[18] Thus construed, it isn't a work of "theory" (not that some haven't taken it that way, a position of which you have rightly been critical). Rather, it seems to flaunt its "phoney" character within the philosophical genre, being a collection of affected* *ruses and dissimulations; these might operate those non-theoretical "sentimental phrases," to which you call attention. This character isn't unique to that text; some element of ruse seems integral throughout Lyotard's work, albeit a ruse that indicates itself in order to gesture towards that muteness that might otherwise escape. Where does this leave us, as readers of Lyotard who might seek to follow texts that seem to resist us, and which perhaps enjoin us not to obey them?*

GB: All of these terms, "rhetoric," "ruse," "phoney," are intrinsically paradoxical (at least once we separate out a certain practice of rhetoric from the discursive policing operations that often characterize the meta-discourse called "Rhetoric," or once we see that "the rhetorical" is not always captured by Rhetoric). If we take "ruse" seriously (as Lyotard likes to do in the wake of Detienne and Vernant's analysis of the Ancient Greek *mētis* (cunning)), then we have to ruse with it.[19] Lyotard's version of this cannot be the same as that famously laid out by Hegel as "the cunning of reason" (known in French as "*la ruse de la raison*"), which operates as a version of dialectical negativity functioning in view of the Result, and which is, of course, one of Lyotard's most consistent objects of suspicion throughout his work. *Libidinal Economy* seemed to Lyotard, I think, to be an extreme example of this reflexively ruseful tendency in his work, and one that he came, if not to regret, at least to deprecate somewhat. But remember that already *Discourse, Figure* opens with an image of what a "good book" might look like, and that would already not at all take the form of a philosophical treatise. All of this is of a piece with a "resistance" in more than one sense of the word (but, in any case, is not limited to "resistance" in the French wartime sense, nor obviously the psychoanalytic sense), and that is in a way already an answer to your "where does this leave us" question: it certainly doesn't leave us anywhere that is confidently determinable in any kind of teleological schema; rather, as it *leaves* us, it always somewhat abandons us to the "where does this leave us?" question, which for its part never leaves us.

IV. The subject of philosophy

Julie Gaillard: *In "Opening Up," you show that, for Lyotard, the activity of thinking is built upon the occultation of the "more or less mute exteriority" which exceeds the scope of any historical account. Lyotard alternately calls it "figure," "aisthēsis," "phōnē," "affect," "infancy," "the Other," "the Thing." Calling this exteriority "a kind of archi-passivity of thinking," a "passivity 'before' thinking can*

get started,"[20] you show that Lyotard, through his reading of Kant, locates this
infancy of thought as a condition of the domain of (adult) knowledge. Because this
archi-passivity is an archaic stratum of experience which subtends and gives rise to
subjects and to intersubjectivity, it lies "under," as it were, the "argumentative" or
"rational" adult age, and remains ever-present, ghosting it, doubling it, while
remaining concealed.

This "more or less mute exteriority," while being the milieu that precedes the
formation of anything like a "subject" or like "intersubjectivity," seems to unsettle
the very activity of thinking. This is perhaps not to dispense entirely with the notion
of the subject—the term is still invoked in the late essay on the sensus communis,
but no longer as foundational, self-identical, or universal. What is it that affect does
to the subject of philosophy? And how are we to understand this latter term?

GB: That "more or less mute exteriority" exceeds more than merely a "historical"
account! The claim is not only that this is inaccessible to *any* of the human
sciences, but that many forms of philosophy also fail to encounter it. That's the
point of the long engagement with "metapragmatics" in the early parts of the
"Foundation Crisis" encyclopedia article I was glossing in "Opening Up" (I guess
nobody much reads Karl Otto Apel these days . . .). And it seems clear to me that,
for Lyotard, any philosophy of the subject is always going to foreclose this
dimension that Lyotard was always trying to address: in a sense his whole
thinking is devoted to showing that philosophy is not grounded in "the subject"
(be it Cartesian or Hegelian), or perhaps that it is not thinking to the extent that
it tries to ground itself that way. This still seems to me to be a radical aspect of
work done in France from the 1960s, and one that is still in some sense "to come."
Along with Derrida and Deleuze, Lyotard has an admirably intransigent view of
this: I'm confident he would have thought that the more recent attempts to
rehabilitate "the subject"—often enough because of rather superficial concerns
about "agency"—represent what he might have called a "slackening." (Incidentally,
this would be part of why recent attempts to generalize a supposed "correlationism"
depend on a failure to read that work, and why Lyotard would be extremely
scathing about the so-called "new realism.") This does "unsettle the very activity
of thinking," as you say, insofar as it places thinking in a secondary, "passive"
position with respect to the event of that "mute exteriority." "I" is not the "first
person" in this approach, though, again, one of the great strengths of Lyotard's
thinking is that it doesn't simply re-instate a primary subject on the side of the
"thou" or the "you": Lyotard's work certainly does not claim that ethics is first
philosophy, however interested he is in Levinas. Of course, just as part of Lyotard's

philosophical task was always to account for the possibility of the positions he is attacking (remember, for example, the analysis in *Discourse, Figure* of how something like a "signified" might have seemed a plausible, or even unavoidable, concept even as we show that it really isn't), so it does seem important to account for the tenacity of the concept of the subject, which then has to be reconstructed, whether on the basis of the phrase-talk in *The Differend*, which has that lovely analysis of the *cogito* and its presupposition of a possible synthesis of the "I" in the "I think" with the "I" in the "I am," or on the basis of the pre-articulate aesthetic "touch" of alterity in the later work. But it is pretty clear, I think (I'm also remembering conversations with Jean-François during which he was often humorously scathing about any "philosophy of the subject," and puzzled that an otherwise smart man like Badiou would want to write a *Theory of the Subject* at all) that he was not at all interested in *reinstating* a "subject of philosophy." As you rightly observe, this should unsettle "the very activity of thinking," and, first of all, by implying that thinking is not straightforwardly an "activity" at all. All sorts of paradoxes and difficulties still remain in this situation, of course, and not least because all the ways he finds of formulating or hinting at that "mute exteriority" are necessarily lateral and allusive: "infancy," for example, is not an identifiable state that precedes adulthood, but something that inhabits adulthood in a way that can never be brought into the light, just as, to use an example I've always liked from *Discourse, Figure,* any attempt to bring lateral vision into focus loses exactly what makes the lateral lateral.[21] (Though, if you'll allow me a digressive thought, maybe just this is part of what makes photography so fascinating, in that it can apparently allow us to focus on the blur.) This general set-up appears to me to be consistent across all of Lyotard's thinking: finding a way of "seeing" the lateral (without which there would be no sight), of "presenting (that there is) the unpresentable," of articulating the inarticulable—that's the very task of thinking, and intrinsically calls for an element of invention in response to the event that I have not constructed or even chosen. Given that by definition these tasks could never be achieved, because they are intrinsically aporetic (if we succeeded in presenting the unpresentable we would have failed just by presenting it—which is why there's an "anaesthetic" dimension to what Lyotard calls the aesthetic), then there's a "fail again, fail better" logic at work which in principle keeps thinking going indefinitely and, with luck, inventively.

JG: *In* The Differend, *this non-foundational, secondary character of the subject that you describe, is thought of in terms of a primacy of the phrase. As you note in* Writing the Event, *the phrase does not presuppose a preexisting subject: on the* *contrary, it is the phrase itself which positions the subject, as an effect of its articulation into a universe. Subjects, alternating between the position of addressee and addressor ("I" and "you"), are "effects of the concatenation of sentences."*[22] *There already, "'I' is not the "first person,'" as you say. With the unarticulated affect-phrase, the primacy of the subject is further dismissed. As Lyotard writes, "unarticulated would signify: this phrase does not present a phrase universe; it signals the meaning; this meaning is of only one kind, pleasure and/or pain . . .; this meaning is not related no any referent . . .; ultimately, this meaning does not proceed from any addressor (I) and does not address itself to any addressee (you)."*[23] *As for the concatenation of sentences, the affect-phrase suspends or interrupts it: it does not "allow itself to be linked on to according to the rules of any genre of discourse."*[24] *How are we to understand the continuities and differences between these two dismissals of the subject?*

GB: Let's perhaps be careful about the term "dismissal" . . . *The Differend*'s analysis tries to show that what is traditionally called "subject" cannot (even in canonical formulations, and exemplarily that of Descartes) have the foundational privilege inscribed in its very concept and that concept's name. Once the event of the phrase is seen to precede the subject, then that foundation is undermined. In some ways, and formulated like that, it could seem as if all Lyotard were doing were a kind of rigorously formulated version of a whole trend (the now decried "linguistic turn") of making "language" in some way the foundation instead of the subject. But, in fact, if I am right in what I was saying earlier about the signs within *The Differend* of a kind of internal collapse of the phrase-talk that gives it its scaffolding, then the "inarticulate" is, analytically in fact, already at work in those analyses: the affect-phrase's failure to present a universe (and therefore even to "be" a phrase) must already be at work in *The Differend* itself as, precisely, "the differend itself." So there is a rigorous continuity between these two analyses, even as the second appears to overtake and undermine the first. I guess another way of thinking about this would be to say it also flows from the priority of the *quid* over the *quod* in *The Differend*: once the "that it happens" (or even the "does it happen?," the *arrive-t-il?*) precedes the "what happens," then making the *phrase* (a *quod*, like it or not) the privileged way of thinking about the *quid* can only be provisional.

JG: *If the task of thinking is "to present (that there is) the unpresentable," it is condemned, as you show, to remain lateral, allusive, aporetic, and interminable. You associate the task of thinking with "an element of invention"—also echoing the* *famous passage of* The Differend *where Lyotard sets out for literature, philosophy, and politics the task of inventing new idioms, of bearing witness to differends. In the case of affect, "the differend itself," this task of bearing witness is as impossible as it is necessary. Pulled by and pushed toward the event of this mute exteriority of affect, writing remains with it in an irreducible differend, and will always "fail again" to grasp it. We know that Lyotard often defines writing as a "working-through" comparable to anamnesis. And indeed, in a passage of* Heidegger and "the jews," *he defines writing as "this 'work' that is nourished by the thing excluded in the interior soaked with its representational misery, but which sets out to represent it (this thing) in words, in colors. . . . [I]t devotes itself, through the most diverse concerns . . ., to marking on its body the 'presence' of that which has not left a mark. It develops as deferred action, but it tries not to be symptomatic, simple phobia, the crude forgetting of the unforgettable secret."*[25] *How are we to understand the task of thinking as a "response" to the event of affect? And how will philosophy, marked by this lateral and aporetic character, invent forms and approaches to articulate this response? How will it "fail better"?*

GB: If I knew how it will "fail better" we would already be outside the logic we're trying to understand! *Knowing how* to fail better would consist in succeeding, and therefore "failing worse" (and concomitantly being guilty of the self-righteous piety Lyotard always detested). So the quick answer to your question is: I don't know. Of course, there's something intrinsically, and interestingly, disappointing about this kind of response: if Lyotard (he's not alone) is saying to us "be inventive!," then we are on the edge of a classic double bind. Many people are impatient or uncomfortable with that situation, whence perhaps the recent tendency to resort to all the kinds of political gesturing and identifications that Lyotard tried so (im)patiently to undermine, in *Just Gaming* for example, or in that terrific little piece on the figure of the intellectual.[26] Many people really are invested in the figure of what we now call the "public intellectual" who "recalls the world to its lost meaning," and seem quite unaware of Lyotard's very powerful and convincing undermining of that figure. When Lyotard protests so intransigently against all that, in the name of "saving the honor of thought,"[27] he knows that this is not a watchword that could ever *compete* on the same level with the watchwords of classical political programs and platforms. Having said that, the whole point (which necessarily goes missing a little in the type of exercise we are going in for here) is precisely not to attempt to reduce the "fail better" situation *itself* to any kind of watchword at all (that would precisely be moving towards the "symptomatic, simple phobia, the crude forgetting of the unforgettable secret," as you quote from the *Heidegger* book). Printing "Fail Better" as a slogan across the front of a t-shirt already fails to fail better. "Working through" or "anamnesis" are trying to capture this tenuous and paradoxical situation in which there is a "debt" to what I have been calling "mute exteriority," and which Lyotard's work consists in naming and characterizing in what is in principle a non-finite series of terms and motifs: and just that process of naming and characterization is already part of the "inventive" response to the call of that exteriority. Unlike some thinkers to whom he is otherwise on occasion quite sympathetic (I'm thinking especially of Rorty here, but in different ways his position on this could also be contrasted with Wittgenstein or Heidegger), this view of the task of thinking does not at all project a kind of demise or euthanasia of philosophy in its fulfillment or withering away. Perhaps this (very firm and consistent) understanding of the task of thinking is destined always to be marginal (or, why not, "lateral"): unlike currently fashionable thinking, it certainly does not constantly tell us "what's on the agenda," nor does it indulge any prophetic claim to know that "the time has come" for this or that specific action or thinking. Rather, a proliferation, a multifarious "scatter" (as I like to call it), that affirms unconditionally something of the *poikilon* (motley) quality that Plato (and some modern Platonists) so fiercely denounced in his diatribe against democracy, and that is intrinsically resistant to the teleological patterns that are obviously endemic in political thinking, but also in fact in metaphysics more generally. If the term "philosophy" is mortgaged to that metaphysics, then perhaps "thinking" may be a better name for the (paradoxically passive) activity in question here.

Notes

1 Geoffrey Bennington, "The Same, Even, Itself . . .," in *Late Lyotard* (Lexington: Createspace, 2005), 43–64.

2 Jean François Lyotard, *The Differend: Phrases in Dispute,* trans. Georges van den Abbeele (Minneapolis: University of Minnesota Press, 1988), 68–9.

3 Ibid., 59.

4 Ibid., 62.

5 Ibid., 135.

6 Ibid., 21.

7 See for instance Bennington, "The Same, Even, Itself . . .," 46.

8 Jean François Lyotard, *Discourse, Figure,* trans. Antony Hudek and Mary Lydon (Minneapolis: University of Minnesota Press, 2011), 133.

9 Jean-François Lyotard. "L'extrême réel : Entretien avec Gérald Sfez," *Rue Descartes*, special issue, "Passions et politique," ed. Gérald Sfez and Marcel Hénaff, 12–13 (May 1995), 200–4.

10 Jean François Lyotard, "One of the Things at Stake in Women's Struggles," trans. Deborah J. Clarke, *SubStance* 6/7.20 (Autumn 1978), 9–17.

11 Jean François Lyotard, *Toward the Postmodern*, eds. Robert Harvey and Mark S. Roberts (Atlantic Highlands, NJ: Humanity Books, 1993), 147.

12 Geoffrey Bennington, "Childish Things," in *Late Lyotard*, 1–42.

13 Geoffrey Bennington, *Lyotard: Writing the Event* (New York: Columbia University Press, 1988), 93.

14 Published as *La Faculté de juger* (Paris: Les Editions de Minuit), 1985.

15 Lyotard, *The Differend*, 139.

16 Jean François Lyotard, "The Affect-Phrase," in *The Lyotard Reader and Guide*, eds Keith Crome and James Williams (New York: Columbia University Press, 2006), 107–8.

17 Geoffrey Bennington, "Political Animals," *Diacritics* 39.2 (Summer 2009), 34.

18 Jean François Lyotard and Jean-Loup Thébaud, *Just Gaming*, trans. Wlad Gozich (Minneapolis: University of Minnesota Press, 1985), 4.

19 See Marcel Detienne and Jean-Pierre Vernant, *Cunning Intelligence in Greek Culture and Society* trans. Janet Lloyd (Chicago: University of Chicago Press, 1991).

20 Geoffrey Bennington, "Opening Up," in *Rewriting Lyotard: Figuration, Presentation, Resistance, Cultural Politics* 9.2 (2013), 205.

21 Lyotard, *Discourse, Figure*, 155.

22 Bennington, *Writing the Event*, 125.

23 Lyotard, "The Affect-Phrase," 105–6.

24 Ibid., 105.

25 Jean François Lyotard, *Heidegger and "the jews*," trans. Andreas Michel and Mark Roberts (Minneapolis: University of Minnesota Press, 1990), 33.

26 Jean François Lyotard, "Tombeau de l'intellectuel," in *Tombeau de l'intellectuel et autres papiers* (Paris: Galilée, 1984), 11–22.

27 Lyotard, *The Differend*, xii.

Bibliography

Works by Jean-François Lyotard

Discours, figure. Paris: Klincksieck, 1971. Translated as *Discourse, Figure* by Anthony Hudek and Mary Lydon. Minneapolis: Univerisity of Minnesota Press, 2011.

"Psychanalyse et peinture." In *Encyclopedia Universalis*, vol 13. Paris: Encyclopedia Universalis, 1972.

Dérive à partir de Marx et Freud. Paris: Union Générale d'Editions, 1973. Partially translated in the volume *Driftworks*, edited by Roger McKeon. New York: Semiotext(e), 1984.

Des dispositifs pulsionels. Paris: Union Générale d'Editions, 1973. Partially translated in the volume *Driftworks*, edited by Roger McKeon. New York: Semiotext(e), 1984.

Economie libidinale. Paris: Les Editions de Minuit, 1974. Translated as *Libidinal Economy* by Iain Hamilton Grant. Bloomington: Indiana University Press, 1993.

"Sur la force des faibles." *L'Arc* "Lyotard" 64 (1976), 4–12.

"A Conversation With Jean-François Lyotard" (With Bernard Blistène). *Flash Art*, 121 (March 1985), 32–9.

Instructions païennes. Paris: Galilée, 1977. Translated as "Lessons in Paganism" by David Macey in *The Lyotard Reader*, edited by Andrew Benjamin. Oxford and Cambridge: Basil Blackwell, 1989.

Rudiments païens: genre dissertatif. Paris: Union Générale d'Editions, 1977. Partially translated in *Toward the Postmodern*, edited by Robert Harvey and Mark S. Roberts. Atlantic Highlands: Humanities Press, 1993. The chapter "Féminité dans la métalangue" is translated as "One of the Things At Stake in Women's Struggles" by Deborah J. Clarke, *SubStance* 6/7.20 (Autumn 1978), 9–17.

"The Unconscious as Mise-en-Scène." Translated by Joseph Maier. In *Performance in Postmodern Culture*, edited by Michel Benamou and Charles Caramello. Madison, WI: Coda Press, 1977.

"On the Strength of the Weak," *Semiotexte* 3.2 (1978), 204–14.

"Petites ruminations sur le commentaire d'art." *Opus International* 70–1 (1979), 16–17.

Les Transformateurs Duchamp. Paris: Galilée, 1977. Translated in a bilingual edition as *Les Transformateurs Duchamp/Duchamp's TRANS/formers*. Edited by Herman Parret. Leuven: Leuven University Press, 2010.

Au Juste (with Jean-Loup Thébaud). Paris: Christian Bourgois, 1979. Translated as *Just Gaming* by Wlad Gozich. Minneapolis: University of Minnesota Press, 1985.

La Condition postmoderne: Rapport sur le savoir. Paris: Les Editions de Minuit, 1979. Translated as *The Postmodern Condition: A Report on Knowledge* by Geoffrey Bennington and Brian Massumi. University of Minnesota Press, 1984.

"The Works and Writings of Daniel Buren: An Introduction to the Philosophy of Contemporary Art." Translated by Lisa Liebmann. *Artforum* 19.6 (Feb. 1981): 56–64.

"La Performance et la phrase chez Daniel Buren." In *Performance, Text(e)s & Documents*, edited by Chantal Pontbriand, 66–9. Montreal: Parachute, 1981.

"Theory as Art: A Pragmatic Point of View." In *Image and Code*, edited by Wendy Steiner, 71–7. Ann Arbor: University of Michigan Press, 1981.

Le Différend. Paris: Les Editions de Minuit, 1983. Translated as *The Differend: Phrases in Dispute* by Georges Van Den Abbeele. Minneapolis: Univerisity of Minnesota Press, 1988.

Tombeau de l'intellectuel et autres papiers. Paris: Galilée, 1984.

L'Enthousiasme, la critique kantienne de l'histoire. Paris: Galilée, 1986. Translated as *Enthusiasm: The Kantian Critique of History* by Georges Van Den Abbeele. Stanford: Stanford University Press, 2009.

"Sensus Communis, le sujet à l'état naissant." *Cahiers Confrontation* 20 (Winter 1989), 161–79. Translated as "Sensus Communis" by Marian Hobson and Geoffrey Bennington. In *Judging Lyotard*. Edited by Andrew Benjamin. New York: Routledge, 1992.

"It's as if a line . . ." Translated by Mary Lydon. *Contemporary Literature* 29.3 (1988), 457–82.

Le Postmoderne expliqué aux enfants: Correspondance, 1982–1985. Paris: Galilée, 1986. Translated as *The Postmodern Explained: Correspondence, 1982–1985*, edited by Julian Pefanis and Morgan Thomas. Minneapolis: University of Minnesota Press, 1993.

Que Peindre?: Adami, Arakawa, Buren (2 vols). Paris: Editions de la Différence, 1986. Translated in a bilingual edition as *Que Peindre?: Adami, Arakawa, Buren/ What to Paint ?: Adami, Arawaka, Buren*. Edited by Herman Parret. Leuven: Leuven University Press, 2012.

Heidegger et les "juifs." Paris: Galilée, 1988. Translated as *Heidegger and the "jews"* by Andreas Michael and Mark S. Roberts. Minneapolis: Univerisity of Minnesota Press, 1990.

L'Inhumain: causeries sur le temps. Paris: Galilée, 1988. Translated as *The Inhuman: Reflections on Time* by Geoffrey Bennington and Rachel Bowlby. Stanford: Stanford University Press, 1991.

Leçons sur "l'Analytique du sublime": Kant, "Critique de la faculté de juger," paragraphes 23–29. Paris: Galilée, 1988. Translated as *Lessons on the Analytic of the Sublime: Kant's Critique of Judgment §§ 23–9* by Elizabeth Rottenberg. Stanford: Stanford University Press. 1991.

"Emma" in *Nouvelle Revue de Psychanalyse* 39 (1989), 43–70. Translated by M. Sanders (with R. Brons and N. Martin) as "Emma: Between Philosophy and Psychoanalysis."

In *Lyotard: Philosophy, Politics and the Sublime*, edited by Hugh J. Silverman, 23–45. New York and London: Routledge, 2002.

"Universal History and Cultural Differences." Translated by David Macey. In *The Lyotard Reader*, edited by Andrew Benjamin, 314–23. Oxford and Cambridge: Blackwell, 1989.

"L'inarticulé ou le différend même." In *Figures et conflits rhétoriques*, eds Michel Meyer and Alain Lempereur (Brussels: University of Brussels, 1990), 201–7. Translated as "The Affect-Phrase (From a Supplement to The Differend)" in *The Lyotard Reader and Guide*, edited by Keith Crome and James Williams. Edinburgh: Edinburgh University Press, 2006.

"That Which Resists After All (an Interview with Gilbert Larochelle)." *Philosophy Today* 36.4 (1992), 402–17.

Lectures d'Enfance. Paris: Galilée, 1993.

Moralités postmodernes. Paris: Galilée, 1993. Translated as *Postmodern Fables* by Georges Van Den Abbeele. Minneapolis: University of Minnesota Press, 1997.

Political Writings. Translated by Bill Readings, Kevin Paul, and Kevin P. Geiman. Minneapolis: University of Minnesota Press, 1993.

Sam Francis: Lesson of Darkness – "like the paintings of a blind man." Translated by Geoffrey Bennington. Venice, CA: Lapis Press, 1993. Also in a bilingual edition as *Sam Francis: Leçon de Ténèbres – "like the paintings of a blind man"/ Sam Francis: Lesson of Darkness – "like the paintings of a blind man."* Translated by Geoffrey Bennington. Leuven: Leuven University Press, 2010.

Toward the Postmodern. Edited by Robert Harvey and Mark S. Roberts. Atlantic Highlands, NJ: Humanities Books, 1993.

Un Trait d'union (with Eberhard Gruber). Sainte-Foy: Les Editions le Griffon d'Argile. Translated as *The Hyphen: Between Judaism and Christianity* by Pascale-Anne Brault and Michael Naas. Atlantic Highlands, NJ: Humanities Press, 1993.

"Nietzsche and the Inhuman" (with Richard Beardsworth), *Journal of Nietzsche Studies* 7 (1994), 67–130.

"L'extrême réel : Entretien avec Gérald Sfez." *Rue Descartes*, special issue, "Passions et politique," edited by Gérald Sfez and Marcel Hénaff, 12–13 (May 1995), 200–4.

"Resistances: A Conversation of Sergio Benvenuto with Jean-François Lyotard," *JEP: European Journal of Psychoanalysis* 2 (1995–1996), n. pag., accessed March 12, 2014, www.psychomedia.it/jep/number2/lyotard.htm.

"Freud, Energy and Chance: A Conversation with Jean-François Lyotard" (with Richard Beardsworth). *Teknema: Journal of Philosophy and Technology* 5 (1999).

Signé Malraux. Paris: Grasset, 1996. Translated as *Signed, Malraux* by Robert Harvey. Minneapolis: University of Minnesota Press, 1999.

Chambre sourde: l'antiesthétique de Malraux. Paris: Galilée, 1998. Translated as *Soundproof Room: Malraux's Anti-aesthetics* by Robert Harvey. Stanford: Stanford University Press, 2001.

La Confession d'Augustin. Paris: Galilée, 1998. Translated as *The Confession of Augustine* by Richard Beardsworth. Stanford: Stanford University Press, 2000.

Karel Appel: Ein Farbgestus, Essays zur Kunst Karel Appels mit einer Bildauswahl des Autors. Translated by Jessica Beer. Berlin: Gachnang und Springer, 1998. Translated in a bilingual edition (with the French) as *Karel Appel: Un geste de couleur/ Karel Appel: A Gesture of Color*. Edited by Herman Parret. Leuven: Leuven University Press, 2009.

Misère de la philosophie. Paris: Galilée, 2000.

"Emma: Between Philosophy and Psychoanalysis." Translated by M. Sanders (with R. Brons and N. Martin). In *Lyotard: Philosophy, Politics and the Sublime*, edited by Hugh J. Silverman, 23–45. New York and London: Routledge, 2002.

"Music and Postmodernity." *New Formations* 66 (Spring 2009), 37–45.

Textes dispersés I: Esthétique et théorie de l'art / Miscellaneous Texts I: Aesthetics and Theory of Art. Edited by Herman Parret. Leuven: Leuven University Press, 2012.

Textes dispersés II: Artistes contemporains / Miscellaneous Texts II: Contemporary Artists. Leuven: Leuven University Press, 2012.

"Argumentation and Presentation: The Foundation Crisis." Translated by Chris Turner. *Rewriting Lyotard: Figuration, Presentation, Resistance. Cultural Politics* 9.2 (2013), 117–43.

"What to Paint?" Interviewed by Bernard Marcadé. Translated by Kent Still and Peter W. Milne. *Rewriting Lyotard: Figuration, Presentation, Resistance. Cultural Politics* 9.2 (2013), 212–18.

General bibliography

Albertini, Rosanna and Guillermo Kuitca. "Guillermo Kuitca: Body of Painting: Abstraction According to Kuitca." *Art Press*, 249 (1999), 30–3.

Arendt, Hannah. *The Jewish Writings*. New York: Schocken, 2007.

Ashton, Dore. *A Critical Study of Philip Guston*. Berkeley: University of California Press, 1990.

Bamford, Kiff. *Lyotard and the "figural" in Performance, Art and Writing*. New York and London: Continuum, 2012.

——. "A Late Performance: Intimate Distance (*Yingmei Duan*)." In *Rereading Jean-François Lyotard*, edited by Heidi Bickis and Rob Shields, 81–95. Burlington, VT: Ashgate, 2013.

Barker, Stephen. "The Weight of Writing." In *Rereading Jean-François Lyotard*, edited by Heidi Bickis and Rob Shields, 55–68. Burlington: Ashgate, 2013.

Bauman, Zygmunt. *Wasted Lives: Modernity and Its Outcasts*. Cambridge: Polity, 2004.

Benjamin, Walter. "Central Park." Translated by Lloyd Spencer. *New German Critique* 34 (Winter 1985), 32–58.

Bennington, Geoffrey. *Lyotard: Writing the event*. New York: Columbia University Press, 1988.

——. *Late Lyotard*. Lexington: CreateSpace, 2005.

——. "Childish Things." In *Minima Memoria: In the Wake of Jean-François Lyotard*, eds Claire Nouvet, Zrinka Stahuljak, and Kent Still, 197–217. Stanford: Stanford University Press, 2006 and in *Late Lyotard*, 1–42.

——. "Political animals." *Diacritics*, 9.2 (2009), 21–35.

——. "Translation in the Dark." In Jean-François Lyotard, *Sam Francis: Lesson of Darkness*, trans. Geoffrey Bennington, 216–23. Leuven: Leuven University Press, 2010.

——. "Opening Up," in *Rewriting Lyotard, Figuration, Presentation, Resistance, Cultural Politics*, 2 (2013), 203–11.

——. "Go Figure." *Parrhesia* 12 (2011), 37–40.

Berkson, Bill. "The New Gustons," *Art News* 69.6 (October 1970): 44–7.

Bernstein, David. "Europe's Jews: Summer, 1947. A Firsthand Report by an American Observer," *Commentary* (August 1947): 101–9.

Blackwood, Michael. *Philip Guston, A Life Lived*. Michael Blackwood Productions, 2012. Film.

Bonnefis, Philippe. "Passages of the Maya." In *Minima Memoria. Essays in the Wake of Jean-François Lyotard*, edited by Claire Nouvet, Kent Still, and Zrinka Stahuljak, 166–75. Stanford: Stanford University Press, 2007.

Brügger, Niels, Finn Fransen and Dominique Pirotte, eds. *Lyotard, Les Déplacements philosophiques*. Brussels: DeBoeck-Wesmael, 1993.

Butler, Judith. "Contingent Foundations: Feminism and the Question of 'Postmodernism.'" In *Feminists Theorize the Political*, edited by Judith Butler and Joan W. Scott, 3–21. New York: Routledge, 1992.

Cariolato, Alfonso. *"Le Geste de Dieu" Sur un lieu de* l'Ethique *de Spinoza*. Chatou: Editions de la Transparence, 2011.

Carlson, Marvin. *Places of Performance: The Semiotics of Theatre Architecture*. Ithaca: Cornell University Press, 1989.

Carroll, David. *Paraesthetics: Foucault, Lyotard, Derrida*. New York and London: Routledge, 1987.

Caygill, Howard. "Stelarc and the Chimera: Kant's Critique of Prosthetic Judgment." *Art Journal* 56.1 (Spring 1997), 46–51.

Cooper, Harry. "Recognizing Guston (In Four Slips)." *October* 99 (Winter 2002), 96–129.

Deleuze, Gilles and Félix Guattari, *What is Philosophy?* Translated by Hugh Tomlinson and Graham Burchell. London and New York: Verso, 1994.

Derrida, Jacques (with Vincent Descombes, Garbis Kortian, Philippe Lacoue-Labarthe, Jean-François Lyotard and Jean-Luc Nancy). *La Faculté de juger*. Paris: Les Editions de Minuit, 1985.

——. "Writing Proofs," and Jean-François Lyotard, "Translator's Notes." Translated by Roland-François Lack. *Pli: Warwick Journal of Philosophy* 6 (Summer 1997), 37–57.

Detienne, Marcel and Jean-Pierre Vernant. *Cunning Intelligence in Greek Culture and Society*. Translated by Janet Lloyd. Chicago: University of Chicago Press, 1991.

Dreishpoon, Douglas. "Sometimes Walking is Enough." In *Guillermo Kuitca: Everything: Paintings and Works on Paper, 1980–2008*, edited by Douglas Dreishpoon and Andreas Huyssen, 36–51. London: Scala Publishers, 2009.

Dubery, Fred and John Willats. *Perspective and Other Drawing Systems*. London: Herbert Press, 1983.

Durafour, Jean-Michel. *Jean-François Lyotard: Questions Au Cinéma*. Paris: Presses Universitaires de France, 2009.

Duville, Matias and Guillermo Kuitca. "Guillermo Kuitca." Translated by Margaret Carson. *Bomb*, 106 (2009), 50–7.

Elias, Norbert. *The Civilizing Process*, 2nd edition. Oxford: Blackwell, 2000.

Enaudeau, Corinne, Jean-François Nordmann, Jean-Michel Salanskis and Frédéric Worms, eds. *Les Transformateurs Lyotard*. Paris: Sens & Tonka, 2008.

Felman, Shoshana. "Crisis of Witnessing: Albert Camus' Postwar Writings." *Cardozo Studies in Law and Literature* 3.2 (Autumn 1991), 197–242.

Freud, Sigmund. *Gesammelte Werke*. Frankfurt am Main: Fischer Verlag, 1946.

——. *The Standard Edition of the Complete Psychological Works of Sigmund Freud*, 24 vols, edited by James Strachey. London: Hogarth, 1957.

Fuente, Eduardo de la. "Music as Negative Theology." *Thesis Eleven* 56 (1999), 57–79.

Garcia-Düttmann, Alexander. *The Memory of Thought: An Essay on Heidegger and Adorno*. New York and London: Continuum, 2002.

Gasché, Rodolphe. *The Honor of Thinking: Critique Philosophy, History*. Stanford: Stanford University Press, 2007.

Genette, Gérard. *Figures III*. Paris: Editions du Seuil, 1972.

——. *Narrative Discourse*. Translated by Jane E. Lewin. Oxford: Basil Blackwell, 1980.

Grosz, Elizabeth. "Bodies-cities." In *Sexuality and Space*, edited by B. Colomina, 241–54. New York: Princeton Architectural Press, 1992.

Guston, Philip. *Philip Guston: Collected Writings, Lectures, and Conversations*, edited by Clark Coolidge. Berkeley: University of California Press, 2011.

Hansen, Mark. *Bodies in Code: Interfaces With Digital Media*. New York: Routledge, 2006.

Härle, Clemens-Carl. "Tautégories. Lyotard lecteur de Kant." In *Les Transformateurs Lyotard*, edited by Corinne Enaudeau, Jean-François Nordmann, Jean-Michel Salanskis, and Frédéric Worms, 43–59. Paris: Sens & Tonka, 2008.

Hershman Leeson, Lynn and Michael Shanks. "Here and Now." In *Archaeologies of Presence*, edited by Gabriella Giannachi, Nick Kaye, and Michael Shanks, 222–34. London: Routledge.

Highmore, Ben. "Bitter After Taste: Affect, Food and Social Aesthetics." In *The Affect Theory Reader*, edited by Melissa Gregg and Gregory Seigworth, 118–37. Durham, NC: Duke University Press, 2000.

Hudek, Anthony. "Seeing through *Discourse, Figure*." *Parrhesia* 12 (2011), accessed July 14, 2015, http://parrhesiajournal.org/parrhesia12/parrhesia12_hudek.

Husserl, Edmund. *Ideas Pertaining to a Pure Phenomenology and to a Phenomenological Philosophy: First Book.* Translated by F. Kersten. Dordrecht: Kluwer Academic Publishers, 1982.

Huyssen, Andreas. "Guillermo Kuitca: Painter of Space." In *Guillermo Kuitca: Everything: Paintings and Works on Paper, 1980–2008*, edited by Douglas Dreishpoon and Andreas Huyssen, 24–33. London: Scala Publishers, 2009.

Ingraham, Catherine. *Architecture and The Burdens of Linearity.* New Haven, CT: Yale University Press, 1998.

Ionescu, Vlad. "Figural Aesthetics: Lyotard, Valéry, Deleuze." *Cultural Politics* 9.2 (2013), 144–57.

Jones, Amelia and Heathfield, Adrian, eds. *Perform, Repeat, Record.* Bristol: Intellect, 2012.

Jones, Graham. *Lyotard Reframed.* New York and London: I.B. Tauris, 2013.

Kahn, Laurence. "D'une lecture apathique de Freud." In *Les Transformateurs Lyotard*, edited by Corinne Enaudeau, Jean-François Nordmann, Jean-Michel Salanskis, and Frédéric Worms, 43–59. Paris: Sens & Tonka, 2008.

——. *Le Psychanalyste apathique et le patient postmoderne.* Paris: Editions de l'Olivier, 2014.

Kant, Immanuel. *Kritik der Reinen Vernunft.* In *Kant's Gesammelte Schriften*, 29 vols. Berlin: G. Reimer, 1910–. Cited as KRV with accompanying translation.

——. *Kritik der praktischen Vernunft.* In *Kant's Gesammelte Schriften*, 29 vols. Berlin: G. Reimer, 1910–. Cited as KPV with accompanying translation.

——. *Kritik der Urteilskraft.* In *Kant's Gesammelte Schriften*, 29 vols. Berlin: G. Reimer, 1910–. Cited as KUK with accompanying translation.

——. *Kant's Political Writings.* Translated by H.B. Nisbet, edited by H.S. Reiss. Cambridge: Cambridge University Press, 1970.

——. *The Conflict of the Faculties.* Translated by Mary J. Gregor and Robert Anchor. In *Religion and Rational Theology*, edited by Allen W. Wood and George di Giovanni, 233–328. Cambridge: Cambridge University Press, 1996.

——. *Practical Philosophy*, edited by M.J. Gregor. Cambridge: New York: Cambridge University Press, 1996.

Kaufmann, David. *Telling Stories: Philip Guston's Later Works.* Berkeley: University of California Press, 2010.

Kirby, Kathleen. "RE: Mapping Subjectivity: Cartographic Vision and the Limits of Politics." In *Bodyspace: Destabilizing Geographies of Gender and Sexuality*, edited by Nancy Duncan, 45–55. New York: Routledge, 1996.

Kleist, Heinrich von. "On the Marionette Theater." Translated by Thomas G. Neumiller, *The Drama Review: TDR* 16.3 (1972), 22–6.

Laplanche, Jean. *Life and Death in Psychoanalysis.* Translated by Jeffrey Mehlman. Baltimore, MD: The Johns Hopkins University Press, 1976.

——. *The Unconscious and the Id.* London: Karnac Books, 1999.

Leclerc, Annie. *Paedophilia ou l'amour des enfants.* Paris: Actes Sud, 2010.

Lefort, Claude. "The Interposed Body," in *Writing: The Political Test*. Translated and edited by David Ames Curtis, 1–19. Durham, NC: Duke University Press, 2000.

Locke, Kirsten. "Lyotard's Infancy: A Debt that Persists." *Postmodern Culture* 23.1 (2012).

Logan, Marie-Rose. "Graphesis . . ." *Yale French Studies* 52 (1975), 4–15.

Lydon, Mary. "Veduta on *Discours, figure*." *Yale French Studies* 99 (2001), 10–26.

Lyotard, Dolorès "Perpetual Letter." Translated by Rob Shields, in *Rereading Jean-François Lyotard*, edited by Heidi Bickis and Rob Shields, 69–71. Burlington, VT: Ashgate, 2013.

—— "L'écriture Migrante De Jean-François Lyotard," in *Contemporary French and Francophone Studies* 18 (2014), 18–30.

Mackay, Robin and Armen Avanessian. *Accelerate: The Accelerationist Reader*. Falmouth: Urbanomic, 2014.

Massumi, Brian. *Parables for the Virtual: Movement, Affect, Sensation*. Durham, NC and London: Duke University Press, 2002.

Mercer-Taylor, Peter, ed. *The Cambridge Companion to Mendelssohn*. Cambridge: Cambridge University Press, 2004.

Michalczyk, John J. *Filming the End of the Holocaust: Allied Documentaries, Nuremberg and the Liberation of the Concentration Camps*. New York and London: Bloomsbury, 2014.

Milne, Peter W. "Exceeding the Given: Rewriting Lyotard's Aesthetics." *Rewriting Lyotard: Figuration, Presentation, Resistance. Cultural Politics* 9.2 (2013), 107–16.

——. "Lyotard's 'Critical' 'Aesthetics'." In *Rereading Jean-François Lyotard: Essays on His Later Works*, edited by Heidi Bickis and Rob Shields, 189–207. Burlington, VT: Ashgate, 2013.

——. "Sensibility and the Law: On Rancière's Reading of Lyotard." *Symposium: Canadian Journal of Continental Philosophy* 15.2 (2011), 95–119.

Milne, Peter W., Heidi Bickis, Rob Shields, and Kent Still, eds. *Rewriting Lyotard: Figuration, Presentation, Resistance*. Special issue of *Cultural Politics*, 9.2 (2013).

Muñoz, José Esteban. *Cruising Utopia: The Then and There of Queer Futurity*. New York: NYU Press, 2009.

Nikolchina, Miglena. "It Always Gives Watching: The Nothing and the Parahuman in Rilke's *Duino Elegies*." *Filozofski Vestnik* XXVI, 2 (2005), 161–71.

Nouvet, Claire, Kent Still, and Zrinka Stahuljak. *Minima Memoria*. Stanford: Stanford University Press, 2007.

Nouvet, Claire. "The Inarticulate Affect. Lyotard and Psychoanalytic Testimony." In *Minima Memoria. Essays in the Wake of Jean-François Lyotard*, edited by Claire Nouvet, Kent Still, and Zrinka Stahuljak, 106–22. Stanford: Stanford University Press, 2007.

Orwell, George. *Dickens, Dali and Others*. Cornwall, NY: Cornwall Press, 1946.

——. *1984*. New York: Signet, 1961.

Pascal, Blaise. *Oeuvres complètes*, 2 vols. Edited by Michel de Guerin. Paris: Gallimard, 2000.

Phelan, Peggy. *Live Art in L.A.: Performance in Southern California, 1970–1983*. London: Routledge, 2012.

Prince, Gerald. *A Dictionary of Narratology*. Aldershot: Scholar Press, 1988.

Quignard, Pascal. *Petits Traités*, 6 vols. Paris: Maeght, 1990.

Rancière, Jacques. *Aesthetics and its Discontents*. Translated by Steven Corcoran. Cambridge: Polity, 2009.

——. *The Politics of Aesthetics*. Translated by Gabriel Rockhill. New York: Continuum, 2004.

Readings, Bill. *Introducing Lyotard: Art and Politics*. New York and London: Routledge, 1991.

Rogozinski, Jacob. "Lyotard: le différend, la présence." In *Témoigner du différend : Quand phraser ne se peut*, edited by Francis Guibal and Jacob Rogozinski, 61–79. Paris: Osiris, 1989.

Ronell, Avital. *Loser Sons: Politics and Authority*. Champaign: The University of Illinois Press, 2012.

Rosenberg, Harold. "Liberation from Detachment: Philip Guston." In *The De-Definition of Art*, 132–40. Chicago: University of Chicago Press, 1972.

Roth, Philip. *Shop Talk: A Writer and His Colleagues and Their Work*. New York: Houghton Mifflin, 2001.

Schmitt, Jean-Claude. "'Gestus'—'Gesticulatio'. Contribution à l'étude du vocabulaire latin médiéval des gestes." In *La Lexicographie du latin médiéval et ses rapports avec les recherches actuelles sur la civilization du Moyen Age*. Paris: CNRS, 1981.

Sedgwick, Eve Kosofsky and Adam Frank. "Shame and the Cybernetic Fold: Reading Sylvan Tomkins." In Eve Kosofsky Sedgwick, *Touching Feeling: Affect, Performance, Pedagogy*, 93–122. Durham, NC: Duke University Press, 2003.

Sfez, Gérald. *Jean-François Lyotard, la faculté d'une phrase*. Paris: Galilée, 2000.

Shandler, Jeffrey. *While America Watches: Televising the Holocaust*. New York and Oxford: Oxford University Press, 1999.

Shields, Rob. *Spatial Questions: Cultural Topologies and Social Spatialisation*. London: Sage, 2013.

Shilling, Chris. *The Body and Social Theory*. London: Sage, 2012.

Slifkin, Robert. *Out of Time: Philip Guston and the Refiguration of Postwar American Art*. Berkeley: University of California Press, 2013.

Speranza, Graciela and Guillermo Kuitca. "Conversations with Guillermo Kuitca." In *Guillermo Kuitca: Everything: Paintings and Works on Paper, 1980–2008*, edited by Douglas Dreishpoon and Andreas Huyssen, 76–101. London: Scala Publishers, 2009.

Still, Kent. Introduction to *Minima Memoria. Essays in the Wake of Jean-François Lyotard*, edited by Claire Nouvet, Kent Still, and Zrinka Stahuljak, xi–xxiv. Stanford: Stanford University Press, 2007.

Theweleit, Klaus. *Male Fantasies: Volume I: Women, Floods, Bodies, History*. Minneapolis: University of Minnesota Press, 1987.

Tomiche, Anne, "Rephrasing the Freudian Unconscious: Lyotard's Affect-Phrase." *Diacritics. A Review of Contemporary Criticism* 24.1 (Spring 1994), 43–63.

——, "Rephrasing the Visible and the Expressive: Lyotard's 'Defense of the Eye' from Figure to Inarticulate Phrase." In *Philosophies of the Visible*, edited by Wilhelm S. Wurzer, 7–20. New York and London: Continuum, 2002.

——, "Phrasing the Disruptiveness of the Visible in Freudian Terms: Lyotard and the Visual." In *Afterwords. Essays in memory of Jean-François Lyotard*, edited by Robert Harvey, 29–54. New York: Occasional Papers of the Humanities Institute University at Stony Brook, 2000.

——, "Le canon littéraire de Jean-François Lyotard." In *Les Transformateurs Lyotard*, edited by Corinne Enaudeau, Jean-François Nordmann, Jean-Michel Salanskis, and Frédéric Worms, 99–116. Paris: Sens & Tonka, 2008.

Toronyi-Lalic, Igor. "Edgard Varese Dropped Bombs on the 20th Century." *Times Online*, 2010, last modified April 9, www.thetimes.co.uk/tto/arts/music/classical/article2470662.ece.

Trifonova, Temenuga. "A Nonhuman Eye: Deleuze on Cinema." *SubStance* 33.2 (2004), 134–52.

Williams, James. *Lyotard and the Political*. London: Routledge, 2000.

Wittgenstein, Ludwig. *Philosophical Investigations*. Translated by G.E.M. Anscombe. Malden: Blackwell, 2001.

Wolf, Bryan. "Between the Lines: Philip Guston, the Holocaust and 'Bad Painting'" (forthcoming).

Woodward, Ashley, *Nihilism in Postmodernity: Lyotard, Baudrillard, Vattimo*. Aurora, Colorado: The Davies Group, 2009.

Index